Sentimental Journey Home I (1965-2018)
Stamping out ignorance in Aggieland: One professor's memories and reflections

Arnold LeUnes

© Copyright 2018, Arnold LeUnes

All Rights Reserved

No part of this book may be reproduced, stored in a retrieval system, or transmitted by any means, electronic, mechanical, photocopying, recording, or otherwise, without written permission from the author.

ISBN: 978-1-64204-289-4

Jilly Pankey, formerly of the Art faculty at Texas State University and presently a freelance artist. More of her work can be viewed at www.jillpankey.com

BOOK ONE

Sentimental Journey Home I (1965-2018)
Stamping out ignorance in Aggieland: One professor's memories and reflections

Reflections on Life in Academia 1
   Accepting All Compliments 15
   Student Evaluations of My Classes 15
      Putting a Positive Spin on Teaching 16
      The Anti's Have Their Say (As Well They Should!) 24
      A Department Head Chimes in on the Conversation 27
   The Outsider 30
   Who Am I? 33
First Females and the General 41
   Women at A&M: A Chronology 42
      My Personal Perspective on the History and Current Status of Women at A&M 45
   1960's Females 49
      Barbara Williams: A 1960's Prototypical Female Student 49
      Barbara X: A Different Kind of 1960's Student 50
   The General 52
      Decorated War Hero 54
      The General Ascends to the Presidency of the University 54
      A "Wild-Eyed Liberal" Takes on the A&M Administration 55
      "Pot-Bellied President" Vows a "Hell of a Fight" 56
      A Ranger Casualty 57
      Post-Mortem on the General 58
First Faculty Colleagues 59
   Arnold LeUnes, Meet Fillmore Sanford! 60
      First Faculty Friends: Professors Varvel, Barker,
      Elliott, Bourgeois, Christensen, and Levenson 61
      Al Casey, aka Little Albert 62
   Other Colleagues of a More Quirky Persuasion 68
      Bill: The Con Man 68
      Virgil: A Case of Paranoia 73

Alexander Kemos: Wannabee Tufts PhD and Navy Seal.. 74
Department Heads I Have Known 75
    Administrator X: A Case of Hysterical Muteness?.. 75
    Bill Reed 76
    Cless Jay... 77
    Fran Bevans and the "Suck-Ass Six"... 79
    The "Normal" Department Heads.. 82
First Students, Like First Loves, Are the Most Memorable 85
    Memorable Students From Those Early Years.. 85
        "Old Bushy Brows"... 85
        Francis Euel "Doc" Savage II, aka "Elijah".. 86
        Raymundo Rodriquez... 89
        Doobwa, Dick, Walton Warriors, and Pressed Ham Under Glass....................................... 94
        Paging Mr. Meoff!... 94
        Charles Jones Does His Best Tim Conway Imitation.. 95
        William Kenneth "Ken" Gray, PhD, Entrepreneur.. 96
        Reverend Don Young, Meet Hamed el-Feky 98
        Larry Godfrey and Deep Sea Fishing: Not My Cup of Tea... 99
American Life in the 1970's... 100
Brenham-Washington County Counseling Service (BWCCS).. 103
    Mr. Ed Wachholz, MSW 105
    The Drano Lady 105
        Trapped Housewife Syndrome. 106
        Grandma Gets to Babysit.. 107
        Entering Blinn College... 108
        Teacher's Aide, Brenham State School. 110
        Back to Dirty Dishes and Dirty Diapers? 110
    School Phobics: Debbie P. and Dale D... 111
        Debbie P.. 112
        Symptoms of School Phobia. 112
        A Behavioral Baseline.. 112
        Treatment Phase. 113
        Dale D. 114
        The Psychologist Takes a "Shyness Pill" 116
        Postscript on Sandra Siemsglusz. 116
    Benita, Meet Buster Lejeune.. 117
    Johnny Mae, I Hardly Knew Ye 118
    A Prostitution Ring 121
    Minor in Possession: "The Meanest, Toughest, and Fastest Guy in the Fifth Grade" 122
    Marcie, the Poetess 123
Other BWCCS Cases 125

Silent Sara, a Six-Year Old Mute 129
Henry: A Bedwetter. 130
Tameka: Is There Such a Thing as a Zero IQ? 132
Travis the Troublemaker. 133
Chareka, a Schizophrenic. 134
Miss Marlene: Borderline Personality Disorder. 135
Jasmine: A Schizophrenic Prostitute. 135
Fred: An Epileptic. 135
Edgar: A Chronic Schizophrenia. 136
Eleanor: A Case of Schizophrenia in Remission. 136
Luke: My Lenny. 136
Interesting Clients from Other Venues 137
   Brenham State School 137
      Self-Destructive Serena. 137
   Central Brazos Valley MHMR Center 139
      Lobotomized Larry. 139
   The Community 141
      Mimi, a Six-Year Old Bedwetter. 141
I Meet Judy Webb LeUnes 143
   School Marm 144
   Community Servant 145
   Judy as Politician 148
   Cancer Raises its Ugly Head 149
   Lucky Me 151
The LeUnes Children 153
   Leslie Katherine LeUnes Stiteler. 154
   Natalie Jean LeUnes Allen. 156
   Christopher Chay Blythe LeUnes. 157
   Amy Kendall LeUnes Norland. 158
   Are President Bill Clinton and the LeUnes Children
   Descendants of Thomas Jefferson? 158
   Katie Elizabeth LeUnes Cryer. 161
   Lyndon Webb LeUnes. 166
   A Soccer Dream. 169
   Personal Heroes 173
      Grace Jones Kiser. 173
      Homer Hardy Blythe 179
Aberrant Aggies: An Axe Murderer and a Pedophile 185
   Mike R., Axe Murderer. 185
      Dr. Death Number Two. 186
      Beginning of the End for Pam. 189

- The Case Begins to Come Apart 190
- My Psychological Workup on Mike 191
- Request for a Change of Venue 193
- The Unfortunate Demise of Dr. Death Number Two 195
- Brian Lancaster: Pornographer and Pedophile 195
  - Brian Visits My Study Abroad Program in Germany 196
  - Jekyll and Hyde Personality 196
  - Trial and Sentencing 198
  - This Stranger Beside Me 199

Slow-Pitch Softball, 1974-2007 201
- From Bad News Bears To Bullies on the Block 201
  - Tony Takes One For the Team 202
  - Our Slow-Pitch Fortunes Take A Turn For the Better 203
  - Richard Benning, Duddley's Draw, and the "Bar Team" 203
- "Bubba's Briefs" 208
- My All-Time All-Star Slowpitch Team 209
- My All-Time Favorite Umpires 210

Hearne, Texas 1968-2017 211
- A Brief History 211
  - Poverty and Despondency 212
- Mr. Norris McDaniel, Mentor and Friend 213
  - Judy LeUnes Rejoins Hearne ISD 214
- Camp Hearne: A German Prisoner of War (POW) Camp 215
- A Dedicated Teacher 218

American Life in the 1980's 221
Anecdotes and Remembrances From the 1980's 223
- Two Psychologists Induce Catatonia in an Adolescent Bus Boy in Mississippi 223
- "The Body" 225
- A Merle Haggard Sighting in Chicago's O'Hare Airport 226
- LeUnes Look-A-Likes 229
- John Lucas, Kyle Rote, Jr., and Dexter Manley 230
- The Loneliness of the Long Distance Runner Redux` 232
- Life Can Get Pretty Kinky 234
- Angelo Bartlett "Bart" Giammati 237

American Life in the 1990's 239
The 1990's: Australia, New Zealand, and the Fiji Islands 241
- Australia, 1991 241
  - Rob de Castella and Plantar Fasciitis 244
- New Zealand 246
- Nadi, Fiji Islands 247

American Life in the 2000's: The "Naughtie Aughties", aka "The Uh-Ohs" 251

Study Abroad in Italy, Germany, and Oceania ... 253
    Castiglion Fiorentino. ... 254
    The Staff and the Fabulous Chefs. ... 255
    Excursions. ... 256
    The Faculty: Joe, Gary, and Howie. ... 256
    A Climb in the Alps. ... 260
    Our Twelve-Year-Old Has the Time of His Life. ... 261
    Memorable Students. ... 262
Germany 2003, 2004, 2005, 2007, 2008, 2009, 2010, 2011, 2012, 2013, 2014, 2015, 2016, 2017. ... 267
    Dr. Rainer Zaeck. ... 267
    Dachau and Georg Elser. ... 268
    Cities and Sites Visited. ... 269
    Group Characters, Characteristics, and Idiosyncrasies. ... 272
Guido, Team T-Mobile, and the "Tour de Farce" ... 277
Trouble in Vienna ... 278
Packing Light and Traveling Easy ... 283
Christmas Down Under, 2004-2005. ... 285
    Tiffany Tracy is our First (and Only) Casualty. ... 285
    Sites to Behold. ... 285
Iran: A Texas Yankee in King Khomenei's Court. ... 287
    Mohammad, Hassan, and Fari. ... 289
    Brothers Mohammad and Habib. ... 291
Preparing to Visit Tehran. ... 292
A Welcome Layover in Dubai ... 294
    In Search of a $12 Bottle of Guinness. ... 295
Wonderful Experiences in Iran ... 296
    Meeting Mostafa. ... 298
    Westerners in the Olympic Hotel. ... 299
Qatar's Mohammed bin Hammam of the Asian Futbol Confederation ... 300
Gridlock to End All Gridlock ... 303
ICSF Opening Ceremonies ... 304
    Maryam Abargoueinejad. ... 305
    Gilda Khalaj. ... 307
    An Iranian Runway Model. ... 307
    In Summation. ... 309

Lagniappe 311
    Miss Hispanic Texas 312
    The Death of Willie Zapalac 314
    The Untimely Passing of Coach Jim Culpepper 316
    Student Cries for Help 318
    Letters of Recommendation 321
    Butchered Words 323
    The Cell/Smart Phone: Can One Person's Drivel be Another Person's Spinach? 325
    Who Is It? 328
    There Oughta' be a Special Place 329
    You Ain't Just A' Whistling Dixie 330
    Academia at Its Boring Best 331
    Hot Item on My Personal Bucket List 331
    Favorite Sayings 333
    OK, OK, OK, Oooooooooooooooookay 336
    "Daddy, Your Students Are Pigs" 336
    Karen Pays the Price 337
    Descendants, Diogenes, and David's Ditzes 337
    A Coed Kicks the Book Habit 339
    Things I Forgot to Tell Rosario 340
    Do Big-Time College Coaches Have Wives? 341
    Beer, Beer for Old Dewey High 342
    International Coffee Wars 343
    Playgirl, Inc. 344
    New York, New York 345
    Things That Can Go Wrong With the Body 345
    In Search of the Ultimate Barbecue Experience 347
    The Gospel According to Arnold the Skeptic 348
        What Religious Outsiders and True Christians Think About Religion. 350
        Origins of Religion as Personal Mystery. 350
        Dragging A "Slow One" Across Harlene as Religious Experience. 351
        Adult Experiences and Misgivings.. 352
        Jesus as a Charismatic Middle Eastern Peasant. 352
        Religious Intolerance: A Redundancy? 352
        George W. Bush as Tartuffe.. 353
        Sigmund Freud on Religion. 355
        U. S. Founding Fathers Views of Religion. 356

Dr. James Kaufman Takes on Dr. Laura Schlessinger 358
    Power of Prayer... 359
    Brann the Iconoclast. 360
    Christians as Infidels... 360
    Animal Rights and Religion.. 361
    A Positive Perspective. 361

For Aggies Only

"Rekindlers" and Others Who Made a Difference 363
All Names Team 370
    All-Alliteration Team.. 370
    All Four-Letter Word Surname Team... 371
    All First-Names Team... 371
    All Last-Names Team 371
    All United Nations Team.. 371
    All European Names Team (Plus Canada) 372
    All-Time Ex-Student A&M Football Team.. 373

PROLOGUE

Sentimental journey home I
Stamping out ignorance in Aggieland:
One professor's memories and reflections

"My yesterday's walk with me. They keep step; they are grey faces that peer over my shoulder."

William Golding, Novelist, Playwright, Poet (1911-1993)

"In everyone's life, at some time, our inner fire goes out. It is then burst into flame by an encounter with another human being. We should all be thankful for those people who rekindle the inner spirit."

Albert Schweitzer, Philosopher, Physician, Theologian, Organist (1875-1965)

During the past eighty years, I have been an infant, child, school boy, adolescent, athlete, college boy, master's and doctoral degree candidate, Army officer, husband, father, great-grandfather, university professor, Yellow Dog Democrat, and proud quasi-pagan, pretty much in that order. Of the preceding, I have mostly wonderful memories and harbor few regrets. However, it pains me greatly to consider relinquishing my long-held grip on my status as a life-long Yellow Dog Democrat. Recent events have compelled me to issue at least a partial caveat or disclaimer because I have seen up close and personal what mindless, straight-ticket voting can do to outstanding candidates for elected office. I have in mind here my lovely wife, Judy, who lost spirited races for the Texas House of Representatives in 2011 and 2012 to what most sources, including many local Republicans, regarded as a lesser qualified opponent. Having to confront this reality at my advanced age is vexing, but I still plan to go to the great voting booth in the sky as pretty much a Yellow Dog Democrat.

I spent most of my early childhood as an imaginary friend. I once bobbed, weaved, and danced the salsa in bar on the beach near Pula, Croatia. More recently, I was commissioned by The Vatican to crochet multi-colored beanies for the newly-appointed His Holiness, the Pope himself. I paid $65,000 to scale Mount Everest a couple of years ago, but on the day of our ascent the Sherpa's left me in my cabin, unaware that I had slept through my alarm. I was Facebook friends with the

President of Lichtenstein for a couple of weeks but he unfriended me because I posted some kind words about the French. I have supplemented my income as a retired, for-hire Mafia hit man by re-lacing baseball gloves (for a substantial fee, I might add) for major league stars Miguel Cabrera of the Detroit Tigers, Jose Altuve of the Houston Astros, and Mike Trout of the California Angels. Thanks to Rosetta Stone and late night sessions with a lovely Teutonic tutor from the Tyrol, I became fluent in German in less than two weeks but forgot everything I learned when a dark-eyed, tawny Portuguese enchantress from the Iberian Peninsula taught me her native tongue. I was at Disney World the day Snow White used the F-word after a hard day with the brats (thanks Zoe Lewis for that one)! Speaking of Disney World, a spokesperson for former first lady Barbara Bush asked me to assist in redesigning King Ludwig's Schloss Neuschwanstein to make it look more like the Disney castle. It makes me livid when an innocent man escapes the gas chamber. Last Christmas, I used my office printer to forge a dollar bill to buy a candy Santa. I once had a summer job in college placing whoopee cushions in the seats at Carnegie Hall. And most significantly, several Irish friends and I discovered the meaning of life a month ago in Dublin while quaffing a quantity of Guinness Stout at O'Donoghue's, but the bartender threw away our notes while we were taking a much-needed potty break.

Dear reader: I am only kidding about these exploits; my everyday life is largely humdrum by any estimate and pales in comparison with those assorted fantasies. I was just making sure I had your attention for what is to transpire over the next several hundred pages.

The major players in my life include my parents, George John LeUnes and Marion Katherine Chamberlain LeUnes, both deceased. My grandparents on both sides of the family, John and Gertrude LeUnes and Paul Richard and Edith Maud Chamberlain, all passed away before I reached adolescence. The first to go were Paternal Grandmother Gertrude and Maternal Grandmother Maud, both dying in 1922, or sixteen years before my arrival in Oklahoma, or what was once known as the Indian Territory. Grandpa John LeUnes outlived Gertrude by twenty-five years, dying in 1947, and Grandpa Chamberlain was the last grandparent to die, in 1949, when I was eleven years of age. I have had two wives, the first being Barbara Laverne Blythe LeUnes (later Pearson) and the second Judy Webb LeUnes (still LeUnes). If you combine my years of marriage to each wife, I celebrated fifty-five years of wedded bliss on January 13, 2017. Judy and I made it to year thirty-eight on that date, and coupled with my seventeen years of marriage to Barbara, I reached my own personal golden anniversary, after a fashion, in 2012. Barbara and I had four children, Leslie, Natalie, Chay, and Amy, and Judy and I are parents of Katie and Lyndon. The kiddos, in turn, have produced ten grandchildren ranging in age from four to twenty-nine years. Oldest granddaughter, Kayla Allen Cline and her husband, Mark, became parents of baby Noah in the summer of 2015, thus making me a great-grandfather for the first time. The Clines added a new great-grandchild, Anna Katherine, to the fold in December of 2017. The other grandchildren are, in order of age, Lauren Allen Powell (mother of great-grandchild, Henry Declan, in February, 2018), Dylan Stiteler, Blake Stiteler, Ryan Allen, Jackson LeUnes, Julian LeUnes, Emma LeUnes, Ashlynn Grace Cryer, and Kendall Cryer.

It is with considerable sadness that I report the death of Barbara Laverne Blythe LeUnes Pearson on the morning of May 28, 2017 (Memorial Day) at the age of seventy-five. Her health had been a source of much family concern for quite some time, and the situation came to a head on Friday, May 26 when three of the children found her semi-comatose at her home in College Station. After some painstaking deliberation, they called 911 and had her transported to St. Joseph's Hospital in Bryan for treatment. She experienced a reasonably good day on Saturday, and the children had their hopes raised that she would recover and be able to go home in a few days. However, she took a fatal turn for the worse late that day and on into Sunday and died of what proved to be uncontrollable internal bleeding early Monday morning. I was notified of her passing by the oldest daughter, Leslie, at around 0900 that day.

BARBARA BLYTHE LEUNES PEARSON OBITUARY, 2017

For all of her numerous admirable traits and substantial intellect, Barbara served as the gold standard for neglecting one's health. Over the years, she stubbornly refused to seek medical preventive and treatment procedures, and no doubt died a few years prematurely as a result. Alternately, it could be said that she may well have died on her own terms, devoid of those interventions the medical profession can do to prolong life. In summation, Barbara was a good woman, a dedicated educator of major proportions, a faithful wife to her two husbands, and the consummate mother, grandmother, and great-grandmother to her four children, eight grandchildren, and one great grandson. I was always awe-struck at the degree of love and devotion showered on her by the children and grandchildren, and words fail when trying to capture the depth of their love for her (and her for them). What better tribute can one have? She will be greatly missed.

Other significant people in my life sphere include old childhood chums from Dewey, Oklahoma and Texas City, Texas, and college pals from Texas A&M University and the University of North Texas. As well, I retain cherished memories of a friend or two left over from my days in the U.S. Army, and many of more recent vintage accumulated during my half century-plus as a Professor at Texas A&M University.

One notable friend from my A&M days is my often cantankerous, sometimes curmudgeonly, Cajun compadre, Anthony Emile "Tony" Bourgeois, whose tenure at A&M began nine months after mine, in September of 1966. Tony kicked around the department teaching mostly the unwashed and unwanted undergraduates for nearly fifty years until retiring in May of 2015, thus abandoning his eternal quest to stamp out ignorance wherever it reared its ugly head. Considering the abundance of ignorance among the unwashed and unwanted, his task (and mine, for that matter) was/is indeed a daunting one.

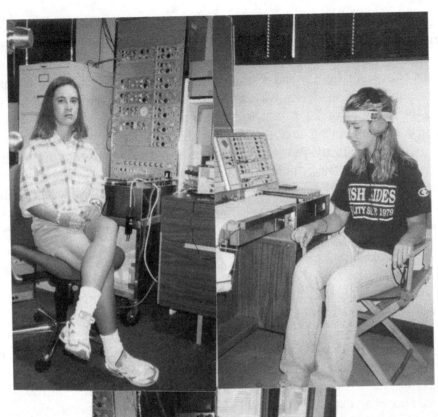
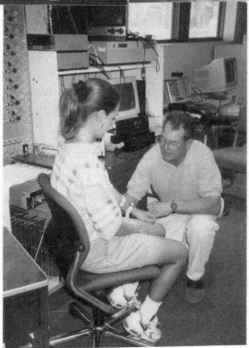

TONY BOURGEOIS CONDUCTING BIOFEEDBACK
WITH A&M GOLFER, LISA ALLEE, AND ANOTHER FEMALE STUDENT

Unfortunately, Tony was temporarily slowed in this worthy pursuit four years ago by replacement surgery on his left hip. In an effort to replace every worn-out body system with a new one, he had two cataract surgeries in May, 2014, and for a while had the vision of a bald eagle (well, sort of). In the past two years, he has had a stint operation, completely lost the vision in his left eye due to a freakish emboli that made its way from his heart to his brain, and had a heart monitor installed early in the summer of 2016 due to disturbing irregularities in that vital organ. Finally, Tony has had considerable hearing loss for about a decade, due in some measure in my humble opinion to his propensity as a thirty-year old to turn his home sound system up to decibel levels that would cause the jets at George Bush International in Houston to blush. (I know, I know…inanimate objects do not blush, but perhaps I have gotten my point across). Health-wise, the man is living proof that the so-called Golden Years can be a real bitch! Despite these considerable physical setbacks, Tony appears to be in amazingly good spirits considering the circumstances, and power to him! I mentioned this to him recently and he attributed what appears on the surface to be a positive perspective to his infinite capacity for self-delusion.

I wish "The Tone-Man" the best as he seeks out new adventures in cooking, fishing, traveling, and visiting with relatives and friends. Speaking of fishing, I marvel at how little our colleagues really knew Tony during his time in the department. I have in mind a recent retirement party in which Tony was showered with all kinds of fishing paraphernalia and several hundred dollars in cash as a gesture of appreciation from his colleagues to supplement his rods, reels, and supply of lures. Interestingly, the man had not wet a line in well over forty years until he participated in a random fishing expedition on the Gulf Coast with his grandchildren a few months ago. This is hardly the stuff of which avid fisherpersons are made.

In addition to my close relatives mentioned earlier, a number of dear friends have fallen along the way, most notably Jack Nation, my fellow Okie colleague, textbook co-author, jogging partner, kindred spirit, and dear, dear, dear friend who died far too early on May 27, 2008 (I miss you more than you'll ever know, Jack). Another notable departure is that of my college roommate for three years at Texas A&M University, Dorsey Dwain Blue. Dorsey died in the summer of 2016.

This cast of characters mentioned in the preceding paragraphs will pop up here and there throughout the entire narrative, but I mention them now so they will need minimal or no introduction later on.

JACK R. NATION, DEAR FRIEND AND COLLEAGUE

As I tried to get these thoughts together over the past decade or so, several shortcomings became obvious. One is that I never possessed the wisdom and foresight to keep a diary and, secondly, I have never been a pack-rat collector of old letters, news clippings, photos, emails, and the like. To compound matters, I also failed to keep memorabilia from my youth, items such as old baseball cards or the hundreds of oft-read and tattered comic books stored under my bed. Fortunately, when my father's ashes were laid to rest in the family plot in Arkansas City, Kansas, in October of 2008 (two years after his death), family members gathered in the city of his youth for some parting words to send him off to whatever eternity awaits him. In the process, they presented me with several boxes of photographs and assorted other memorabilia, and these items have been invaluable in writing sections of the book dealing with family history.

The stories, anecdotes, and observations that follow are reminiscences from my past, admittedly susceptible to the shortcomings of memory distortion, memory loss, and, in some cases, unintentional embellishment. Actually, if I were totally honest and upfront, I might admit to a smidgeon of intentional embellishment, or what is more popularly known as artistic license. However, a modicum of dishonesty has served me well over the years, so I will deny any embellishment in these many pages. Speaking of memory, I do not have "senior moments" as is the case with some of my aging peers; rather, I prefer to label my occasional lapses as "septuagenarian slips!" When I reached eighty on April 16, 2018, I suppose these memory lapses are better thought of as "octogenarian omissions."

Where possible I have supplemented my recollections with newspaper accounts, Internet postings, library archival material, historical notes and anecdotes, pictures, legal documents, and other objective sources commonly used to shore up memory and assist in achieving a more accurate portrayal of people and events. I have tried my best to exercise precision in my recollections and have refrained where possible from recounting things I do not feel secure about with regard to accuracy. There will most certainly be differences of opinion about people and events among friends, acquaintances, family members, and others, and I am willing to live with the ambiguity. I learned a long time ago that my recollections do not always jive perfectly with those of others who have experienced the same people or events. In the final analysis, however, these next several hundred pages represent life as I have experienced it, limited prism and all, and I am willing to take hits from critics wherever disagreements may arise. I know I have given this enterprise my best shot, and hope the readers are sometimes intrigued, often amused, and occasionally even made uncomfortable by my words. The challenge of the professor is to educate, provoke new thought, ignite a spark of creativity, and attack old shibboleths. I see my mission as a writer to be much the same. I am particularly fond of taking on old shibboleths!

This memoir arose in part out of repeated requests over the years from students and friends who asked that I recast the stories, reflections, observations, opinions, anecdotes, and experiences I have related to them in person. Some requests came from students in my classes and others from friends or colleagues over a cup of coffee in my office, on the golf course or softball diamond, or in the midst of a beer served up ice cold at a popular local watering hole. These friends and acquaintances suggested I take these reflections from the oral to the written domain so others not privy to them in person might share them second-hand, if you will. One person, a memoir-writing mentor, William "Bill" Harper, once suggested I should put them to music and take them on the road. Ah, to be as talented in both music and story-telling as Bill seems to think I am. It is also a source of flattery to think some people believe this collection of thoughts and ideas might be of interest to a wider audience. It is almost certain some things were lost in translation from the verbal to the written domain, but I am optimistic I have captured the essence of these stories, anecdotes, and observations.

One lingering concern is whether or not the readership will find my reflections and recollections to be interesting. In this regard, Kyle Norland, the husband of my number three daughter and number four child, Amy, provided an interesting anecdote at a graduation party held a couple of years ago in honor of my oldest granddaughter, Kayla Cline (nee Allen) when she received her master's degree in Accounting. I was telling several people at the gathering about the state of this writing project at that time, and the ever-diplomatic Kyle chimed in his two eurocents worth as follows: "Why would you write a book about your life? You are not interesting." Whether or not I am interesting lies in the eye of the readership but I responded to Kyle's assessment by assuring him that one does not have to be personally enthralling in order to write fascinating things. Some of the best authors are as bland and boring as broccoli in social situations. Though I did not say so at the time, I also thought Kyle might also profit from brushing up on his interpersonal skills since he is in the marketing business. Ultimately, the answer as to whether or not I am interesting will be determined by you, the reader, as you make your way through the next several hundred pages. As for Kyle, he has grown on me over the years and I like him very much. It helps that he is a devoted husband to my daughter, Amy.

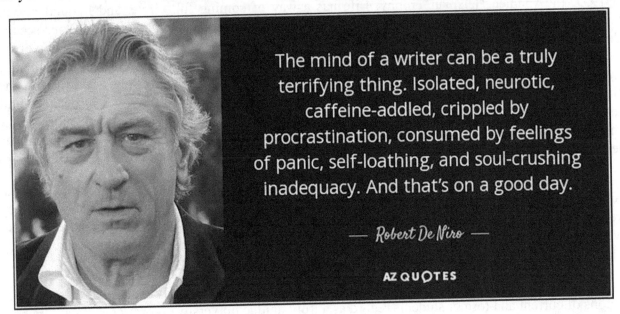

ROBERT DENIRO ON BEING A WRITER

Because of the length of this total document, a decision was made to publish what amounts to two books which may be purchased separately or as companion volumes. The first book focuses on my faculty years at the university along with a collection of random observations about life that I think will help the interested reader get a better feel for who I am and what I think, however quirky. Most of the latter are intended to be humorous or light-hearted and aimed at poking fun at life's foibles. The second book is dedicated to my first eighteen years growing up in the halcyon 1940's and 1950's in semi-rural Dewey, Oklahoma, and semi-urban Texas City, Texas. Also fleshed out in some detail are my mostly wonderful undergraduate and graduate years, along with my quasi-obligatory but intrinsically rewarding experiences in the US Army, and those from my graduate school days. Overall, the second book covers my life and experiences from birth through most of my twenty-seventh year, or what might be described in some quarters as a coming of age story.

It is my fondest hope that the readership will be interested in what a natural-born Okie, transplanted Texan, Texas Aggie two-percenter, Army veteran, and long-time college professor has to say. Two-percenter, by the way, is local jargon of a pejorative nature used to describe people who have not fallen victim to the incessant brainwashing on the part of the formidable Texas A&M University propaganda machine. I love this university but find the pervasive lockstep, one-size-fits-all mindlessness to be depressing and difficult to embrace. In this regard, the oft-mentioned quote variously attributed to comedians Groucho Marx and Woody Allen comes to mind: "I would not want to belong to an organization that would have me as a member."

I began my undergraduate days at A&M in the midst of a great deal of publicity about one of our most accomplished football players, John David Crow, who won collegiate football's highest honor in 1957, the vaunted Heisman Trophy. Life has a way of coming full circle, and I found myself caught up fifty-six years later in 2013 in the multi-million dollar madness surrounding our second Heisman recipient, Johnny Manziel, aka "Johnny Football." It is estimated that the university received nearly forty million dollars in free publicity in a twelve-month period thanks to Manziel's prodigious, at times mind-boggling, gridiron exploits. I would like to thank John David Crow and "Johnny Football" for being symbolic bookends for what has been a wonderful five decades-plus voyage at this university. Unfortunately, due to series of bad decisions on his part, most of the publicity since 2012 surrounding "Johnny Football" has not been positive or profitable. He has taken dead aim and shot himself in the foot, life-wise and on the football field.

While the preponderance of my recollections are specific to people and events associated with Texas A&M, this book is much more about commonalities people share irrespective of where they were raised, attended school, or their place of current residence. People are people and events are events, and hopefully my characters and experiences are ones with whom anyone can identify regardless of mindset, experience, university affiliation, or geographical locale.

The reflections about A&M are mine alone and they represent a highly individual take on what legions of current and former students regard as a truly unique university. Words cannot capture how pleased I am to say that I have spent the majority of my life at Texas A&M, the village of College Station, the great state of Texas, and the good old US of A; I have had a life-long love affair with each of those entities.

I am also pleased to report that my views of people and events are occasionally contrarian. My observations and utterances are not always in agreement with those of the legions of students, former students, parents, flacks, publicists, and erstwhile cheerleaders who view the university from a mythical, mystical, rose-prismed, Pollyanna-ish perspective. With regard to this sugar plum vision, I am especially intrigued by what seems to be a smugness on the part of many Aggies suggesting you could not possibly know school spirit if you did not attend Texas A&M. The Aggies seem to think they invented and thus have a patent on school spirit. I have long labored under the suspicion that current students and past graduates of Notre Dame, Alabama, Oklahoma, USC, Michigan, or even venerable old John Harvard think they know something about loving their school, too. Just a few months ago during basketball season, I was reminded of this issue while watching the raucous Kansas Jayhawk fans. I suspect you would have a hard time convincing those "Rock, Chalk, Jayhawk, KU" folks that anyone could love their school more than they do.

There is a less attractive underbelly, if you will, to every organization, and Texas A&M University is no exception. I have a few reflections that may not be especially popular, but I think they are relevant to a broader understanding of the evolution and current status of this fascinating institution that has been so good to my family and me. At the same time, I have devoted the overwhelming preponderance of my remembrances to the fun, funny, and fascinating faculty, students, and other people I have met over what is rapidly approaching six decades if you factor in my tenure as an undergraduate from 1956-1960. I think I have portrayed my friends and acquaintances as interesting and, in some cases, funny people with forgivable foibles and lovable, laughable, and occasionally laudable idiosyncrasies. Some names are global and will be instantly recognized, but many I speak of in this modest document are of local origin and largely unknown to a wider audience. However, there are people similar to my friends and acquaintances in every city, state, university, and other walks of life, so it is possible to view them in a symbolic sense with application across the human experience. The names I cite may be different from those with which the individual reader is most familiar, but the wants and wishes, dreams and schemes, and emotions and experiences are really quite universal.

As a caveat, I have been a student at only two universities and professor at one, and thus am limited in generalizing about all institutions of higher learning. However, as stated earlier, I think there are commonalities that cut across all universities, personalities, and academic disciplines which I hope will pique the interest of a broader readership. Universities, like people, are more alike than they are different, and I think I have captured some of this common ground binding us together in academia and life.

Reflections about college life, life in general, and observations related to sport, politics, male and female students, interesting professors, and famous personalities are numerous. There is an equal abundance of anecdotes and observations with which almost everyone can hopefully identify. I also see my reflections as cutting across several academic disciplines including anthropology, history, philosophy, psychology, and sociology. I particularly love history and almost certainly would be a professor in that discipline if I were to repeat my life as an academic. While I have persevered and prospered to a fair degree in the world of Psychology, my heart is not with the paradigms my colleagues espouse to explain human and animal behavior. I am a modest methodologist at best and the murky nuances of statistics remain elusive to this day, so it is probably more descriptive to think of me as artist by disposition and temperament rather than scientist. More often than not, I find my colleagues to be adept at taking an interesting psychological issue or problem and analyzing it to death with endless sophisticated statistical applications, eventually rendering it virtually uninterpretable to anyone other than fellow research psychologists and statistics buffs. We in the social and behavioral sciences tend to obfuscate with numbers and our contemporaries in the arts and humanities are prone to do so with flowery and often obscure words.

My secondary goal, one guaranteed to be a success if only through its novelty, was to create a historical document for my relatives, particularly my children and grandchildren (and future generations of children). To my knowledge, no relative has ever taken the time and trouble to chronicle family events and memories with one exception. Shortly before her death in 1922, my maternal grandmother, Gertrude LeUnes, wrote a memoir of sixty-seven pages from which I have borrowed some material to be discussed later.

By way of summarizing the preceding paragraphs and pages, the "grey ghosts" and the "rekindlers" will have to share the stage with sentiments expressed in two additional adages or proverbs. First, there is a quote from an anonymous source stating, "A bird who wants to sing will always find a song." Second, the seventeenth century poet John Milton once wrote: "I am a part of all that I have met." I am the bird who wants to sing, this is my song, and these words are dedicated to all I have met, for they are an inseparable and cherished part of all that I am. They are, at once, my "grey ghosts", my "rekindlers", and me.

Reflections on Life in Academia

"Every day I get up and look through the Forbes list of the richest people in America. If I'm not there, I go to work."

Robert Orben, Author, Humorist

The trail that led to my becoming a Professor at Texas A&M University is both complex and convoluted. The wonderful, half-century journey essentially began in the fall of 1965 where I was in my fifth semester of doctoral studies at what was known at the time as North Texas State College (NTSC) and now the University of North Texas (UNT). It seems that my all-time favorite Professor, Dr. Merl E. Bonney, sought me out and asked if I would be interested is assuming a one-semester teaching position at my old alma mater, Texas A&M University, in College Station. As the two of us talked, I became quite interested in the position for it offered teaching experience which I did not have at that time. To heighten my interest, the job also paid $500 a month more than I was making with my NTSC "assistantship." At the conclusion of our meeting, I indicated my interest pending a discussion with my wife. Dr. Bonney subsequently sent my name to the A&M search committee along with that of my good friend, John Ed Wilhite. This dual nomination put the two of us in the somewhat uncomfortable position of competing against each other for the A&M teaching position. Following a day-long interview with selected members of the A&M faculty, I was chosen over John Ed and subsequently offered and took the job.

When I left Denton, ostensibly for the spring semester of 1966 only, I still needed to complete four courses, the much-dreaded preliminary examinations over the totality of my coursework, and the daunting dissertation requirement. My plans were to complete my four-month contract with A&M and return to Denton in the summer of 1966 to resume my life as a full-time doctoral student. That four-month stint became fifty-two years in December of 2017.

It eventually became obvious I would be staying at A&M on a more-or-less permanent basis when they asked me to sign on for the following academic year. I thus had to make arrangements to move the family down to College Station and complete my degree while working full-time. Making the 450-mile round trip drive between College Station and Denton for three-plus years was problematic, and teaching full-time made completing those requirements no easier. However, I eventually finished the twelve hours of course work at A&M, transferred the credits back to UNT, and dispatched the other hurdles over the next couple of years. I officially received my doctoral degree at the end of the summer of 1969, three-and-a-half years after leaving Denton and good old UNT for good.

All in all, I regard the eighteen months I was in residence as a doctoral student in Denton as some of the best in my life. I was blessed with mostly fabulous professors, a few good friends, and a wonderful and supportive family. It simply does not get much better than that!

I would like to shift the focus to my half-century as a faculty member at Texas A&M University, with highlights of the most memorable things that have happened during that time. Some of my vignettes are historical, others are meant to be humorous, a few unfortunately may be sad or depressing, and one or two are tragic, but all express the humanness that I have experienced in the past five-plus decades.

I am not going to attempt to shed incisive insights on the inner workings and political nuances of a Tier One, big-time, high-dollar research institution such as Texas A&M. I will leave that discussion to others more attuned to the topic and more astute in their observations. I have frankly enjoyed being for the most part a minor player on a big field, and my goal here is to write about "little people" and their impact on my life. There is a rich and fascinating human side to a university, and it has been my goal to capture some of it for the reader.

It seems only natural as I experience my eightieth year to reflect back on the vicissitudes of life, and at that advanced age, perhaps one better damn well get on with the process. Actuarial prediction and a modicum of good old street smarts suggest that one is living pretty much on borrowed time while wending one's way through the eighth decade of life. No one is guaranteed anything, longevity-wise, and the young die just as do the aged, though not nearly as frequently. The transition from youth to the egregiously euphemistic "Golden Years" is made more difficult by limitations sometimes imposed by failing health and/or the discriminatory practice of ageism.

Speaking of health concerns, I recently saw an American Association of Retired Persons (AARP) blurb indicating that only eleven people per hundred over the age of sixty do not use any prescription medications. I was one of those eleven until a couple of years ago when I ended up on Flomax, one of the drugs of choice for dealing with the malevolent, mean-spirited, balky prostate gland. As a much younger man I used to falsely gloat about how inferior and medically nettlesome the genito-urinary system of the female was in comparison with that of males. I was overbearing and cocksure in my dissing of the "female plumbing system", as I so smugly put it. Little did I know what was in store; no one ever warned me about the out-of-sight, covert, sneaky, mean-spirited, malevolent, and at times downright evil prostate gland with its propensity to wreak every bit as much havoc on my gender as the dreaded uterus does with the so-called "weaker sex." I will have more on this topic shortly as it has a lot of bearing on my present and future.

The advertisements for these Flomax-like drugs indicate that going to the bathroom frequently, waking up repeatedly at night, getting little warning about an impending urinary event, taking forever to get the stream started, flat out dribbling, and a host of other aggravations are signs of

Benign Prostatic Hyperplasia/Hypertrophy (BPH), or the enlarged prostate so common to older men. I have experienced every one of those symptoms and several others probably as yet undocumented by medical science.

Thanks to my training in the fields of clinical and counseling psychology as well as the sub-field about which I have written extensively, sport psychology, I found a way to convert frequent BPH-related night-time excursions to the bathroom to an advantage. We in psychology often ask our clients to reframe and restructure negative, counterproductive thoughts into efficacious and positive ones. I have been provided with plenty of practice about what I preach with the nagging nocturnal trips to the bathroom.

My typical night for the past fifteen years or so, and prior to 2017, went something like this: Bedtime around midnight followed by the first trip to the bathroom an hour later. It would then be an hour or so between visit one and visit two, and the others would occur every ninety minutes to two hours until I got up for good in the morning. Rather than cursing my fate, I looked at each episode as a chance to go back to bed, rearrange my covers, and get some additional blissful sleep while counting warm and woolly women. I would also get to wallow in the ecstasy of thumbing my nose at the twin tyrannies of the pernicious prostate gland and the eternally aggravating alarm clock.

The turning of a negative to a positive reminds me of an old Texas City friend and fellow college student in the 1950's, Sam Welch, who had a summer job at the Carbide Refinery. Sam would pack his lunch in the evening prior to heading off to work the next morning. Consistent with his Sunday through Thursday evening ritual, Sam would also prepare a nice lunch on Friday evening before turning in for the night. He would then get up early on Saturday morning, dutifully dress himself in the appropriate garb for refinery work, grab his hard hat, and head to the car. A few steps shy of his vehicle, Sam would stop and say to no one in particular, "To hell with Carbide! I'm not going to work today." He would then go back in the house, undress, and jump joyously back into bed and sleep another hour or two. Of course, Sam knew he did not have to work on Saturday's but it felt so good to tell "The Man" to stuff it. In your face, buddy! Sort of reminds me of country singer Johnny Paycheck's old hit song, "Take This Job and Shove It."

To get on with this tale, my health is decent but problematic of late; great sugar reading, solid liver functioning, not so great but passable kidney functioning, borderline acceptable blood pressure, a healthy balance between high and low density lipoproteins or the good and bad cholesterol, and no signs of prostate cancer (or any other malignancy, for that matter). Several years ago, I survived the highly-cherished colonoscopy for the first time ever, and that went well enough. The SuperPrep, that God-awful mixture designed to clear the intestines prior to the final examination, was ghastly, and fasting for twenty-four hours was no fun. One unanticipated bonus, however, was being asked to pass gas upon waking up from the procedure. Being able to fart with social approval and medical sanction is literally a license to kill! You could hear healthy farts echoing off the walls and down the halls of the endoscopy center. My wife, having the usual female abhorrence for the passing of gas, human or canine, found the whole exercise reprehensible, of course.

I take six pills a day, three of which require a prescription. With regard to prescription drugs, I take a low dosage of Crestor to control cholesterol, and the lowest possible dosage of a beta-blocker to regulate heartbeat. As for the others, I take a multi-vitamin, an aspirin on the chance it may help ward off heart problems, and two Instaflex to prevent hip pain.

The latter compound has been a life-saver; I had reached a point several years ago where my hip pain was at times excruciating. In order to treat the pain, I tried several of the hypochondroitin-based compounds with absolutely no success. Finally, in a stroke of serendipity, I stumbled on to a miracle cure several years ago known as Instaflex, and it continues to work like a charm. I was peering at my computer screen one afternoon and saw an advertisement up in the upper right hand corner for a pill to control joint pain. The advertisement promised a free one-month supply and I thought, "What the heck. It probably won't work but it won't cost me anything." I fired off an email and received the Instaflex a few days later. It says on the label to take three a day but, ever the optimist, I decided to see what two would do. Literally within twenty-four hours, I was pain-free and have remained so for the past six years, plus or minus. Because I get the desired effect with two pills, a thirty-day prescription lasts forty-five. I pay around $50 for each bottle but it is worth every penny and then some. Why this formula works and others of reasonably similar composition did not remains a mystery. I suppose there is some subtle ingredient in this product that is absent in the others. For me, Instaflex is an absolute wonder drug.

Speaking of cholesterol, that artery-clogging substance is a bane to many adults, and is a constant source of concern among professional and patients alike. Strangely enough, during one of my most recent annual physical examination, it was revealed that my cholesterol reading was *too low*. As a result of this rather unanticipated finding, it was suggested we reduce my Crestor from ten milligrams a day to five to deal with the low reading. Who ever heard of cholesterol being too low?

The reasonably sunny health report characterizing my first seventy-eight years has taken an adverse turn in the past eight or ten months due to two unforeseen events. Number One: It seems that my prostate gland, yes, the pernicious little entity which is normally the size of a lemon has grown considerably to the size of a baseball and apparently is blocking my urinary tract. In turn, I have not been fully evacuating urine from the bladder, and the urine has backed up in the bladder and destroyed a fair amount of my kidney functioning. I am presently dealing with the kidney and urinary tract issues, ably assisted by Dr. Richard Morgan, a nephrologist, and Dr. Charles Peirce, a urologist, and the three of us are optimistic about my future.

Number Two: I took off for Germany in July of 2017, fully intending to spend five weeks with the students who were studying abroad with me. For three days, I felt as good as I have in several years, but my moments of well-being were interrupted by a series of serious falls. On the fourth fall which took place in my apartment in Bonn, I split the back of my head open and had to be rushed to the emergency room to patch up my wound. A dozen stitches later, the doctor in charge of my case at the time told me I had a mysterious secondary infection and they were looking into it. Their first hypothesis was that I had a urinary tract infection based on a reading of my medical history reported above. Eventually, that hypothesis was replaced with a more definitive one, namely pneumonia, of all things. And my falls were directly attributable to the pneumonia.

The pneumonia was accompanied by several subdural hematomas associated with the aforementioned falls. Also, the stress of it all triggered off some transitory panic attacks and a brief flirtation with atrial fibrillation which eventually put me in the cardiac intensive care unit for a brief stay. I was treated with enough antibiotics to immunize half of Germany. As well, I was x-rayed, MRI-ed, CT-Scanned, PET-Scanned, ECG-ed, and transfused endlessly. Just to make sure each and every based had been touched, toward the end of my stay I was administered the coveted, much-sought-out colonoscopy which like all the other tests turned out to be negative.

Overall, I spent four miserable weeks getting acquainted up close and personal with medical care, German style. I was treated capably and well, though the language barrier was huge. The physicians I met had some command of English, some of the nurses did, but as one worked down the medical hierarchy to student nurses and other trainees, hearing my native tongue became a scarce commodity. All I can say is being sick in an American hospital is bad enough but at least people here speak English! Some of this English language deprivation was buffered by the presence of a number of my multi-lingual Study Abroad associates from Germany, a handful of American colleagues, and my oldest daughter, Leslie, and oldest son, Chay who took it upon themselves to spend a couple of weeks in Bonn. Neither had been in Europe before, so the experience was quite an eye-opener for them, and their efforts on my behalf were most appreciated.

Another disconcerting issue was the fact that the left hand seldom was in communication with the right hand, and lots of conflicting treatment information and unnecessary drug prescribing took place. Lest we think poorly of our German friends in the hospital administration business, observing my wife's hospital stays due to her soon-to-be discussed cancer revealed that American hospital administrators and physicians are equally afflicted with the left hand-right hand problem.

At the end of a month stay that was prolonged a few days by concerns (legitimate) about my ability of withstand a flight home to the US, I boarded a plane in the company of a medical escort who deposited me safely in the hands of my wife once I arrived home in College Station. Judy was quite perplexed when the emergency room staff decided I did not need hospitalization, but one more night in a hospital might have sent me over the edge. I honestly do not know if I could make another night in hospital confinement, getting drugged, scanned, scoped, poked, gouged, invaded, transfused, x-rayed, and otherwise enduring a plethora of uncomfortable scenarios designed to purge the pneumonia demon(s) from my system.

**IRISES HARVESTED FROM MONET'S GARDEN
AND PLANTED AT MY HOUSE IN TEXAS**

Once home, I tried to shake the cobwebs associated with the whole ordeal. I had overcome a life-threatening malady but the after-effects of the pneumonia, compounded by weeks of inactivity, medication hangovers, and battle fatigue from the flight home, were physically and mentally devastating. I pretty much stayed in bed for three weeks, sleeping mostly but watching the Little League World Series and the world track and field championships from London. Once up and about, I was so weak I could only ambulate with the assistance of a walker which, thank goodness, I discarded after several weeks of use. Thanks to a better diet, physical therapy, and the passage of time, I feel reasonably good and am able to do most of the things I have always done. I piddle around our house some, whether I want to or not, washing clothes, doing dishes, and other menial household tasks. I also work outside a bit, mainly picking up small broke limbs caused by Hurricane Harvey which dropped two feet of rain on the area but left us pretty much unscathed otherwise. South Texas and Houston, of course, were not spared.

There is never a down day when you own a home and eight acres of land. Making normal house repairs, mending broken fences, taking down drought-stricken trees and limbs, terrorizing the infernal fire ants, mowing or replacing grass, feeding the assorted tame and feral animals, planting ornamental trees, transplanting or fertilizing this that, and the other, repairing the lawn thanks to burrowing wildlife, digging dogs, brown spot, and chinch bugs, and just dealing with a huge assortment of seemingly endless chores keeps me on my toes. Another onerous task yet to be confronted is removing filamentous algae, hyacinths, and other invasive vegetation from my two-thirds acre tank (or what we called a pond in Oklahoma). Overall, I feel reasonably normal and healthy and am teaching again this semester. I did take this fall semester off to recuperate, and I am convinced it was a wise decision.

Health issues aside, at work I am pretty much regarded as part of the furniture and no one pays much attention to me any more except for a handful of undergraduate students. I have spent many wonderful, rewarding years as a professor at my alma mater. As noted elsewhere, I came to the university as an undergraduate student late in the summer of 1956, largely unaware of the true nature of the military, all male environment. I liked females well enough and had an aversion to uniforms, so the shock of not being around the former and having to wear the latter was substantial. A&M was affectionately known as "Sing Sing on the Brazos" in the 1950's, in reference to the famous California prison and the mostly lazy river that runs through this part of Texas. The nickname also spoke to the reputation of the university, at least among its students, as an alternate placement for borderline delinquents whose parents could afford to send their sons to college instead of having them confined in a treatment facility for wayward youth.

At this point, it is probably apt to say I am in the twilight of my academic career, and I have informed the powers-that-be I am going to hang it up in May of 2019 at the latest. In the past, I always told my classes my intentions were to keel over on the podium in front of their grandchildren due to a fatal heart attack. It has struck me of late that these "threats" are now passé. Conservatively, I would have to live to the age of one hundred or more to await the grandchildren of my present students. Not going to happen, in all likelihood.

I had long entertained illusions of setting the all-time record for longevity at the university but an article in the student newspaper a number of years ago gave me pause. The news item focused on a colleague in Political Science, Dr. Paul Van Riper, who retired for good in the spring of 2008 at the age of ninety-one. To be honest, though, Dr. Van Riper retired from full-time duties many years ago, I think when the mandatory retirement age was sixty-five, so much of his longevity was accumulated in sporadic or part-time increments. Nevertheless, I have decided not to challenge the good Dr. Van

Riper. I am thrilled, for the most part, to be at the end, not the start, of my career. I really do not think I would like academia twenty years from now, and probably would not even recognize it.

Recently, the university powers-that-be gave me something to think about with regard to the retirement issue. To wit, in order to get rid of the old geezer element on the faculty, the university administration has agreed to write us a check equivalent to our nine-month salary (minus deductions) if we will take a hike. Quite a number of the older faculty make a nice salary, though I am not remotely one of them, and it would be a financial coup if the administration could get rid of us old guys and girls. I have taken them up on the offer, and relinquished my tenure on August 31, 2017. I then resumed work the next day for two additional years as what the university calls "Senior Professor." Being the recipient of a check for $60,000 after deductions, give or take, has eased the pain of giving up something that has been so precious for so long.

My career has been marked by well over one hundred publications in a variety of professional journals dealing with the teaching of psychology, crime and delinquency, and, for the past thirty years, sport psychology. I have also delivered roughly an equal number of conference presentations which lends a certain visibility among one's peers. A couple of books have emerged from the train wreck that is my office, and one, a textbook on sport psychology, came out in its fourth edition in the summer of 2008 and is scheduled to come out as a fifth edition in 2019. I started working on the initial drafts of the book in 1984 and entertain apprehensions from time to time that I may not have another edition in me after thirty-four years. I will know soon when I start the next round of revisions.

Authors often complain that their books make them no money, and I happy to say the sport book has put around $300,000 in my bank account, or about $10,000 a year. Not a lot of money per year but it is $300,000 I would not have had otherwise. I also wrote a 208-page version of my larger text designed for the layman, and that book hit the market in the summer of 2011. It sold 3,000 copies during its first six months and I made about a dollar a book in royalties. I was just informed two months ago that some cosmetic changes have been made with the latter book in an attempt to pump some new life into its sales. Perhaps it will sell at a decent rate and provide me with some future beer money.

Sentimental Journey Home I (1965-2018)

SPORT PSYCHOLOGY TEXT, FIRST EDITION, 1989

SPORT PSYCHOLOGY TEXT, SECOND EDITION, 1996

SPORT PSYCHOLOGY TEST, THIRD EDITION, 2002

SPORT PSYCHOLOGY TEXT, FOURTH EDITION, 2008

SPORT PSYCHOLOGY: A PRACTICAL GUIDE, 2011

PLAY STRONGER, BETTER, HAPPIER: A PRACTICAL GUIDE TO
SPORT PSYCHOLOGY, SECOND EDITION, 2018

I have also been nominated for and/or received a number of teaching and student relations awards, and those probably mean the most to me of all my other modest achievements. Being named Fish Camp Namesake, T-Camp Namesake, Delta Gamma Teacher of the Year, Panhellenic Professor of the Year, Pi Beta Phi Professor Honoree, and receiving the prestigious Distinguished Award for Teaching from the TAMU Association of Former Students are accolades that are near and dear to my heart. Even more gratifying is the daily verbal and written feedback provided by current and former students. Someone once remarked that one of the great things about being a professor is there is no other profession where you are told each and every day how wonderful you are. I am told at least once a day how wonderful I am by someone, past or present, and that trumps tangible rewards any day. When I mentioned this idea to one of my classes this past spring, several students suggested there are probably some in my profession who are seldom if ever told they are wonderful. I know, and I am blessed. In this regard, when I returned from my five-week sojourn in Europe in 2016, I found a warm note attached to my office door from Matt Blume, Class of 1990, and an equally gratifying missive from Amy (Robinson) Gilmore, Class of 1980. In 2017, upon returning from the ill-fated trip to Germany, I had a long note on my desk from none other than Rosario Grajales, a cherished students from the early 1990's who is discussed fondly elsewhere in her capacity as a "rekindler." Remembrances from people such as Matt, Amy, and Rosario many years removed from their largely carefree undergraduate days is indeed a blessing.

I have always enjoyed my students and have had gratifying professional and personal relationships with many of them. It is an immense source of reward when I run into or receive emails from students from the 1960's, 1970's, and 1980's and beyond. I have kept up on a continuing basis with quite a number of them, and have been fortunate enough to see them prosper in their careers and personal lives.

Accepting All Compliments

One of the greatest compliments among thousands I have received over the years was given to me nearly twenty years ago by an ex-student and at one time my greatest cheerleader, Scott Cummings, who took my Abnormal Psychology class in the fall of 1984. Scott left A&M with his bachelor's degree and later earned the Doctor of Public Health degree from the University of Texas Health Science Center in Houston. He now wears two hats in A&M's Department of Agricultural Leadership, Education, and Communications, one as Associate Professor and Extension Specialist and the other as Associate Department Head and Program Leader. When Scott first returned to A&M as a faculty member in 1997, we crossed paths in the weight room at the university recreation center where we visited a bit. In the process of updating each other about our lives since his departure for graduate school and other challenges, Scott mentioned to me an excerpt that goes roughly as follows: "I received two degrees from and later worked at the University of Texas Health Science Center in Houston, and I do not think a day passed that someone did not mention your name and how fortunate they were to have known you and taken one or more of your classes." That is indeed high praise coming from people who are now physicians, nurses, psychologists, physical therapists, and hospital administrators working in that impressive professional setting. Scott's daughter, Lauren, enrolled in my Sport Psychology class in the fall of 2012, and I hope her father's hype did not set the bar too high.

Student Evaluations of My Classes

Separate and apart from the comments of Scott Cummings, for the past fifty years, the university has mandated evaluations of teaching performance be conducted in every class each fall and spring semester. Some emphasis is placed on these ratings in our annual evaluations so they do serve a purpose beyond personal feedback. In the process of filling out these forms anonymously (though a few gutsy students do sign their names), the respondent may add comments on the back side if they so choose. Probably three-fourths decline the option but others find it to be a good opportunity to pat us on our backs or paddle our butts, so to speak. I wish I had saved the more interesting comments throughout the years for they have often been rich in emotion and feeling. In any case, I typically read the comments, process the criticisms and suggestions for what they are worth, and pass the evaluations on to the shredder.

When I started writing these memories eons ago now, I decided to hang on to some of the more recent comments for they are illustrative of the totality throughout my career. In general, I find that my numbers are good but not nearly as good as they were in the halcyon early days when I had a much stronger age-related bond with the constituency. The most oft-repeated criticism of my teaching style is that I tell too many stories and thus do not focus enough on the actual course material. However, I can honestly say that I seldom spin a yarn I consider to be extraneous to my subject matter. I try to tell tales that illustrate various teaching points, and they may sometimes seem irrelevant to the students but I do not see them as tangential to my teaching goals. However, if I get the sense the group may be losing focus, I occasionally lapse into a story of limited didactic value just to keep everyone awake and on their toes. I will say that students may respond to me differentially on the ratings but they do not sleep in class. Whatever else I may accomplish, I am largely successful at keeping them awake which seems to give me a leg up on teaching them something. I almost never see a student nod off in my classes, and it seems to me that they are far more likely to learn if awake rather than asleep.

I also feel obligated because of my longevity and fascination with history to enlighten them about the world around them and the roots of their university. And, occasionally, I may take a few minutes to talk about current events and modern life. These diversions sometimes are only tangentially related to my course content, but I think the students should know a bit about from whence their beloved little university sprung or what is going on in their world beyond school, football, Greek parties, Corps of Cadets shenanigans, student leadership activities, and whatever else lights their post-adolescent fires.

Putting a Positive Spin on Teaching. I am including here a random sample of some of the more positive responses I have received. The reader will note far more positive than negative responses, and the nice thing is that I receive far more good ones than negative ones, perhaps at a ratio of five to one or thereabouts.

***"I would take all my Psychology classes with him if I could."

***"Dr. LeUnes is the BEST! GREAT class, GREAT speaker, GREAT Professor....a very fun person out of class, too."

***"Dr LeUnes is a BOMB. You have to take his class!" (Dear Reader: I am assuming being a bomb is a positive thing).

***"You have a great teaching style and have led such an interesting life. It was fun."

***"Pay this man more $$$!"

***"...very approachable, very knowledgeable, always excited and enthusiastic, and very understanding."

***"He is a great teacher, easy to talk to, and I am glad that I am taking another course from him this fall."

***"Dr. LeUnes is a great professor and most of all, a great human being."

***"I thought you were a fantastic teacher. And would take a class again from you anytime!!!"

***"It is a pleasure to take a class from a man who cares so deeply for the knowledge of his students. He shows his enthusiasm for life through his lectures & nothing is more motivating. Always eager to answer questions & invites a camaraderie between students, a complete joy of a class & not a better person to guide this experience."

***"He was an awesome professor and an awesome human being. One of my best collegiate experiences."

***"I never met a professor I respect more than I respect you. Thanks for your kindness and approachability. I will miss you." (This one was signed "Nichole" which was Nichole Loup from the 2001 Italy Study Abroad experience discussed elsewhere, and her kind words I regard as high praise indeed).

***"The best professor I have had so far. You came down from being a professor to become our friend, and that is such an incredible thing for us as students. Thank you so much." (This one was also from the Italy 2001 experience and signed by Heather Howbert. She was one of my favorite students as will be noted elsewhere and I appreciate her kind words more than she will ever know).

***"Best professor I have ever had. Sweetest professor ever. Love you, Dr. LeUnes."

***"It was never dull and I always looked forward to coming (A rare phenomenon)."

***"…when I learned of the field trips with the class, I considered switching out. Good thing I didn't. Those were some of the most meaningful & educational experiences I've yet had in college. Thanks for caring about your class, caring about your students, and teaching me so much."

***"I really enjoyed taking your class this semester. You have had the most interesting experiences of anyone I've ever met!"

***"I just wanted to let you know that I really enjoyed your class and your style of teaching. Your real-life stories really bring the class to life and the field trips were true eye-opening experiences. Thanks for putting so much effort so that we may get a good education."

***"I am also always really impressed with how you remember your students. It is nice to not be just a face in the crowd."

***"I just wanted to thank you again for a great class. I really enjoyed it and I wish there was an Abnormal Part Two I could take…I'll be stopping by next semester on more advice from you on what direction I should take in terms of what I should do when I 'grow up'. Thanks again!" This note was penned by Daryl Ryan in 2012 while she was still at A&M, and I received a follow-up thank you note from her in August of 2015. Daryl wrote: "I wanted to send a note thanking you for the encouragement and opportunities you presented me as a wonderful teacher. I would have never made it through without your guidance. Whether you know it or not, you have significantly impacted my life and I am truly grateful! Thank you for helping this passion of mine become a reality." Daryl is now a licensed Speech Language Pathologist, married, and the proud mother of two young infants.

***"I have absolutely LOVED your class and am going to miss it dearly. You are a wonderful professor and person: don't let any student tell you otherwise. I hope to remain friends. I've enjoyed getting to know you! One of your favorite students ever (Is it safe to say that?)."

***"…I'd like to say that your class has been the most motivating and enlightening I've taken in my time at Texas A&M. I knew about you for quite some time through my parents, but I didn't anticipate loving this class as much as I have. In light of this, I've been looking into delving deeper into my study of psychology by doing some research with a faculty member." This one came from Andre Arizpe, the son of two of my favorite students from the past, Bob and Shirley Arizpe. Bob has been the Superintendent of the San Antonio State Mental Hospital for quite a few years and Shirley is in Human Relations for a corporation.

*** "Set the field trips in stone. Trying to rearrange my schedule for Giddings was a pain in the ass. And don't pull the 'you can still get an A in my class without going'. Liked your class though."

***"It is a blessing to be in your class. God bless." (Written on team poster from Katerina Ruzickova, former A&M golfer from Czech Republic)

***"The first day of class, something you told us really stood out to me. You told the class to always tell the people we love, admire, look up to, etc. that we do before the opportunity is not there. I actually gave a speech to my whole high school about never taking anything for granted. My point is to tell you that I am extremely grateful that I get to have the opportunity to take a class with you. Any time I mention your name to a psychology major, they respond with 'I love that guy!' I can tell you love what you do and it is obvious, which makes me excited to use my psychology knowledge when I start my career. I am not going into sport psychology, but I know that I will use a lot of the information learned in your class when I am an occupational therapist and in life in general. I love all your stories, and I honestly could sit in your class for hours without getting bored. I don't think I have ever taken a college class where I haven't wanted to run out of the room the minute it was over. Thank you for letting me express my appreciation for all your stories, life lessons, and psychology knowledge." (Jordyn Logue, undergraduate)

***"Mr. LeUnes, you are a wonderful teacher and person. I have learned so much from you and wish I could stick around for more of your entertaining stories! I will be back in College Station in the spring after graduating from Rice, so I may be looking into volunteering at Giddings—I haven't decided yet! I will keep in touch with you. Best, Guess Who!? (Since I have had only one Rice student in class in the past twenty-five years, and two altogether, it was easy to identify "Guess Who?" as Georgene Jalbuena, a science major from that esteemed center of learning in Houston).

I would like to save some of the best for last, and seven comments, two from the distant past and five of recent vintage, stand out among my favorites. One from my second year of teaching came from Karen Allen, a student in 1967. She checked the numbers portion of the evaluation and then added a quote from the esteemed Lebanese poet and philosopher, Kahlil Gibran (1883-1931): "If he is indeed wise he does not bid you to enter the house of his wisdom, but rather leads you to the threshold of your own mind." I am not sure I was as successful in that endeavor as she thought I was, but the sentiment expressed through the words of Gibran says much about Karen Allen those many, many years ago.

A second "golden oldie" is from 1974 and came from a most unlikely source, a woman I barely knew. The student, Patricia Simpson, and I were talking casually during one of my class field trips in Austin, and she said she started off the class with quite a negative view because of my laid-back, conversational, story-telling style. She eventually reached a turning point, and said my approach to teaching was best summed for her in the lyrics of a musical hit of that year, *Killing Me Softly*, sung majestically by Roberta Flack. Patricia said it came to her one day in class that I was killing her softly a la Roberta Flack, and her favorite stanza, followed by the chorus, was:

> I heard he sang a good song
> I heard he had a style
> And so I came to see him
> And listen for a while
> And there he was this young boy
> A stranger to my eyes.
>
> Strumming my pain with his fingers
> Singing my life with his words
> Killing me softly with his song
> Killing me softly with his song
> Telling my whole life with his words
> Killing me softly with his song.

What a poetic tribute!

Another favorite is of an entirely different genre, and came to me in the spring of 2012 from the pen of a student named David Schares (he signed his name to the course evaluation). David wrote:

***"I would like to let you know that I enjoyed your class very much and always enjoyed coming to class. I found all your past experience very informational and if it weren't for the Hispanic guy on the commercial, Dos Equis could have used you as the most interesting man in the world!" In 2016, Dos Equis replaced the original most interesting man in the world but, strangely enough, did not come looking for me when they were in the searching stage!

In a similar vein, two of my undergraduate research assistants from the 2013-2014 year, Abby Demiano and Morganne Blackstock, offer the following tribute:

***"We cannot thank you enough for the amazing opportunity to do student research alongside you this year. The experience is one we will never forget! Neither one of us would have guessed this journey was going to occur when we signed up for your Abnormal Psychology course- what a fun and memorable journey it was. Getting to know you personally has been such an honor, you may be "the most interesting man in the world" (Dos Equis should consider promoting you) or at least as topnotch BBQ expert! Having you guide us and teach us the ropes of research truly paid off – still in shock that the cell phone study is being published. Again, **thank you** so much for the lessons you taught us and the memories you've given to us!"

Another tribute, this time coming from a most interesting young man from Denmark, adds sort of an international perspective. The student in question, Ahmed Issa (and known by all simply as "Issa") is an Iraqi who has lived all his life in Copenhagen prior to coming to A&M. He took part in my 2013 Germany Study Abroad program and has been most visible since your return in August of that year. Issa wrote:

***"Dr. LeUnes, you come both with so much wisdom and experience, and you care so much about students. I have meet [sic] a lot of professors, but I can easily say that you stand out above them all. You portray a certain person that everybody embraces, and you certainly know how to have fun. I grew such a great bond with you in Germany that I from time to time would think of my own father teaching me how go about life as a child. From my experiences with you, I have learned that you are a great individual with an old school sense of humor. A superb professional and a world citizen with an immaculate taste for beer."

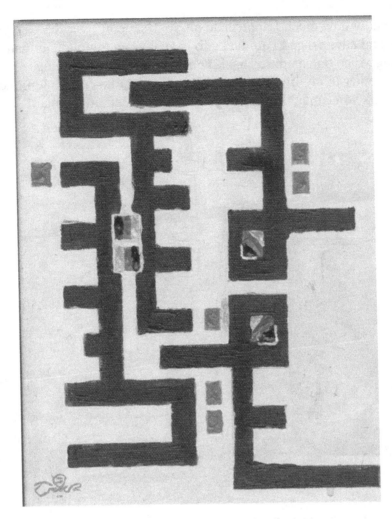

AHMED ISSA GIFT, LEUNES IN ARABIC

Allison (Alli) Van Ness, a student in both of my classes in 2013-2014, wrote a very touching letter, one of the most heartfelt I have seen:

***"Thank you for the absolutely wonderful past two semesters. I loved waking up and starting my days in your class. I have learned <u>so</u> much and owe you a huge thank you. Your enthusiasm about psychology has furthered my interest in the subject. You will be the face and name I remember when I think back about my college professors and college days. I appreciate all of your dedication to students and love for Texas A&M. A&M is extremely lucky to have such a lovely professor to teach and mentor students. It was a <u>pleasure</u> to be one of your students. And once again, **thank you** for all of the wonderful knowledge you have passed on to me."

A tribute from Faith Williams is another favorite:

***"I want you to know how much I appreciate all your support over the past year. You are both a great professor and advisor, and I am lucky to have chosen to go to Germany with you and have you as a guiding voice on campus. Thank you so much for everything. Please know as I move onto this next chapter in my life, you have played an instrumental role in helping me reach my goals. I can't thank you enough. Bis spater." ["See you later" in German].

I LOVE LEUNES, ANDREA DIGUARDI, GERMANY, 2013

VALENTINE FROM STUDENTS, CIRCA 1985

Faith Williams was the most adventurous of all my four hundred Study Abroad students, always trying out novel European cuisine, traveling to other countries, and most of all, setting a goal to return to Europe as soon as possible. The second Faith set foot on US territory after the summer in Germany, she started looking for other opportunities to return to Europe. She quickly found a program in Italy that eventually fell through for reasons too complex to discuss here. Ever the opportunist, Faith sought and landed an internship in DC for the spring semester of 2015 which has resulted in a dream situation for her, moving and shaking in the excitement of the Halls of Congress and Washington, DC as a Congressional Intern. Once the internship was concluded, Faith stayed in DC, moving on to a full-time paid position in the animal welfare business if my memory serves me right. Faith Williams epitomizes what the Study Abroad experience ought to do for students, namely expanding their horizons and opening their eyes to the great big world which is out there for their taking if they have the initiative.

Finally, kind words from Alexandra (Alex) Burks, a student for whom I developed a profound fondness during her stay here, are most meaningful given the source. Alex wrote:

***"I also wish the class size was not so large this semester, but again it has still proven to be a wonderful experience. I can assure you that if you taught a third course that I would take it as well. I would love to keep in touch throughout the remainder of my collegiate career and afterwards as well, once again, thank you for aiding in making my time here at A&M so extraordinary."

The Anti's Have Their Say (As Well They Should!). Lest you are about to decide I walk on watercress, please read on to get a feel for what my detractors have to say. I am pleased to report that most of the more negative evaluations are greatly outnumbered by the positive ones. Among my favorite student comments of a negative nature were received for three consecutive semesters forty years ago from what turned out to be a young female. Since these evaluations are filled out anonymously, I had no idea the first time who might be casting the negative stone. Once the identical verbiage appeared a second and then a third time in subsequent semesters, the list of possible perpetrators was easily narrowed down to one. In checking, I found that the woman in question was in a major that did not require any of my courses; all were electives for her, for heaven's sake! I could only conclude that she took those three courses with me because she enjoyed the pain. Her first assessment went as follows:

***"The man should not be allowed to appear in the presence of young people in a college classroom setting. He is an evil influence on young minds and should be sent to the College of Education to learn how to teach. Only then should he be allowed back in the classroom." Subsequent evaluations used almost identical verbiage to describe my didactic (and perhaps character) shortcomings.

Another assessment with considerable impact was not so much a course evaluation but rather was forwarded in a note during the middle of a semester. In this case, the student was not so much critical of me as she was a chapter in the abnormal psychology textbook on human sexuality:

***"I'm not trying to get points or sound like a religious fanatic, but I could not – did not read – Chapter 10 because of its graphicness (?). I had not read the chapter before I did my book evaluation, so I think the book should not be used. If it is used, I think Chapter 10 should not be a required chapter to cover. I'm not trying to be critical. I just believe in righteousness and morality because it is God's standards. You are an excellent teacher. Thanks for a great semester and class." Signed Melody (693-2704 if any comment)

Speaking of sex, I received a call maybe twenty years ago from a female student prior to the start of the semester, complaining about my required textbook in the Psychology of Adjustment course. The text contained what she, like Melody, deemed to be an offensive chapter on human sexuality, and she requested that I find a text that did not discuss such material. I politely informed her that all texts in human adjustment contain a chapter on sexual behavior due to its relevance to the continuation of the human species as well as its ostensible relationship to physical and psychological well-being. She then let me know she would not read the chapter on sexuality, attend any classes in which material of a sexual nature was presented, and would not respond to exam questions pertaining to human sexuality. I told her that those were all choices open to any student at any time, but such a decision might have negative consequences for her course grade. I also suggested she might choose to enroll in something more innocuous and less offensive. I ended our conversation by telling her, "If you think sex is objectionable, wait until you meet me. You will truly understand the full meaning of the word objectionable at that point."

Interestingly, she enrolled in the course despite it being a free elective and thus not required in her major. True to my prediction, she found me objectionable and ultimately filed sexual harassment charges with the university administration. I never talked to the woman after the phone call mentioned in the previous paragraph, and she lodged the complaints against me based on mostly random comments I made in class about human sexuality. Despite the absurdity of her claim about my lectures specifically sexually harassing her, I spent a good portion of the next year defending myself against this woman's groundless charges. This nonsense is political correctness gone awry, but I did finally receive a letter of apology from a top university administrator, exonerating me of all charges. The university administrators honoring this frivolous complaint should really be ashamed of themselves for giving this woman the time of day. It is truly political correctness at its worst, not to mention professional cowardice. The fact that I talked to this woman once on the phone and never in person and thus would have had a hard time personally harassing her apparently was only factored into the university administration's last-minute decision to dismiss her allegations. Shame on someone (and I know exactly who this someone is)! Moral cowardice is not a virtue!

Another favorite negative evaluation came up in the spring of 2009, again from a young coed who went right for the jugular vein:

***"The only thing I hate more than Sport Psychology is Professor LeUnes." I have absolutely no difficulty imagining that some students would not like me as a person or as a professor, but hatred does seem to be an extreme emotion. I was discussing this evaluation with a current student the other day and she was of the opinion that this little ditty says a lot more about the person expressing the emotion than it does the professor in question. I suspect she is correct in her assessment.

One I received in the spring of 2011 went as follows:

***"Dr. LeUnes does not care if his students succeed. He makes his tests very unfair and he favors students. If you aren't one of his favorite students he will make no exceptions for you even if put in a similar situation. He leaves during exams and has no one in class watching the students. We can't ask questions and the students cheat."

In this regard, I monitor exams using a two-part model borrowed from Rice University and the Aggie Honor Code which tells me that Aggies do not lie, cheat, or steal. I am told that Rice students do not cheat either so professors do not monitor exams. At the same time, the local honor code says that Aggies do not cheat. Thus, if you take those two philosophies at face value, there should be no need to monitor exams. Interestingly, I get far more praise than reproach about this approach to monitoring exams; some students say cheating actually is <u>less</u> likely under my conditions. Other students say they like the fact that I treat them as if they were honest adults. Of course, when I am assigned a teaching assistant, I ask them to monitor exams but give them plenty of freedom to work on their course assignments or other tasks while doing so. I refuse to be a policeman.

I guess I am deteriorating as a teacher right in front of my own eyes for the negative comments are more common of late, and certainly more vitriolic. A couple of samples from my Abnormal Psychology course in 2102 read as follows:

***"I am going to first say that I am so thankful for the education this university has given me, but with all due respect I cannot believe this man is still allowed to teach courses here. He forgets what he is trying to say halfway through saying [occasionally] and handed out the wrong test on the wrong day [never happened].

A second negative evaluation read as follows:

***"He is teaching from an old edition of the book [absolutely untrue; always use the most current edition] but requiring us to use a newer one, therefore many discrepencie {sic} arise. You are TRULY doing a disservice to your students in this course with him teaching it."

Yet another dissenter wrote:

***"I was really excited about this class, and it was a huge let down. Class was somewhat a waste of time because too much time was spent on setting up a story. The set up often had nothing to do with the point. Also, out of the chapters in the textbook, I think a lot more interesting material could have been chosen [True; I do not cover eating disorders, sexual disorders, sleep disorders, among other things].

Another dissident iterated:

***"I was upset that we hadn't focused or really learned about a mental disorder until almost halfway through the semester [Guilty as charged; I talk of mainly the treatment team, types of treatment, and psychological testing before launching into the disorders themselves]. Basically, I didn't learn anything I didn't already learn in Intro Psych [Must have had a very limited, biased, unbalanced introductory course]."

Someone else offered up the following:

***"Dr. LeUnes never presents A&M University in a positive light. He tells pointless and probably made up stories the whole time." (I cannot control whether one finds my stories aimless, but they are not made up. Life happens.)

Yet another student finds me offensive on other grounds:

***"I did not like this professor. Very interested in abnormal psyc but hardly learned anything from him. He says a lot of rude, condescending, and offensive comments."

The latest negative evaluation occurred in the spring semester of 2015 and was penned by an Honors student in Abnormal Psychology:

***"I think I never had to write such a negative evaluation before. While Dr. LeUnes is clearly intelligent and has years of experience in his field, his expertise is very narrow and the class consisted largely of him relating personal anecdotes to us. We had no textbook, he was regularly late to class, would forget his lecture material, or both, and when he would give lectures, he regularly devoted 20 minutes of our 50-minute class the relating to us goings-on in the community. We were not given a "syllabus" until week two of the class, and it was regularly revised. No clear set of expectations was provided. The course was wholly disorganized and I would not take another class from him. In fact, I may need to re-take this class altogether because I learned so little."

Yikes! To show that there is balance to our classroom world, the following evaluation came from a member of the same class:

***"I LOVE Dr. LeUnes. I have learned more in this class than I have in all of my other college classes combined. His vibrant stories & years of experience allows him to give his students real-life examples & really connect with the material. I cannot imagine anyone who could possibly teach this class better than he does."

All in all in that particular Honors course, there was one negative comment, as detailed above, and ten highly positive ones; eight students chose not to make any written comments. Despite this one very negative evaluation, the overall numerical rating for that semester course was my highest in maybe thirty years. Clearly, however, someone was not impressed!

***Finally, I had the ageism thing thrown at me by a male student: "Too old. Needs to retire."

A Department Head Chimes in on the Conversation. A cherished compliment from a non-student source came from one of my former department heads many years ago. His name was Dr. Cless Jay (not his real name) and he once related the following anecdote to me: "You know, Arnold, I travel around a lot in Texas extolling the virtues of the university and the department. I often cite the many achievements of my top researchers who have the lucrative federal grants and publish in the best journals. When I am talking to former students, they listen politely, seem to be impressed with all those achievements, but when all is said and done they eventually get around to saying; "All that stuff is well and good but what I really want to know is how Arnold LeUnes is doing." Again, high praise!

In this same vein, a colleague of many years, Dr. Brian Stagner, sent me an email in August of 2015 with the following message: "Hi Arnold. Every time I go to a conference and somebody reads the TAMU on my badge I get asked about you. Every time. It's all good, or at least when I press them for scandal and mayhem your former students are discreet. It happened again in Toronto." Unfortunately, there is scant scandal and only modest mayhem in my life to be discreet about, but it was nice of Brian to send along his thoughtful vignette.

I relate these vignettes and anecdotes not to boast but because they in some small way sum up a philosophy that has guided my behavior with students over the years. Simply put, I have always tried to treat them like I want to be treated, namely with dignity and respect. At times, my resolve gets tested by that infinitesimally small number of students who are out to beat the system, those who feel entitled because of some misguided sense of their own celestial significance, and the unfortunate souls who now and probably for the rest of their lives will always have an excuse for their failings and shortcomings. This latter group seems to view their excuse-making as admirable or at the minimum, forgivable. But again, such students are in the minority and only in a minuscule way detract from the whole.

Over the years, however, and particularly of late, I have seen a reasonably major shift in the way students respond to me. For my first twenty-five or thirty years, I was literally besieged by students with a variety of interests, requests, and motives. My calendar stayed completely full of appointments on almost any given day, and students lined up outside my door to visit about academic issues, life, careers, or whatever. If I left the building and went out on campus, I became a human pinball, bouncing from person to person and conversation to conversation as I made my way from Point A to Point B. It was nice to be recognized and sought out, but it was also difficult to find much privacy in that environment. However, I have always viewed my apparent popularity with students to be a blessing to be cherished. Being treated like a rock star, and I was, is not all bad…

Today, lines seldom form outside my door. There are far fewer frequent visitors. There are some who seek my counsel about graduate school, career issues, or life in general. There are those who need letters of recommendation for this, that, and the other, and I do more than my share. For example, in the fall of 2010, at her request I hired a delightful young coed named Annie Willis to help me around the office four hours a week. My original goal was to have Annie assist with a variety of tasks, but all we did for each of those four-hour periods in September, October, and November was write letters of recommendation together. Interestingly, I find that all are eager to seek out letters for graduate programs, professional schools, or jobs but only a small number, maybe one out of every four or five at most, ever indicate in person or by emails how their applications turned out. I now make them take a blood oath to let me know how the process plays out, and that strategy appears to have upped my response rate from twenty-five percent to maybe thirty-three.

All in all, I feel good, appear from all indicators to be reasonably healthy (for an old geezer), have a positive outlook on life, and my children (six), grandchildren (ten), and great-grandmonsters (three) are doing about as well as anyone could hope or expect. I enjoy my family life, and work is a wonderful refuge for me. I show up for at the office virtually every day of the year, paid or unpaid, except for the five weeks I spent with my summer Study Abroad students in Germany. Being at work orders my life and keeps me focused, and this is one big reason I have not retired. I have many sources of enjoyment besides work but showing up at the office almost daily has a grounding effect I am hesitant to lose. Another thing that keeps me going is that I am eighty but each semester my students in abnormal and sport psychology allow me, three times a week for fifty minutes each, to feel like I am twenty-nine years old again.

I dread the thought of joining a group of retirees for morning coffee and chitchat at the nearest McDonald's. Or the morning walk about town with my hand wrapped around a cup of Starbucks or convenience store coffee. Or the neighborhood power walks in the evening with the wife and/or the dogs. Spare me these indignities for they look like a form of water torture. This is just my humble opinion, happy retirees. It just is not for me. I have numerous retired friends and all of them think I am stark-raving mad for continuing to work; that is, except for my old high school comrade, college professor, and professional newsman, Mike Rhea, who has found periodic bouts with retirement to be less than exhilarating.

What makes all of this more remarkable is that I feel good almost all the time in spite of what my body is telling me to the contrary. Starting at the top and working downward, an objective inventory tells me the following: (1) My hair is gray, there is far less of it, and the curls and waves which I disliked and now would love to have back are almost totally gone; (2) My hearing is not as good as it once was and my ears are the source of a good deal of unwanted hair growth; (3) My eyes still work reasonably well but less efficiently all the time; I seldom use glasses except for reading fine print. Still, I do not see as well as I once did; (4) I am anosmic, and my nose, like my ears, is the site of much undesirable hair growth; (5) I have maybe eight percent fewer teeth than I had forty years ago and the ones I have are fragile and worn (as my dentist, Curtis Kaiser said at my last checkup, "Your teeth are beaten up but still working." I assured Curtis that the state of my dentition serves as a metaphor for my entire life, beaten up but still working; (6) My neck cracks and pops and does not allow full range of motion, particularly when backing up my Toyota truck; (7) I have nowhere near the upper body musculature I once had; (8) My hands shake a bit from time to time; (9) My right hip would like to be painful but Instaflex will not let it, thank goodness; (10) My balance is good but leaves something to be desired; (11) The skin on my upper arms is becoming more chicken-like; and (12) My feet bother me after a long day.

It seems paradoxical in light of these assorted aches, pains, and system failures that I can possibly feel good, but I do. There are occasional days when I feel like I am in my twenties or thirties, and I am blessed. Overall, things are good.

The Outsider

My high school yearbook has a section in which predictions are made about the future of each of the Class of 1956 graduates, and I am the subject of the first two lines where the prognostication goes as follows: "Arnold LeUnes is the head coach of the University of Podunk." At least the part about being affiliated with a university was correct. However, I have none of the psychological traits or professional credentials that would make one a coach at any university, let alone a high-powered football factory such as Texas A&M. Rather, I have adopted the role of outsider at my university, and as stated earlier, I proudly adhere to the old adage variously attributed to both Groucho Marx and Woody Allen which goes as follows, "I would not want to belong to a group that would have me as a member." The trenches have been my milieu, down there with the ragtag undergraduates, the downtrodden and oft-browbeaten graduate students, and a small contingent of faculty friends of similar philosophical and life perspective. As the lovely lady in the harbor says, "Give me your tired, your poor, your huddled masses yearning to breathe free The wretched refuse of your teeming shores."

As partial documentation of my self-nominated outsider status, I had never met, conversed with, or shaken the hand of any President of this university from 1966 until April of 2012. On that momentous 2012 day, I walked from The Zone Club in Kyle Field to the newly-renovated Memorial Student Center conversing with Dr. R. Bowen Loftin, aka "President Bow-Tie." President Loftin later left the university to assume the duties of Chancellor at the University of Missouri, but was widely known prior to his untimely departure for his student-friendly demeanor and ever-present assortment of colorful bow ties. The bow ties were the source of much light-hearted discussion around campus and at athletic events where our fearless leader could be seen shaking hands and good-naturedly posing for photo-ops with all takers.

Speaking of sartorial accessories, Dr. E. Gordon Gee, President of The Ohio State University, was the subject of a fairly recent Huffington Post article which reported he had spent $64,000 of state money on bow ties and spin-offs thereof. As part of his shtick, President Gee presents each entering freshman a bow tie cookie when he or she sets foot on the campus in Columbus.

I have not, to my knowledge, ever been invited to any of the myriad receptions held at the houses of either the President or the Chancellor. I have not walked the hallowed halls of the George Herbert Walker Bush Museum and Library, and until August of 2012, had never attended one of the faculty convocations where multi-colored and resplendent academic regalia are the norm. Shortly before that fateful date, my department head trapped me, backed me into a corner, and forced me at gunpoint (not really!) to represent the department at the 2012 Freshman Convocation ceremonies. I most reluctantly did as requested, and despite my direst predictions of doom and gloom, it actually was not especially painful to sit through the ceremony.

That disclaimer aside, however, these formal events and those who revel in them are largely alien to me. They are people with a very different frame of reference, seemingly from another line of work or perhaps a different universe. I simply cannot comprehend resplendent robes, the toting of the mace, the utterance of predictable platitudes and bromides, and the worship of pomp and circumstance. Speaking of old shibboleths, graduation is the ultimate pomp and circumstance event in the life of an academic, and platitudes and bromides abound. I have to agree with a quote from writer and humorist, Robert Orben: "A graduation ceremony is an event where the commencement speaker tells thousands of students dressed in identical caps and gowns that individuality is the key to success."

To rub additional dirt into the gaping wound of being an outsider, I have never been asked to attend a university football game in one of the celebrity boxes that encircle the newly redone Kyle Field, A&M's football stadium, and leased by wealthy former students or even wealthier corporations. Oh, indignity, where is thy sting?!

At a level lower in the pecking order of academia, I have visited with the Dean of the College of Liberal Arts on a couple of occasions, but only when summoned for disciplinary comeuppances for crimes that were usually more trumped up than real (for example, the sexual harassment case reported earlier). On one occasion early in my career, I was confronted by Dr. David Maxwell, the Dean of Liberal Arts and an economist by training, with allegations lodged by an "anonymous mother" to the President of the university, Dr. Jack Williams. The "anonymous mother" alleged that I had told her daughter she could not make an A in my class unless she came across with the proverbial "Lay for an A" sexual encounter. While I am no angel and have committed way more than my share of character indiscretions, the seduction strategy suggested by this "anonymous mother" has not once been my style. And only once have I been offered sex for a grade, and that was thirty-five years ago. The student who made the offer remains etched firmly in my memory but I will not divulge her name for obvious reasons.

At about the same time all this nonsense was taking place, my on-the-edge-of-the boondocks home situated between Bryan and Hearne was trashed and house plants thrown around and broken while I was away for the day. The timing of the two events seemed somehow less than coincidental which, in the course of our conversation, I related to Dean Maxwell. I was able to eventually convince the Dean that I had not committed the dastardly deeds dredged up by my detractor. After deliberating about this issue for an hour or so, we parted company, with the Dean giving me a friendly, almost fatherly admonition as I departed that went something like this: "Arnie, Old Bean, I don't care if you fuck every woman on campus, just don't do it while they are in your class." I am not sure Dean Maxwell's words of wisdom about frolicking with the friskier *femme fatales* on campus would hold up in our modern politically correct environment. But, then, it may not have been a good way to proceed in 1975 either!

Speaking of "Old Beans", one of the Dean's most notable idiosyncrasies was his liberal use of the phrase when referring to younger faculty members, particularly those whose names he did not know or remember. This gambit reminds me of an old Sociology professor from the 1960's, Dee Kutach, who called each of his male students "Fireball." Almost any hormonal, macho young male, particularly those in the Corps of Cadets where being a man reigns supreme, would swell up with pride and feel just a little bit better about his masculinity knowing he was a "Fireball" in the eyes of one of his most esteemed professors.

Wherever possible, I have avoided talking to most of my twelve department heads, all male by the way until 2016 when Heather Lench assumed the "reins of power." Daily psychological, occupational, and geographical proximity dictates a certain amount of interaction whether one likes or actively seeks it. While most of these men (and one woman) had basically good hearts and meant well, at least four could be characterized without stretching the psychiatric diagnostic criteria too much as antisocial, alcoholic, hysterically mute, or depressive and suicidal. I will enlighten the reader about these notables at a later juncture.

One of the good guys of recent vintage who ascended (descended) to that dubious department head throne was Dr. Leslie (Les) Morey, a highly respected clinical psychology researcher and professor by day and a more than passable bass guitarist by night. Les has played locally and regionally with a band known as Tubie and the Touchtones for several years now, performing in an interesting assortment of cabarets, taverns, watering holes, and out-and-out dives where, in the latter instance, dodging beer bottles thrown by drunks is part of the price of performing. Les got out of the department head business after one four-year term because, as he put it one day in a casual conversation in my office, "I am tired of waking up each morning trying to figure out which faculty member I am going to hate the most today." The parallels between his experiences as a department head in 2010 and mine as an Army officer nearly five decades earlier were spooky; I never knew which of my enlisted men would be whining or complaining the most when I got to my office each morning.

As a fledgling second (and later first) lieutenant, I was in charge of a fifteen-man section at Fort Hood from April 1962 through August of 1964. As a result of my experiences in that situation, I knew by age of twenty-five I would never seek nor hold a position of administrative authority ever again. Governing my own life is more than I can handle most of the time, and shepherding the lives of others is simply not my calling. I lack the discipline, mental toughness, or depth of character or whatever trait it is that allows one to make the tough call. Too many administrators will not make that tough call, instead penalizing those who do the right thing while failing to demand accountability from those who violate the rules. The typical administrator response is to punish all for the transgressions of a few. The mantra seems to be, "Don't ever confront the rule breakers, the ne'er-do-wells, and the scoundrels; it is too painful. Send out a general memorandum or email to all and hope the ones you really would like to punish turn their behavior around." Punishing all the for the sins of a few takes less courage and, paradoxically, saves the cowardly administrator from incurring the wrath of the miscreants he or she should not care about in the first place. And the misbehavior of the guilty goes on unchecked.

As an aside, I think one of the greatest problems with the public schools today is the apparent unwillingness of school administrators, particularly principals, to evaluate, document, and dispatch those who are unfit or incapable of teaching. It is easier to sit in the office and fire off memos that penalize the innocent and empower the incompetent. There is a widely held sentiment among critics of our educational process that you cannot fire a teacher. In reality, there are actually strictures in place that make firing the incompetent teacher relatively easy, but it requires administrators who will do the right thing and make the tough call when it comes to evaluation and documentation.

Who Am I?

I have been a fair-to-middling professor, a public speaker of some facility, a passable researcher and writer, a steady and amiable colleague, a willing mentor to students, a patient listener (to students if not family), a facilitative sponsor of annual study abroad experiences for young Aggies, a decent husband, a loving if sometimes distant father, and a good friend to many.

I am a tad overweight, have consumed entirely too much beer, thus freeing up water to wash dirty cars, dirty clothes, dirty dishes, and dirty people, laugh loudly and frequently, curse like the proverbial sailor when provoked (or just for the hell of it), and have a flash-point temper but carry no grudges. I like nice guys and absolutely adore pretty women. My lovely wife says I am partial to tall, blonde, athletic Amazons, but then again, short, dark-haired, non-athletic Italians or Uruguayans will do, too. Or, to paraphrase the actress, writer, sex symbol, and master of the double entendre, Mae West, whose words about men could apply equally to women: "I only like two kinds: domestic and imported."

I am fascinated with sports of almost all persuasions, but would shed nary a tear if professional football and the even more repugnant cousin, professional basketball, disappeared overnight. I still have some patience with viewing the ruffians who play professional football but watching the tattooed hooligans in the NBA is painful for it bears little resemblance to entertainment. And this is the only sport entity I know of where the spoiled brats have a substantial say-so about who gets fired as head coach, a la the recently retired and easy to dislike Kobe Bryant. On top of that, the fighting, wrestling, and taunting during the games, the "in-your-face" macho bullshit, and the constant tearful, heartfelt apologies from the crybabies for their gay bashing, wife and girl-friend beatings, alcohol-related automobile accidents, late night drinking sprees, and other excesses cancel out the positives for me. To put these comments in context, all this comes from a guy who has missed maybe a hundred A&M men's home basketball games in the past fifty years. Clearly, my problem is not with the game of basketball itself; I am just not terribly fond of miscreants. In the interest of fairness, there are some great organizations in the NBA (i.e., the San Antonio Spurs) and some really first-class people playing the game (i.e., LeBron James), so I do not want to paint with too broad a brush here.

I like visiting at home and abroad, and adore Paris beyond words. Munich is a close second, partly because the Bavarians seem nonplussed if visitors are not drinking one of their absolutely elegant beers. The trendy, touristy Hofbrauhaus is a major venue for fun and frivolity in Munich, and merry maids often are seen carrying six and eight liters of beer at one time, using their oft-ample breasts to balance the inordinately heavy load. I have an abiding fondness for the French people and a begrudging admiration for the lean, loud, and lax Italians who as a group are capable of screwing up an anvil. I am absolutely blown away at the beauty of Slovenia and Croatia, and words fail me miserably when I try to describe those two enchantingly different islands on the other side of the world that make up New Zealand. The Kiwis love their country, seem to like us Americans well enough, and enjoy a lifestyle that is the envy of many. I cherish the laid back lifestyle in Amsterdam, and revel in German, Dutch, Czech, and Belgian culture and their unwavering devotion to brewing truly remarkable beer. I am partial to dunkel (dark) beers but their hefeweizens (wheat beers) are phenomenal, too. It has taken American brewers and beer drinkers a long time to figure out that the Europeans have us beat hands down when it comes to putting a good beer on the bar. The presence of more and more brew pubs and the burgeoning craft beer industry serves as testimony to this awakening here in America.

WAITRESS AND STEINS, HOFBRAUHAUS, MUNICH

I cringe to the very core of my existence every time I hear the pompous, pretentious, and politically correct term so dear to academia, "Africana Studies." The "Studies" part gives me no real pause but my skin crawls akin to a woman pulling her long, dainty, beautifully decorated fingernails across a blackboard every time someone says "Africana." And, oh my goodness, the skin starts to literally pull away from the bones even more when I hear the consummately pretentious area of "inquiry" known as the "African Diaspora." I wish I could help it folks, for I believe in the cause, but "Africana" and "Diaspora" just do not get it done for me. Academics are prone to pretension, and my colleagues in the more artsy-fartsy side of the equation seem most prone to its usage.

Far more vexing, however, is "Scholar", a term used and abused so hopelessly and gratuitously in academic circles. The status as "Scholar" is almost always self-conferred, particularly among young, neophyte professors who would not know a scholar if one hit them upside the temple with a transcendental, transformative, titillating tome. When I think of scholar, I think of someone who writes or speaks in terms that transform the human condition in some significant way. If one accepts my definition, true scholars are indeed few and far between, which has been my experience. I certainly am not willing to grant scholar status to a 25-year old newbie fresh out of graduate school, though many of them seem to have no hesitancy to do so themselves. One of the absolute dumbest, least accomplished professors I know at A&M constantly refers to himself as a scholar. Shame, shame!

I love a good joke (clean or off-color, domestic or imported), beautiful music of several genres, and creative works of art. I love a juicy home-grown tomato and am most fond of the hundred crepe myrtles in my yard. For more years than I am willing to admit, I tolerated my wife's horse (now deceased) who was hell bent on killing me when I was not looking. What kind of beast would kill the person who feeds it? Yes, it would be a horse! Being seriously neuronally-challenged, only two thoughts ever enter their feeble little minds: (1) I'm hungry, and (2) How can I harm a human today! But I truly enjoy our three dachshunds and the homely-to-the-point-of-being-almost-cute one-eyed Chihuahua. I also greatly enjoy the domestic ducks and their countless wild cousins, the black-bellied whistling ducks, sometimes up to fifty or more at a time, who frequent our pond. I am fascinated by our two feral cats, Baby and Domino, the legions of raccoons, opossums, and an occasional skunk that congregate nightly outside my bedroom window. It is a source of continuing amazement that this ragtag collection of wild animals can co-exist side by side, dining on the cheap cat and dog food we provide. Cheap, like many other things in life, is in the eye of the beholder for I suspect we spend upwards of $400 per month on food, snacks, shots, and medical care for our domesticated and adopted wild animals. However, they return the favor in considerable measure through their playful hijinks and didoes. And it doesn't get too much better than the night late in June each summer when the raccoons bring their babies out for the very first time.

I love a good scarf in the winter, and am still young and financially strapped enough to derive great pleasure from finding a twenty-dollar bill in a jacket that has been tucked away in a closet since the last cold snap of the previous winter. And the feel of clean sheets on the bed is still a pretty big high for me. I also often wonder how many home runs Mickey Mantle would have hit if he had played in the era of the designated hitter and performance enhancing anabolic-androgenic steroids.

I never watched an episode of *Dallas* or *Cheers* or *The Cosby Show* (How about that Bill Cosby?) nor have I ever seen *The Simpsons'*, *How I Met Your Mother*, or *Grey's Anatomy*. And I absolutely refuse to watch the unreality of reality TV! Speaking of television, David Letterman once read an excerpt from his 1993 book *Late Night Fun Facts* indicating the phrase, "No shit, Sherlock" first appeared in Leviticus. I never knew! But, then, Leviticus and LeUnes would constitute an unlikely and unholy alliance.

    Among the legions of comedians, commentators, and social critics who show up on the tube, Keith Olbermann, Bill Maher and Michael Moore have always been favorites but I must reluctantly admit that sometimes Maher can get a bit shrill and over the top, even for me. Moore may have seen his better days, too, though his 2016 film, "Where to Invade Next", offered a potential rebirth. We also agree that we as a people could profit from retaining the best things about our country while borrowing the best practices of Germany, France, and the Scandinavian countries to make us even greater. My fifteen summer trips abroad since 2000 have convinced me the Europeans do many things better than we do (i.e., health care, education, workplace harmony, family life, gun control, the death penalty) and we could profit by learning about and implementing their philosophy and practices into our own society.

    I am ashamed to admit it in public like this, but I got so bored the other night I watched fifteen minutes of *Cheaters* on television. There is something imbedded in the most remote depths of the human psyche, something very base, ugly, and reptilian, that would lead a writer or producer to concoct a television show which has as its central theme men and women being publicly videotaped in confrontations with their significant others who have been caught red-handed in romantic trysts outside the "love honor and obey" relationship. Such shenanigans add a whole new dimension to tasteless and the term "filthy lucre." And what can one say about the people who actually watch this trash?

    I also have yet another quirk: Every time I hear the name of the current Hollywood heart-throb Brad Pitt, an automatic image of Sean Penn pops into my brain. How can that possibly be? What kind of electrical malfunction would make that happen? And while I am at it, what is in our DNA that makes us thirst for details about the tawdry lives of an endless array of intellectually challenged movie ingénues? Almost without exception, these women add new and deeper meaning to the term "brainless twit" every time they open their mouths. And while we are lionizing actors and actresses, one should remember they make their living reading script written by professional writers who are blessed with infinitely more functional neurons than they.

    I have never been a fan of the Beatles, Michael Jackson, or Whitney Houston. I never cared much for watching the immensely talented Michael Jordan in his day or LeBron James in his, and you would have to put a gun to the side of my head to get me to watch the recently retired (thank goodness) Kobe Bryant play basketball. By the way, did I tell you what I think of professional basketball? I did? Sorry, I have been known to digress! Just ask my students.

    When he was at the peak of his game from 2000 to 2010, I hoped against hope that Eldrick "Tiger" Woods would smile at least once when his game was not going well. Tiger was all arm pumps and toothy smiles when the shots were falling, but the clubs were thrown and the air blued with strings of obscenities when they were not. On those increasingly frequent occasions when he struggled with his game, the skin around his eyes would tighten, the pouty lower lip would drop, and he became a club-throwing, epithet-generating machine. And I do not suppose his personal life, especially events in 2010 and then again to a lesser extent in 2017, have been sources of much contentment for him, either. His public persona is that of a robotic, tortured, soul-less, shell of a man. He talks, between multiple back surgeries, of eventually making a comeback, and we shall see how that goes. I personally think he is a physical wreck and a psychological basket case.

For a small retainer, maybe as paltry a sum as $100,000 which is pocket change to the Tiger, I could have saved him a lot of grief (and money) that November night in 2010 when his wife walloped him upside the noggin with a sand wedge. All he had to do was dial me up on the old cell phone, agree to my modest $100,000 retainer, let me arrange a press conference with the media, and grab the microphone and tearfully confess every one of his sins, real and imagined, and, for good measure, one or two of mine, too. As part of our agreement, he would have to publicly name every woman with whom he had been involved so that none of them could pop up periodically to keep the rumor pot boiling. My reasoning is that the public is forgiving of its icons for most of their transgressions, particularly sexual ones, and getting the tawdry details out there and over with would be the most prudent policy. For about the same money, I could have saved William Jefferson Clinton some grief, too! Actually, I would have given the president a cut rate as he did not possess anything approximating the wealth of "El Tigre." By the way, do you suppose rumors started by David Letterman at that time linking Tiger to Flo, the insurance woman from Progressive, have any substance?

My list of least favorite celebrities is led by George W. Bush though he has been seriously challenged of late with the unfortunate and unlikely emergence of our new President, Donald Trump. Like many, I am vexed, perplexed, astounded, dumbfounded and rendered speechless by Mr. Trump's unexpected rise and election. His almost daily trampling on the Constitution, incessant lapidation of the press, counter-productive dissing of the intelligence community, scary saber-rattling with Iran and North Korea, and fanciful creation of false bogeymen with which to stir up the masses reminds me of other narcissistic madmen in recent history.

Though my hopes are not high and become less so with each passing day, I wish Mr. Trump well for the country does not prosper if he is not successful. However, it is scary to contemplate the continuation of a Trump presidency, and it is made even more frightening when one compares what we now have occupying the Oval Office with the man who just left it. My sentiments on this matter are summed up well by Johnathan Giftos, a faculty member at the Albert Einstein College of Medicine, some months ago: "[It is sad and scary] when a faithfully married black president who was the son of a single mother, the first black editor of Harvard Law Review and a professor of constitutional law is considered unintelligent, immoral, and anti-American by the right while a xenophobic, misogynistic, serial philandering trust fund kid who quotes from the National Enquirer, peddles conspiracy theories, routinely calls women ugly and fat, calls McCain a loser for having been a prisoner of war, and who has advocated torture and the bombing of women and children has captured the hearts of a majority of Republicans."

But let's get back to George W. Bush. What "The Shrub" did to the people of Iraq, the young men he sent to die or get mutilated in the misguided, useless wars in Iraq and Afghanistan, the American people in general, the political and economic destabilization of the Middle East, our relations with the rest of the civilized world, and the economy of our own country borders on the criminal.

Mr. Bush is joined in my personal fraternity of unlikeable public figures by his fellow Texan, the seriously intellectually- and informationally-challenged former Governor and several times failed Presidential candidate, Rick "Let Me Shoot Myself in the Foot" Perry, the resident hatemeister Rush Limbaugh, the off-the-top-of-the-chart, insufferably sanctimonious, bible-thumping boor and one-time NFL poseur Tim Tebow, and the increasingly invisible (thank goodness) Sarah Palin. Glen Beck, Ann Coulter(geist), Bill O'Reilly, and Sean Hannity occasionally intrude on my consciousness but they are merely minor nuisances in my hierarchy of least favorite characters. And how about the baggage generated by the loose cannon Congressman from Texas, Ted Cruz, who many fancy to be a modern-day version of the 1950's witch hunter, Senator Joseph McCarthy. Bush…Perry…Cruz…? What is it about my beloved home state of Texas that spawns these misguided, malevolent political misfits? Where are Barbara Jordan, Molly Ivins, and John Henry Faulk when we need them so badly?

Speaking of Tim Tebow, help me out on this one: Is it Tebow or his mother who once proclaimed him to be the new Messiah? At the peak of his popularity as a Heisman trophy winner a few years ago, Tebow elevated dropping to his knees in a publicly prayerful pose to the level of a fetish. I would like to know if Tebow, the man with unbelievably errant arm and the equally incredible belief in the inerrancy of the Bible, ever read Matthew 6:5-6 where one can find some interesting thoughts about public displays of prayer? To wit:

"And when you pray, do not be like the hypocrites, for they love to pray in standing in the synagogues and on the street corners to be seen by others. Truly I tell you, they have received their reward in full. But when you pray, go into your room, close the door and pray to your Father, who is unseen. Then your Father, who sees what is done in secret, will reward you. And when you pray, do not keep on babbling like pagans, for they think they will be heard because of their many words. Do not be like them, for the Father knows what you need before you ask him."

Had there been professional sports in his day, Matthew would no doubt have extended his prohibitions concerning prayer to football and baseball, two sports played by men who are prone to embrace a wide assortment of superstitions (such as organized religion).

I once again thought of the insightful Matthew just yesterday morning while clogging some arteries at McDonald's. Looking up from my newspaper, I observed a four-some of septuagenarians praying at length over their coffee and breakfast burritos. I am guessing Matthew would have sent them home to conduct their business with the lord in private.

But this is enough about unlikeable lamentables! I would like to devote the next several hundred pages to more positive things such as my mostly fun reflections from fifty-two years as a Professor of Psychology at Texas A&M University and eighty as an amateur observer of human behavior and life events. To that end, I would like to kick things off by talking about two transformative events in the history of previously all-male and predominantly military Texas A&M University, the full admission of women in 1963 and the massive changes orchestrated by President Earl Rudder from the late 1950-s until his untimely death in 1970. When General Rudder took over the leadership of the university, women (and black students, for that matter) were non-existent and the place was dying on the vine, impaling itself on its own sword of inefficiency and historically bad choices; change was long overdue; A&M was never to be the same and that is a wonderful thing!

First Females and the General

Two Powerful Forces Reshape the University

It has been a distinct privilege to have witnessed up close and personal the admittance of women as fully-sanctioned, degree-seeking students, a process that was instrumental in saving and ultimately transforming Texas A&M University. Another powerful influence with transformative significance was the indomitable presence of General James Earl Rudder. He was a major influence in the admittance of women as well as the general restructuring of the university at a critical juncture in its history. These events and people made for some interesting times in the late 1950's, throughout the decade of the 1960's. Let us first look at how women changed the landscape of what was once an all-male military bastion.

HUTSON SISTERS, FIRST FEMALES AT A&M, 1903

Women at A&M: A Chronology

A major transformation with profound implications for the future of the university took place in 1963 with the admission of women as fully-sanctioned, degree-seeking students, a process that picked up considerable impetus during my first years on the faculty. A&M's history with regard to women had been a checkered one, populated with occasional points of light and more than a few dark periods. A few of the more salient highlights of the female "movement" at A&M from 1893 to the present are:

1893. Ethel Hutson is first woman to attend A&M.
1903. Mary and Sophie Hutson complete engineering degrees but not awarded diplomas. Both practiced engineering and remained involved with and supportive of A&M.
1909. Women attend summer school
1923. Fourteen females listed in yearbook as "Special Women Students."
1930. First lawsuit filed on behalf of full admission of women.
1940. Women were not in attendance at summer school for the first time since 1909.
1946. Student wives are allowed to take "extension" courses. Women return as summer school students.
1953. State Senator, William T. Moore, the legendary "Bull of the Brazos", introduces a resolution to force the A&M Board of Regents to admit women. The measure is defeated in the Senate by 27-1 margin. Moore threatens to take the issue to the courts.
1954. Faculty Academic Council recommends to the Board that women be admitted and military training be made voluntary. On a larger societal note, women are allowed to serve on Texas juries for the first time.
1956. President David Morgan asks Chancellor M. T. Harrington to petition the board to consider co-education. Harrington refuses to send the proposal to the Board.
1957. President David Williams recommends admission of all women. The Board rejects his recommendation.
1957. Compulsory military training reinstated.
1958. *The Eagle* and *The Battalion* recommend admission of women.
1958. The YMCA sponsors student referendum on admitting females. The vote is two to one against the proposal.
1958. Judge W. T. Mc Donald, Class of 1933, orders A&M open to women. His decision is reversed by a higher court and Judge McDonald is hanged in effigy on campus. Attorney John Barron, an outspoken advocate of female admission, seeks police protection for his family.
1959. Sterling Evans, class of 1921 and a strong advocate of admitting females, joins the Board of Regents.
1960. Attrition rate among freshmen reaches 56%.
1962. Between 1952 and 1962, A&M's enrollment grew by 29%. The University of Texas grew by 70% and Texas Tech by 117%. A&M was the fifth largest university in the state.
1962. According to results of an unofficial poll, the student body favors co-education.

1963. The Board permits limited enrollment by wives of faculty, male Aggies, and staff members. Eligible females may also attend graduate school and College of Veterinary Medicine. 183 women are enrolled but are required to sign a waiver stating they will not file a lawsuit if A&M once again becomes an all-male institution.
1963. A&M College of Texas becomes Texas A&M University.
1963. An organization for Aggies over age seventy, the Sul Ross Group, comes out strongly against co-education.
1963. Racial integration approved.
1963. Women are variously referred to as "Maggies" and "Waggies."
1965. Student Senate passes resolution that prevented women from being honored at Silver Taps. Another resolution is passed stating that women should have their own unique ring as opposed to the traditional Aggie Ring available to males.
1965. Andy Rogers, a former student serving in the state Senate, introduces bill in the legislature to reinstate all-male status at A&M.
1965. President Rudder, Board Chair Evans, the Corps Commander, and the Student Body President all testify on behalf of co-education.
1966. New changes in wording concerning admissions effectively negate prohibition against co-education.
1970. Nancy Neilson earns a B. S. degree in Nuclear Engineering, making her the first woman to receive an engineering degree.
1970. Wording is put in place that officially makes A&M a co-educational institution.
1970. General Rudder dies on March 23.
1971. Nearly 2,000 women are enrolled.
1974. Participation in the Corps of Cadets opened to women.
1975. More than 7, 000 women are enrolled.
1976. Linda Cornelius Waltman becomes A&M's first female scholarship athlete. She later made the ill-fated 1980 US Olympic track team (the US boycotted because of the Russian invasion of Afghanistan), and was the first female to be inducted into the A&M Athletic Hall of Fame.
1977. Dr. Jarvis Miller named President of the university.
1978. Females participated in cutting wood for the Bonfire for the first time. Prior to that, they were allowed only to work as parts of the "Cookie Crew" or the "Water Wenches."
1979. Melanie Zentgraf, a member of the Corps of Cadets, files a class action suit focused on integrating women into several elite Corps organizations. The suit goes on for five years.
1980. Over 12,000 female are enrolled. Total enrollment is 33,000.
1980. Dr. Miller refuses to shake the hand of Melanie Zentgraf during graduation exercises. Dr. Miller was reassigned on July 10.
1985. The first women join the Aggie Band.
1987. Mandy Schubert is named Deputy Corps Commander, the second highest leadership position in the Corps.
1994. Brooke Leslie becomes the first female student body President.

1996. For the first time in school history, there were more females than males in the entering freshman class.

1998. Women make up 46% of the student body.

2000. Susan Rudd Wynn, class of 1978, becomes first female graduate to serve on A&M Board of Regents.

2007. Brooke Rollins, nee Leslie, becomes the first female speaker at the College Station campus Muster ceremonies held in honor of deceased A&M former students. She received a law degree from the prestigious University of Texas program and later assumed the position of Executive Director of the conservative right-wing Texas Public Policy Foundation which has caused much rancor among the faculties of A&M, UT, and several other universities with its wrong-headed "Seven Solutions" for changing higher education.

2008. Dr. Elsa Murano becomes the first female, first minority, first under fifty years of age President of the university on January 3. Her reign ended unceremoniously June 15, 2009, amid a firestorm of political in-fighting at the local and state levels. There were allegations from many circles that meddling in the affairs of the university by one its former students and present Governor of Texas, Rick Perry, was at the heart of the controversy. Bill Flores, an A&M former student, wealthy businessman, and US Congressman summed up the situation in a quote from an article on the controversy from *The Eagle*: "One, they [Board of Regents] had an opportunity to choose from world-class candidates. Two, they succumbed and abdicated to political pressure and appointed a candidate who was less than ideal. Three, once they appointed that candidate, they gave her no support and no mentoring. And then they threw her to the wolves when she didn't cave into their every request. Aggies everywhere ought to be outraged." I do not know that I was outraged but I can say for certain this is the only time I have ever agreed with the unrelenting Obama-bashing Texas Congressman Bill Flores on anything.

2013. Women's Former Student Network (WFSN) sponsors a three-day celebration of the fiftieth anniversary of the admittance of women to A&M as full-time, degree-seeking students. A parallel celebration took place honoring the admission of blacks to the university for the first time, also in 1963.

2015. Alyssa Michalke is named Corps Commander, the first time a female has been appointed to this most prestigious student leadership position.

2016. Cecille Osorio becomes the second female to lead the Corps of Cadets, and twin sisters, Hannah and Claire Wimberly are elected as Student Body President and Senior Class President, respectively. This situation represents the first time in the history of the university the top three student leadership positions have been held by females.

JUDY LEUNES AND ALYSSA MICHALKE

My Personal Perspective on the History and Current Status of Women at A&M. As indicated in the time line, the university had an on-again, off-again, often contentious relationship for many years with regard to female admissions. There were periods in which females could go to summer school but not attend during regular semesters. At other times, they could enroll on a sporadic basis in extension or special courses. Then there were on-again, off-again periods when Aggie wives could attend classes. There were also occasions when local political figures would champion the cause of women, only to be confronted with public and private threats against their well-being. Various legal and legislative initiatives were sponsored by advocates in favor of integration of women. The local and campus newspapers ran articles, pro and con, about the issue. Straw polls were taken on campus to assess student attitudes. These events are testimony to the over-the-top emotionality on the part of both the supporters and the opponents. Women finally began the painful, arduous, slow process of integration into the core fabric of the university in the 1960's.

My own experience with women at A&M was non-existent as an undergraduate since none were allowed, and precious few were here when I joined the faculty in the spring semester of 1966. For example, that first spring I taught Introductory Psychology to four classes of eighty-eight students each and none were females. Shortly thereafter, in the summer of the same year, I taught an Introductory Psychology class with a dozen females and thirty-three males. By the start of the 1970's, my classes typically had more females than males though this was most certainly not the case in disciplines such as agriculture, engineering, and the hard sciences.

I remember teaching Developmental Psychology in the fall of 1967 in Scoates Hall which at that time was home to several departments in the College of Agriculture. That male-dominated college had few if any female students or professors so my class with fifteen females and twenty-one males was a novelty, literally a sight to behold. By way of illustration, I was lecturing along one day and I could hear feet scurrying and people murmuring in the hall. Through the commotion, I detected a muffled male voice saying: "Hey, guys, come here. Look! This guy has females in his class! Look!" I looked into the hall and saw three or four Agriculture professors rubbernecking to get a view of those scarce-as-hen's teeth females. Those of us teaching in the fields of Psychology and Education took it for granted that females were commonplace, but their presence was clearly a rarity in most departments and colleges on campus.

As noted earlier in considerable detail, the transitioning of women into the University was not an altogether smooth process. There were many among the alumni, aka "Former Students", who had graduated with lasting positive memories and fanatical worship of the all-male, military bastion that had been A&M for most of its first century of existence. These hardliners saw no place for women in their ultra-conservative little military university and were outspoken in their opposition. To compound the problem, there was a small but vocal contingent of faculty members who shared similar sentiments.

A couple of brief vignettes are representative of the indignities women faced in those early years of full admission. Though it was not a common practice at all in the 1960's, on occasion, professors would walk in the first day of class and announce that women were free to stay in the class but they would definitely make an F if they did so. In those days, mechanisms for redressing grievances about academic matters such as this egregious violation were minimal or non-existent.

I also remember a Professor in Business who routinely referred to the females in his class as "split-tails." On one occasion to get the semester started on the right foot, he asked the females in his class to move down to the first two rows and sit with their legs crossed. He then supposedly said, "Thanks, ladies. Now that the gates to Hell are closed, we can begin the lecture." The preceding anecdotes suggest that for a handful of professors and a sizable segment of former students, women had no place as students at A&M, plain and simple, end of story!

As mentioned in the timeline, another example of out-and-out discrimination was requiring female students to sign a waiver each semester indicating if A&M ever returned to being an all-male institution, the ladies would pack their bags and go away without a fuss, especially an ugly, legal one. Further discrimination was found in the coursework titles. For example, a common requirement in a number of majors was "Professional Speaking for Men", a title that endured in the catalog and schedule of classes until the late 1960's.

Perhaps my favorite symbol of the close-mindedness with regard to female students was the prevailing attitude about one of the most hallowed symbols of all that is good about A&M, the highly-coveted, much-ballyhooed, and, of late, extremely expensive Aggie Ring. It seems that for several years after their admission, females were not allowed to order, purchase, or wear the Aggie Ring. Instead, they could purchase the PHT ring which stood for "Putting Hubby Through." That same item is still available to students from that era in A&M's history but is now more euphemistically referred to as a "Companionship Ring", so-named I suppose because so many of the early female students were wives of and thus "companions" to male students. It was not uncommon in the 1960's and 1970's for women to work full-time and attend school part-time, often serving as the main source of financial support for their families.

My first wife, Barbara, while working on her PhD degree in History in the late 1960's and early 1970's, was afforded a first-hand, up-close and personal glimpse into this misguided, misogynistic mentality. The incident took place toward the end of her doctoral coursework at a time when she coincidentally happened to be pregnant with child number four, Amy. Amy was born on May 9 (Mother's Day) of 1971 which, among other things, was smack dab in the middle of semester final examinations. Barbara took two exams prior to Amy's arrival and two shortly afterward. While walking toward class for one of the two she finished before the big event, she overheard one cadet say to another, "Good God! They even let pregnant ones in this place now!" His partner in crime replied, "Yeah, the place is going to hell in a handbasket."

A particularly egregious and unpardonable individual act of discrimination against women at A&M was an unfathomably stupid *faux pas* committed by none other than one of the university presidents, Dr. Jarvis Miller, and he did it in front of thousands of students and parents attending the 1980 spring commencement ceremonies. As is the custom during graduation, the President hands each student their diploma and sends them on their merry way with a hearty handshake as they make the transition from the protective womb of college life to the endless ecstasies and boundless blisses of the cold, cruel world. When the activist Melanie Zentgraf mentioned in the timeline reached the podium, Dr. Miller refused to shake her outstretched hand as he handed out the diplomas.

As noted earlier in the timeline, Ms. Zentgraf had filed a landmark class action suit to force the university to allow women to participate in several elite organizations including the Corps of Cadets. Dr. Miller thus viewed Melanie Zentgraf as a rabble-rousing, trouble-making feminist who was out to undermine all that A&M holds sacred. She stuck out her hand on three separate occasions and each time he openly and blatantly refused to acknowledge her gesture, resting his right hand on his hip until she finally got the message and left the stage with diploma in hand sans the ritualistic handshake.

Dr. Miller was widely regarded, at least among people I knew, as presiding over a failed presidency, and the Zentgraf graduation gaffe apparently did little to help his cause. He was terminated in the summer of 1980 after two-plus years at the helm, and I cannot help but believe the unforgivable public relations *faux pas* surrounding the Zentgraf snub was pivotal in accelerating his dismissal. It seems more than mere coincidence that graduation took place early in May of 1980 and his resignation was tendered two months later in July.

Dr. Miller had another nettlesome idiosyncrasy, apparently believing that the job of the college professor was essentially the time-honored 0800 to 1700 hours operation (You know, the eight to five job!). There were rumors he had spies go through the various buildings to make sure faculty members were still in their offices or laboratories during that specified time frame. He was said to have accosted a professor from Veterinary Medicine who was jogging around campus early one afternoon, berating him for not being on the job during working hours. In another instance, he found an eminent Chemistry professor at home mowing his yard in the middle of the afternoon. He called the professor's Dean and requested a meeting with himself, the miscreant, and his department head to discuss this act of "professional misconduct." At the meeting, the "villain" informed Dr. Miller that he had gone home to rest after spending the previous thirty-six hours in his laboratory, supervising a critical phase in an experiment he was conducting with some associates. The culprit further stated that he would be glad to rein in his laboratory personnel, put his own professional ambitions on hold, and proceed to work the luxurious forty-hour week so endorsed by Dr. Miller. He further told the President that he did not think ideas, inventions, and innovations recognized a clock. Rather, they occurred at the oddest, sometimes most serendipitous times, and most likely would not thrive in a narrowly defined, eight-to-five corporate environment. These lapses in judgment and leadership provide a microcosmic glimpse into the man and his deservedly brief tenure as leader of this university. These events are reminiscent of more recent attempts by ex-Governor Rick Perry and our sometimes misguided Board of Regents to "corporatize" the university by employing a business model to what it is we do here. Fortunately, these attempts to corporatize have met with dismal failure.

Old customs sometimes die inexorable, painful deaths and such was the fate of gender discrimination. For example, the number of undergraduate females admitted to the university for most of the past two decades has been equal to or greater than that of males, and life today goes on pretty much as if women have always had equal rights and privileges at A&M. Such has not always been the case, and those early female pioneers had to overcome some real trials and tribulations to succeed. Today's female students cannot begin to imagine what their early counterparts endured to integrate the deeply entrenched macho, male, military A&M culture of old. I truly do not think the women of today have any idea there has been a long and strong history of discrimination against women at their beloved university.

Lest one get the impression that all is well on the equality issue, even today there are vestiges of discrimination cloaked in the "preservation of Aggie traditions" escape hatch. Any time a female challenges the status quo, particularly the sacrosanct, all-male, yell leader positions, the naysayers all rise up in unison to defend the past. The litany goes something like this: "We have always had males as yell leaders and it has to remain that way or we have violated a sacred tradition", as if it was ordained somewhere that traditions, particularly those that protect the all-male hegemony, should not be subject to challenge. It was encouraging that in the 2012 student elections on campus, a female yell leader candidate actually received over 3,000 votes. I am hopeful this is a portent of things to come; it would be gratifying to see a female topple that all-male "tradition" and joins her rightful place on the sidelines at athletic events.

Another tempest in a teapot has focused attention on whether the Aggie Dance Team, created in 1995, should be allowed to perform on the sidelines at A&M football games. Not surprisingly, there is plenty of opposition to this proposal from status-quo, old Army diehards. I am again hopeful that dancers will take their rightful place, performing on the sidelines at football games. Who, in their right mind, would deny women the right to exercise school spirit in the same way as male students?

1960's Females.

Two females from my earliest days stand out as memorable, though for quite different reasons. Coincidentally, both were named Barbara, and I spent many an hour with each of them.

Barbara Williams: A 1960's Prototypical Female Student. In my mind, Barbara Williams was the prototypical female student at A&M during the late 1960's. She was a bit older than most undergraduates of today, maybe in her late twenties, married, mother of several children (three as I remember), and attending school while her husband pursued graduate work. She was a blonde extrovert with a nice personality and great sense of humor, and I enjoyed visiting with her about school, careers, children, and life beyond A&M. She was an exceptional student and went on to earn the PhD degree in Clinical Psychology from the University of Houston.

I remember once talking to Barbara about her doctoral dissertation which focused on various treatment strategies designed to treat and hopefully cure court-committed alcoholics, all male. As part of the treatment regimen, each client was asked to think about consuming his favorite alcoholic beverage in a comfortable, cozy environment with dim lights and soft music. Each was asked to visualize taking a soothing drink, rolling its cool, refreshing contents around on the tongue and roof of the mouth, allowing it to retreat to near the uvula, all the while tickling the throat with its tanginess. The visual scenario concluded with the client swallowing his drink, at which time it would turn into a collection of wiggly, crawling bugs, small spiders, earwigs, brown Louisiana cockroaches, pill bugs, praying mantises, and other creepy crawlers.

In theory, this aversive conditioning paradigm should render the alcoholic forever incapable of consuming alcohol. Though Barbara reported short-run success with her regimen, my suspicion is that good, hard-core, court-committed alcoholics might need something more substantive in the way of aversive consequences in order for the change to achieve permanent sobriety.

I still use Barbara's anecdote in class as an attention-getting example of how aversive procedures so useful, though controversial, in psychological practice can be applied to everyday life. My adapted scenario goes something like this: "You have had a particularly long, difficult week in which you had many exams, a term paper due, and an in-class presentation to make. On top of these school demands, your best friend calls to let you know she has been dating your fiancée on the sly for months and they are getting married tomorrow. She further says, "I'm not sure we will be best friends anymore, huh?" Then you get a call from your parents announcing they have both lost their jobs, and you are on your own financially.

Your friends tell you everyone is getting together at 1700 hours at a popular student hangout, a cantina that serves two-for-one $1 Margaritas. When you get there after an absolutely wretched week, you find that your friends cheated by getting a two-hour head start on you. To catch up, you order a Pina Colada, your favorite drink, also on special for $1. You are tired, ragged out from school, generally fed up with life, and in need of a good, stiff jolt of alcohol. The waiter brings the drink, and interestingly he is a Brad Pitt (Sean Penn?) look-alike which only adds to the effect. The drink looks absolutely wonderful, too; there are multi-colored layers of alcohol in the frosty glass, with orange slices, cherries, nuts, and whipped cream in abundance (shows you what I know about Pina Coladas!). You pick up the drink, savor the cold glass, look around at your wonderful friends, and take a sip. As was the case with Barbara's court-committed alcoholics, the drink erupts into a phantasmagoric, revolting, stomach-churning amalgam of every insect known to entomological science.

This scenario, however absurd and unlikely, might lead one to forgo and not seek solace in a liquid happy hour at the end of an unbelievably stressful week. As a postscript, I always conclude the vignette by asking the class to think of me at their next happy hour. Just doing my part to foster a more alcohol-free world!

At last report, Barbara Williams had retired from her practice in clinical psychology as well as from her faculty position with a local university, and was living in Louisville, Kentucky.

Barbara X: A Different Kind of 1960's Student. Another most memorable student in the spring of 1968, a young woman from Bryan named Barbara X (not her real name). The two of us came to know each other well because she spent several hundred hours (yes, hundreds!) in my office over a two- or three-year period, talking almost entirely about her disordered thoughts and seemingly tortured life. Barbara was maybe 5' 8" of 5' 9", nice-looking, with big brown eyes and full lips, and spoke with a pronounced slow Texas drawl. She had a good mind but consistently underachieved, due in great measure I am sure to her emotional difficulties. She was the only child of parents who were in their fifties at the time of her birth, and the degree of parental overprotection was as pronounced as any in my experience.

The overprotective parenting style was designed to limit her exposure to evil thoughts and deeds which, in turn, prevented Barbara from dating boys or hanging out with the other girls in high school. The pattern continued into college, where Barbara was dropped off on campus each day by her mother just in time for morning classes. To complete the circle of control over Barbara's college life, she would be picked up immediately after her last class and driven to the family home. In order to exert total control and to heighten Barbara X's dependency, the mother would force her to go through the additional indignity of calling each day to get a ride home. The mother would then begrudgingly agree to come out to campus to pick Barbara up, all the while going out of her way to make sure she understood what an imposition it was to do so. These events, of course, took place far in advance of the cell phone era, so Barbara was forced to prevail on professors who would agree to let her use their phone to make the obligatory, dependency-entrenching call. She came to my office on many occasions to call home, and you could hear the mother saying things that went something like this: "Okay, I will come pick you up. I am right in the middle of making your father's favorite cookies and they will probably be ruined, but I will come out there to get you anyway. I wish you could find a more convenient time to make these calls." This exchange is patently bogus psychologically and designed to foster the already pathological love-hate, dependency relationship in existence between this mother and daughter.

Another goal of this dominating parental style was to make sure temptation never reared its ugly head. For example, if she mentioned dating a boy she liked, her mother had a series of ready-made rejections for each overture:

"You can't go with him. I don't know his mother."
"You can't go out with him. He's not Catholic."
"You can't go out with him. He's not Czech."
"You cannot go out with him. His father is a womanizer and the apple does not fall very far from the tree."
"He is not acceptable because he isn't in the Corps of Cadets at A&M."
Conversely, if Barbara attempted to date a guy in the Corps, that effort was met with:
"Corps guys are all animals who after only one thing. Sex! You don't want to go out with that kind of person, do you?"

Interestingly, Barbara's parents were nearing seventy when she started college and as is often the case with folks in their age cohort, they retired quite early in the evening. She learned to wait until the parents were fast asleep, at which time she would quietly make an exit via a bedroom window to meet up with one or two guys waiting nearby. She never really revealed much about these interludes in our conversations, but I had the impression the interactions were more social than sexual.

Barbara once related a vignette about a "boyfriend" from a city in north Texas who supposedly regaled her with tales of sneaking in late at night to bugger corpses in the family-owned funeral home. By chance, it turns out I knew the young man in question, a star athlete at the local high school, and was familiar with the family business. As a result, I entertained some reservations about the veracity of her stories concerning her necrophilic, buggering beau, but stranger things have happened, have they not? Certainly, the details of these nocturnal necrophilic encounters as she related them to me second-hand suggested something nefarious might well have taken place in the midnight hours at the family funeral parlor.

Barbara was fascinated with weapons, and often talked of a recurring obsession born of long-simmering resentment toward her parents in which she shot both of them while they slept. She also claimed to be an accomplished marksman and talked at length about the many idle hours she spent at home perfecting her shooting skills. The fantasy about killing her parents dominated her consciousness for the greater part of the adolescent and young adult years, and I am not sure it ever completely vanished. Fortunately, she never acted on her fantasies. Deep down, I never thought she would kill her parents as she depended on them so heavily. She may have hated them, but the love-hate mixture seemed to serve as a deterrent to double homicide.

I have seen Barbara on occasion since the late 1960's. One time was at a softball game, where I was setting up in the batter's box, awaiting the first pitch, when my attention was diverted by a comment from the catcher who turned out to be none other than Barbara. She proceeded over the next few pitches to tell me she was "doing well." She also boasted of being "the leading marijuana grower in Grimes County" of which Navasota, twenty miles south of College Station, is the largest city. Again, I had no idea as to the veracity of her boastful claim about the alleged marijuana crop, but it was an interesting revelation, or at least one important to her.

After that brief interlude on the softball diamond, I saw Barbara out in the community on occasion, and once she called my home phone just to talk. There were lingering signs of paranoid ideation on every occasion. I have not seen or heard of Barbara in fifteen or twenty years. Hopefully, the demons that plagued her are in abeyance and she is at peace as she enters the euphemistic "Golden Years." She would be well into her sixties by now.

The General

"In 1963 Earl Rudder opened the doors to women and saved A&M."

Writer Paul Burka in a 1997 <u>Texas Monthly</u> article

A second major force in the revitalization of Texas A&M in the 1960's was its 21st President, General James Earl Rudder (May 6, 1910-March 23, 1970). General Rudder went by his middle name, Earl, but was known widely on campus as "The General." He is credited with changing the face of the university by (1) paving the way for the full and unqualified admittance of women, (2) making sweeping changes in the curriculum in the liberal arts, education, and business, disciplines that had been largely neglected throughout A&M's history, and (3) reformulating the role of the Corps of Cadets, thereby reducing its influence on everyday university life.

Sentimental Journey Home I (1965-2018)

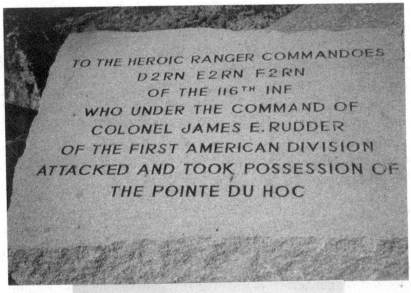

RUDDER MEMORIAL AND MUSEUM, NORMANDY BEACH, FRANCE

Decorated War Hero. The General was a genuine World War II hero, and his most notable combat achievement was leading the Second Ranger Battalion up the treacherous one hundred-foot cliffs at Pointe du Hoc on Normandy Beach, D-Day, the Sixth of June, in 1944. The General was a Lieutenant Colonel at that time, and his battalion suffered fifty percent casualties while wresting Pointe du Hoc from the hands of the Germans. Rudder himself was wounded twice in the fighting. His leadership in combat was considerable, and for his efforts was awarded the Distinguished Service Cross, Legion of Merit, Silver Star, Bronze Star, Purple Heart, French Legion of Honor, and several other meritorious citations. About the only honor missing is the Congressional Medal of Honor and one can wonder if his achievements at Pointe du Hoc could easily have earned him that one. In any case, the General was a legitimate war hero.

Today, there is a museum near the French city of Caen dedicated to the heroic feats of Lieutenant Colonel Rudder and his gallant men. After visiting the museum for the first time in 2001, I came away with the feeling The General may actually be more of a hero in France than he ever has been in the US, though his reputation as a soldier stateside, or at least in Texas, was and is considerable. Earl Rudder was promoted to Colonel before World War II was over, and advanced to Brigadier General in the Army Reserves in 1954 and to Major General in 1957.

The General Ascends to the Presidency of the University. Shortly after World War II ended in 1945, General Rudder was elected Mayor of his hometown, Brady, and served in that capacity from 1946 to 1952. In 1955, he assumed the position of Land Commissioner for the state of Texas. His political connections in Austin and Washington led to his appointment as Vice-President of A&M in early 1958, and he ascended to the Presidency of the university the following year. There is evidence suggesting that President Lyndon B. Johnson was a major force in the rise of "The General" from small city mayor to major political office in Austin to university president. As one example of President Johnson's support, General Rudder was the 1967 recipient of the Distinguished Service Medal, our nations' highest peacetime civilian award.

Rudder's appointment to a position of leadership of an academic institution was regarded in some quarters as a bit curious. As a student, he played on the A&M football team, was decent but not outstanding in the classroom, and graduated in 1932 with a degree in Industrial Education. His military accomplishments aside, there was nothing in his academic background suggesting he was prepared for handling the position of university president.

From my viewpoint as fledgling professor in the late 1960's, I was taken aback at his mostly thinly-veiled but sometimes blatant disdain for the faculty. The General had what appeared to be a deeply-rooted paranoid streak about academicians and seemed distrustful of faculty motives concerning him personally as well as those related to the broader issues of academia and the university.

My feelings about The General were greatly shaped by a one-time exposure during my early tenure at A&M. The encounter in question centered on a meeting in which our fearless leader spoke at great length to a large segment of the faculty. He strode into the Chemistry Building Auditorium which was probably the only facility of campus at that time large enough to hold such a sizable faculty group. The General took his place on the stage, surrounded by two or three aides or what several of us thought were really "goons", for lack of a better term. As The General spoke, the enforcers who had stationed themselves on his left, center, and right sides, glowered at the faculty members with their most menacing, threatening glares. The air was full of threat and paranoia, with the "goons" continuously scanning the audience for signs of dissent or disagreement, all the while protecting The General from his faculty enemies, real or imagined. Given the image they were trying to project, it would not have surprised me at all if the presidential protectors had reached into their coat jackets and brought out loaded weapons. I am pretty sure they were not armed, but I had the feeling they wanted us to think they were packing heat. It was that paranoid an event.

In the course of the meeting, The General commended us for our efforts on behalf of the university and its students, but was quick to let us know that if we did not like it at A&M, Highway 6 ran both ways. To the uninitiated in the ways of A&M, it has long been a tradition for students to use the popular phrase "Highway 6 Runs Both Ways", meant as a directive for students who take issue with the accepted party line or the hallowed traditions of the university (known in A&M parlance as "two per centers") to hit the road. In other words, if you don't like it here, Highway 6 runs north or south and get the hell out. I always thought it was corny enough that the students used the "Highway 6 Runs Both Ways" mentality in exchanges with each other in normal conversation or in letters to the editor of the student newspaper, but for the president of a university to use that kind of language and its implied threat came across as a demeaning slap in the face to the faculty.

A "Wild-Eyed Liberal" Takes on the A&M Administration. Speaking of paranoia concerning the faculty as well as the absence of due process, there was an episode in the late 1960's in which a professor got crosswise with the leadership in the hallowed College of Veterinary Medicine (i.e., "The Vet School"), mentioned at the time in hushed, reverential terms as if there was something transcendent about its existence. The professor in question was fired without cause, ostensibly due to a rumored illicit affair with a student. It was further intimated he had stopped going to the "right" church (i.e., the one attended by the Dean of the "Vet School"), and had committed an assortment of other violations of local norms from the perspective of General Rudder and the Vet School Dean.

Legend had it that The General called the culprit in, accused him of the aforementioned assorted improprieties, and fired him on the spot. The professor balked at being summarily dismissed and threatened a lawsuit. The university powers-that-be apparently responded to the threat of a legal, and possibly embarrassing public relations black eye by relenting on the summary dismissal. By way of retaliation, however, they took away the professor's classes for a year, at which time measures were instigated to have him dismissed for inferior teaching performance. When that strategy did not work, his laboratory was put under lock and key, and an attempt was made to dismiss him on grounds that his research work for the year was lacking in both quality and quantity. That strategy did not work either, so as a last gasp measure, his parking place was relocated from near the hallowed "Vet School" to a spot adjacent to the football stadium, Kyle Field, which meant the culprit in question had to walk fifteen or twenty minutes each way to work and back.

The perpetrator eventually tired of the harassment and filed a grievance with the American Association of University Professors (AAUP), a watchdog organization with expressed interests in protecting the rights of professors with regard to due process in higher education. This filing led A&M to be placed on AAUP censure in 1968. AAUP censure, then and now, essentially sends a message to professors and college administrators across the country that academic freedom and due process do not exist at universities on their blacklist. Eventually, the perpetrator in this case left the university, financial restitution was made, and the AAUP censure was finally lifted in 1982, a period of fourteen years. As I remember, getting off the blacklist cost A&M $250,000.

By now, the attentive reader has no doubt surmised the major player in this drama was some wild-eyed liberal, trouble-making, hippie, Commie sympathizer, and this would seem on the surface to be a reasonably safe assumption. However, our professorial protagonist later married the woman with whom he ostensibly was having the affair and they named their first-born twin children, Ronald and Reagan. What does this anecdote tell you about the guy? Sounds like a wild-eyed, hippie, liberal trouble-making leftist to me, alright!

One of the more depressing aspects of this entire incident occurred around the time of the original attempts to fire the wild-eyed, hippie perp. There was lively debate among the faculty on campus about whether or not a university president should have total control over hiring and firing, particularly the latter. The essence of the argument was: Should a university president have total say-so, with absolute authority to fire people because of the way they look, the clothes they wear, or their political persuasion or religious affiliation? To hopefully shed some light on this issue, a straw vote was conducted, as I remember, by the leadership of the local AAUP chapter. Support for the unilateral powers of General Rudder to fire without cause was almost unanimously upheld by the faculty in every college except two, Liberal Arts and Education.

To put it mildly, I was appalled at the California F-Scale-like, blind-obedience-to-authority vote of my colleagues in most of the colleges within the university. Fortunately, the creation and adoption of a tenure policy that protects faculty from whimsical and capricious decision-making by university administrators was an outgrowth of the incident. The right to be different and the right to dissent without fear of capricious retribution are two of the driving forces that propel universities to greatness.

"Pot-Bellied President" Vows a "Hell of a Fight." Another interesting vignette which provides insights into the way The General's mind worked concerned the student rebellion so widespread across the country in the late 1960's. At the height of the angst about the Vietnam War, the civil rights movement brought about by the huge racial divide in the country, and life in general, The General delivered a speech to the Texas A&M University chapter of the Future Farmers of America (FFA). Aspects of the talk were reported in the local newspaper, *The Eagle*, where The General was quoted liberally on several issues. The article bore the headline, "Pot-bellied President Vows 'Hell of a Fight'." The General promised his audience that if student troublemakers caused a ruckus at A&M, they would be in for a "hell of a fight" and "this pot-bellied President will be in the front ranks leading it." When asked about dissident students, The General said, "….beards on students are just a means of seeking identification they can't get any other way." Of professors with similar propensities, he remarked, "A prof who wears a beard in the classroom is just trying to substitute a beard for knowledge." He ended his diatribe against non-conformity by stating, "If he were personally in charge of hiring professors, none would be sporting beards or wearing sandals." Once again, we are reminded of The General's paranoia, suspicion, and distrust of his faculty.

Additional insight into the psyche of The General took place in the late 1960's when I put forth a proposal to add an undergraduate course in Abnormal Psychology to the departmental offerings. According to Al Casey who represented the department in the deliberations about the fate of the course, it was approved over much objection from our fearless leader. According to Al, The General's resistance was expressed as follows: "If you teach such a course, the next thing you know a bunch of nuts will start attending the university." In a similar vein, he was said to have opposed hiring additional psychologists for the student counseling service on the grounds that such organizations coddled people with mental problems. To paraphrase his eloquence on the issue, he said, "Aggies do not have mental problems and students with mental problems are not true Aggies and should go home where they belong."

Another Rudder gaffe came to light via a 1960's article in Time in which he took a backhanded, and I suspect unintended, slap at the few women attending the university by alluding to the tough "John Wayne types" who were the heart and soul of the university. I hope I never meet a female at A&M who reminds me of "The Duke." Speaking of John Wayne, my father was fond of relating details of two chance meetings he had with the iconic movie star. The one I remember had the two of them conversing for maybe thirty minutes while waiting for and riding a ferry somewhere in the Galveston-Baytown area. My father came away from his two brief interactions with John Wayne with a most favorable impression, and regarded him as an amiable, unassuming, and a genuinely nice, regular guy.

A Ranger Casualty. The General was often accompanied on his strolls across campus or trips to the countryside by his loyal English bulldog, appropriately named in honor of Rudder's Rangers of Pointe du Hoc fame. Ranger II had been a fixture at the university from the time The General arrived in 1958 until the dog's death in 1965. A replacement canine companion, Ranger III, soon followed.

Ranger III was often seen hanging around the campus, and one of his favorite activities was watching students retrieve candy bars from the vending machine located at the foot of the stairs in the Nagle Hall basement. For several years my office was located in that building just adjacent to those vending machines. From time to time for the sake of amusement, I would watch unsuspecting students deposit the necessary coins, pull the lever, and wait briefly while their favorite candy bar fell into the tray. Ranger had learned through good old Pavlovian conditioning to pair the sound of the lever being pulled with noise created by the candy bar falling into the tray. While the naive, unsuspecting student was waiting to retrieve the newly-dispensed candy bar, Ranger would bolt down the stairs, place his front paws on the tray, put the candy bar in his mouth, run up the steps and out of the building, and head south toward home. Ranger's foraging skills were documented by a photographer from *The Battalion* who captured him on film trying to pull a candy machine knob with his teeth. The resulting picture went viral (in today's jargon) among the various wire services and was printed in newspapers throughout the country, thus affording Ranger III his richly-deserved fifteen minutes of fame.

There is a sad aspect to this otherwise warm-fuzzy, feel-good story. It seems that The General and his beloved canine companion were out boating one day, and for some reason the overweight Ranger of candy bar foraging fame jumped overboard and sank. Unfortunately, he failed to resurface. His lifeless body was eventually retrieved and he was buried beside his predecessor, Ranger II. That was a sad day for The General and for those of us who knew Ranger III, for he was a 1960's campus icon. Hanging around Nagle Hall was never the same without him.

Post-Mortem on The General. The General died at the age of fifty-nine on March 23, 1970, of an embolism caused by a bleeding ulcer. Some believed his demise was attributable to his macho insistence that things would be fine if he just toughed it out, which is the stance one might expect from a genuine tough-guy, war hero. Undoubtedly, The General would have lived much longer if he had been more attuned to his psychological and physical health needs.

A statue has been erected featuring The General and it sits near the Memorial Student Center, and prominently featured in his left hand is a book. There were detractors who not so facetiously have suggested The General, much like our forty-third President, George W. Bush, may have never read a book. It was thus gratifying to those detractors to find out the volume in his hand was not Goethe, Shakespeare, Freud, or heaven forbid, Marx, but rather a copy of the student yearbook, what many viewed as a more appropriate read for him. In 2008, a new high school bearing his name opened in Bryan. It seems ironic that someone who was so paranoid about and harbored so much contempt for his professors would have an educational institution named in his honor. I do not begrudge him or his family the accolade, but the irony simply will not go away.

In all fairness to General Rudder, he was a genuine war hero, and the evidence very much supports his efforts on behalf of advancing (saving?) the university in the 1960's. He took a hard line on the full admittance of women, broadened the curriculum and upgraded the faculty, and made the Corps of Cadets non-compulsory. On a number of occasions, he confronted and generally subdued his numerous and powerful critics. The changes he championed were highly emotional but absolutely critical to A&M's ultimate survival. His willingness to stand behind his beliefs and face down his adversaries is most commendable. Though his life was apparently never threatened during the fight to save A&M, the times were hectic and the issues emotional. It could easily be argued that the stress of campus events contributed in some measure to The General's premature demise.

Despite some misgivings about The General which have been chronicled here, I have a begrudging admiration for the man for much of what this university is today is traceable to his courage under fire, not on the beaches of Normandy but on the campus at Texas A&M.

First Faculty Colleagues

As noted in the preceding pages, significant changes took place at A&M in the 1950's and 1960's that substantially redefined the institution. One, of course, was the admission of women as noted in great detail. Another change was a softening of the perception of the university as an all-male military school. To help accomplish this change, the role of the Corps of Cadets was redefined. By 1958, one could join the Corps, decide that it was not the right decision, and become a regular, non-military (i.e., civilian) student and remain in school. That option was not available during my first two years as a student; if you resigned from the Corps of Cadets, it was mandatory that you simultaneously withdraw from the university! Pretty draconian stuff, I would say.

Another change with major implications for the growth of the university was expansion of the curriculum in the early 1960's in the areas of Education, Business Administration, and the Liberal Arts. As well, initiatives were put in place to effect a general upgrading of the faculty in all academic areas. A&M has always had isolated pockets of excellence in agriculture, engineering, and the hard sciences, but the overall quality of the faculty was, in a word and to put it generously, "unremarkable." Interestingly, there was little change in terms of the quality of the faculty during the ten-year period from my entry into the university as a freshman in 1956 and the time I joined the faculty as a lecturer in 1966 after a short hiatus for graduate school and military service which were discussed elsewhere.

To document what at first blush might appear to be a random, biased, highly individual, off-the-cuff observation, I analyzed the contents of the university catalog for the academic year 1965-1966, or my first year on the faculty. I was specifically looking for degrees and university affiliations of the professors in place at that time. Among the more significant findings were: only forty-nine percent of the faculty possessed a PhD degree; another five percent were Doctors of Veterinary Medicine (DVM). The remaining forty-six percent of the faculty possessed either a master's degree (thirty-eight percent) or, in a minority of cases, only a baccalaureate degree (eight percent). Of the totality of professors listed in the catalog, one-third had their terminal degree from A&M and scant few of the non-A&M PhD's were from prestigious schools. Several faculty members in the College of Agriculture had PhD's from a somewhat predictable source, Cornell University with its outstanding agriculture program, thus making it the most prominently represented of the more elite universities at that time.

By way of contrast, and to illustrate how much things have changed over the past fifty years in terms of faculty pedigrees, I took a quick look at only the first three pages of the faculty roster in the catalog for 2010-2011. I selected only the faculty members whose last names began with A or B, hoping that would satisfy the readership that I have analyzed something resembling a representative sample. I further assumed the data would be representative of what I would find if I scrutinized the other twenty-four letters of the alphabet.

What I found was that five of every six faculty members possessed a doctoral degree, only one in six of which had been granted by A&M; both figures represent considerable improvements over the 1965-1966 analysis. 2011-2012 faculty whose last names began with A or B received PhD's from outstanding institutions including The University of Texas-Austin, Massachusetts Institute of Technology (MIT), Georgia Institute of Technology, University of California-Berkeley, Stanford University, Rochester University, Rice University, University of Chicago, McGill University in Canada, and a total of twenty-one graduates of the academically prestigious universities in the Big Ten Conference. Clearly, there has been a substantial, yea even monumental, upgrading of faculty quality at A&M over the years. This pedigree upgrade is absolutely essential if A&M is to achieve the overriding goal of Vision 2020 which is for the university to assume a place among the truly elite institutions of higher learning.

It was in the midst of these three university-altering changes, the full admittance of women, diminution in the influence of the military, and broad expansion of curricular offerings and faculty quality, that I began my career as a faculty member at Texas A&M University.

Arnold LeUnes, Meet Fillmore Sanford!

My first few years on the faculty were interesting for reasons having little to do with the aforementioned earthshaking issues, namely the increasing visibility of women on campus, expansions in curricular offerings, the upgrading in faculty pedigrees, and the indomitable presence of General Rudder. Frankly, I was pretty intimidated by the whole scene, and particularly by the older, more established and what I correctly or incorrectly perceived to be august professors in the department. There was something like fifteen of us at the time, ten in the field of Education and five who identified with the discipline of Psychology. Officially, we were all members of the Department of Education which was headed by a long-time public school administrator, Dr. X.

The department offered baccalaureate, masters, and doctoral degrees, with the latter a generic program featuring critical elements associated with public school administration. The doctoral students joked among themselves about getting a PhD in "Heat, light, and ventilation" and "How to keep your lunch lines straight" which I suppose are high-priority concerns if one is a public school administrator. Those of us in Psychology were seen as auxiliary to the main focus, but a bachelor's degree program was initiated in 1964, two years prior to my joining the faculty.

I spent the first semester at A&M "teaching" Introductory Psychology through canned television lecture tapes featuring Dr. Fillmore Sanford, a prominent member of the Psychology faculty at the

University of Texas in Austin. Each of the Sanford tapes lasted forty-eight minutes which, in a fifty-minute class, essentially ruled out any questions or observations from professors or students. Also, the tapes, maybe thirty in number, left room for only six live lectures and six major exams during the semester. My role, and that of several junior (and sometimes senior colleagues), was essentially reduced to turning a television set on and off and administering, scoring, and recording a handful of exams for classes of eighty-eight students per section.

The class was held in Room 402 of the venerable old Academic Building. Well above eye level in the front of the classroom rested two television monitors, and two more were situated equally high on platforms located at the mid-point of the room on each side. Thus, the students theoretically had equal opportunity to be regaled and, at the same time, educated by the unending excitement generated by our portly and no doubt erudite host, Dr. Sanford. Students in the front half of the room would grimly hang on, watching dry lectures on psychological statistics, research methodology, and the brain and nervous system. It took those of us teaching the course several "lectures" to figure out the students seated in the back half of the room were having a very different learning experience by surreptitiously switching the rear monitors from Dr. Sanford to Andy Griffith and Gomer Pyle reruns. To cover their chicanery, the students would turn the volume down on those two rearmost sets, and while the poor students in front bore grim, tortured faces in their attempts to unravel the mysteries and nuances of statistics and the nervous system, those sitting in the back would periodically break into uncontrollable guffaws at the antics of Andy Griffith, Gomer Pyle, and Don Knotts. It was this more than occasional laughter that proved to be their undoing since there was little funny about Dr. Sanford and his eccentric, dry, and quirky sense of humor. The switch to the comedy shows was a certainty if we faculty members did not sit in the back of the room to squelch the inventive students. All in all, this experiment with televised introductory psychology was a disaster and the program was deep-sixed shortly after its inception in favor of good old live, professor-driven lectures. Professors and students alike rejoiced, and there was joy in Mudville again.

First Faculty Friends: Professors Varvel, Barker, Elliott, Bourgeois, Christensen, and Levenson. I had the good fortune to meet several very interesting colleagues during those first couple of years on the job. Some were highly positive role models and others merely curious; you learned what to do from the former and what not to do from the latter. Chief among the psychology folks on board at that time were Dr. Walter "Marvel" Varvel, the resident statistician, Dr. Donald Barker, Dr. Jim Elliott who taught learning theory, and the wiry, pugnacious, professorial Irishman, Dr. Albert Casey, whose expertise was substantial in two areas, the psychology of learning and experimental psychology. Each of these gentlemen exerted a huge impact on me, both personally and professionally, and I thank them for their friendship and collegiality as well. Walter Varvel and Al Casey passed away of old age, Jim Elliott died quite young of a mysterious neurological disease, and Barker to my knowledge is still kicking about. I used to see Don fairly often, but have not had a Barker sighting in several years.

Walter, Al, Jim, and Don were joined shortly after my arrival by cherished colleagues, Drs. Tony Bourgeois, Larry Christensen, and Hanna Levenson, in that order. Tony and Larry are now both retired, the latter after serving for many years as Department Head in Psychology at the University of South Alabama in Mobile, Alabama. Hanna has lived in San Francisco for nearly four decades, and is still working full-time, balancing the dual demands of being a Professor and private clinical practitioner in that fascinating if cold, rainy, foggy city.

Tony, Hanna, and I had a joyful reunion over brunch in Waco in 2012 in the midst of a three-day workshop she was conducting at Baylor University. We had not seen each other since 1977 when the three of us attended the American Psychological Association (APA) convention in San Francisco. Hanna looked great and has enjoyed a highly rewarding career as a professor and practicing psychologist. It was interesting to note that she was on her way back home from Waco by way of Dallas where she was spending a couple of days with a new boyfriend who happened to be a rabbi. I have not had the privilege of knowing anyone who was dating a rabbi, so I was impressed!

Al Casey, aka Little Albert. A most interesting colleague and erstwhile informal mentor was the aforementioned Al Casey who received his PhD in Experimental Psychology from the University of Kansas, coincidentally the same bastion of learning that gave us the immensely erudite Walter Varvel. Al Casey was a Semper Fi, true-believer, no-holds-barred, hard-core, card-carrying, kiln-dried, hell-fire-and-brimstone, born-again, died-in-the-wool, never-say-die, never-give-an-inch, orthodoxy-spouting experimental psychologist steeped in the teachings of B. F. Skinner of Harvard University. Skinner was the major proponent of the behavioral approach to learning which placed heavy emphasis on data gleaned from animal and human experimentation. To Professors Skinner and Casey and their acolytes, behavior was the proper subject of inquiry and the numerous vague and fuzzy imponderables generated by two competing schools of thought, psychoanalysis and humanism, were viewed as unscientific, mystical, and maybe even voodoo-like.

Casey had a huge following among the undergraduates and I always thought of him as A&M's version of the Pied Piper of Hamlin. He mesmerized our students with his etched-in-stone Skinnerian verities, avidly converting the huddled masses to rabid behaviorism. The process was not difficult at all for Al Casey for he was armed with irrefutable certainties about how the world was constructed. He tolerated little ambiguity and dispensed swift and not always gentle punishment for departure from orthodoxy, and his students reveled in the notion that there were no shades of gray in the black and white psychological world he had created for them. This quasi-religious conversion was greatly facilitated by Casey's pronouncements of eternal truths from the three Skinnerian bibles of that era, *Behavior of Organisms*, *Walden Two*, and *Beyond Freedom and Dignity*.

As noted earlier, Casey taught undergraduate courses in the Psychology of Learning and Experimental Psychology. It was not unusual for his classes to have a handful of students, affectionately known as "lettermen", mostly guys who were trying to pass one or both of his courses for the second or even the third time. The students actually seemed to possess a vague, unstated sense of pride in being a second-year or third-year letterman with Al Casey.

A unique feature in his experimental course was the requirement that everyone conduct a rat experiment, and neither gender nor queasiness about handling rodents constituted grounds for granting an exception. It was enchanting to see our students, male and female, comfortable or queasy, get up close and personal with their rats. Women with morbid fears of all manners of rodents and guys with nervous stomachs became adept handlers of the ill-tempered, obstreperous, slippery, nippy, prone-to-bite, shitty-dispositioned little varmints.

Casey had wheedled some research dollars out of a granting agency to conduct radiation research with goats in a laboratory on the west side of campus. From time to time over coffee in the departmental lounge, Al would lament the loss of a goat, attributable in his mind no doubt to bands of marauding, nocturnal coyotes or bands of wild dogs. Little did he know but the scavengers were far more human than animal, more two-legged than four. In reality, the "coyotes" were students, his animal caretakers with an abiding fondness for cabrito, the roasted goat delicacy long associated with Mexico and south and west Texas. Professor Casey died in his eighties, and so far as I know went to the big Skinner Box in the sky without anyone ever letting him in on the little secret about his goats.

Overall, Al Casey was a good friend and a facilitative colleague and to this day I regard him as an insightful and helpful mentor, though I am not sure he relished or ever saw himself in that role. He was a good researcher and a committed, enthusiastic teacher, and seeing those twin talents working in combination was infectious. I greatly admired his dedication to the teaching process and for the first time I understood why accomplished researchers were almost always the best teachers. I have long since rejected the idea that some people should stake their careers on research while others do so with teaching. For one thing what constitutes good teaching is almost impossible to accurately assess and, secondly, the evidence strongly suggests that professors who teach in universities without a research mandate do not really spend any more time at teaching than do professors at research institutions. At conventions, I used to marvel at my friends from so-called "teaching universities" (i.e., UT-Pan American (now The University of Texas Rio Grande Valley), Angelo State University, Tarleton State University, to name only a few) who talked of teaching in the morning and golfing, hiking, sailing or napping by one o'clock in the afternoon. That certainly was not the A&M model I knew.

My friend and colleague, Al Casey, was sort of front and center in an ugly 1981 episode involving three members of the A&M football team. Of the incident, sportswriter Ed Fowler of the *Houston Chronicle* penned a byline on November 26 entitled "Justice at A&M Disappears During Texas Week." A related headline showed up twelve days later in *The Houstonian*, the student newspaper at Sam Houston State University (SHSU), and read: "Music Major Mum After Mauling." Both headlines were in reference to an altercation involving A&M All-American safety Billy Cannon, Jr., reserve linebacker and backup quarterback John Elkins, and a third-string tight end named John Kellen.

It seems that the protagonists in this melodrama had ventured some sixty miles east from College Station to Huntsville in search of new scenery and, I suppose, some female companionship. In the process, they apparently over-imbibed and were totally blitzed, to use a sport metaphor, when they pulled up to the Jack in the Box fast food establishment near the SHSU campus at midnight. Two musicians, Don Slocomb, Jr. and Brian Casey (Al's son), had finished practicing music shortly before the bewitching hour and had adjourned to the Jack in the Box where they were drinking milk shakes in the parking lot when our football heroes pulled up. The hulking behemoths, weighing a collective seven hundred pounds, got out of the car, walked over near the entrance to the Jack in the Box, lined up three abreast, and urinated on a side window of the fast food vendor. This unanticipated moment of levity apparently amused the merry music makers who were watching from afar and, for whatever reason, their enjoyment of the proceedings seemed to annoy the football players. Cannon proceeded to pummel Slocomb who had played professionally with some top jazz groups, and there was a lingering fear that irreparable damage had been done to the mouth structures that compose the embouchure so critical to playing a wind instrument. Chronicle sportswriter Ed Fowler put it this way in his article: "But then Cannon just busted up the mouth of a professional saxophonist. Maybe someone needs to put that action in terms the coach (Tom Wilson at that time) can understand. It's like breaking a place-kicker's toe, or a quarterback's hand. Saxophonists with busted-up mouths do not make sweet music, although sometimes their lawyers do." Speaking of attorney's, the Slocomb's and Casey's were poised to file suit against Cannon and his henchmen if damage to either of their sons proved serious. Fortunately that did not turn out to be the case and so far as I know no lawsuit was ever filed.

While Slocomb was taking his licks from Cannon, John Kellen stood on Brian Casey's head, thus pinning him to the pavement. The third member of the party, John Elkins, apparently was not fond of what was going down in the parking lot so he jumped into a nearby bar ditch, hiding there until the police arrived and the melee ceased. I was dismayed to hear of John's involvement in all this nonsense as he was a very likeable softball teammate for a summer or two. John came across as a nice, sensible guy, and I was pleased to hear that his role in this incident was relatively benign.

At some point in the unfolding mayhem, Cannon wrapped both arms around Don Slocomb's back, ran several yards across the parking lot, and propelled the two of them through a plate glass window and onto the floor of the Jack in the Box. The falling glass slid down, forming a guillotine of sorts, and Cannon received cuts that required dozens of stitches. The injury caused him to miss the Texas Christian University (TCU) game the following weekend.

Eventually, the Huntsville police arrived on the scene and restored some degree of serenity to the chaos. In response to their presence, Kellen was said to have yelled: "You can't arrest us, we're A&M football players." Despite Kellen's cheeky assertion, he and Cannon were both written up for public intoxication. In addition to the $100 fine, Cannon paid $780 in restitution for damages to the restaurant. For his actions, Kellen was suspended for the Texas game but Cannon was allowed to play. As sportswriter Fowler noted so saliently in a second *Houston Chronicle* column, third team players who commit misdemeanor crimes get suspended for a game but All-American safeties who commit simple assault do not. He deemed it strange that public intoxication is a violation of team rules but attempting to restructure the face and mouth of a talented young musician is conveniently overlooked. This led Fowler to conclude his article with the following quote: "Justice, Aggie-style, has become a laughing matter."

Some months later, Cannon was chosen in the first round of the NFL draft by the Dallas Cowboys but his career was cut short after seven games due to damage to two vertebrae in his neck. Apparently, Cannon had a congenital narrowing of the spine that raised the ugly specter of permanent paralysis should he continue to play football. I cannot help but think that the Casey's and the Slocomb's secretly had smiles on their faces at this turn of events. I know from conversations with Al Casey that he felt that some degree of poetic justice had been served. Cannon retired, returned to A&M, and completed his undergraduate degree.

Al Casey played a pivotal role in another memorable event for me, also involving the city of Huntsville, when he arranged a tour of selected units of the Texas prison system for our Psychology faculty. We arrived in Huntsville, were admitted to the prison, but found our tour was delayed for maybe thirty minutes because of a *faux pas* unwittingly committed by yours truly. It seems that some months earlier, I had decided to grow a beard, but had no way of knowing the facial hair was going to trigger off a minor firestorm with our prison tour guide that day.

The guide in question was none other than fifty-ish Dr. George Beto, the director of the prison system and one of the most renowned and respected figures in the history of penology in this country. It seems that the distinguished Dr. Beto, for whom two prison units are named, was a bit on the conservative side, or maybe he just had a burr under his saddle (or fire up his ass) that day, but whatever the triggering event, he took umbrage at my beard. Mincing nary a word, he indicated to the group that I was not welcome to tour his fiefdom with my colleagues. Al Casey intervened on my behalf, and apparently persuasively so, for I was eventually if reluctantly allowed to take part in the tour. I privately concluded that Dr. Beto was afraid my beard would, in some way, exert a corruptive force on his murderers, rapists, robbers, arsonists, wife beater, and sadists. My guess is that Dr. Beto's collection of societal misfits paid little attention to the beard, and I will bet my sweet bippy none were made more violent by my presence.

Interestingly, I had been through the system nine or ten years earlier as a college sophomore enrolled in an A&M criminology class. Our professor was an old-timer named Professor Dan Russell who was a nice man and decent teacher, but as I look back on his behavior now with a bit more insight, he easily could have been in the early stages of dementia.

An endearing quirk of Professor Dan Russell (We called him "Doctor" but I think he only had a master's degree) was his unique system for checking class attendance each day. He assigned everyone a number according to our alphabetical listing on his course roster, and we were instructed to call out our individual number in sequence once the person designated as number one started the process at the beginning of class each day. If Dr. Russell did not hear a number called out, he concluded the student was absent and he would thus note it on his roll sheet. Once someone uttered

"One", we would all chime in with our own numbers as appropriate and, unbeknownst to Dr. Russell, most of those of our missing classmates as well. It was important that we not call out all numbers for fear that perfect attendance each day would attract Dr. Russell's attention. Periodically, then, there would be a random moment of silence, thus allowing him to record an occasional absence. Once the process was concluded, Dr. Russell would remark, "My, my, it is nice to have everyone in class again today. It makes professors happy when students attend class so faithfully." A quick scan on the room would typically show maybe half or three-fourths of the class was actually in attendance. At the time, I thought this quirky method for checking roll was merely a personal idiosyncrasy, but I have wondered since if this was not one of the early manifestations of the onset of his apparent bout with dementia.

Dr. Russell at one time had been on the Board of Directors of the prison system and used this influence to get our group a first-class tour. The rumor among my classmates was that he had done his master's thesis in Chicago during the heyday of the old gangster, Al Capone, and the famous FBI agent, Frank Nitti. Additional rumors, however apocryphal, held that the highly visible scar on his nose was supposedly a "gift" from one of Capone's hitmen. Whether or not Capone or one of his confederates performed the surgery on Professor Russell's nose was never really confirmed or denied, but we thought it made a great story. It also added a certain "romance" to his life story and afforded him considerable clout as a criminologist in our minds.

Two events took place during that tour I guess will stick with me until I meet my merrymaker, the clown in the sky who orchestrates this gigantic comedy known as life. One incident took place in the area where prisoners were commissioned to make license plates for the citizenry of Texas. The license plates were metal and demand was high as they had to be replaced each year up until 1995 when applying a sticker to the inside of the windshield became the new norm for license renewal. The process whereby the metal plates was made required incredible rhythm, for the operators had to manipulate two hand-held devices and two foot pedals at the same time, thus creating an effect reminiscent of the percussion section in a band.

The unit director touring us through that part of the prison gathered everyone up in a circle and said with complete, cocksure authority: "Gentlemen, look across this room. You will notice that everyone who we have making these license plates is a round-headed nigger. Everyone here was selected to work in this area because they are round-headed, which means they have rhythm. As you can tell from the syncopation in the room, it takes incredible rhythm to operate these license plate machines. Long-headed niggers simply lack the necessary rhythm, and do I need to address the rhythmic shortcomings of white prisoners?" I was not especially worldly as a college sophomore, but I suspected that rhythm was probably distributed reasonably equally between blacks with round heads and those with long ones. And maybe a white guy or two probably had rhythm, maybe a genetic freak like the now-deceased drummer *par excellence*, Buddy Rich. However, if you accept the premise that only individuals who are black and have round heads can accomplish the task, then you will probably select only those prisoners for your license plate work detail. The bias then becomes a self-fulfilling prophecy. As our guide held forth, I could not help but think Tony Dorsett, the Dallas Cowboy Hall of Fame running back of the 1970's and 1980's, or the immensely popular comedian of the same period, Flip Wilson, would have been a prolific producer of license plates had they chosen careers in crime. Today, I would probably add former President Barack Obama to my list of potential license makers in another time and space.

A second memorable event that day was the tour of the women's unit. We were met at the entrance to the cell block by a solidly built, middle-aged, fireplug of a woman named Dobbs. She started off her part of the overall tour as follows: "Howdy, Gentlemen. I am Warden Dobbs. I am in charge of the women's unit of the Texas Department of Corrections. There are four hundred women in my unit, or two hundred homosexual pairs." After that introduction, almost anything seemed possible. As we navigated our way through the unit, laughter and catcalls, many laden with crude sexual overtones, poured forth in profusion from the cells. My tender, late adolescent ears were bombarded with language and sexual innuendos unheard of in my previous experience, and it was obvious we were not in the presence of a collection of vestal virgins.

We eventually arrived at a cell decorated from top to bottom and side to side with attractive, eye-catching paintings. The incongruity between the human grit and grime and real-life pathos we had been exposed to all day and the beauty of the works of art was palpable. It turns out the artist was Annie Laurie Williams, a convicted child-killer widely known for her murderous actions and artistic talents. Her work was indeed eye-catching and made us wonder what circumstances could have led this seemingly gentle artist to kill her two boys, ages nine and seven, dismember them, and dupe a friend into burying them in Galveston County. For her grisly crimes, she was incarcerated in the Goree Unit in 1955, or two years before our visit.

The unit was originally opened in 1911 and was known as the Goree State Farm for Women. Females served their sentences there until 1980, at which time the state moved them to a facility in Gatesville, a small central Texas town near Fort Hood. In this regard, a 2013 graduate of our Psychology program who was also one of my 2011 Germany Study Abroad participants served a year in Gatesville while in high school, having killed her cousin who was also her best friend in an intoxicated manslaughter automobile accident.

Warden Dobbs told us Annie Williams was a prostitute and her husband a robber of banks. The shady reputations of the two parents played a big role in the boys being alternately rejected or taunted and bullied by their peers at school and in the neighborhood. This rejection apparently was a big factor in the unconscionable murders committed by Annie Williams who rationalized her acts as follows: "I killed my kids because the world was not good enough for them." For those slayings, she was sentenced to life in prison. Despite the life sentence, she was released on parole in 1980, fled her assigned Halfway House in Houston shortly thereafter, and lived a "normal life" in California and Idaho for more than a decade. She was eventually re-arrested, her parole revoked, and at last report (1997), had been returned to prison where she occupied much of her time braiding yarn to be used as hair for dolls being made by other women inmates.

For a couple of years in the late 1960's, I attended the annual prison art show in Huntsville and the works of Annie Williams were prominent and award-winning. We were also told by one of our guides she had shown her wares in many major national art galleries and her paintings were typically bought up by a large hotel chain for display in their various units across the country.

As a post-script to these events of the late 1950's, when I returned to campus as a faculty member in the mid-1960's, I recall seeing Dan Russell in the company of his wife who was leading him around more or less like he was a little boy. Rumors had it that Dr. Russell was fully senile by that time. I must say my memories of him are most fond and his sponsorship of class field trips is something I have incorporated in my own classes for nearly a half century. I owe Professor Dan Russell big-time on that one!

Another person who felt he owed the man an eternal debt of gratitude was one William O. Adams, A&M Class of 1944, who endowed the Daniel Russell Memorial Scholarship in his honor. It seems that Mr. Adams was a student in 1942 and in the middle of the semester his appendix burst, leaving him upon recovery with a sizeable medical debt by standards at that time, the princely sum of $100. Mr. Adams thought he would be forced to drop out of school, but fortuitously someone suggested he discuss the situation with Professor Russell first. After their visit, Professor Russell handed him a check for $100, asking only that he someday repay the debt on behalf of another student in need. In the words of Dan Russell as quoted in a 2014 edition of *Spirit*, an A&M publication, "This is not a loan. If you can ever afford to repay me, I ask you to use the money to help another student." Today, the Dan Russell Scholarship is used expressly for that purpose, helping young Aggies with their tuition. This anecdote speaks volumes about Dan Russell's charity and integrity, and I am pleased to have known him. And thanks to Mr. William Adams for a wonderful remembrance of Professor Dan Russell.

Other Colleagues of a More Quirky Persuasion

Bill: The Con Man. Another of my noteworthy colleagues, though not entirely for the right reasons, was a middle-aged, well-dressed, dapper, handsome "educator" by the name of Bill R. I was told early on by our Department Head, Dr. X, to milk Bill for all he was worth and to model myself after him in light of his vast experience and distinguished national reputation. I assured Dr. X I would watch Bill in action where possible, pick his brain, and generally try to profit from exposure to someone with such a superstar academic pedigree and impeccable professional credentials.

Bill quickly developed a less-than-stellar reputation, and was widely viewed by students and colleagues as somewhat of a quirky eccentric. My initial inkling that something might be awry with him occurred late one afternoon at the University Terrace Apartments where my family lived the first two years we were in College Station. I inadvertently found myself smack-dab in the middle of a somewhat animated conversation at poolside with a couple of professors from the Department of Mathematics. In the course of our discussion, they ascertained my departmental affiliation and asked if I knew Bill R. They went on to tell me they had paid the man a tidy sum of money to consult on a research study they were conducting but had not heard a peep from him for months. I acknowledged that I knew their man but not well, and thus could not account for either his typical behavior or the alleged delinquency in responding to their calls.

Shortly after that conversation, I got another salient glimpse into the character of the idiosyncratic Bill R. He was the designated speaker for a bi-weekly seminar sponsored by our department in which specialists from the faculty held forth for two hours for peers in other disciplines who might be interested in what each one of us might have to say. The guiding philosophy behind the creation of the seminars was the belief that professors in our department would hold forth in their designated areas of expertise for other professors across the campus who desired to improve their teaching. How to motivate students, the best ways to construct a classroom examination, and characteristics of college students were among the items discussed in the individual sessions.

In the course of his stint in the box where had been asked to hold forth on learning disabilities, Bill mentioned something about getting a PhD at the University of Heidelberg in Germany after World War II. It was my understanding he had been stationed in that consummately lovely German city after the war but in the course of looking at his credentials later on, his doctorate had actually been conferred by Temple University in Philadelphia in the area of Educational Administration. I temporarily attributed the error to an inadvertence, maybe a slip of the tongue or a memory lapse. However, he continued to embarrass himself and the department by putting his listeners down with assertions about his intellectual and experiential superiority. Further, he made numerous mispronunciations of words (social millenniums instead of social milieus) and proper names (Henslinger instead of Hensarling, Gravitz instead of Graves, Levine instead of LeUnes), and generally put on a dismal display for his increasingly inattentive and borderline rebellious audience. The talk was a total embarrassment, and attendance at our seminars dropped by half after Bill's disaster. The department head came up to me after the talk and said: "What did you think? Wasn't Bill interesting?" I agreed that it was indeed interesting and left it at that.

Bill's total disregard for punctuality added to the growing legend. He seldom if ever made meetings on time and more often than not completely failed to show up for appointments with students and colleagues. On one noteworthy occasion, he had been scheduled to give an in-service talk to a group of A&M Consolidated Middle School teachers at the end of their long, demanding work day. He showed up nearly an hour late, offered no apology for his inconsideration, and proceeded to go on with his hour lecture as if nothing happened, never sensing or seeming to care that he was talking to a very hostile and mostly female audience who just wanted to go home, feed their families, and get on with the evening.

Another noticeable failing was the cavalier approach he brought to his teaching duties. He taught three courses each semester which was standard in those days. One was a sophomore level introductory course, another was for master's degree students, and the third a doctoral seminar. He used the same text, pretty much identical notes, and essentially the same examinations in all three courses, and the assigned text was unrelated to the content domain in each instance. His students and a few faculty voiced reservations about what he was doing but, in the name of protecting his academic freedom and thus our own, we reasoned that he should be free to do as he wished with his courses. In retrospect, our reasoning was probably flawed, but most of us were neophytes at the time with a poorly-developed awareness of what constituted academic freedom.

One day Bill R. was walking down the hall in the Academic Building, resplendent in a gold, glittery sport coat, and I just could not restrain myself, in my most phony manner, from congratulating him on his good taste in clothing. At the same time, I felt compelled to pose a question for which I pretty much already knew the answer. The terse interchange was as follows: "Hey, Bill. Good looking sport coat, man. Do you mind if I ask where you purchased it?" As I said, I already knew the answer but I wanted to see what he would say. He rambled on about picking it up in Hong Kong during his most recent trip to the Orient. What he had actually done was special order the sport coat from Chet's Hong Kong Clothes, a business in Bryan specializing in tailor-made clothing ostensibly crafted from exotic fibers flown in from the Far East. The business was housed on the first floor of what was then the Ramada Inn just northeast of the campus. The area is now the home to Northpoint Crossing, a visually hideous three-phase commercial and residential development. Phase One opened in 2014 with 928 beds and 50,000 square feet of space for clothing, retail, and restaurants.

I watched the televised demolition of the original building in 2012, literally hours before departing for Germany for five weeks with a gaggle of undergraduates. The company hired to set the charges to bring the structure down obviously knew their craft, for the implosion took maybe ten seconds.

But I digress; let us get back to Chet's Hong Kong Clothes. Though I had seen advertisements for Chet's for some time, I walked around in the store for the first time a few days before the hall incident with Bill R., trying to get a feel for what Chet was all about. In the midst of my exploratory expedition, I happened to spy two loud, glitzy sports coats, a glittery gold one and the other an iridescent blue. I asked Chet if he would think me presumptuous if I inquired about their ownership, and he said no. He further indicated a Psychology professor at A&M, Bill R., had special ordered them a couple of weeks earlier. Importing your clothes in Hong Kong is one thing; buying them from Chet's Hong Kong Clothes in Bryan-College Station, Texas, is quite another! But that was Bill R. in a nutshell, all fluff and pretension, or as the Texans would put it, all hat and no cattle!

The penultimate event, a straw that helped break the back of the proverbial camel for me personally, was an incident in which he brought a witch doctor (my terminology) to one of his classes as a guest lecturer. In the course of his talk, the witch doctor posing as a guest "expert" made a comment to the effect that failing to crawl in a rhythmic fashion in infancy causes faulty wiring in the brain, with attendant motor problems and learning deficiencies. He further stated that crossing one's legs while sitting also disturbs these neural pathways, and urged his listeners to put their hands on their desks and feet flat on the floor lest they exacerbate the neural wiring problem. He then uncorked a whopper, asserting that 40% of the optic nerves go to the eye, 40% to the elbow, and the remaining 20% to the knee. That distribution of optic nerves, he continued, is why people watch television, elbows resting on the knees with hands placed to both sides of the head. This coalescence of electrical contact points unites the optic nerve fibers going to the eye with those in the elbows and knees, thus creating a maximal connection of all possible components of an intact, smoothly functioning electrical circuit. Chihuahua and God Praise the Queen!!!

It was at this point that curiosity really started to kill this cat (and other feline friends). Faculty colleagues Jim Elliott and Tony Bourgeois, doctoral student friends John Badgett and Norvell Northcutt, and yours truly were increasingly convinced that something was amiss with our supposed superstar. On the other hand, being mid-twenties neophytes in the world of academia, we were still willing after all the input to the contrary to concede the problem could, alas, rest with us. We acknowledged the possibility that Bill may simply have been too celestial and thus beyond the powers of comprehension for us mere earthlings. Simply put, we were overmatched and the problem was ours, not his. As someone has said, one of the great things about being a celebrity is when you are a bore, your listeners think it is their fault. Bill was our celebrity, for sure, and the lack of insight was our problem, not his.

Jim, Tony, Norvell, John, and I decided that since we were incapable of comprehending Bill on any other basis, perhaps it might make sense to read the research articles he had published in the various professional journals. He had listed somewhere upwards of two hundred articles on his vitae, and we decided to divvy them up five ways and see what insights could be gleaned from our independent analyses. The five of us agreed to get back together in a few days to discuss our findings.

What we found was the creation of a gigantic ruse. Bill had randomly selected numerous articles from a variety of educational and psychological journals and doctored them to make it appear he was the author when he was not. He would find articles with a unifying, cohesive theme and add the titles to his vitae verbatim, with all details intact other than the author name; that is, the title, journal, volume number, and page numbers were correct but the name of the actual author(s) was omitted and replaced on his vitae with his own. Simply stated, the articles existed but Bill R. was not the author of any of them!

At this point, John and Norvell, the two doctoral students, took it upon themselves to schedule a meeting with the department head. When John and Norvell informed Dr. X of the irregularities in Bill R.'s vitae, the chair's first reaction was to kill the messengers. He called a meeting of all PhD students and informed them they were no longer on financial assistance. This decree essentially relieved them of their teaching and research duties. It became obvious almost overnight that his hastily-made decision was flawed; this institution and most other major universities would simply collapse under their own weight if the graduate students were banned from the classrooms and laboratories. Within a day or two after the initial, ill-considered overreaction, the head called the students back together and reinstated them. At the same time, he gave them a stern warning about spending time in the library engaged in nefarious activity that might be used to impugn the integrity of his most esteemed professors.

After a while, the lunacy of banning graduate students from the library also became apparent, so a decision was made to confront the villain rather than continuing to impale the messengers. Bill R. was summoned forth for a "Come to Jesus Meeting", but as anyone familiar with the psychological makeup of the antisocial personality can tell you, his response to all charges was more one of defiance than contrition. He told the chair that he had been brought to the department with great media hoopla and fanfare, had been widely hailed as the savior of the department and perhaps the university itself, and his departure under such checkered circumstances would reflect poorly on those who had hired him in the first place. He defiantly asked our leader what he was going to do about the situation given the potential embarrassment it could cause him, other at-fault administrators, and the university as a whole.

Approximately ten days later, Bill received his long-awaited answer. Someone in authority in the administration took advantage of A&M's long tentacles in the so-called "real world" and orchestrated a deal whereby Bill R. would resign his post at A&M and become the Vice President of Education for a major conglomerate, which I remember as Pepsico Corporation. He was to receive a sizeable salary increase, a generous housing allowance, and a robust budget with which to operate his section of that giant corporation. All the A&M administration asked was that Bill R. set up meetings with the local media and apprise them of the fact that after weeks of painful soul-searching, he felt compelled to accept the lucrative position in industry despite his professed "undying love for Texas A&M University." Also, he was to let everyone know that if things did not work out with his new venture, he would happily return to the first love in life other than his family, that of being a faculty member at Texas A&M University. Of course, the truth was that he was never coming back and that message was spelled out to him in no uncertain terms by the administration. He was essentially told that if he ever showed up on campus ever again, he would be shot on sight, figuratively speaking, of course. The public relations gimmick was merely a feeble attempt at damage control concocted to protect the image of the university (and a few red-faced administrators with extremely tight anal sphincters, no doubt).

Several months after his departure, we in the department received a note from our man Bill R., along with a vita that listed him as former Head of the Psychology Department at A&M, which did not exist at that time. He also listed himself as a graduate of the William Alanson White Psychoanalytic Institute which under no circumstances admitted people into training who possessed doctoral degrees in his area of expertise which was public school administration. He listed quite a number of other accomplishments and honors, and all entries were slight misstatements of fact, gross distortions, or out-and-out prevarications.

Rumors were that Bill R. had held ten different jobs in twenty years when A&M brought him aboard, and, if true, that should have sent up all kinds of red flags to those who hire new faculty members. Essentially, it took each employer one year to find out our man was a fourteen carat fraud and one year to cut him loose. For whatever reason, it took Pepsico three years to drop the axe, at which time Bill R. became an Assistant Superintendent for Research in one of the largest school systems in Texas which I will never identify as San Antonio Independent School District. One can only speculate about his ability to conduct and supervise school district research, given that he had never done any himself, other than looking for random articles with which to falsify his vita.

He was a mentor alright, but not in the manner that the department head had in mind when he sent me in Bill's direction in 1967. Bill R. vanished from our awareness around 1970.

Virgil: A Case of Paranoia. Another fascinating colleague from those early days was Virgil C. I did not know much about Virgil for he was not around A&M very long after I arrived. He was a late thirtyish, maybe fortyish, long, tall, drink-of-water who fit the popular stereotype of the nerdy, absent-minded professor. During my first months at A&M, I really never gave much thought to the non-descript Virgil until he accosted my friend, John Badgett, in the hall on the fourth floor of the Academic Building where our offices and classrooms were located. John was nearing completion of his PhD work, and he and I were walking down the hall near Room 402 one day, undoubtedly talking about school, football, or women when Virgil walked up, grabbed John by the shoulders, spun him around, and said, "John Badgett. I heard you call me a son-of-a-bitch. I heard you! I heard you call me a son-of-a-bitch. No one calls me a son-of-a-bitch and gets away with it. I am a respected veteran in the field of education and I can make or break your career with one phone call. You are just starting out but I can ruin your career, and I will if I ever hear you call me a son-of-a-bitch again." With that message reeking of paranoia, Virgil strode away. Badgett looked at me with a dumbfounded, quizzical, what-the-hell-just-happened look. I quickly turned my palms up and out in feigned confusion. Then John said, "He's not going to get away with that." I said, "I agree, Johnny, I wouldn't let anyone talk to me that way." Isn't it fun to get your friends into fights when the cost to you is zero?

John intercepted Virgil at the elevator and gave him a pretty good shove. As the two combatants entered the elevator, it was obvious this episode might escalate and become very interesting, so I ran down the four flights of steps in the Academic Building as fast as my legs would carry me. I arrived at the first floor elevator stop just in time to see the door open and John give Virgil a pretty good forearm across the chest. Pretty quickly, wiser, cooler heads intervened, the two combatants were separated, and sent their separate ways, both muttering inaudibly to themselves.

This same elevator had earlier been the source of mystery in some quarters, with a suggestion it might be possessed by evil spirits. The concern with the elevator emanated from an old, bent, thin, gray, black gentleman who worked in the building as a custodian in the 1960's. I watched him from time to time and noticed he carried his cleaning materials up and down the steps, studiously avoiding the elevator when moving from one floor to the next. Curiosity finally got the best of me one day so I approached him to get his take on this elevator thing. He let me know in no uncertain terms he was not setting foot in the elevator because there were "haints" in there, and it was best to avoid them. "The thing is 'hainted'", he said. "It's 'hainted', man. There are 'haints' in there, and they'll get you if you don't watch out. Be careful and stay away from those 'haints.' There may have been a moment or two when Virgil thought he had been victimized by one of those 'haints.' Come to think of it, John Badgett did strike me as a little bit "hainted."

John and I (and others) subsequently found out through a "snitch" in the Dean's office that Virgil had an interesting caveat attached to the end of one of his letters of recommendation from The Ohio State University where he received his PhD degree. The letter indicated Virgil was prone to episodes of paranoia and should not be hired anywhere until he received intensive treatment for his disorder. We also found out from our informant that Virgil had accosted somewhere between two and three dozen other people on campus, always invoking the "No one calls me a son-of-a-bitch" mantra.

Enter the image-preservers once again. Virgil was called on the carpet and reluctantly admitted there was a problem. After a few days of deliberation and behind-the-scenes maneuvering, Virgil was given an offer that was simply too good to pass up. It seems that Harvard University, quite coincidentally and conveniently, was looking for an outstanding mid-career Education professor to fill a recently created and lucrative one-year postdoctoral position. All Virgil had to do to land the position, other than going through the application process, was to call a meeting with the local media, professing his undying love for A&M with the addendum that if things did not pan out as anticipated in the hallowed halls of John Harvard, he would return to resume his first love, other than his family, of teaching young Aggies. Of course, coming back was never an option in his negotiations any more than they were in the case of Bill R., but it looked good for such a distinguished educator like Virgil to profess his undying love and affection for the university and its students as he was escorted unceremoniously out the door. I somehow had the feeling the message about being shot on sight if he ever returned to campus was not figurative in Virgil's case!

Those were rough years for A&M as they tried to overcome decades of lethargy in hiring and nurturing good faculty. During the Bill/Virgil era, another Education professor was hired with the understanding he was to complete his PhD within the year. Three or four years later, he still had not received his degree, and an inquiry into the matter revealed that the culprit had been dismissed from the doctoral program at his university prior to accepting the A&M position. He was quietly and summarily canned by A&M sans public fanfare, for obvious reasons. That same year, it was learned that a chap in the Department of English had manufactured all three of his degrees, and he was deep-sixed for academic dishonesty. Those were difficult times and tougher strictures were put in place related to the hiring of faculty as a result of these multiple misadventures. As we were to see decades later, those strictures were not without holes.

Alexander Kemos: Wannabee Tufts PhD and Navy Seal. Ironically enough, a similar scenario unfolded forty-plus years later involving the third highest ranking administrator at A&M, a slight man named Alexander Kemos. Kemos was hired in 2009, and his title was Senior Vice President for Administration, As such, he was in charge of facilities, the campus police, and assorted university business enterprises. It came to light in his second year, 2010, that two of his most sterling credentials, the advanced degrees (MS and PhD) from Tufts University Fletcher School of Law and

Diplomacy and his status as a Navy Seal, were bogus. He had indeed been a graduate student at Tufts but never finished, and there is no record whatsoever that he ever began or completed Navy Seal training. Claiming to be a Seal was a violation of the federal Stolen Valor Act, since repealed by Congress, and carried with it a possible year in jail at that time. Actions such as those of Kemos make a mockery of the "Brothers with Different Mothers" mantra of Navy Seals, but with the repeal of the Stolen Valor Act, Kemos will never face prosecution for his bogus claim. My guess is that legal action in these cases was typically reserved for violations deemed more egregious than those committed by Kemos anyway.

When the twin indiscretions came to light, Kemos was dismissed from his $300,000 a year position. Apparently, our friendly impostor was very close to Dr. Bowen Loftin, the university president at the time, and his dismissal took place while the two were preparing to vacation in Maine. As I remember, Dr. Loftin was already at the vacation site awaiting the arrival of Kemos when he was informed of his friend's indiscretions. The situation had to be most uncomfortable for both parties, and newspaper descriptions of their parting suggested more than passing unease for all.

It is perfectly predictable that the university administration would want to institute some damage control by applying lipstick to the Kemos pig. Not long after the incident made headlines, a university spokesman pointed out to the various media that Kemos' falsification of his credentials was a first of its type for A&M. I beg to differ! All one has to do is go back four decades to find multiple examples of unprofessional behavior in the academy. Faking or overstating credentials was not really new in the 2000's and, in fact, was a way of life in the 1960's.

Department Heads I Have Known

Administrator X: A Case of Hysterical Muteness? Dr. X (not his real name) was quite a case. He was a professional school administrator from the "heat, light, and ventilation" school, distinguished looking, probably in his mid- to late-60's, and departmental chair for a time when I first arrived on the scene. It seems he spent the last few years of his life in a state of muteness for which there seemed to be no identifiable anatomical or physiological cause. The younger faculty and graduate students, waxing analytical, figured it was a good case of Freudian hysterical muteness brought on by an alleged but virtually certain illicit extramarital affair with a divorced, middle-aged graduate student exacerbated by the guilt often inherent in such dalliance.

Coffee room chatter among her graduate student peers had it that the woman in question whose name I remember vividly but will not reveal was receiving a stipend equal to two or three times that typically offered to other graduate students, thanks to the largesse of her benefactor, our honorable department chairperson. Other rumors had wrecker companies towing his Cadillac from the alley behind her home on several occasions. Retrieving the vehicle from the wrecker yard was apparently a ticklish problem, a "sticky wicket" as the British say, given the events that led to it being towed in the first place. Other rumors had his wife confronting the two of them in potentially incriminating circumstances. And from the looks of the betrayed wife, she was no trivial adversary! "Bulldog" Turner (the football version) would have been impressed!

I think Dr. X was essentially a good man, a moral man, a self-professed religious man, and amateur and professional psychologists alike proffered opinions over coffee in the faculty lounge about guilt over the affair being the root source of the muteness. We reasoned that muteness served as a protective mechanism to keep him from confessing his sins to a critical public. To put it another way, one cannot confess if one cannot talk! How much of our psychodynamic interpretation is true is obviously speculative, but the man reportedly went to his grave in a state of silence.

Bill Reed. Speaking of department heads, we had a succession of interesting clinical cases assume that position in my first years. The hysterically mute Dr. X was followed by a refugee from Xerox Corporation by the name of Dr. Bill Reed (not his real name). Bill Reed was trained as an Industrial-Organizational psychologist, (i.e., Human Resource Management in Colleges of Business), and had held corporate managerial positions prior to assuming the job as our department head. Bill was a survivor of the Bataan Death March in World War II and a decent fellow at heart but bless his tortured soul, he was a lousy leader. He was indecisive and had a reputation among the other heads as a weak advocate for his faculty. In meetings with the Dean of the College where the infighting for resources among the various heads is legendary, he apparently was feckless. "Skip" Leabo, the head of the Department of Journalism, once told me the other heads would shuffle about prior to those meetings with the Dean in an attempt to be the last one to talk to Bill. The operative assumption was that if you needed a swing vote on an issue and you were the last person to have Bill's ear, you could count on him regardless of what he had previously promised others and his own personal sentiments.

After a couple of years as department head, Bill went into a pronounced depressive funk and started faking illness and injuries. He even resorted to showing up for work with one arm in a sling, what in retrospect was an obvious plea for sympathy, literally a desperate cry for help. His antics were pretty much totally ignored, ironically enough, right in the midst of a group of psychologists, some of whom are trained to detect and minister to such conditions. It was clear that Bill was suffering a serious depressive episode but no one seemed to suspect he was suicidal. Bill eventually killed himself with a shot to the head.

We were, of course, taken aback at the news of his sad and untimely demise. On the day of his self-inflicted death, Bill had reportedly driven to Lake Somerville where he tried to drown himself. However, he was simply too adept at swimming. I would guess the will to survive that led him to live through Bataan must have also reflexively kicked in, preventing him from being able to consummate the suicidal act by drowning. He then headed back in the direction of College Station, drove out to a lonely country road near Cook's Point which is halfway between A&M and Caldwell, and shot himself in the head. This method of suicide pretty much takes reflexes out of the equation. Bill Reed left a wife and eight children.

From all indications, Bill was estranged from most if not all of his family, his career was in shambles, and he was at philosophical odds with the teachings of the Mormon faith in which he had been raised. At his funeral which I attended, an unpopular one with some of the local Mormon brethren because of the nature of his death, Bill was characterized as being seriously out of step with his religion, and was described at one point by the minister presiding over the services as a "Philistine."

Cless Jay. Bill Reed was replaced by Dr. Cless Jay (not his real name), a brilliant psychologist with an absolutely pathological addiction to alcohol. Cless was a graduate of Alma College and Michigan State University. While at Alma, a university founded on extreme fundamental religious beliefs, Cless became a minister, and sermonized for a few years before giving up the calling. I once asked him why he gave up the ministry and he said: "I was making two souls for everyone I saved and that behavior flew in the face of my vows as a man of the cloth."

I will say one thing about his religious persuasion…he knew an unimaginable number of hymns. On a lark, no doubt fueled in part by alcohol, Cless and I motored over to Austin one evening to meet up with an old friend from the Bill R. episode, Norvell Northcutt. It seems that Norvell left our department in a what I have always felt was a justifiable philosophical snit shortly before completing his PhD because of the nonsense taking place within the department involving the aforementioned Bill Reed, Virgil C., and Dr. X. I thought his decision to continue the pursuit of the doctorate at the University of Texas, yes the dreaded "tu", was an honorable one, and I admired him for his stand on what he considered to be major ethical violations taking place in his department at A&M. He eventually received the PhD there, taught for many years, and retired as Vice President of Austin Community College. He later came out of retirement and joined the faculty at "tu." Norvell was one of the brightest people I ever met, and in addition, he was a talented singer and guitarist.

Not too long ago, I was rummaging around, looking for an old study I conducted on the group dynamics of a college gymnastics team, and came across a letter from Norvell dated February 6, 1970. At the time, Captain Northcutt was stationed just outside of Saigon in Vietnam and his letter described his duties and apprehensions about the situation there. Of these stresses and strains, he said: "…everyone here seems to be a little apprehensive, particularly at night. Accordingly, I've been carrying my bullet shooter with me. I'm the operational definition of a Saigon warrior—M-16 in one hand, can of beer in the other." This was vintage sardonic Norvell Northcutt. Well-stated, my friend!

Though his music preference was country-western, Norvell had quite a repertoire of hymns as his disposal, too. Knowing this, Cless, Norvell, and I decided to get together at Norvell's home off of Bee Caves Road in Austin for what we eventually labelled as a good old "hymn-off" featuring my two friends. The three of us drank copious amounts of beer while playing our guitars (Norvell adroitly, and Cless and I loudly to disguise our numerous and glaring inadequacies), singing hymns well into the wee hours of the morning. Two or three hours past midnight, the two hymn meisters agreed to call the gathering of eagles a draw and Cless and I headed back to good old College Station.

Cless was a talented workaholic and made Professor at Michigan State by age twenty-nine, a rise to eminence seldom seen in a university of such academic stature. For whatever reason, and it might not be too big a reach to invoke alcohol-related explanations for his departure from Michigan State, he decided to interview for our department head position. Cless accepted the ensuing job offer, but it was not long before he went on drunken spree after drunken spree spanning a period of several years. The university was so small and simple to operate in those days that Ruth Ann Powell, our departmental administrative assistant, pretty much ran things when Cless was on one of his legendary benders. On one occasion, Ruth Ann got a call at the departmental office at 0800 from a desk clerk at the local Holiday Inn South indicating that Cless had passed out in a flower bed near their front entry. Several of us went over, retrieved him from his resting place, and took him home to sleep it off.

On another occasion, Cless had been sequestered for treatment at the local mental health center but left against medical advice. He immediately headed for Denny Seal's place just off of Dexter Street in College Station and adjacent to the university. Denny was a master's student in our department (he later received a PhD in Industrial Engineering), and occasionally looked after Cless when he was on one of his drinking sprees or rampages.

On that particular evening, Denny dialed me up on the phone and asked if I would help him babysit Cless. Keeping our drunken friend entertained and thus out of the public eye was a daunting task, given his tendencies toward gregariousness and combativeness when drinking, and it challenged our collective ingenuities. We started our vigil early one Friday evening and watched him drink up every alcoholic beverage in Denny's house. When the beer, wine, and liquor were gone, he proceeded to drain the cough syrup and any other concoction containing even the slightest trace of alcohol. He stayed drunk until Sunday morning, at which time he asked if we would take him to the Chicken Oil Company, a popular burger and beer hangout, to shoot pool. Denny and I were pretty much ragged out by then and greatly welcomed his request as it offered respite from the weekend-long ordeal we had inadvertently created for ourselves.

Cless' reputation as a legendary drunk preceded him, making him a well-known figure by virtually every proprietor and bartender in town. Part of our reasoning for taking him out was we were positive someone in the Chicken Oil would recognize him and call the mental health authorities or the police, at which time Cless would be taken off our hands. That is exactly what happened, and Cless was returned to the center to resume treatment.

Cless was a nasty, surly, mean, and mouthy drunk, always looking for a fight. It was a miracle he survived his frequent verbal assaults on friends, acquaintances, and strangers, particularly the latter. He often attacked his friends with vicious verbal barrages which we eventually learned were largely harmless and soon forgotten, washed away in an alcoholic haze. However, when Cless frequented low-life establishments like the "Cajun We No Tell Number Two" near Navasota and insulted the locals, things could get dicey real fast. He was also known to verbally confront the race track crowd from the local motor speedway, and there are some pretty tough and ready-to-fight-at-the-drop-of-a-hat types in that assemblage. Miracles being what they are, Cless was never to my knowledge beaten within an inch of his life, but it was not for lack of provocation and effort on his part.

Things rocked along unsteadily for several years, and the *coup de grace* occurred when Cless got into a well-publicized shootout with his wife, herself a psychologist and former student in our department, in their home. I do not know if shots were actually fired but apparently a gun or guns were drawn. At that point, the domestic drama was picked up by the local media, and the publicity generated by the incident led the university administration to decide it had endured enough of his drunken didoes. He was let go, went to work for the US government, and eventually overcame his alcohol addiction.

I corresponded with Cless a few years ago and he was doing well. I later learned that Dr. Cless Jay died June 10, 2010 at the age of seventy-three. He was cremated and his remains were scattered in the Pacific Ocean off the coast near Monterey County, California. This scattering of the ashes seemed a fitting end for a man who was tortured for so long by demon rum but was able, in his last years, to find peace and tranquility living on or near the sea.

Fran Bevans and the "Suck-Ass Six." Cless Jay was replaced by Dr. Fran Bevans (not his real name) who came to our department with credentials as a historian of psychology. Bevans ascended to the headship of the department through a most interesting set of circumstances. It seems that an external search for department head was granted by the administration, and several well-known psychologists from other universities including Dr. Robert Blanchard from the State University of New York (SUNY) system and Dr. Robert Solso from the University of Idaho were interviewed. Blanchard was impressive and well-regarded by our faculty, but removed his name from consideration shortly after his visit to campus.

The truth in the case of the Robert Solso is murky at best, and multiple rumors circulated for weeks concerning his application. He appeared to be quite interested in coming to A&M, but his candidacy was short-circuited by a smear campaign rumored to have been hatched by Bevans and his bevy of ass-kissing lackeys in the department. To discredit our final external candidate, not-so-subtle rumors were circulated here and there, carefully planted and suggesting Solso had a habit of indiscriminately hitting on young female students. There was an added inference that these victims were easily influenced undergraduates who were no doubt virginal, naïve, and powerless to stand up for their rights. In the words of one of my former departmental colleagues, a statistician by training: "There is nothing lower than a professor who would dick an undergraduate." The truth of the matter was Solso had been dating a former graduate student for some time, and she had moved away from Idaho upon receiving her PhD degree and accepting a faculty position elsewhere. From all appearances, the two of them were carrying on a healthy, above-board, long-distance relationship with all the problems inherent in such an arrangement. To use this relationship to try to paint Solso as a predator who sexually harassed students did a real disservice to a good psychologist. Perhaps Solso learned of this skullduggery, but whatever the reason, he withdrew his name from consideration. With the external job candidate pool depleted, the faculty was then faced with the task of choosing among an assortment of internal candidates.

Solso spent the last twenty-three years of his life at the University of Nevada-Reno, and died in 2005 at the age of seventy-one. He listed among his many accomplishments and accolades the authorship of thirty-seven books and eighty-eight articles. It is a shame when those books and articles were published, they did not have the Department of Psychology at Texas A&M University listed as the affiliate institution!

Out of the ashes of what was once an external search emerged Bevans who had the blind and unwavering support of six people who ate lunch with him and French kissed his ass daily and royally to curry favor. Six votes in what was then a small faculty carried a lot of weight, and when it came time to select a new head, Bevans received the support necessary to secure the appointment. In honor of their accomplishments, and as a token of my undying affection for the man and his aiders, abettors, and henchpersons, I affectionately dubbed the sycophantic lunch cabal as the "Suck-Ass Six." All six of those people have since left the university and Bevans, as will be noted, is also long-gone.

My opposition to Bevans getting the department head position was considerable, a sentiment shared by my deceased friend and much-admired colleague, Jack Nation. We were both vocal in committee meetings about our vehement opposition to Bevans, and our negative stance and vote of no-confidence were leaked to him by one of his six, servile, suck-ass supporters on the selection committee and thus privy to all aspects of the deliberations. Once installed as department head, Bevans proceeded to spend the next eight years trying to destroy two careers, Jack's and mine. If ever there was an instance in which having a tenure policy served its purpose, this was it. Jack and I, without such strictures in place, would have been long gone. Since neither of us could be fired without cause, Bevans tried to strangle us, salary-wise. I figured his payback during those eight years cost me maybe a quarter of a million dollars on my retirement alone, not to mention annual salary raises.

My friend and now-retired colleague, Ludy Benjamin, took note of what was going on around the department and decided to look into the relationship between Bevans, the "Suck-Ass Six", and faculty productivity. Ludy, like others of us outside the inner circle, entertained suspicions that being in the lunchroom with Bevans was strongly related to pay raises and other perks. Being a good scientist, Benjamin brought some numbers to bear on the issue, and found the correlation between pay raises for a one-year period and the production of scholarly articles to be a negative .69 or some such figure. Clearly, the fewer articles one published, the greater the pay raise. Or in the case of Brothers Benjamin, Nation, and LeUnes and other productive faculty, the greater the number of articles published, the lower the raise. The single biggest predictor of pay raises, then, was merely eating lunch with, and being servile to Fran Bevans.

Related to this episode, I was stacking up some dead soldiers at a local watering hole one day with an off-duty Dallas police officer who happened to also have a Master of Science degree in

Psychology. During our quasi-beery deliberations, I somehow got off on the topic of our fearless leader and his curious ascent to power within the department, likening the machinations that led him to power to those of Hitler on an obviously smaller, less earth-shaking scale. In response to my apparently woeful lamentation, my drinking companion posed a blunt question that took me by surprise and for which I had no immediate answer. He asked, with a touch of obvious venom spiced with cop language: "You want the sorry son-of-a-bitch killed? I can get him killed for practically nothing. All I have to do is drive my police cruiser over to South Oak Cliff (in Dallas) and let it be known that I have a shithead in College Station that needs killing. I can get the motherfucker killed for fifty bucks. Thugs will line up outside my cruiser six deep to pick up that easy money. Now if you just want him busted up real good, you know, maimed, it will cost you a hundred. When people are maimed, they usually survive and can thus possibly identify their attacker(s). A murder will cost you fifty bucks but I need a hundred if you want that prick maimed. Pick your poison!"

I assured him the problem had not yet reached such dire straits but I would mull over my options during the next days and weeks. He then said, "I'll tell you what else you can do and no one will be the wiser for it. You don't need any money or thugs for this one and no one can pin the murder on you. What you do is go out to the parking lot adjacent to your building and locate his vehicle. When no one is looking, drain the oil out of the crank case and fill it up with Phillips 66 nitrogen fertilizer. He will come out after work, fire up his car, and head home. In no time, the engine will heat up real nice, the fertilizer will expand, and Ka-Fucking-Boom!!!! All of a sudden, his sorry ass will fly through the roof and the motor will exit through the fucking floorboard. The city may try to sue you for destroying their streets but your guy will be vaporized and a distant memory by then. End of story!"

Ironically and sadly, what I knew to be a tongue-in-cheek proposal put forth by my merry minion of the law was essentially a mini-version of what Timothy MacVeigh and his cronies did in 1995 at the Murrah Building in Oklahoma City. The misguided antics of that tormented trio led to the death of 168 innocent people, many of them children. Similar scripts were played out in the Texas City disaster in 1947 in which five hundred people were killed, and the calamity in West, Texas, in 2013, in which fifteen people died. In both disasters, nitrogen fertilizer was the villain.

Not too many years later, I was walking down the halls of our building when the department head at the time, Paul Wellman, stopped me and asked if I was still in touch with that Dallas cop. Paul had just come from a contentious meeting with some of our more obstreperous colleagues, and was primed to make the call. He was joking of course, but I do have the cop's phone number handy just in case it is ever needed. You never know in this business!

Bevans left A&M under a cloud of rumor-filled suspicion, and joined the faculty at the University of Maryland-Baltimore County (UMBC). Shortly after his arrival in Baltimore, word got back that he was had been fired or asked to resign his position there, supposedly for engaging in shady dealings similar to those rumored to have led to his demise at A&M. I cannot speak to the veracity of the rumors at either university but he left UMBC less than a year after arriving in Baltimore and assumed a position at East Carolina University. I think he retired there.

I always thought Fran Bevans was about the sorriest person I had ever met who was not serving time in the Texas Department of Criminal Justice. I stand by that assertion three decades later. My father, a student of the Bible and a true believer in its kinder, gentler messages, once told me I should seek peace through forgiveness in his case. The peace I have derived over the past several decades from detesting Bevans has been immeasurable and a daily source of never-ending joy, peace, solace, comfort, and serenity that simply cannot be matched by any amount of turning-the-other-cheek, bullshit forgiveness. The more astute observers among the readership are probably thinking I do not care much for Bevans. What would ever give you that idea?

Hysterical muteness, paranoia, depression and suicide, alcoholism, and anti-social personality disorder in your leaders and role models…it just does not get any better than that for a newbie, neophyte faculty member with a specialty area in abnormal psychology. I could not have dreamt a more interesting introduction to the college teaching profession!

The "Normal" Department Heads. Things have tamed down a good bit since those early days and most of our department heads in the past twenty-five years have been reasonably sane, maybe even "normal", whatever that is. Bevans was replaced by Dr. Steve Worchel, or "Stevie Wonder" as Jack Nation and I affectionately referred to him, partially for his wondrous ability to covertly shuffle money and personnel coupled with an absolute mastery of the filibuster when things were not going his way in faculty meetings. Steve was widely known among his department head peers as a strong advocate for his faculty, in stark contrast to the wishy-washy and hapless Bill Reed. Steve's reputation was that of a fighter for his faculty, and the head of another department summed him up to me as follows: "If you go into a Dean's meeting, you better have your ducks in a row or Worchel will walk out of the room with all the resources." Steve left A&M for a Dean's position at the University of Southern Maine, but at last report was enduring the considerable rigors of living in Hawaii while professing and subsequently retiring at the University of Hawaii-Hilo.

Dr. Worchel's successors to the throne, Paul Wellman, Steve Rholes, Les Morey, Ludy Benjamin, Doug Woods, and Heather Lench have been sources of reasonable stability and not particularly noteworthy in terms of outwardly observable psychopathology. They did their jobs as best they could, and after four or eight years, stepped down from the headship without fanfare to return to their "first love of teaching", that time-honored and worn-out euphemism used when administrators return, willingly or unwillingly, to a faculty position.

Bless his baseball-loving heart, Ludy Benjamin served as department head for two years prior to his retirement in May, 2012, simply because no one else would take up the mantle. I think it was also comforting to Ludy to know he would only be saddled with the thankless job for a short period of time. Rather than return to his first love of teaching, Ludy and his wife Priscilla retired to Virginia to be near their two daughters and two grandsons. To escape the relatively warm summers in Virginia, the Benjamin's spend several weeks in a home overlooking the Atlantic Ocean in Nova Scotia. I hear from Ludy periodically and he is living a life that would be the envy of almost any retiree. I miss him greatly as a colleague but am thrilled that retirement has been everything he thought it would be and then some.

Upon Ludy's retirement, Paul Wellman reluctantly stepped back into the department head gauntlet for 2012-2013 while a search was conducted to hire a new head from outside the university. We were blessed with an outstanding new hire from the University of Wisconsin-Milwaukee, a clinical psychologist by the name of Douglas Woods. Doug stayed at A&M for three years and did a great job of leading the department. Unfortunately for us, late in the summer of 2015, Doug accepted a position as Dean of the College of Arts and Sciences at Marquette University, so back to Milwaukee he went. He is a good guy, a damn good psychologist, and he is sorely missed.

Dr. Heather Lench is our newest leader, and she brings a voice of reason and moderation to the task as she learns the ropes, so to speak. Heather is unique in the sense that she is the first female to have the headship since our department was created fifty-five years ago.

COLLEAGUES TONY BOURGEOIS, JACK NATION,
LUDY BENJAMIN AND WIFE PRISCILLA, CIRCA 2000

First Students, Like First Loves, Are the Most Memorable

"I am part of all that I have met."
John Milton, Poet (1608-1674)

"Mi taku oyasin" ("We are all related").
Lakota Sioux Belief

These two quotes are the underlying influences behind the crafting of those portions of this memoir that pertains to students I have known since joining the faculty in 1966. It is most gratifying to be able to say that many of these students, or "All I have known", became good friends as well. Their contribution to my emotional well-being in the vast majority of cases over the past five decades has been considerable. Each of these people I am going to mention said or did something along the way that left an indelible mark on my psyche. Unfortunately, there are too many of them to provide a personal anecdote about why each is so memorable, though it is tempting to do so. Time and space limitations quickly bring me back to reality.

The females I have met are at once admirable, atypical in mostly charming ways, likeable, and unforgettable. Included in this group are everyday students seeking advice about school, career, and philosophy of life. Others I regard as friends, and "rekindlers of the inner spirit." I thank each of you very much for enriching my life.

As for the males in my life, there have been hundreds who were great students, talented athletes, graduate school or career path advisees, softball teammates, beer drinking buddies, domino partners/opponents, plain old dear friends, and, yes, "rekindlers of the inner spirit." I cannot thank you all enough for also being a part of whom I am. A very long list of these memorable students, females and males alike, can be found at the conclusion of this memoir.

Memorable Students From Those Early Years

Having said all this, I find it both intriguing and remarkable that the most memorable students were among the first I met those many years ago. There is something about them, at once a near and yet distant familiarity, that just will not let go. Here are some of the more memorable of those first students.

"Old Bushy Brows". One of my very first acquaintances upon assuming my faculty position circa 1966 was a forty-ish PhD student by the name of George, known affectionately among his peers as "Old Bushy Brows", a sobriquet coined in reference to his substantial and unruly dark eyebrows, a la Andy Rooney, the recently-deceased nonagenarian curmudgeon on *Sixty Minutes*. George could be described as average: average size, average looks, average intelligence, average in every respect except for the eyebrows and some pronounced behavioral quirks, both of which greatly exceeded average. George was divorced and the father of a female teenager with whom he was estranged, and he seldom mentioned the child and her mother. It did not seem my business to pry, so I never knew any of the circumstances that led to the divorce and subsequent estrangement.

George spent a lot of time hanging around our popular coffee room on the fourth floor of the Academic Building. The lounge was shared by professors from Education, Psychology, English, Modern Language, and History, thus creating an interesting mix of people with divergent interests, backgrounds, and points of view which, in turn, made for some very stimulating conversation. At that time in the evolution of the university as a research institution, there was no real mandate for research or scholarship in our department and a number of others, so the coffee room was a popular meeting place when we were not in class. George, through some sort of osmotic process, became the *de facto* official coffee-maker for the group and his efforts were most appreciated. He brewed strong coffee and that was fine with the group. By popular demand, our colleague, Larry Christensen, was never allowed to do so for he brewed what I would describe as coffee-deprived, ever-so-slightly brown, colored water. You could read your newspaper while looking through a mug of his coffee.

George was a smug sort, convinced he was right about pretty much everything and as is the case with most people of that persuasion, he was never hesitant to offer an opinion. Some of his views struck me as unusual, but the first real inkling that there might be something seriously strange about the guy emerged from a discussion he and I had about movies. Apparently, George lived a life that was variously described by his doctoral student peers as Spartan, Monastic, or stoic, but he did allow himself a night out once or twice a month. His chosen destination typically was the Circle Drive-In, an outdoor theater (no longer in existence) on the north edge of the campus located near what is now the Zachary Engineering Building. Strangely enough, those nights out on the town always seemed to coincide with a triple feature highlighting ex-Mouseketeer Annette Funicello and a glamorous gaggle of near-naked nubiles cavorting on the beach in their itty-bitty, teensy-weensy, purple polka dot bikinis, playing beach blanket bingo and sand volleyball. To add spice to his nights out on the town, George would grab a couple of greasy chili dogs from the concession stand. Consuming greasy chili dogs while ogling nimble nubiles and nymphets in itsy-bitsy bikinis spiking volleyballs into the sand turned out to be more than George could take. He would become nauseated, throw up, go home, and come to work on Mondays, ranting and raving about lewd and licentious movies being shown right here in River City. His lament went roughly as follows: "There is something wrong with the modern American film maker. I saw three of the most disgusting movies this weekend, and they set a bad example for young people with their depravity." If Annette Funicello and her 1960's Mouseketeer buddies were laden with lewdness, licentiousness, debauchery, and depravity, what would George think of the movies of today? For example, my wife and I watched *The Wolf of Wall Street* a few years ago and if any of you readers have also seen that movie, you know it would no doubt send George into an apoplectic, life-threatening fit.

It is interesting in this regard to note that one of my recent and most cherished students had a father who apparently made a fortune on Wall Street, so much so he was able to retire as a very young man. In discussing the movie with her, he indicated it was spot-on and an incredibly accurate representation of life in the world of high finance.

An interaction George and I had shortly after the beach blanket bingo episode gave me additional pause concerning the condition of George's psyche. I was monitoring an exam one morning, killing time gazing off into space, when I heard a *Pssst!* emanating from the hallway. George signaled me over, gave me his most stern, most earnest, bushy-browed look, and asked, "Do you allow women to sit that way in your classes? When I look at the way the women are sitting in your class, I see immorality everywhere. You have an obligation to teach abnormal psychology as best you can but you have an equal and important obligation to teach morality. You need to talk to those women about their morals and do so immediately!" I told him I would most assuredly visit with the offenders of propriety at the start of the next class period, lying through my teeth with every spoken word. Somehow, I never believed that being the guardian of student morality was one of my charges as a professor. If it was, however, I most certainly would intervene at some other level than how women choose to sit in class.

At the end of that spring semester in 1966, George and I were leaning over the rail on the fourth floor of the Academic Building, watching people come and go on the third floor below. All of a sudden, he blurted out a comment about two young females who appeared to be checking their semester final grades. In those politically incorrect days, class roll sheets and thus grades were tacked haphazardly to bulletin boards in the various hallways by full name for all to see. The Family Educational Rights and Privacy Act (FERPA), with its restrictions on what can (rightly) be revealed about college students, long ago deep-sixed that ill-conceived practice.

George, leaning heavily on the rail with fingers clinched and breathing in short gasps, said, "Have you ever seen anything so disgusting? Look at the way those two girls are dressed. Let's run down there and get their names and see if we can get them kicked out of the university. There is definitely something wrong with the modern American mother, letting children dress like that in public." I said, "Ease up, George, They are just checking grades and will go away soon." In reality, both girls were wearing modest mid-thigh length shorts and sleeveless blouses sans plunging necklines and bare abdomens, and pretty much looked like models of youthful, casual dress decorum to me. I talked George out of taking any action and the girls quickly disappeared. As they went their merry ways, I could not help but think that immorality, like beauty, lies in the eye of the beholder! One man's poison ivy is clearly another man's spinach, for sure.

It was about this time that George decided he would start an exercise regimen to work off tensions, sexual or otherwise. He started his quest for physical and mental health by jogging, but was nearly sideswiped by a car on College Avenue adjacent to the campus. This near-death experience caused him to hit his head on a telephone pole, opening up a gash that required a couple of stitches. He then decided he needed to change up his exercise routine, so he took up handball. He broke a bone in his hand the very first day, so he switched from handball back to jogging. Shortly after making the decision to again alter his exercise agenda, George ended up in Saint Joseph's Hospital in Bryan where he underwent a hernia operation for a pre-existing condition that was apparently aggravated by jogging.

Being every bit the Good Samaritan, I went to the hospital the day after the surgery and asked George how he was doing. He responded in his own inimitable fashion, "I would be fine if they would just leave me alone. I know this is a Catholic hospital and I also know there is a post-recuperative period to hernia surgery, but every time I look up there is a nun pulling back my covers and checking me out. Everyone knows that nuns are just oversexed females who are hiding behind their habits." The next day, I went back, only to find him in an even more agitated, apoplectic state. As he put it, "I thought the nuns were bad, but now they have Candy Stripers checking me out. Everyone knows that Candy Stripers are just oversexed teenage girls."

George overcame these multiple hurdles and adversities and ultimately received his PhD degree by sheer tenacity and force of will. He then hit the job market and landed his first faculty position with a Department of Education at a small university in Missouri. As fate would have it, his major responsibility there was supervising prospective elementary education majors in their student teaching assignments. Where else in the world could a misogynist find more women to dislike than in an elementary education teacher preparation program? Unable to handle the stresses of such an undertaking, he resigned at the end of the first year and came back to town for a short stay while looking for a more suitable job. I asked him how it went up there in Missouri and he told me, "The women there are like women everywhere…available and oversexed. I did not have one young lady that I could, in good conscience, put in front of elementary school kids as a role model…lipstick, powder, paint, sex, drugs, rock and roll…it was an absolutely awful experience."

Two years later, he rolled back into College Station after a stint as Superintendent of Schools on a Sioux Indian Reservation in one of the Dakotas. I asked him how it went up there in Sioux country, and he said, "The Indian women are oversexed just like all the others, and I don't know how I lasted two years in that job. It was dreadful!"

Speaking of George's antipathy toward women, my old friend John Badgett of "You better not call me a son-of-a-bitch again" fame involving the consummately paranoid professor, Virgil C., approached me one day while he and George were still fellow doctoral students and asked, "Do you know a girl that's a good sport? She has to be a risk taker, a true-blue good sport with a thirst for adventure. Know anyone like that?" I responded: "How good a sport does this woman have to be, John? I know some interesting women but there may be limits on their good sportsmanship." In response, John said, with a slight smirk on his face, "She has to be a good enough sport to go over to George's house tonight and seduce him." I replied, "Can't help you there, John. I don't know any woman who is that good a sport."

I was aware John was playfully yanking my chain. We both knew any woman put in the position of seducing George would be at high risk for violence, and we were not about to do that, even if we could. The thinly veiled sexual hostility and the constraints keeping such deep-rooted animosity toward women in check were fragile. The specter of having a sexual liaison with one of the "enemy" might just be enough to trip a fuse and trigger off a major aggressive episode. This is very Freudian, I know, but the George's of the world have been known to commit some pretty heinous acts when confronted with temptations they cannot handle.

Rumor had it that George entered the doctoral program at A&M after being dismissed from a teaching job in Fort Worth, ostensibly for molesting fifth grade girls. By his own admission, he had been dismissed from a seminary prior to going to teaching, though he gave no reasons. The psychodynamics that made this guy tick were fascinating to contemplate… the failed refuge in the seminary, possible/probable molestation of young school girls, imaginal encounters with immoral college coeds, fantasies of oversexed nuns, candy-stripers, and Sioux Indian maidens, and viewing lewd and licentious movies. Immorality everywhere and not enough time for one crusader to stamp it all out. I lost touch with George in the early 1970's but I would predict he became a reclusive, increasingly bitter old man who never abandoned his antipathy toward women.

Francis Euel "Doc" Savage II, aka "Elijah". Yet another fascinating character from those early days was an eccentric undergraduate student named Francis Euel Savage, aka "Doc", and later, "Elijah." He, like George, aka "Old Bushy Brows", was among the very first people I met upon taking my teaching appointment in 1966. "Doc" had acquired his nickname from Lester Dent's fictional "Doc Savage" character who was created in the 1930's to subdue evil wherever it might raise its ugly head.

I got to know "Doc" a bit in the spring of 1967 when he enrolled in my Developmental Psychology course. About midway through the semester, he came up during a break in the class and asked if I knew the name of a cute little brunette who sat on the front left side of the room. I did, and volunteered her name to "Doc", assuming his request was borne of simple curiosity. Little did I know! The damsel in question later told me that "Doc" drove to her house on his way out of town for spring break, coaxed her to come out on the porch, and blurted out a hasty proposal of marriage. He further told her the offer was final and required an immediate response for he was leaving town as soon as their conversation was over. She responded immediately alright, but apparently not in the manner our man had hoped. This little episode was my first glimpse into the warped psyche of the man, but it was a harbinger of things to come.

"Doc" had a notorious reputation among his peers (and a few faculty members) for panicking during final exams. This panic reaction would then precipitate a hasty retreat to assorted houses of ill-repute along the Texas-Mexico border. After a few days of "rest and relaxation", he would return to campus and beg for forgiveness from his professors. More often than not, he was bailed out by his overly magnanimous, forgiving professors and remained on target to receive his degree.

Prior to the beginning of the senior year, "Doc" presented his resume' to several of us, and it contained a most intriguing entry. The item of interest was: "Invited address, annual faculty convocation, Fairleigh Dickinson University, New Jersey, summer of 1967." The likelihood that a decidedly average, not especially verbal, not particularly engaging, largely non-descript undergraduate student from Texas A&M would be invited to deliver a summer address at a major university convocation when faculty are typically scattered all over the globe seemed improbable. No one took the entry seriously, but it was the source of considerable lighthearted discussion around the department among faculty and students alike whenever "Doc's" name came up.

After graduation from A&M, "Doc" entered Southern Methodist University (SMU) in Dallas at some point where he received an MBA degree. He then went into the restaurant business in the Texas Panhandle city of Lubbock, but ultimately left his job and family behind because God spoke to him at work one day, directing him to go to Israel and spread the word of Yahweh. As he put it in a 2006 interview with the A&M campus newspaper, *The Battalion:* "My heavenly Father pulled me out of the business, sent me to Israel walking with a pack and a sleeping bag and a canteen and the budget of a penny." He walked and hitchhiked his way across Israel, distributing food to needy Israeli's while preaching the gospel to anyone who would listen. And, no doubt, to some who would rather not listen!

His missionary work in Israel completed, "Doc" returned to the US. Apparently confused and at loose ends at this point, he made a strategic retreat in the late 1980's to the secure womb, if you will, of good old Aggieland. He immediately took on a new name and identity, transforming himself from "Doc" to "Elijah."

"Elijah" became an instant celebrity around town, with his easily identified and ornately decorated vehicles festooned with outrageous adornments and assorted religious messages; the Star of David soon became his signature with the locals. The first time I saw "Elijah" after his return to College Station, he pedaled past me on his bicycle which was decorated with a high-flying flag extolling his love for Yahweh. I later saw "Elijah" driving an old, huge, gas-guzzling General Motors sedan decked out in a mind-boggling assortment of six-sided stars, religious icons, multi-colored flags, and citations of selected scriptures. His vehicle has been variously dubbed the "Chariot of Fire of Elijah", the "Jewmobile", and the "Art Car of Israel." I think "Elijah's" ultimate dream was to be invited to take part in a parade in Jerusalem as guest of the Israeli government, with his "art work" on display while music from the Texas Aggie Band blared in the background!

"Elijah" frequented local eateries, coffee shops, and popular campus hangouts, regaling listeners with tales of his religious conversion and love for Jesus Christ. In the process, he became a local legend, and for a decade or more almost everyone in Bryan, College Station, or A&M had experienced several "Elijah" sightings or had an "Elijah" story to tell.

At some point, "Elijah" decided he needed to build a nose cone dubbed "The Millenium Eagle" to be pulled behind "The Chariot of Fire", the purpose of which was three-fold. First, the cone served as a mobile camping unit in which to sleep. As well, the structure protected him from roving bands of nettlesome teenagers who occasionally bombarded him late at night with fruits, vegetables, and garbage. The third and perhaps most important function of the nose cone has not been put to use yet but is in the wings waiting for the Rapture. Apparently, "Elijah" has predicted an incendiary end to the world, a fiery Armageddon, and the nose cone was to be used to lift him from the earth, propelling him to a safe haven above the apocalyptic fray. The man and his assorted vehicles have been the subject of much discussion locally for quite some time. As well, he has been featured in several pictorial displays and articles in the campus and local newspapers.

In his search for eternal truth, "Elijah" decided that two more pilgrimages to the Holy Land would be proper and fitting for a man of his deep religious convictions. To finance this operation, he solicited donations from local churches, ministers, assorted donors with fervent religious convictions and deep financial pockets, and just plain old everyday Christian do-gooders. Apparently, "Elijah" made a deep impression on the Israeli's during his first and second visits. To wit, he was met by authorities at El Al Airport in Tel Aviv as he deplaned on his third trip and given a return ticket to the good old U S of A. It appears Israel was not in need of another prophet, particularly a false one, so I suspect "Elijah's" better days as a religious emissary to that country are over.

"Elijah" held forth at Denny's, The Kettle, Sweet Eugene's, and an assortment of parking lots near Walmart, Sam's, and anywhere else where his idiosyncratic presence was tolerated. I have often asked my students for the location of the latest "Elijah" sighting, and the sites were always different, probably because a moving target is hard to hit. "Elijah" was often asked to move by nervous proprietors with misgivings about his odd behavior and habits and the effect his idiosyncrasies would have on business.

One of "Elijah's" favorite campus hangouts when he first came back to town was the open area between the Memorial Student Center and Rudder Tower. He delivered sermons, "enthralled" believers and non-believers alike with his religious rants, and sold simple, crudely made religious crosses and other handcrafted religious items. His only other visible means of support was painting house numbers on curbs in the local neighborhoods.

"Elijah's" presence on campus was brought to an abrupt halt some twenty years ago when his one-man campaign to rid the campus of whores, lesbians, members of the National Organization of Women (NOW) or what he called the National Organization of Biblically Disobedient Women, gay men, leftists, liberals, radicals, fuzzy-thinking psychologists, and other wimps, weirdo's, and weaklings was viewed unfavorably by A&M administrators.

For starters, "Elijah" left a threatening note on the office door of Dr. Wendy Stock, one of my female colleagues in the Department of Psychology. Wendy was openly bisexual, a controversial authority on female abuse and degradation via pornography, and her alternative views on sexual behavior were bothersome to some people. Because of his aversion to her bisexuality and views that ran counter to societal norms, "Elijah" put a note on Dr. Stock's door, making it clear she had thirty days to get out of town or else. Shortly after Dr. Stock got the word, Dr. Steve Worchel, our department head, found a similar message attached to his office door. Steve pretty much dismissed the note as that of a harmless crank and attached no great significance to the threat. But the *coup de grace* for "Elijah" came when he left a "get out of town or else" notice on the door of the university president, Dr. William Mobley, an Industrial-Organizational psychologist by training and a member of our faculty, though no one can recall him ever entering our building nor teaching a class during his tenure as President.

The Mobley threat earned "Elijah" a face-to-face meeting with the chief of security at A&M, one Bob Wiatt. Wiatt sported a black patch over one eye, and this adornment lent a menacing look to the man who, except for the patch and his Federal Bureau of Investigation (FBI) tough-guy reputation, was pretty much unassuming and not the least bit threatening in size or demeanor. I guess the sweet nothings Bob Wiatt whispered in "Elijah's" ear at their meeting of the minds had a lasting impact, for Elijah has not been seen on campus in two decades. I suppose one can get cross-wise with the system by threatening the life of a university President! One can only imagine the fate of "Elijah" if he had threatened the life of Robert Gates, a more recent university president and former head of the Central Intelligence Agency (CIA). I am guessing our peripatetic prophet would have just vanished without a trace! Poof, and he would be gone!

This anecdote reminds me of another involving the immensely popular Dr. Gates and his reputation as the nation's top spy. It seems Dr. Gates chose to fire Wally Groff, the Athletic Director, and that dismissal was grist for the mill of the local media for some time. Shelby Metcalf, the basketball coach and resident humorist opined in an interview that Mr. Groff had indeed been lucky. As Coach Metcalf so aptly stated, "Wally is lucky. He just got fired. He could have simply disappeared." This tongue-in-cheek quote from the consummately witty Metcalf was in obvious reference to the far-reaching powers of the top man in the CIA.

Bob Wiatt had been a larger-than-life figure in the annals of the FBI with a richly-deserved reputation as a tough guy. He had been a key agent in investigating the assassination of President John F. Kennedy and was a central figure in a case involving a kidnapped Texas State Trooper. The trooper case was eventually fictionalized and made into a movie by then fledgling film maker Steven Spielberg. The movie, *The Sugarland Express*, came out in 1974 and jumpstarted Spielberg's career.

Wiatt was also a major player in a 1974 shootout at one of the Texas Department of Corrections facilities in Huntsville, an event that has been eloquently chronicled by my friend and writing mentor, William T. "Bill" Harper. In his book, *Eleven Days in Hell: The 1974 Carrasco Prison Siege in Huntsville, Texas*, Bill Harper provides a gripping account of the entire saga, and for his efforts was awarded the Violet Crown Book Award for best non-fiction from the Writer's League of Texas in 2005.

What happened during those eleven tension-filled days, in a nutshell, was a small group of prisoners took several employees hostage, and when the siege ended, two civilians and one prisoner had died. In the process, Wiatt took several bullets in his flak jacket, thus avoiding serious injury or death. Wiatt killed two men in his FBI career, firing fatal shots that brought an end to both the kidnapped state trooper incident and the Huntsville prison hostage takeover.

Bob Wiatt retired in 1980 after serving three decades with the FBI, and became the Director of Security at A&M in 1982, a job he held for a little over twenty years. Bob Wiatt, along with his wife, Ann, were major forces in bringing the arts to the Brazos Valley, and many area citizens mourned his passing at the age of eighty-four on August 13, 2010.

The "Elijah" sightings on the part of my more recent students are approaching zero. For the past two semesters, I have asked my classes if they know "Elijah" and I pretty much get no response. "Elijah" no longer has the quasi-iconic status he enjoyed in the 1990's. Perhaps age and the passage of time has caught up with him. I see him around town occasionally, and while he himself is pretty non-descript, his vehicle is still the subject of much discussion and photo-op sessions for the locals.

My last face-to-face meeting with "Elijah" was maybe twenty-five years ago when he was undecided about moving from west Texas to make College Station his new home. At that last meeting, he told me he was working on a play in which he wanted to focus on using the Fighting Texas Aggie Band as a metaphor for solving the problem of the homeless in Texas. My metaphorically-challenged brain could not wrap itself around that concept, so I was of little help to "Elijah" in bringing his play to fruition.

"Elijah" loved the Corps of Cadets and the Texas Aggie Band almost more than life itself, and disparaging remarks about either were fighting words. As a gauge of "Elijah's" fascination with those hallowed A&M entities, the following excerpt from some of his writings is illustrative. "Elijah" wrote:

"….back in 1963 … that code of honor meant something. Today, for some in Aggieland, the feminists from N.O.W. (National Organization for Biblically Disobedient Women) rule the psychology department, and launch media attacks through the New York media, attacking the Parsons mounted Cavalry, the Texas Aggie Corps of Cadets, and the reputations of young men and women now training as military warriors to fight in the most important of all wars … the next one!

At the same time, the homosexuals have become part of the Texas Aggie faculty, and with their reprobate minds join in conspiracy with other homosexuals in the journalism media to attack the Texas Aggie Corps of Cadets.

Are all the men in the journalism department at Texas A&M in cahoots with the feminists, the homosexuals, and other biblical reprobates? Are they?

The Battalion back in 1963 was an honest reporter of facts and truth. Today there is not much truth nor many positive facts about the fightin' Texas Aggie Band at all. Why? Who's calling the shots at A&M?"

This excerpt also demonstrates the dysfunctional thought processes my colleagues in clinical psychology would call "paranoid ideation" with its projection of hostile impulses, persecutory themes, and topical flight. It would be interesting to know what the original "Doc" Savage would think about the efforts of his latter day namesake to stamp out evil at Texas A&M.

Raymundo Rodriquez. Raymundo Rodriquez was a big favorite of mine early on and, after graduation, enjoyed a successful career as an administrator with the Hogg Foundation for Mental Health in Austin. He was known as Ray Rodriquez during his stay at A&M, but later became Rrrrrrraymundo Rrrrrrrrodriquez with much rolling of the r's to accentuate pride in his Mexican-American heritage. Some of the older readers may remember when it was not fashionable to be Hispanic, leading the opportunistic newsman and erstwhile gadfly Geraldo Rivera to adopt the more anglicized Jerry Rivers. At about the same time Ray Rodriquez made his transformation from Ray to Rrrrrrraymundo, Jerry Rivers conveniently reverted back to being Geraldo Rivera. There had been a shift in cultural values and it became hip to be Hispanic. By the way, I do a disservice to Raymundo Rodriquez with the Geraldo comparison, and for that I apologize profusely.

Years later, Raymundo's son, also Raymundo, came to A&M where he struggled academically for a while. He ultimately graduated, and I am pleased to say I was able to play a small part in getting him admitted and helping him graduate. Raymundo, the elder, swore eternal allegiance to me for the assistance I lent his son, and told me that if I ever sought a grant through the auspices of the Hogg Foundation, it was in the book. Unwisely, I never took Raymundo Rodriquez up on his generous offer.

Doobwa, Dick, Walton Warriors, and Pressed Ham Under Glass. Richard Dubois, whose name was alternately pronounced as "doo-bwah" and "doo-boys", was truly a hoot! He was bright and talented, with a shag Beatles haircut, an eternal, toothy smile, and an open, friendly brown face. Richard always looked as if he had just pulled off a prank or was in the process of committing one. We shared many a laugh together over the years because of his jovial nature and endless hijinks.

In the late 1960's I received an early evening phone call from the city jail in Huntsville, Texas. It seems that Dubois and his raffish associates, Richard Vitek, Mickey San Miguel, and Frank Pontelandolfo, had made the short trek to Huntsville in search of some female companionship which was in short supply locally. En route to Huntsville, the fun-loving guys thought they were being tailgated so all but the driver dropped their jeans, propped their rear ends in the back window, and mooned the car behind them. As it turned out, the person being mooned was a highway patrolman who proceeded to pull the offenders of propriety over. From there, they were escorted to the city jail. Their distress call was sent in hopes I would provide either bail or, at the very worst, spiritual consolation. Being long on consolation and short on cash, I told them, "You guys rot in jail, Dubois!" I was kidding of course and they eventually were turned loose without my intervention on their behalf. After some reflection, Dubois et al. filed that episode away for later retrieval as the "Pressed Ham Under Glass" caper, in obvious reference to the buttocks pressed firmly against the rear window.

Some weeks later, Dick Vitek invited me to an end of the semester get-together sponsored by Walton Hall, the dormitory where most of the guys lived. It seems that the Walton Warriors, as they were known, decided they were going to celebrate the end of the school year by depleting their treasury. They rented Fort Shiloh (razed in 2013 to make way for a new business), an old beer joint and dance hall on the south edge of town, and had their end-of-year soiree catered by Tom's Barbecue, an iconic eatery of the era. Not surprisingly, there were also several kegs of beer on hand. My friend, Tony Bourgeois, was also invited to the gathering, and the two of us arrived to find the tables situated so they formed several adjoining long, rectangular walkways.

I thought the tables had been arranged to promote conversation and foster camaraderie, but it became obvious later on that the Men of Walton had a more sinister goal in mind. Around 2100 hours, the true method in their madness began to unfold when a dark stretch limousine pulled up to the Fort Shiloh entrance. Like quail spooked by hiking intruders, a contingent of young, attractive, scantily clad strippers emerged from the vehicle. The ladies promptly ascended to the table tops and began plying their seductive skills, gyrating along and around those carefully planned rectangular walkways for the rest of the evening. The girls did the usual stripper things but topped off the evening with some lagniappe for the very attentive Warriors. To wit, the girls began dunking their breasts in random cups of beer and if the owner of said receptacle stuck a dollar bill in their bikinis, he was entitled to lick the beer off their ample appendages. Before the evening was over, the girls had so many dollar bills hanging from their abdomens they looked like female versions of the old comic strip character, Alley Oop!

Promptly at midnight, the limousine reappeared and the girls vanished as rapidly as they had arrived. Thanks to the delicious barbecue, endless bumping and grinding, and beer made even tastier by the intrusion of female breasts, the Walton Warriors agreed to a man that they had ended the year on a high note, and then some!

Paging Mr. Meoff! There was a well-known professor at A&M in the 1960's and 1970's whose name was O. D. "Olive Drab" Butler. Dr. Butler was also a General in the Army Reserve and widely known for his red-ass, no-nonsense military bearing and Prussian mentality. The latter traits and his first two initials gave rise to his well-known nickname. Dr. Butler had a son, O. D. III, or "Duke" who was, among other things, a golfer with the university team. "Duke" played two years on the PGA tour after graduation, and later presided over the Houston Golf Association (HGA). He ended his illustrious career as Senior Vice President of Tournament Relations for the PGA, retiring in 2007. For his various efforts on behalf of the game, "Duke" Butler was inducted into the Texas Golf Hall of Fame in 1987.

Though the truth will never be known, my friends and I were convinced that "Duke", while still a student at A&M, may possibly have been a co-conspirator in pulling off one of the best pranks we had ever witnessed. At the very least, the man was guilty by association. It seems that three A&M doctoral students in Physical Education (now known as Kinesiology) and yours truly were headed off to Lake Somerville to fish for black bass one Sunday morning. My compadres were Tom

Semper, later the best man when Judy and I got married (and vice versa), childhood friend Earl Yarbrough, and legendary local angler and story-teller, Jim "Super Aggie" Terry. Jim earned his nickname for his resemblance to the "Super Aggie" caricature so popular at the time.

To get the day started on the right foot, we stopped off at a restaurant on Texas Avenue in Bryan to grab some breakfast. About halfway through our eggs, bacon, and pancakes, a waitress came waltzing through the room, loudly paging the infamous, mysterious, ephemeral, and heretofore thought to be mythical "Jack Meoff." She kept hollering, "Jack Meoff. We have a phone call for Mr. Jack Meoff."

Everyone in the restaurant was mesmerized by her plaintive calls, and a dead silence fell over the place, the only exception being the muffled sounds of a hirsute, near-nonagenarian who was spitting pancakes all over the counter. Our waitress friend continued valiantly but unsuccessfully in her search, asking if there was a "Jack Meoff" in the building. She concluded her frantic attempts to find the elusive mythical character with a final plaintive request: "Is there a "Mister Meoff" in the building? There is an urgent call for "Mr. Jack Meoff."

The reason we thought that "Duke" Butler might have been in on this prank is that he and some of his National Guard buddies were in the restaurant earlier, laughing, carrying on, and generally having a good time. They finally chugalugged what remained of their coffee, paid the tab, and departed the premises. In almost exactly the number of minutes it would take to get back the nearby National Guard Armory in Bryan and locate a phone, the paging of the mysterious "Mr. Jack Meoff" began. We reckoned those weekend warriors hatched the plot over breakfast, thus accounting for the devious laughter coming from their table. We opined that upon arriving back at the Armory with not much else to do, they fired off a phone call to the restaurant, asking if someone would page the now famous "Mr. Meoff."

The Meoff caper is one of those urban legends that young guys talk about but even in their wildest dreams cannot imagine they would ever experience it in real life. Boy, were we ever wrong! The poor, naïve waitress fell for it hook, line, and sinker, bringing the entire house down in the process. I fear, however, that the poor old fellow at the counter may have choked to death on his pancakes! Of course, whether or not "Duke" Butler was involved I suspect will never be known, and it may be unfair to link him to the events of that morning. However, some person or group deserves credit for pulling off the "Jack Meoff" prank, and slick as a whistle if I do say so myself!

I ran into "Duke" Butler recently at a local restaurant, Smitty K's, but did not have the heart (guts) to ask him about the "Jack Meoff" caper. My guess is "Duke" either does not remember the episode or does not want to remember it. There are many things we all do as young people that we would rather not be reminded of twenty, thirty, or forty years later.

Charles Jones Does His Best Tim Conway Imitation. Bless his heart, it is hard not to think of slow-moving, slow-talking Charles Jones when I hark back to those earliest days. My first office at A&M was located on the fourth floor of the Academic Building, and I was toiling away one afternoon when I heard a faint knock on my cubbyhole divider. I say cubbyhole because we did not actually have offices but rather partitions which afforded little privacy to conduct our business, some of which could be pretty sensitive when student academic or personal matters were involved. In any event, I looked up and a young man asked if he could have a few minutes of my time. I invited him to sit down though I had serious misgivings about whether he would make it across the room or not. He talked in a slow drawl and moved at a snail's pace, obviously suffering from an advanced case of what my friend John Badgett of Slippery Rock fame would call "The slows." Charles had the worst case of "The slows" I had ever seen. In fact, I was not sure Charles was alive at all, and seriously considered having my colleague, Tony Bourgeois, hook him up to some biofeedback equipment to see if there were functioning vital signs. There were indeed signs of life, as I was to find out later, but they were effectively masked by "The slows."

After a careful evaluation of the situation, I decided my affable and unassuming visitor was more alive than dead, so I politely asked what he wanted to talk about. The young man, handsome, with an open face, curly hair, and blue eyes, looked at me and said in a slow southwestern drawl: "My name is Charles Jones and I want to be a Psychology major. My advisor in Biology told me to talk to you, so here I am." My first thought, based on his almost total absence of speed in both speech and locomotion, was that I had another reject from Biology on my hands, seeking refuge in what was perceived by some on campus to be the a less-demanding major, Psychology.

I said to Charles, "What motivates you want to make this switch?" He said, "I want to go to medical school, but I would like to get a liberal arts education in addition to taking the science requirements in the pre-medicine curriculum." With a mix of both trepidation and fear, I asked the next and perhaps obvious question, "Charles, what kind of grades do you have? Can you even get into our college, let alone medical school?" Though it took an inordinate amount of time to get the answer out of him, Charles said, "I think I am okay on grades. I have approximately forty-five hours and have made all A's except for one B in a Calculus. That B lowered by grade point ratio to 2.96 (A&M had a 3.00 system in place at that time which has since been replaced by the more contemporary 4.00 standard).

I was somewhat taken aback by this revelation, but once I digested the news, the two of us went to work, ironing out the specifics of what it would take for him to get the degree in our department while completing the science prerequisites for medical school. Charles was ahead of his time in seeking a liberal arts education, for A&M students were strongly discouraged from majoring in anything other than the hard sciences if they intended to go to medical school.

Charles and I developed a nice relationship over the next three years. As might be expected, he excelled in the classroom and graduated with his near-perfect grade point ratio intact. A year prior to graduation, he started the application process for medical school and as I remember applied to six or seven schools and received acceptances from all. He eventually chose to attend the University of Colorado in Boulder.

At the end of his first year in Boulder, Charles dropped by my office once again just to chat about how things were going with his studies and life in general. In the course of our conversation, he told me that he was going to specialize in surgery. Perhaps having a case of "The slows" is actually an asset in surgery. I think I would prefer a surgeon with "The slows" to a frenetic one with a case of Attention Deficit Disorder with Hyperactivity (ADHD).

Prior to finding out about his choice of specialization, I asked Charles if he had ever entertained becoming a psychiatrist. He responded as follows: "I would pick up trash in the bar ditches before I would practice psychiatry. You learn to hate those students almost instantaneously. While you are pulling thirty-hour rotations in the emergency room, they are up in the library studying and cutting important things out of the assigned readings with razor blades. They even have the gall to sell you the ill-gotten material so that you might have access to it for exams. Also, they only help in the Emergency Room (ER) with its usual run of domestic fight victims, drunks in toxic states, victims of automobile accidents, and emergency births if you march them out there at gun point. Their mentality is: 'I know I will never do this stuff once I am out of medical school, so why should I do it now? You learn to hate the psychiatry students early on in your training."

As a postscript, one of the students in my Abnormal Psychology class in the summer of 2010, Laurie Guerra, Googled Charles Jones after I mentioned the preceding vignette. It turns out that Dr. Jones is indeed a surgeon, still in Boulder, a member of the American College of Surgeons, married with three children, and a golfer, hiker, skier, and photographer. In 1990, he served as the group physician for a team of climbers from Boulder who scaled Mount Everest. Way to go, Charles!

William Kenneth "Ken" Gray, PhD, Entrepreneur. Ken Gray was representative of several students passing through A&M in the late 1960's and early 1970's who went on to become successful entrepreneurs as a result of their psychology training and subsequent work experience in the state-supported intellectual disabilities, mental illness, or juvenile delinquency networks in Texas. Ken had flunked out of the University of Texas as a "not-ready-for-college" teenager, worked in the private sector selling shoes, started a family, and then came back to school when he was around thirty years of age. Ken subsequently got his undergraduate degree at A&M, a master's in Psychology from Stephen F. Austin State University in Nacogdoches, and a PhD in Educational Administration back here at A&M.

For a number of years, Ken worked at the Travis State School, a residential treatment facility for intellectually disabled persons under the aegis of the Texas Department of Mental Health and Mental Retardation (TDMHMR). As a result of our prior association, Ken conducted many a wonderful, informative tour of his facility for my students. He and I also had some great times in Austin after the trips, quaffing a beer or two (pitcher or two?) at several local watering holes in that wonderful city. More often than not, our pub/restaurant of choice was storied old Scholz Garten on San Jacinto Street in downtown Austin. Speaking of Scholz's, Judy and I attended a political rally there in October of 2017 and it was a *déjà vu* experience and haunting reminder of good times past. It was my first visit in probably twenty years or more.

After years at the Travis State School, Ken decided that he could do for himself what he had done for years for TDMHMR. He thus started his own operation providing care for intellectually disabled persons, but at a considerable boost in salary. Ken was the first of several of our early master's degree graduates who went on to bigger and better things in the entrepreneurial domain after working for a decade or more with various state agencies.

Another TDMHMR psychologist who joined the entrepreneurial ranks was Bob Steronko who started a business in the Austin area and at last report had forty-one people working for him. Two others, Bob Cavin and Bob Shaw, followed the lead of Gray and Steronko but in the Texas Youth Commission (now Texas Juvenile Justice Department) network. Yet another person with an entrepreneurial flair was Jim Karhan who moved from the juvenile justice system to form a corporation called Brown-Karhan whose niche was providing care for people with head and spinal cord injuries.

I often cite these former students as examples in my classes of how young people with degrees in Psychology can diversify and maximize their talents (and income) if they are willing to work in the trenches while learning the necessary ropes. With a modicum of moxie, some people skills, and a touch of luck, they should be able to follow the template laid down by people like Gray, Steronko, Cavin, Shaw, and Karhan. My hat goes off to these guys for opening my eyes to a whole new world, entrepreneurship, separate and apart from working for a state agency or the more traditional private practice in clinical or counseling psychology.

Reverend Don Young, Meet Hamed el-Feky. For the better part of a half-century, I have organized field trips to various area institutions providing treatment/rehabilitation to criminals, delinquents, intellectually-challenged persons, and the mentally ill. Many of my former students will tell you that being involved in the experiences was unforgettable and in some cases transformative. On one of these early field trips, two undergraduate students, Reverend Donald Young and Hamed el-Feky, and yours truly traveled together by car for a morning tour of the Austin State Hospital and an afternoon walk-through of the Travis State School, both TDMHMR institutions. Our driver, Hamed, an Egyptian, was short, stocky, and dark, and Reverend Young, the pastor at a local fundamentalist church, was tall, rangy, and circumspect. How this unlikely triumvirate ended up riding together remains a mystery. It was certainly the most unholy of alliances, thanks primarily to my presence; a Coptic Christian, a fundamental Protestant minister, and a practicing philistine, all co-existing relatively peacefully.

I had no idea how long Hamed had been in the US or what his driving credentials were in his home country, but he was an out-of-control, demolition derby-esque driver who seemed hell bent on destruction, his and ours. We took Highway 21 from the west side of Bryan, turned right on Highway 290 and headed toward Manor and Elgin, took a left on Interstate 35, and a right which led us to the mental hospital located on 45th Street just north of the University of Texas. On the various highways, Hamed constantly crossed the mid-stripe separating us from the potentially fatal oncoming traffic; he passed on hills and curves with excessive speed and reckless abandon; in the city itself, he repeatedly ran stop signs and ignored red lights, treating them pretty much as suggestions rather than laws.

The trip to Austin was scary enough but Hamed saved the best for last as darkness had overtaken us by the time we headed back to College Station! The entire return trip was a nightmarish flirtation with vehicular suicide/homicide with Hamed driving at high speed, veering across the mid-stripe, forcing oncoming cars onto the shoulder, and passing once again on steep inclines and blind curves.

Thankfully, Reverend Young had the presence of mind to get in touch with God and call in a chip or two on our behalf. He sat in the back seat, praying for forgiveness for ever sin he had ever committed, and I am convinced, though he never said so, that he also threw in several of my many transgressions for good measure. I am also pretty sure I overheard Reverend Young telling the good Lord that if he survived he would be an even more devoted servant. He definitely pulled out all the stops on our behalf, and the young minister's fervent requests were appreciated at the time and even more five decades later. I harbor little doubt that I owe my life and the wonderful things that have happened to me and mine for the past half century to the power of prayer invested in the Right Reverend Donald Young.

Larry Godfrey and Deep Sea Fishing: Not My Cup of Tea. In the summer of 1969, an affable, outgoing chap named Larry Godfrey enrolled in Psychology 307, Developmental Psychology, a course I taught for quite a few years before a specialist in that area, Emily Davidson, joined our faculty. Larry grew up in College Station and attended A&M Consolidated where he was an all-around high school athlete, though golf was his specialty. Larry later became an outdoorsman and even wrote a hunting and fishing column for the local paper in the 1960's. We got to know each other pretty well through class and impromptu conversations and one day he proposed to take it on himself to teach me the nuances of his consuming passion, catching black bass. I had fished a bit in my youth, but his serious approach to the sport was novel and appealing and his fervor for catching bass contagious.

On several occasions that summer and the ensuing fall, Larry and I made the half-hour trek to Lake Somerville, near the city of the same name. The lake was created by damming up the Yegua River, and as Texas lakes go, Somerville was small, relatively shallow, and murky. Despite these apparent limitations, the lake has produced some excellent bass fishing for many years.

Larry was an ardent proponent of fishing for bass with artificial worms, and took it on himself to teach me the intricacies of tying a hook firmly to the fishing line. That lesson was followed by a tutorial on how to put a worm on the hook so that it makes the best presentation in the water. Tying the line to the hook is accomplished by running the line twice through the eye of the hook which gives you two complete loops. You then wind the end of the line around the two loops five or six times, grabbing the loose end of the line with your teeth, pulling the line snug against the eye of the hook. Sometimes, line is left over so it is important to lop off the excess with your fingernail clippers or rat nose pliers in order to for it to manifest a more unobtrusive presence in the water. Once the worm is threaded properly on the hook, it is cast into the water and allowed to sink to the bottom of the lake where a periodic upward jiggling motion is made with the tip of the rod. The intent is to make the worm look as if it had just fallen into the water and subsequently climbed over a rock or a submerged log. There is an alternate school of thought that suggests that bass are prone to strike the worm, not because of an attractive presentation, but rather because it represents an intrusion into their watery life space which, in turn, causes them to attack the intruder out of aggravation, meanness, or self-defense.

Over time, I became a passable worm fisherman, and Larry and I caught quite a number of good-sized bass on our occasional expeditions. Thanks to Larry, I became quite attached to bass fishing and spent many a day on various lakes and ponds in Texas and Mexico over the next five years before my pathologies changed and I became a softball addict. I will address that thirty-year aberration elsewhere.

Larry called me one afternoon, proposing that we do something very different, namely rounding up some friends and acquaintances to go on a deep sea fishing expedition out of Freeport, two hours south of College Station. The price tag was forty dollars per person and we were able to amass a group of forty people plus a crew of eight, counting Larry.

We left College Station in the early afternoon, hoping to reach Freeport in time to eat some fresh seafood, drink a couple of beers, tell some fish stories, and grab a few hours of shuteye prior to our departure from land which was scheduled for 0300. After sleeping, fitfully in my case, for maybe three hours, we awoke and made our way to the dock where the boat was anchored, swinging from side to side due to the howling wind and frequent, feverish, and foaming waves. I was not sure if the wind conditions would cause the expedition to be cancelled or not, but Larry and his "accomplices" on the boat held a quick summit meeting and decided we should give it a go.

The boat captain then gathered us around and talked a bit about safety, demeanor on the boat, and generally what to expect while participating in a deep sea fishing expedition. He ended his remarks with some ominous comments about the weather, stating that the only reason he was taking us out at all was because we had gone to so much trouble and expense getting to Freeport. He ended his pre-expedition oratory with the following admonition, "Boys, the winds are fierce and the seas turbulent. It is going to be a real motherfucker out there, so get ready!" I never really knew what the word "motherfucker" meant until that morning. I now know motherfucker! Sort of like I know a real ass-chewing when I get one, thanks to Colonel Wing Foo Jung at Fort Hood which is discussed elsewhere.

When we passed the last jetties, the boat went straight up in the air, came down on the far side of a giant wave, settled momentarily on an even keel, and pitched once again like a bucking bronco as we encountered another giant wave. And so it went for the rest of the morning. We should have sensed something was really amiss when the shrimp boats were coming in as we headed out. Those hardy shrimpers are not easily intimidated by the elements, but they were taking proper safety precautions that morning. I suspect they knew "motherfucker", too!

My friend, Tony Bourgeois, ponied up his forty bucks for the trip (Larry let me go free for recruiting a goodly number of the other participants), eagerly anticipating a full day of fishing for exotic breeds not found in the fresh water ponds, streams, and lakes we frequented around central Texas. We had not been at sea more than an hour when Tony started feeling queasy from the torturous tossing and turning of the boat. He must have anticipated upchucking the partially digested seafood meal of the previous evening for he put down his rod and reel, grabbed a nearby coffee can, sat down on the deck, turned several shades of green, and spent the rest of the day throwing up into the friendly confines of his new-found companion, the coffee can. I think Tony actually got in a few casts before attaching his rod and reel to a post and finding a place to throw up out of harm's way.

Larry reported in his fishing and hunting column a day or two later that forty of the forty-eight people on board suffered seasickness at one point or another. It was fascinating to see how people chose to behave in the face of their impending or actual sickness. Several assumed a supine position in the bottom of the boat and vomited straight into the air, perhaps a perverse, projectile tribute to the gods who protect sailors and fishermen in turbulent seas. Others made frequent trips to the side of the boat to purge what remained in their stomachs. Yet others used the restroom facilities for their episodes of nausea. The boat decks and the seas ran thick with the detritus, the flotsam and jetsam, expelled from more than three dozen stomachs.

As for me, I fought a valiant battle but eventually became the fortieth and final victim of the elements. Watching everyone else throw up was contagious and I finally lost it, over and over and over. And then some more! I did get to fish long enough to sacrifice a lure to a lusty ling that lashed it off the line as if it were held by mere thread.

A number of the seasick "partiers" had recovered by the time I started losing it, and I spent the rest of the day in a state of nausea, vomiting, or both. I never got to enjoy any of the expedition except for the immense, indescribable joy of having it end in late afternoon. The waters calmed greatly as the day wore on and our trip back to Freeport went smoothly, giving us a teasing snapshot of what might have been. The Captains' early morning prophesy that we were going to encounter bad seas and then some (i.e., a "motherfucker") was spot on.

Postscript: The night before the ill-fated trip, Tony and I loaded a case of Budweiser Light into a cooler and immersed those twenty-four puppies in five pounds of ice. We got back to College Station with twenty-three beers. Apparently, Larry or one of the crew helped themselves to our more than ample stash; it certainly was not Tony or me! We were too busy experiencing motherfucker!

American Life in the 1970's

U. S. Population is 205 Million
Annual Average Salary is $7,600
Quart of Milk is Thirty-three Cents and Bread Costs Twenty-four Cents a Loaf
Richard Nixon Leaves Presidency in Disgrace over Watergate Affair
Roe vs. Wade Legalized Abortion
Nineteen People Killed In Siege at 1972 Olympic Site in Munich
South Vietnam Falls to Forces of North Vietnam
American Religious Cult Leader James Jones and 900 Followers Commit Suicide
Ayatollah Khomeini Installs Theocracy in Iran, Holds Sixty-six Hostages for 444 Days
Email, Barcode Scanning, Laser Printer, First Electronic Book Invented
The Floppy Disc First Appeared, First Test Tube Baby Born
The Poetry of Rod McKuen is Immensely Popular
Mood Rings, Lava Lamps, Rubik's Cube, Pet Rocks, Smiley Face Stickers Popular
Bell Bottom Pants, Hip Huggers, Hot Pants, Earth Shoes, and Streaking Popular
Era of Soft Rock, Hard Rock, Punk Rock, Folk Rock, and Disco
Bee Gees, Pink Floyd, Three Dog Night, Eagles, Carpenters Dominate Music Scene
Jonathan Livingston Seagull and *I'm OK, You're OK* are Bestsellers
Godfather, Jaws, Exorcist, Apocalypse Now, Star Wars Dominate Cinema
All in the Family, Roots, Happy Days, Brady Bunch, and Sesame Street are TV Hits
U.S. Swimmer Mark Spitz Wins Heretofore Unprecedented Seven Gold Medals in Olympics

Brenham-Washington County Counseling Service (BWCCS)

Mr. Ed Wachholz, MSW

In 1970, I was contacted by Mr. Ed Wachholz, the Director of the Brenham-Washington County (Texas) Counseling Service, to gauge my interest in becoming the consulting psychologist for the center. Mr. Wachholz, a Wisconsin native of German descent, held a master's degree in Social Work and took over the reins of the counseling service after retiring from a twenty-six-year Air Force career where he was as a meteorologist, of all things. The counseling service was created because of repeated appeals from area Lutheran ministers who were frustrated with counseling church members whose psychological problems were beyond the scope of their ministerial training.

There were nineteen Lutheran churches in Washington County at that time (and I suppose even now), due in great part to the German heritage of so many area residents. The ministers of those nineteen churches appealed to the Lutheran Social Service (LSS) to initiate and support the center to provide counseling and related services to their congregations as well as a broad assortment of clients from the county and area cities with no Lutheran affiliation. This agreement led the LSS to hire Ed Wachholz as Director.

Shortly after assuming the position, Ed inquired about my willingness to come in two afternoons a week to assist him and his staff of one, a full-time administrative assistant named Ginger Brandt. For the next five years, I made the short forty-five mile trek every Tuesday and Thursday afternoon from College Station to the lovely city of Brenham, accompanied by as many students as I could cram into my small economy vehicle. I typically had a graduate student and three undergraduate students in tow, and each was assigned to work for the semester (and beyond if they chose to do so) with a schizophrenic, an alcoholic, a geriatric case, and a child or adolescent. One of the beneficial features of that twice per week ninety-mile round trip was the students and I had time on the way over and back to compare case histories, share problems, and seek treatment solutions.

Over those five years, I met an endless array of fascinating clients. My training as a doctoral student had been essentially in counseling psychology yet much of what I did in Brenham and other venues those first ten years at A&M would be considered more clinical in nature. For those unfamiliar with the two domains, the clinical psychologist is trained to work with the more severe psychological conditions such as antisocial (psychopathic) behavior, schizophrenia, major depression, and bipolar illness. By contrast, the focus of the counseling psychologist is on problems of everyday living, things like marriage adjustment, adjustment to the work place, childrearing difficulties, everyday anxieties, and bad habits (i.e., obesity, nicotine addiction, and so on). My cross-domain involvement was born of necessity for there were no clinical psychologists within a fifty- to sixty-mile radius of Bryan-College Station in the 1960's and 1970's. Thus, one had to make do with what one had, and treatment in much of the Brazos Valley became the province of two most unlikely people, namely my good friend and erstwhile mentor and resident behaviorist, Albert Casey, and yours truly.

I would like to focus the ensuing discussion on some of the most memorable clients with whom I worked at the counseling service, mostly as a tribute to their tenacity and positive outlook as they tried to overcome their personal difficulties. In all instances, no actual names have been used. In accordance with that spirit and to protect her privacy and that of family members who may still be living in the area, I have chosen to call this first case "The Drano Lady."

The Drano Lady

The Drano Lady was a 28-eight-year old married woman with three small children, all under the age of six or seven. I guess having three children was not sufficient to satisfy the hard-working, middle-class husband for he was putting constant pressure on his wife to have another child. My client was of average height and weight, attractive and well-groomed, though she seemed largely unaware of her appearance and its effect on other people. She had never dated anyone other than her husband and they married right out of high school. Thus, at age twenty-eight, she was in her tenth year of marriage.

The Drano Lady was referred to the Counseling Service by the family minister who was concerned about her anxiety issues and obsessive-compulsive behaviors. In obsessive-compulsive behavior, the individual is haunted by unwanted and unhealthy thoughts and urges (i.e., obsessions), and reduces the anxiety arising from the obsessions by engaging in ritualistic acting-out behaviors of a highly repetitive nature (i.e., compulsions). The example I use with my classes to illustrate the condition is the old childhood admonition, "Step on a crack and you break your mother's back." To deal with this recurring unwanted and unpleasant thought of harming dear old mom, the child religiously avoids stepping on any cracks in the sidewalk or street. Of course, this is a harmless childhood activity but captures the essence of the obsessive-compulsive disorder.

My client steadfastly refused to take any anti-anxiety medications suggested by her family physician on the grounds that by doing so, she would be in danger of becoming, in her words, "a drug addict." In talking with my new client for the first time, I was struck by the depth of her obsessions, compulsions, and circular self-defeating behavior. She talked at great length about poisoning her husband and children, and was obsessed with putting Drano or some other corrosive or poisonous substance in stews and casseroles as she prepared the family meals. The obsession had reached such poignancy that she could not go near the grocery store aisles where Drano, Oil of Wintergreen, and other harmful household substances were stocked.

Interestingly, as I was relating this case study in my Abnormal Psychology class a few semesters ago, one of the students suggested the inclusion of Oil of Wintergreen in the Drano Lady's list of substances to be avoided was strange since it was harmless. Actually, Oil of Wintergreen is not innocuous at all; it can be toxic and potentially fatal due to the presence of methyl salicylate. As one indicator of its toxicity, one teaspoon of methyl salicylate is equivalent to around two dozen 300-milligram aspirin tablets. On the positive side of the ledger, the substance is often used in much smaller amounts as a flavoring agent in gum, candy, and root beer which is probably why the student believed it to be harmless.

In order to cope with the obsessions about poisoning the family, The Drano Lady developed a ritual in which she walked through her home, turning each light switch on and off ten times.....not nine, not eleven, but ten. She would also pull her appliance plugs from the wall, turn them over, and reinsert them, doing so with the requisite, ritualistic ten times each. Obviously, one could tie up a pretty fair amount of time each day with such rituals, and she did just that.

The family social life was remarkable, if only for its paucity of outside stimulation. Her father-in-law had died and left his wife, my client's mother-in-law, with the responsibility of managing a farm by herself. In order to accomplish the never-ending tasks inherent in farm life, the Drano Lady's husband and his brothers and brothers-in-law would make a trip the first and third weekend of every month to what they all called "Momma's house" in nearby Navasota to work the farm. Thus, her husband was gone every other weekend. As a concession to family life, on the second and fourth weekends, the men all took their wives and children to Momma's where they once again worked the farm. In brief, my client's social life consisted of two weekends a month without her husband in Brenham and two weekends with him and the in-laws in Navasota. One weekend a year with in-laws might be more than enough for some of us.

As another index of her deprived social life, she had never enjoyed a night out with her husband or female friends in ten years of marriage except to deliver each of the three children. I am convinced some of my female readers might view delivering a baby as something other than a "night out on the town." Perhaps it would not be unfair of me to describe her social life as circumscribed, narrow, or limited!

Trapped Housewife Syndrome. I once read the *The Feminine Mystique*, the 1963 landmark book written by the prominent writer, feminist, and activist, Betty Friedan. As a result, I could not shake the feeling that The Drano Lady was a victim of what the feminist advocate Friedan had called "The Trapped Housewife Syndrome." Ms. Friedan would no doubt view The Drano Lady as one of those victims, irretrievably trapped and inundated with dirty dishes, dirty diapers, lingering loneliness, a devoted but undemonstrative husband, and haunting obsessions of committing infanticide or murder.

I gave a great deal of thought to how I might most effectively break this cycle of anxiety, obsessive ruminations, and ritualistic acting out. Accordingly, I set my mind to a course of action that would get her out of the house and into the larger world for some much-needed stimulation and socialization. I had determined in an earlier session she had an intelligence quotient (IQ) on the

Wechsler Adult Intelligence Scale (WAIS) of around 120 which is more than adequate for pursuing intellectual activities such as university class work. It was our good fortune that Brenham is home to one of the finest community colleges in the state of Texas, Blinn College, and I suggested in one of our sessions that she ought to consider enrolling there. She countered that she did not think she was intelligent enough to go to college and the students would look at her like she was an old wrinkled hag who was used up and worn out at the advanced age of twenty-eight. We then discussed the intellectual qualities necessary to prosper in the college environment and I was able to use her test data to break down the argument about not being smart enough to survive in a community college. An IQ of 120 would place her in the upper 14% of the American population, and slightly above the average for college students in general. As I tell my classes in Abnormal Psychology, her IQ essentially equals that of the average student at Texas A&M.

To get her past her haggard, old woman intimation, I asked The Drano Lady to devote our next scheduled session to strolling across the Blinn campus to get a feel for the place. Another homework assignment was to approach some students and offer to buy them a cup of coffee or a soft drink in return for hearing their take on life at Blinn. She came back from that exercise amazed that eighteen- and nineteen-year olds could be warm, nurturing, and accepting of someone in their obvious dotage.

Grandma Gets to Babysit. Once concerns about lack of ability and social fit had been sufficiently dispelled, the major obstacle to progress was good child care, that bane of many working women and older married or divorced college students. It seemed to me that a highly reliable and imminently available source of care in this case might well be residing nearby, namely her mother. There were, of course, obstacles to overcome in this area, too. For one thing, the mother and daughter did not have a healthy adult relationship. For another, The Drano Lady and her family lived in a home owned by the mother on the same block as the mother, and her husband worked for her mother in the family business. To say that her mother owned them lock, stock, and barrel would be an understatement. Of course, mother never let her daughter and son-in-law forget her "generosity."

I suggested to The Drano Lady that she ask her mother to take Tuesday and Thursday mornings off from her business to babysit the grandchildren for four or five hours each of those two days. This concession would allow my client to take three courses and still be home shortly after the noon hour.

Given the unhealthy nature of their relationship and upon hearing the news, the mother lit into her daughter, stating: "You are going to do what? You are going to college? You have got to be kidding me. You have never done one independent thing in your life. You will fail in college just as you have in every other thing in your life, and you will come crawling back to me on your hands and knees asking for forgiveness. And besides that, <u>everyone</u> knows when a married woman goes to college, her husband immediately starts running around with another woman. Everyone knows that!!"

The Drano Lady was devastated though not surprised by the vitriol and venom that spewed forth from her mother. This volatile, counterproductive exchange further convinced me we had reached a crisis point in the therapeutic relationship so I started formulating a plan I hoped would work. What I conjured up would not appear in any standard scholarly treatise on how to conduct counseling or psychotherapy, but I had reached the end of my rope and figured that there was little to lose at this point. My plan might also put me on shaky ethical footing, but I figured the return potentially outweighed the risk. Something drastic had to take place or my client would go under and, at the risk of being melodramatic, possibly for the rest of her life.

I told my client we were implementing some drastic measures to make the mother understand she, her married adult daughter, was going to school one way or another, preferably with the mother's blessing and assistance with the babysitting. I gave her a didactic on normal, healthy mother-daughter relationships by drawing on my experience with young female college students who were in the process of achieving independence from their parents. In essence, I told her that it is normal for first-year college students to be homesick and miss their parents, thus leading them to call or go home frequently. However, in the normal scheme of things, by the third or fourth year, the parents are forced to plead with their kids to come home once in a while. To wit: "Why do you never come home anymore? Please come home. Bring your whole dorm if you like. We'll feed all of them if you'll just come home." As I always tell my students: "Your parents send you off to college to get an education, think for yourself, and stand up for your beliefs but when that independence starts to get a firm hold, it can be a bitter pill to swallow. Your achieving independence is truly a double-edged sword for your parents." In almost all cases of normal distancing, the process is gradual and my client had achieved none of the necessary independence, hence the use of some reasonably drastic measures.

I told her she was twenty-eight, bright, attractive, a good mother and wife, and it was time for her mother to come to an understanding of how the cow ate the cabbage. To accomplish this long overdue goal, The Drano Lady was asked to stretch her powers of creativity to the utmost limits and imagine that I was her mother. Once that image, however difficult, was reasonably imbedded in her consciousness, we role-played requesting assistance with the children while she went to Blinn two mornings a week. I played the part of the mean mother, calling my client every name in the book, and generally setting a tone for failure by destroying her self-confidence. I talked about failure, disappointed and abandoned children, and a husband on the prowl for female companionship no longer available at home. My client had been instructed to let me rave and rant and foam at the mouth, at which time she was to put her nose to mine, look me square in the eye, and say: "Mother, you go square to hell." I urged her to practice the statement, making sure she said it with such conviction that the mother could not possibly misread her intent. She told me, "I do not use such language", and I retorted, "We are talking dirty today, so let's practice!"

She showed up for her appointment the next week looking very much the worse for wear, immediately breaking into tears when I asked how things went. From the looks of things, I figured I had destroyed the poor woman. She talked haltingly of confronting her mother, letting things escalate to a fever pitch with the usual invectives and insinuations, and then putting her nose on her mother's and saying as we had practiced: "Mother, you can go square to hell. I am going to Blinn and you might as well get accustomed to the idea. Also, you will help me out by babysitting two mornings a week!" She told me the two of them had never gotten along better, and her mother agreed to babysit the children as requested. I was, of course, relieved that my unorthodox, quasi-ethical approach to solving a knotty problem had been so successful. Yes, my client's psyche was at short-term risk with what we had done, but I was not willing to entertain the long-term consequences of doing absolutely nothing.

Entering Blinn College. The next obstacles were the bureaucratic challenges associated with entering Blinn College. Application forms, choice of classes, and the nettlesome inoculations had to be addressed. We finally decided that a good start might be to take a business machines course, an introduction to sociology, and a course in college English. The business course was selected in case she decided to seek employment at some point and the latter two were chosen because they were traditional options popular with freshmen students. Also, they would apply to most degree programs at Texas A&M or Sam Houston State University in Huntsville which were her most likely final destinations, educationally speaking.

She entered Blinn in late August and things rocked along nicely until November. She was making a B in each of the three courses and seemed to be enjoying herself. Her newly-found feelings of worth and mastery were palpable and she could barely hide her exuberance at being able to thrive in college. Around Thanksgiving, however, a big change took place. She had been offered a job as Teacher's Aide at the Brenham State School (BSS), a state-supported treatment facility for intellectually disabled adults. The BSS administration struck a deal with my client which required her to begin employment immediately. Another stipulation required her to work ten hours a week at the facility and devote the other thirty hours of the forty-hour work week to classes at Blinn for a period of two years. At that point, she would transfer to either A&M or Sam Houston, both of which offered excellent teacher training programs. As part of the package, upon completion of the undergraduate degree, she would owe the state of Texas five years as a teacher at the state school. Though unhappy that she had to quit Blinn so late in the semester, I agreed it was for all the right reasons. It is hard to argue with a deal that pays a person a full salary for ten hours of work while allowing him or her to devote the remainder of the work week to completing a college education minus the usual money anxieties experienced by many students, particularly non-traditional ones like my client.

Teacher's Aide, Brenham State School. She started the new job around Christmas. Though I thought she was off and running and in need of little support from me, we agreed to have follow-up sessions for as long as they were deemed helpful. During an early session after she started working at the state school, I noticed immediate changes in the way she dressed, how she carried herself, and her outlook on life. It was as if a whole new world had opened up to her. She even started smoking cigarettes for a brief time, belatedly engaging in that time-honored symbol of adolescent rebellion and emerging individuality. Fortunately, she discontinued that egregious habit before it became entrenched.

One day she asked me what I thought about guilt feelings she was experiencing related to some male colleagues at the state school. She related her new-found emotions as follows: "I have never looked at any man in my life except my husband but I must confess that some of the men at work look pretty good." I assured her that such a reaction was normal and it was okay to look. On the other hand, going beyond looking at other men was an issue I hoped we would not have to deal with later. Given her psychological makeup and past character, I did not see this as a serious problem.

On another occasion, she told me that for the first time in her marriage, she and her husband had had a major disagreement. The source of the marital discord was her occasional visits to the Tranquility Club, a local bowling alley and bar, where she would have a mixed drink after work with some of her new girlfriends. He told her only cheap women did such things, accompanying his opinion with a warning to the effect that: "Everyone knows that when three or four women meet for drinks, they are really hoping to be picked up by other men. <u>Everyone</u> knows that!"

Back to Dirty Dishes and Dirty Diapers? I reveled in her meteoric ascendance into self-efficacy and self-worth, but it all came crashing down after four months. Because of her personal growth and newly-found success at work, the husband had to take on more of an active role in raising his children. He had to face the fact that she had no interest in having another child and he also did not always get the five-course meals at lunch and dinner. Her new independence was frightening to him, creating challenges to his masculinity and authority that he had never before confronted. She was no longer the docile, obedient, pliable housewife of old. In the process of dealing with these changes in his previously circumscribed world, he developed bleeding ulcers. Ever the ever-obedient and nurturing wife, The Drano Lady resigned her job at the state school in order to tend to her sick husband. She also discontinued seeing me. Watching a person grow by leaps and bounds in counseling is a psychologist's dream, and it was difficult to hide my disappointment with her decision.

The end of our relationship was complicated by the fact that she claimed during one of our last sessions that she was in love with me. This "infatuation" with one's psychologist, physician, minister, professor, or other person in positions of power and authority is not new, but such emotions do complicate the therapeutic relationship. I tried to navigate my way across that slippery slope by acknowledging the legitimacy of her feelings as well as my appreciation for the courage it took to bring up such an emotional issue. At the same time, I told her I greatly admired her for what she had achieved during our time together but her admiration of me should not be confused with love. We left that most delicate issue pretty much alone, she departed from the center, and I never heard from her again. I hoped against hope she did not return to a life of ruminating over stews, flipping light switches, and rotating wall plugs. If alive today, she would be in her seventies, and it would be fascinating to know how her life has played out over the last forty years.

School Phobics: Debbie P. and Dale D.

Debbie P. A distraught middle-aged mother showed up at the center one afternoon, clearly stressed by the hand life had dealt her. The problem that brought the woman to our doorstep was her fourteen-year old daughter, Debbie, who was a chronic school truant and a very unhappy teenager. In the process of conducting the intake interview, I learned that both parents were unemployed and the family lived in a government housing project. All other children had dropped out of high school, gotten married and moved away to other cities, leaving the parents alone with their youngest child, Debbie.

The family had moved around a good bit, and the frequent relocations led Debbie to attend eleven schools in eight years. Additionally, and more critical to the case, she had never attended school longer than three days successively in any of those eleven school settings. The prospect of attending school triggered off an assortment of vague and not-so-vague ailments and complaints including stomach aches, nausea, and occasional vomiting. As Debbie reached adolescence, she became increasingly rebellious about going to school which caused frequent arguments with her parents.

After relaying the details of Debbie's situation to me, the mother asked what I thought ought to be done. I lied through my teeth to gain some precious planning time, reassuring her all the while that I had a firm grip on the problem. We scheduled another appointment for the next week and I headed back to College Station and the university library where I read everything I could find related to this problem.

Symptoms of School Phobia. I found an abundant literature on what is popularly known as "school phobia." I learned the condition typically manifests itself at two life junctures, either during the kindergarten years or in the transition from elementary to middle school or junior high. In the first instance, the symptoms are probably tied to the first-time separation of the young child from his or her mother and the perceived loss of the comforting, psychologically safe home environment. If the child presents the aforementioned symptoms at this point, the parents can usually handle it by being assertive, patient, and a willingness to make "being sick" an unrewarding experience. To wit: "You can be sick if you like, but there will be no television, no video games, and no ice cream. If you are sick, you are sick and need to stay in bed and get well." Pretty soon, most children find school to be a more desirable option than confinement to bed and being deprived of their favorite foods and the stimulation provided by their friends.

The second manifestation of school phobia may occur during the transition from grade school to junior high or from middle school to junior high, depending on the school structure. In this instance, however, the apprehension is not so much about separation from the home or mother but rather a fear of peer rejection at school. We all know peers can be pretty heartless when a child is not in the social mainstream, and taunting or bullying can become a big issue. Debbie was different to the extent that her family was essentially indigent, plus she lacked the confidence and social skills necessary to fit in with adolescent peers.

When the crying, pleading, whining, stomach aches, nausea, and vomiting set in with an adolescent school phobic, the dynamics are complex and parents are often poorly equipped to handle the situation by themselves. It was this profound feeling of helplessness that led Debbie's mother to seek assistance from our agency.

After two sessions with the mother, I decided it was high time I met the chief protagonist of this drama, Miss Debbie herself. What I found was a small, cute, brown-haired, adolescent female, all of five feet tall and weighing at most 115 pounds. She was shy, retiring, and not at all self-confident but unexpectedly forthcoming in all of our conversations. During our initial discussions, she related a painful incident surrounding her most recent birthday. It seems she had turned fourteen a few weeks earlier and invited twenty "friends" to her birthday party, none of whom showed up. The message conveyed here was one of total rejection, clearly a psychologically devastating blow to a self-conscious, friendless teenager.

In the course of another of our discussions, Debbie told me she had a best friend named Erica (an alias). Erica was also one of my clients, and it immediately struck me that she and Debbie were a most unlikely duo. Both were fourteen for sure, but Debbie was much younger emotionally and had just started her menstrual period while her "friend" was fourteen going on twenty-five physically and, to some extent, emotionally. Erica was a bit of a "wild child", almost certainly sexually active, and had just returned home after running away to New Orleans for a couple of days. I was curious about this unlikely alliance so I asked Erica about her friendship with Debbie. Erica told me her Sunday School teacher requested she speak in the halls at school because Debbie was lonely and friendless. That simple social exchange was the extent of their "friendship."

A Behavioral Baseline. Thanks to my library search on school phobia, I pretty much knew what needed to be done with this case. The first item of business was to secure an index of the severity of the attendance problems at school. In talking with personnel at the junior high school, I found Debbie's attendance record to be problematic and her grades in shambles. She had missed all or part of thirty-five days between August 22 and December 6, most of them consecutively in November and early December. Her grades for the first nine-week session were as follows: English (66), Reading (69), Social Studies (60), Mathematics (66), Science (Incomplete or I), Choir (B), and Physical Education (C). She had received Incompletes across the board for the second nine-week grading period. Clearly, Debbie was in major academic trouble.

Results from a test I administered indicated she had an IQ of exactly one hundred which is at the mid-point for the US population, with fifty percent scoring higher and an equal number scoring lower. She was an average kid intellectually, period and end of story. In the process of administering the test, I witnessed additional verification of her profound lack of self-confidence and fear of rejection. For example, if she knew the answer to an item on the test, it would come out quickly and reasonably confidently. However, if she was unsure of or did not know an answer, there would be a retreat to a ritualistic avoidance response in which she would alternately stare at the floor or gaze at the ceiling, biting her lower lip and moving her head slowly from side to side while looking at nothing in particular. I am convinced she was afraid I would chastise her for a wrong answer and she was simply not going to run that risk. Saying "I don't know" was simply too emotionally-loaded and dangerous.

To get an index of how long she would engage in the mute, staring, head-pivoting ritual, I once let the behaviors go more than three minutes before I called her hand. I interpreted her response (or lack of one really) to be that of a young girl who was friendless but had met someone (me) who was accepting and responsive, in some ways a friend of last resort. And she was not about to put that acceptance and friendship on the line by saying something as psychologically risky as "I don't know."

Treatment Phase. Early on in the decision-making process, I had decided it would be imprudent to begin treatment prior to Christmas and have whatever gains that may have been made wiped out by the two-week holiday vacation. Thus, Debbie spent about a month in Homebound Instruction prior to and following the Christmas vacation. I decided January 18, the date on which the second half of the academic year began, would be a good time to launch our treatment program in full force.

Prior to making the decision about January 18, I called what my wife refers to as a "Come to Jesus meeting" of all concerned parties. This friendly little soiree included our Director, Ed Wachholz, Debbie, her mother, the school principal, the school nurse, a school counselor, a favorite teacher, a student from A&M named Sandra Siemsglusz, and yours truly. The first thing I emphasized with the group was that Debbie had to understand she was going back to class and would not be allowed to leave the school grounds at any time short of the unfortunate acquisition of Ebola or the Bubonic Plague. We further agreed the first line of defense should be her favorite teacher. However, if Debbie got nauseated or sick and could not stay in the classroom, she was to go to the Counselor's office. If all else failed, then the school nurse would become the court of last resort. It was understood by all parties, or so I thought, that in no case would Debbie be allowed to leave school. I was to find out soon how wrong I was in my supposition. The principal generously agreed to waive her failing marks from the first semester if we could get her back on target at school, and her promotion to the ninth grade would be dependent on her spring semester grades alone.

The mother agreed to bow out of the picture in the mornings, thus leaving it to Sandra Siemsglusz to pick up Debbie and transport her to school. I got Sandra involved because she was in my Abnormal Psychology class and I knew she drove back and forth daily from Brenham to College Station to take classes while completing her degree in Education. Sandra was a bit older than the typical college student, probably near my age (the mid-thirties), married to Pastor Jon Siemsglusz, a Lutheran minister, and the mother of several children. She brought a nice mix of maturity, patience, good humor, and understanding to Debbie's case for which I was most thankful.

I asked Sandra to work around her own schedule as best she could to enable her to transport Debbie to school in the mornings and pick her up at the end of the school day. Luckily, their two schedules dovetailed nicely. The beauty of this arrangement was that it got the family out of the picture each morning, thus negating the begging, pleading, screaming, yelling, cajoling, and assorted terror tactics they had employed futilely for the past several years. As an added inducement to cement Sandra's involvement, she enrolled in a three-hour field experiences course (Psychology 484) I had created in the late 1960's so that A&M students like her who were doing good deeds in the community could get college course credit for their efforts.

We got Debbie back in school on the eighteenth of January and things rocked along nicely for a couple of weeks. Then one afternoon in mid-February, Sandra reported that Debbie had incurred nine straight absences. I was incredulous and asked how this could have possibly happened since there had been no news reports of an Ebola or Bubonic Plague outbreak in Washington County, Texas. Sandra informed me that Debbie had complained of menstrual cramps and was sent home by the school nurse. As a male, I am painfully aware of my profound ignorance of the assorted nuances of menstrual cramps but I knew they were not of the magnitude of skin-eating fungi. I thus implored Sandra in my most emphatic, diplomatic fashion to, "Please pick Debbie up tomorrow morning and get her happy little ass back in school."

Sandra picked Debbie up the following day, and it was clear that going back so school was filled with trepidation. Sandra drove her around until the anxiety was defused to the point she could be taken to school. As Debbie walked up the sidewalk, a couple of the cool eighth grade guys (Girls, remember how cool the eighth grade boys were?) spotted her, and one of them turned to Debbie and said, "What are you doing here. We thought you was retarded." She gave her detractors a withering look and entered the school, unaware of the transformative things that were getting ready to happen to her.

Early on in the treatment program, Sandra and I, being at times incorrigibly extroverted, made a couple of minor errors in strategy. We decided that Debbie should join the school Pep Squad; she did not like it. We then decided she should be a Candy Striper at the local hospital; she disliked that activity, also. After those two failed exercises, Sandra and I had an epiphany. Simply put, our client was a low-key, shy, quiet, retiring personality and we were trying to fit that introverted square peg into some kind of pre-selected extroverted round hole as defined by Sandra and me, and it was not ever going to work. She and I then backed off in our attempts to make Debbie the Belle of the Ball.

From February 15 to the end of school in May, Debbie missed nary a day and her grades for the third nine weeks were all passing and those for the fourth were as follows: English (82), Reading (89), Social Studies (81), Mathematics (73), Science (76), Choir (B), and Physical Education (C). True to his word, the Principal promoted Debbie to the ninth grade. To add a happy ending to the story, Debbie missed fewer than seven days total during the remaining four years of high school, and most of the absences resulted from a couple of bouts with the flu.

Of course, the mother was ecstatic with the results and Debbie truly liked herself for perhaps the first time in her young life; she was no longer a reject and a failure. She spent most of her high school years in the company of a female friend and a boy who she later married after graduation.

The last I heard of Debbie was some twenty years ago, and she had just become mother to young twins.

Dale D. Not too long after the successful treatment of Debbie, I took on a school phobia case with quite a few similarities, though it ended on a much sadder note. Again, the client was a fourteen-year old, in this instance a young lady named Dale. Unlike our previous case, Dale had lived all her life in Brenham but the history of school attendance and performance closely mirrored that of Debbie. Dale, like Debbie, was in the eighth grade and had never attended school for more than three consecutive days either. During my initial meeting with Dale and her mother, I told them I knew exactly what I wanted to do to resolve this case, and I did not have to spin a little white lie to buy some time in this instance. I went back to the Sandra Siemsglusz well one more time, and she agreed to assist where she could. As might be predicted from our experience with Debbie, it was not long before Dale had racked up a personal record of three consecutive weeks of school attendance.

However, the dreadful menstrual cramps rose up and bit us in the behind once again. Yes, Sandra learned that our friendly school nurse sent Dale home with menstrual cramps and she had not been seen at school for almost two weeks. Once again, I sent Sandra on a rescue mission, not knowing I was throwing her to the lions, or in this case, an aging lioness known as Dale's mother. The mother related a tale of woe about how her older children were married and gone and she and her husband had a marriage only in the legal sense. Thus, she turned to Dale for companionship. The mother essentially confessed without using the exact words that she needed a sick Dale not a healthy one. To support her pathology, the mother enlisted the counsel of a local physician, a pediatrician whose words of advice were music to her ears.

The Psychologist Takes a "Shyness Pill." Dale's mother told Sandra and I she was instructed by the physician to keep her child away from those" crazy psychologists" for they were going to really mess her up. I countered this asinine assertion borne of either malice or unfathomable ignorance by pointing to our successes for the three weeks leading up to the menstrual cramps episode. As well, I asked if she did not see a much happier, healthier Dale who was proud of herself for setting a personal record (PR) for school attendance. She agreed that the evidence was hard to argue with, but she was going to take the pediatrician's advice anyway and retrieve Dale from our evil clutches. She said her decision had been made easier because the pediatrician had put Dale on medication guaranteed to work faster and better than anything Sandra and I might conjure up.

The label on the medication bottle read "Shyness Pills" which piqued my curiosity along several dimensions. I wondered what they pills could possibly be, and the labeling process seemed ethically problematic to me. To test the waters, so to speak, I told the mother that shyness had been a lifelong curse for me, too, and wondered if I might have one of the wonder pills. She agreed to my request, seemingly thrilled that she might be partner to extricating me from the tyranny of the shyness monster. When I opened the bottle of "shyness pills", I immediately knew I was looking at Thorazine, the most powerful anti-psychotic medication on the market at the time. I know nothing about pharmaceutical ethics but I cannot imagine that labeling a potent anti-psychotic drug as

"Shyness Pills" is remotely acceptable. And the last thing that child needed was something to further enable her withdrawn, asocial condition.

Contact with Dale and her mother was discontinued after that regrettable encounter. I was told later that Dale averaged fewer than two days of school attendance per week over the next four years but was socially promoted out of high school at the end of her "senior" year. The last time I saw the dynamic duo, Dale was around twenty-one and she and her mother were walking cozily around the square in Brenham, arms entwined around each other. I am not opposed to young adults engaging in displays of affection with their mothers, but I smelled a great big rat in this case.

I unashamedly admit to my students in Abnormal Psychology that I do not have the foggiest notion as to the cause of schizophrenia, though the genetic, biochemical, and psychosocial explanations are all intriguing and have their proponents. If in fact the disorder can be psychosocially induced, this case serves as a vivid illustration of how a parent could program a child for failure, and these life failures are sometimes labeled as schizophrenia. Though I know nothing about how Dale's life has played out since 1975, I am putting my money on misery and woe!

Postscript on Sandra Siemsglusz. As a postscript, because of her impressive efforts on behalf of both young women, but particularly with Debbie, I invited Sandra to co-author an article that was published in 1977 in the journal *Adolescence*. The piece was titled "Paraprofessional Treatment of School Phobia in a Young Adolescent Girl" and is in large part a tribute to Sandra's creativity, grit, and determination in her efforts to help Debbie (and the far less fortunate Dale).

Sandra graduated from A&M, was later divorced from Pastor Siemsglusz, remarried, earned a master's degree in Counseling from the University of Houston-Clear Lake, and taught and counseled in several Houston area schools. Sandra died in 1999, once again demonstrating that life is not always fair. She was a good woman with a kind heart and an unbridled optimism about children and their potential to thrive if provided with a helping hand.

In 2010, I met Sandra's grand-niece Lindsay, an A&M Business student from Brenham, through her volunteer involvement in "Wiener Fest™", a dog race event involving literally hundreds of dachshunds. My wife, Judy, started the event in 2006 to raise money for the local animal shelter now known as the Aggieland Humane Society, and Lindsay was a huge help to her that year.

Several months later, Mary Catherine Siemsglusz, also of Brenham, showed up in my Sport Psychology class; she is Lindsay's cousin and the granddaughter of Sandra. Eighteen months later, in the summer of 2012, Catherine took part in my Germany Study Abroad Program where, among other things, I was able to tell her how much I admired her grandmother for her friendship and valiant efforts on behalf of a struggling teenager thirty-five years earlier. Sandra made a difference in at least two lives, Debbie's and mine. I was gratified to hear, also, that despite the fact that Catherine was eight years old at the time of Sandra' death, she has wonderful memories of a grandmother who was actively involved in her life for all too short a time.

Benita, Meet Buster Lejeune

In the mid-1970's, I had the good fortune to meet a most challenging client who will be known as Benita. Her escapades prior to my arrival on the scene were well-documented because she ran for Governor of Texas in 1950 against Allen Shivers from Port Arthur. In that election involving seven candidates, Shivers received 76% of the votes and Benita was the choice of 9,542 voters, or slightly fewer than one percent of the total.

In the 1940's and 1950's, for all practical purposes, the only political party in Texas was the Democratic Party, and it had liberal and conservative wings. The liberal wing was led by Senator Ralph Yarborough from the small city of Chandler in northeast Texas, and Allen Shivers of Liberty, east of Houston, was the leader of the conservative camp, and his followers were known as "Shivercrats." There were sharp philosophical differences between the two factions, and Shivers' support of Republican President Dwight D. Eisenhower led the liberal wing to brand him as a traitor to the spirit and philosophy of the Democratic Party.

Only one female, Miriam "Ma" Ferguson, had ever served as Governor in Texas prior to my first meeting with Benita, so her candidacy was somewhat groundbreaking at the time. Benita contended that the "Shivercrats" were in cahoots with Yarborough's liberal faction, and both wings were generally up to no good. According to Benita, the desire to destroy her political career through intimidation and harassment was a shared goal of both Shivers and Yarborough and their followers. Benita further maintained that supporters of both camps mailed or phoned death threats and, as part of the intimidation tactics, threw bricks through the plate glass windows in her home in the middle of the night. She truly believed that both political camps were hell-bent on putting a woman who had the gall to intrude on a man's world in her proper place.

To protect herself from these alleged assaults, Benita started carrying a shotgun to her elementary school classroom. One can only imagine the shock and dismay among the parents of the children in her class when that little piece of information came to light. Parental complaints to the school authorities eventually led to Benita's resignation and eventual hospitalization for paranoid schizophrenia. Once released, Benita vowed not only to get mad but to get even with several local politicians who she viewed as the instruments of her past and continuing persecution. There were numerous frivolous lawsuits lodged against the County Judge, other important local figures, and her former husband who she said was a bigamist. Benita quickly became known as a town eccentric, and a paranoid and hostile one at that.

Events leading up to Benita's referral to BWCCS were based to a great extent on her continuing misbehavior in various local venues. She showed up at the school board meetings, ranting and raving about the inadequacies of the local schools. At other times, she challenged the leadership of the local mental health agencies to do a better job of meeting the needs of the local community. Then she took on the leadership of the Friends of the Library because their services were not up to her very high standards. Like most paranoid ideation, there was an element of truth to her assertions; yes, the schools could be better, yes, the mental health agencies could function more effectively, and, yes, the library could always be better. However, it was the frequency and the vitriol with which these messages were delivered that got everyone's attention.

But the tipping point that led to her referral was a flurry of seemingly endless, highly charged verbal confrontations with the leadership at St. Peter's Episcopal Church which had been a significant force in the religious life of Brenham since 1848. Benita had been a lifelong member but got herself crosswise with the congregation because of repeated and heated verbal attacks on the pastor and a select woman's group within the church. Benita was articulate, forceful, pugnacious, and armed with righteous indignation, and the vehemence of her attacks on the women began to scare them. These paranoid hostilities deepened, ultimately leading the minister of the large and influential church to refer her to our clinic. Benita had frankly pushed the pastor, a Reverend Swygert (whose son Tommy received a degree in Psychology at A&M), and the other parishioners to the breaking point.

I learned in an initial interview that Benita was the daughter of a once-prosperous local veterinarian who had died years earlier. Through circumstances of which I have absolutely no knowledge, Benita was essentially destitute by the time I met her. Despite her lack of financial resources, Benita gamely tried to maintain the veneer of wealth and Southern-Belle gentility, always showing up for appointments in her best pantsuit outfit and matching white gloves. The seams on her suits and gloves were frayed and worn, but she did the best she could to keep up appearances of fading nobility.

Benita graduated number one in her high school class and her valedictory address was later published. She went on to obtain baccalaureate and master's degrees plus thirty hours toward a doctorate in the field of education. Her master's thesis entitled "Trends in Texas Public School Administration for Women" was completed at Southwest Texas State University (now Texas State University) in 1965. She was also a member of *International Who's Who in Poetry*, published a collection of her poems entitled "Love Notes of a Blue Trillium", and generally regarded herself as both an important poet and a substantial intellect. As part of the façade of intellectual superiority, Benita would speak with me alone because I was the only person in the counseling center who had more degrees than she did. She looked down with disdain on my undergraduate and beginning graduate students, for they were mere underlings, the unwashed and unwanted no doubt wallowing in unfathomable ignorance.

Her brilliance was readily apparent though often masked by paranoid ruminations of past and present political injustices perpetrated against her by various local and state political and civic figures. One example of her occasionally incisive insights surfaced when she told me there was a crazy psychologist over in Liberty County running a camp for wayward or disturbed children, and she predicted he was going to kill someone one day. Sure enough, shortly after her prognostication, an eighteen-year old female resident made what on the surface appeared to be a feeble attempt at suicide by swallowing rat poison on a Friday. To maintain discipline and to keep the girl in her place, the camp proprietor refused to provide medical treatment over a long weekend, and she died on the Monday after the incident. The owner, who was not a psychologist as he had previously contended, was indicted on criminal charges and served time in jail for his willful negligence.

Another instance of insightful illumination came when Benita told me the wealthy and politically powerful Hobby family in Houston was marshalling its considerable resources to topple the presidency of Richard Nixon. When Nixon resigned in disgrace over Watergate a few months after Benita's pronouncement, editorials in several metropolitan newspapers made reference to the millions and millions of dollars the Hobby family spent to take Mr. Nixon down.

No doubt, the Hobby family was influential. They owned the Houston Post, Oveta Culp Hobby was an ambassador under several presidents, and William "Bill" Hobby held down the powerful Lieutenant Governor's job in Texas for nineteen years from 1973-1991. The way the constitution is written in Texas, Hobby often wielded more influence than did the three governors under whom he served (Dolph Briscoe, Bill Clements on two different occasions, and Mark White).

Speaking of Mark White, he died of a heart attack on August 5, 2017, at the age of seventy-seven. He was Governor of the great state of Texas, my beloved home, from 1983 to 1987 and initiated many wonderful changes in our educational system. Among other things, and with the able assistance of Lieutenant Governor William Hobby, White raised teacher salaries by $5,000 in one year, reduced class sizes, and generally re-set educational priorities across the board during his tenure at the top elected official in Texas. He also pushed for much-needed changes in the way protective services for children are provided, got a seat belt law passed, brought numerous hi-tech companies to Austin, and was a driving force behind the creation and promotion of the now-famous anti-litter slogan "Don't Mess With Texas" which brought environmental awareness to the forefront.

Not too many years ago, Governor White was honored for his many years of selfless service to the citizens of Texas at a ceremony in Austin, and though I cannot recall why exactly, he asked that Judy and I be guests at his table. Conversing about the "good old days" of the Democratic Party with someone of his stature was a peak experience for Judy and me. The Governor was particularly impressed that Judy had worked diligently as a teacher leader for his election and even more impressed that she knew so much about him after the passage of so many years. It was a most enjoyable evening and we are both thankful for his largess, kindness, and cordiality. His lovely wife, Linda Gale, was also present and added greatly to our enjoyment of the evening.

But back to Benita. She seemed to like me for the most part, but there were times when we locked horns as a result of her paranoid ideation. The abnormal psychology textbooks often talk about a "pseudo-community", or an imaginary collection of persecutory forces created in the minds of paranoid individuals, and Benita slowly but surely incorporated me into her persecutory world as I increasingly challenged her paranoid ways. When all was going well between us, she would affectionately refer to me as "Doctor Lejeune" which I guess she thought had a nice touch of French elegance to it. When confronted, however, she would grab hold of the table between us, puff up like a battle-tested pit bull, and excoriate me as follows: "Listen, Buster, you can't talk to me like that."

The students who were working with me at the time took to calling me "Buster Lejeune", sort of a multiple personality (now known in the psychiatric nomenclature system as Dissociative Identity Disorder, or DID), in her honor. The name does have an element of the multiple personality in it, and that had appeal for my young students who were becoming familiar with the diagnostic system used by psychologists and psychiatrists. In that connection, I was sitting on the bench outside the Dixie Chicken at North Gate one evening when a female slipped up beside me, kissed me on the cheek, and ran off shouting, "Buster Lejeune, Buster Lejeune". To this day, I do not know the identity of the culprit in this caper, but clearly my fame had spread, thanks to Benita.

My other lingering memory of Benita involved the two Christmases we were counselor and counselee. To celebrate the holiday season, Benita would bring me a two-liter drink wrapped in festive silver, green, and red foil. I knew this gesture was the best she could do financially, and I appreciated the thought behind the gift far more than the drink itself. I have always told my classes I am not in the habit of taking drinks from paranoid personalities who have incorporated me into their pseudo-communities. Thus, what I would do is take the bottle home, set up paper cups for my four children, and let them taste the drink first. If after a short time, they were not in death throes from cyanide poisoning, I would then take a drink myself. I can usually count on my universally bright and insightful students to see the dark humor in this little anecdote.

I eventually alienated Benita with my challenges to her paranoia. One day without much warning, I confronted her about some absurdity, was relegated to my rightful place among her many persecutors, and watched her walk out of my office and vanish from my life forever. Benita died on June 2, 1994, some twenty years after we met; she was either seventy-eight or seventy-nine.

Johnny Mae, I Hardly Knew Ye

Another woman who ran for Governor a few years before Benita and who also made her home in Brenham was Johnny Mae Hackworth (November 6, 1904- April 12, 1980). Johnny Mae was never a client of mine but I mention her here because of the similarities between Benita and Johnny Mae and their aspirations to become Governor of Texas. My knowledge of Johnny Mae was based totally on hearsay and occasional newspaper reports and I have not been able to find out much about her life through the usual media sources.

It seems that Johnny Mae ran for governor on several occasions, and once received nearly forty thousand votes. A self-appointed minister, she had the annoying, non-ministerial habit of threatening the lives of American Presidents, and spent time in jail on several occasions as a result. A major focus of her rancor was John F. Kennedy, and she is described by Gerald Blaine and Lisa McCubbin in their book entitled *The Kennedy Detail* as "Johnny Mae Hackworth: Letter writer, religious fanatic who made threats against the President, arrested in 1955 and 1960." Johnny Mae Hackworth died over three decades ago, and I regret not ever having the opportunity to make her acquaintance.

A Prostitution Ring

Nate, a handsome eleven-year old black child, was referred by his elementary school principal who wanted our professional opinion concerning his mental status. In the process of interviewing and testing Nate, I unearthed what proved to be one of the most bizarre situations I had encountered as a neophyte psychological consultant. It seems Nate was a partner in a family prostitution operation in which virtually every female family member was a participant. Grandma was a prostitute, Nate's mother and several of her sisters were practicing members of the world's oldest profession, and all their female children were scarlet women in training. There was a wide range of ages and body types available to accommodate almost any preference.

Nate was friendly, likeable, and free from demonstrable psychopathology, mostly a kid who occasionally acted out because of adverse family circumstances. Teacher reports, personal interviews, and my assessment of his mental status led us to devote less time and effort to Nate and make his mother, the aunt, and the prostitution operation our major foci.

The two sisters were the prime movers and shakers (pardon the pun) in the family business. As well, both women were diagnosed schizophrenics in remission who required follow-up services to ensure they stayed on their medications and did not lapse back into full-blown psychosis. Our main intervention was involving them in work activities at our sheltered workshop which afforded us the opportunity to monitor both their behavior and their commitment to their prescribed psychotropic medications.

Nate's mother was maybe five feet tall and weighed an easy 200 pounds. In contrast, her sister spread her plus or minus 200 pounds over a strong, athletic, six-foot frame. The two of them were as different in disposition as they were in physiognomy. Nate's mother was sweet, docile, and good-natured but the aunt had the devilish disposition of a cornered copperhead.

One of the more interesting aspects of the case was the foot shuffling, averting of eyes, and feeble excuse-making that took place among the center's staff and student volunteers when it came time to bring the ladies to our workshop each week. The problem had to do with their pungent, offensive body odor; no one wanted the ladies in their car because of the smell. Also, when we knew they were coming in for observation and consultation, all the windows in the building went up, and it did not matter if it was July with temperatures in excess of one hundred degrees or January when temperatures occasionally reached the thirties. The aroma was simply too offensive to endure without fresh air circulating about.

Though socially repugnant, the beyond-offensive body odor problem was in one respect the least of the problems for Nate's mother. It seems she had developed tardive dyskinesia which often occurs when patients are placed on major tranquilizers (aka anti-psychotics), such as Thorazine or Stelazine, for prolonged periods of time. Over-reliance on major tranquilizers causes dopamine depletion in the brain which has a number of adverse consequences, one of which is loss of control of the muscles regulating movement of the mouth and tongue. In turn, this disregulation causes a snake-like flicking of the tongue, incessant lip smacking, and drooling. Some of these same symptoms may be noted in older adults where dopamine has been depleted through the normal aging process. However, in normal aging, the problem develops more gradually and the extent of the damage is usually less dramatic.

Because of her body build, Nate's mother was understandably round. She also dipped snuff, and the laxity brought about by the tardive dyskinesia caused her to dribble small but steady amounts of brown saliva into the juncture of her bulbous breasts and ample stomach, thus creating amorphous, Rorschach Inkblot-like stains on the front of her shirts. All professional or clinical judgments aside, I found it personally unimaginable that someone would pay to have sex with an obese, smelly, drooling, psychotic woman. Nate's mother was proof that there is someone out there for everyone or, alternately, there is no accounting for the lack of taste among some males of the species.

The last time I saw either of the sisters was when Nate's mother showed up at our center convulsing and frothing at the mouth. My first thought was that she was having an extremely adverse reaction to her anti-psychotic medications. However, not knowing for sure what we were dealing with, we rushed her to Saint Jude's, a local Catholic hospital on Highway 36 just north of the town center, for a diagnosis of her condition. We were temporarily rebuffed in our efforts to get our client admitted because the Sister in charge of the hospital insisted that she was a psychiatric problem not a medical one and thus not St. Jude's responsibility. Ed Wachholz pled our case eloquently and eventually got her admitted to the hospital where she died the following afternoon of spinal meningitis, hardly a psychiatric condition.

Following the death of Nate's mother, case workers from local child welfare agencies began legal proceedings that led to dissolution of the prostitution ring. All children including Nate were placed in foster care. Nate's aunt refused any further treatment which was her legal right. We never saw her (or Nate) again.

Minor in Possession: "The Meanest, Toughest, and Fastest Guy in the Fifth Grade"

Another eleven-year-old school referral made his way into our lives, charged with under-age drinking and truancy. The immediate problem that led to the referral was his arrest by the local police for public drunkenness in the company of several older but also underage companions. All received citations for Minor in Possession (MIP) of alcohol for their misguided Saturday night imbibing.

My client was black, exceptionally handsome and athletic, personable, and easy to like. He was the only boy in his family, surrounded age-wise by several older and younger sisters, and was viewed mostly as a source of free labor which accounted for some his failure to attend school regularly. In the initial interview, I asked him to tell me about himself. He tersely summarized who he thought himself to be in eleven words, "I'm the meanest, toughest, and fastest guy in the fifth grade." In checking with a couple of known fifth-grade informants and their teachers, his personal assessment was corroborated; he was widely acknowledged to be "the meanest, toughest, and fastest fifth-grader" around. He was also intelligent as evidenced by his IQ scores on the Wechsler Intelligence Scale for Children (WISC) which I administered as part of his psychological evaluation. His IQ was around 120 which, as stated earlier in the case of The Drano Lady, is about the average of college graduates. As far as native intellect was concerned, he could have pretty much been anything he wanted to be.

One of the more intriguing things noted during the testing session was his response to one of the questions on Comprehension, the WISC subtest designed to assess one's awareness of societal norms and rules. The item asks the client to respond to the following: "What should you do if a boy much smaller than you comes up and starts hitting you?" Appropriate responses include verbal pleas to stop the hitting, getting an authority figure to stop the confrontation, and almost any other response that precludes engaging in retaliatory verbal or physical assault. The boy's response was: "That's the last thing that dude would ever do. I would punch him out and beat him within an inch of his life. He would find out real quick not to mess with me."

I asked him if he thought being belligerent, beating up people, and getting drunk were acceptable behaviors. He partially justified his misbehaviors, most notably the underage drinking, using references to football, his favorite sport. He told me that many of the football players from Brenham High School, particularly the outstanding ones, all played drunk and he planned to do the same when he got old enough to be on the team. Since he obviously liked football, I asked him who his role models were, and he cited three highly visible local athletes with whom he strongly identified. All three young men had solid reputations with the locals in terms of character and seemed to be the kind of people you would want your children to admire and emulate. Unfortunately, it was their imagined rather than actual deviance that drove his hero-worship.

One Brenham High School role model was Roosevelt Leaks who had been one of the most celebrated players in Texas high school history. Roosevelt graduated and moved on to the University of Texas where he had an outstanding career as an All-American running back. As an index of his talent, Leaks was runner-up his senior year for the Heisman Trophy, the prestigious award given annually to the most outstanding college football player in the nation. He went on to play several years of professional football, mostly with the Baltimore Colts in the NFL.

Two other heroes were Cleveland Franklin and Wilson Whitley. Cleveland moved on from Brenham to become a star running back for the Baylor Bears, and Wilson was an All-American defensive lineman for the University of Houston Cougars. Wilson Whitley had a particularly distinguished career in the NFL but died an untimely death in his thirties due to a heart condition.

My client's ultimate role model, however, was Duane Thomas, a stellar running back at West Texas State (now West Texas A&M University in the Panhandle city of Canyon) and later an All-Pro running back for the Dallas Cowboys. Thomas, perhaps the fastest and certainly one of the most elusive running backs in the NFL at the time, threw away an almost certain Hall of Fame career with the Cowboys because he decided he was not going to be a "plantation nigger," as he put it, for the organization's white owners, administrators, and coaches. He quit the Cowboys but tried to make a comeback later when he was in his early thirties. Unfortunately for Duane Thomas, the once mind-boggling running skills had diminished into mediocrity through nearly a decade of disuse. At some point, I asked my young client what it was that he liked so much about Duane Thomas, and he replied: "Cause he doesn't take any crap off of white people!" One can only guess about the dynamics that led to his fascination with the negative traits he conjured up in his idols.

On one occasion, the "meanest, toughest, and fastest guy in the fifth grade" stated that if you are a good player, the high school coaches get together at the end of your senior season, chip in a thousand dollars each, and buy you a brand new car. Of course, he was not aware that high school coaches do not make that kind of money nor would they typically engage in these clear violations of the rules. He was astute, however, in noting that Leaks, Franklin, and Whitley all drove late model vehicles after moving on to college. I will leave it to your imagination to figure out how three money-challenged Brenham boys came into possession of these nice vehicles. While I cannot speak for the University of Texas or the University of Houston, I am certain to core of my very existence that no Baylor booster would violate his or her religious values by engaging in underhandedness on behalf of one of their athletes! Then, again, Baylor is the same university that coveted Dave Bliss who once asked his players to lie and help cover up his complicity in a murder scheme involving members of his basketball team. That same Bliss, unrepentant to the core, took a coaching and athletic directorship position at the local private school, Allen Academy, and almost immediately engaged in some shady recruiting practices that got the school expelled from the Texas Association of Private and Parochial Schools (TAPPS) organization. This, alas, is the same institution that had a pronounced culture of rape among its football players, something conveniently overlooked by Coach Art Briles, his staff, the Athletic Director, and the President of the university, the highly hypocritical Ken Starr. All of these actors have been removed from their positions at Baylor, and it is most gratifying to me that Briles, the father of several female children ironically enough, cannot find another coaching job.

The local child welfare authorities also took over this case and removed "the meanest, toughest, and fastest fifth grader" from his home. He was then placed in the Buckner Boys Home in Dallas where he vanished from my life. Of all my old clients, I probably wonder about his ultimate fate more than others because of his outstanding intellectual and athletic promise. As we all know, the deck of life sometimes gets stacked unfairly, but one can hope that he has played out his hand in a positive and productive fashion. He would now be around fifty-five years of age.

Marcie, the Poetess

Marcie was thirty-three years old, Anglo, clinically obese, single, with a gentle streak and eighteen hospitalizations, seven for manic-depressive illness (now bipolar disorder) and eleven for schizophrenia. The fact that she had conflicting but overlapping diagnoses accentuates the fragile nature of the diagnostic criteria used in psychology and psychiatry. Then again, it may be possible to be both schizophrenic and bipolar or to alternate between the two conditions. If so, we use the label "Schizo-Affective Disorder."

When I first met Marcie, she was working around our operation as part of a treatment program created by our director. He figured, and rightly so, that any outside stimulation we could provide would be healthier than her sitting at home where she lived with her parents in between those multiple hospitalizations referred to in the preceding paragraph.

I assigned one of my students to work with Marcie on weight loss, among other things. At her peak, Marcie weighed 282 pounds and we figured it would not hurt her to shed a few of them. She dropped down to 264 pounds for a short while but skyrocketed back to 282 which piqued our interest, so I had the student follow her one day to see what she would do after getting paid for her work in our sheltered workshop. Marcia took her admittedly small weekly paycheck, maybe twenty-five dollars, to the Dairy Queen just down the street from our clinic. She spent every penny on cheeseburgers, French fries, and milk shakes, and in those days you could buy a boatload of burgers, fries, and shakes if you had that kind of money. I would estimate one could purchase maybe eight or ten cheeseburger baskets with fries and four of five milkshakes with twenty-five dollars.

My most salient memory of Marcie occurred early one Thursday afternoon. Upon arriving at the clinic, I noticed she was unusually giddy and giggly. The giddiness lasted for about a half hour, at which time she went into the restroom and cried for a while. She came out after a short stay and started giggling and acting silly once again. It was not long before she retired to the restroom for another crying jag. She was clearly in the early stages of a rapid cycling manic state which eventually got so out of control that by the end of the evening she had to be committed to the Austin State Hospital (ASH). Ed Wachholz committed Marcie and reported she was in such a delirious manic state at the hospital that she threw chairs, assaulted the male staff sexually, and generally was totally out of control, all 282 bipolar pounds of her.

The sad thing is that she was such a gentle soul when not victimized by her demons, playing the piano and writing poetry to while away what were clearly lonely hours. Marcie's poetry focused on her experiences as a mentally ill person, and I am taking the liberty of including one she generously gave me during one of her visits to the center. I have often kicked myself for not gathering up her work, editing it, and publishing it as a book. I make no claims to understand poetry and would not know a good poem if one slapped me up side the noggin, but I do know something about mental illness and I thought her perspectives were powerful and her pain palpable. Here is a sample poem written in 1965 and given to me a decade later:

The Institutionalized Pussycat

Marcie, 09-10-1965

I sit by the window at the start of each day
And watch Mama Kitty going her way
Her hair streaked with silver, her eyes clear as glass
You can tell at a moment—this girl's got class
What is she doing in a place like this?
Why she has a family, and a husband to miss
She roams the long thoroughfare midst bushes and trash
A forgotten inmate of a place known as ASH (Austin State Hospital)
But when she gain insight and finds life is authentic
Then she can start an out-kitten's clinic.

Other BWCCS Cases

Nearly a dozen other cases stand out from those five years with the BWCCS, and I will briefly synopsize each, beginning with six-year-old Sara the Silent.

Silent Sara, a Six-Year Old Mute

Sara was a first-grader referred by the school principal because of a total unwillingness to communicate with peers and teachers alike. Essentially, the only two people Sara would talk to in the entire world were her mother and maternal grandmother. No one else could elicit so much as a peep from her. She was beautiful, always dressed immaculately, and looked to be the picture of health. She had big, wistful, brown eyes that seemed to be hiding some deep, dark secrets, but the biggest problem was she would not talk, even to me. At our initial meeting, we sat and pretty much stared at each other in silence for the better part of an hour. I told my stupid, kid jokes; I acted like a clown; I stood on my head; I brought out my entire bag of silly, juvenile tricks, but to no avail. At one point, however, I spotted a flicker of light in those beautiful brown eyes when I asked if she had a dog. There was a visible change and you could see the wheels were turning as she engaged in some kind of cognitive activity, perhaps involving a canine friend. She reluctantly admitted with a nod that she had a dog, and when I asked his name, she smiled ever so slightly and said in a long, drawn out fashion, "Brownnnnie." She did not speak another word to me that day, and her father removed her from counseling after two sessions when he found out that she was seeing a crazy psychologist.

In talking with the mother, it seems for the majority of Sara's childhood, the two parents worked different shifts at the same place of employment. When the mother was working, the father provided child care for those eight hours and he demanded absolute silence from his baby girl during his "shift." He cleverly and systematically paired reinforcing the child for silence with punishment for anything resembling vocalization. Essentially, she spent most of her early childhood, as much as sixteen hours a day, counting bedtime, in silence, talking only when her mother was at home and the father working. Over a period of six years, she had become essentially mute, talking only to two people and only on occasion even with them. It was these eternal silent periods with the teacher and her peers that led to the referral.

In relating this case with my students, they have often asked why Child Protective Services (CPS) was not brought into the case. One big reason is that CPS case workers are overworked and underpaid and see far too many clients to be able to do their job as effectively as they would like. The horrors associated with failures of state and local agencies to protect the rights of children are a never-ending source of fodder for the front pages of our newspapers. In the case of Sara, even if one wanted to pursue charges, the fact that the child was beautiful, physically healthy, well-dressed, lived in a comfortable middle-class home, and had nary a bruise or cut on her body would make for a really tough conviction in a court of law. In the vast majority of clear-cut cases of abuse the child is returned to the home, so what is the likelihood a judge would remove this beautiful and outwardly healthy child from what appeared to be a nice home and place her in a foster placement? "Not a chance" is the likely answer.

Henry: A Bedwetter.

Henry, a fifth-grader was another school referral, primarily due to his indifference to academic matters. However, in the course of discussing the school difficulties with his mother, I found out Henry was a bedwetter or enuretic and almost never experienced a dry night. I told the mother of some past successes treating enuresis cases and received her permission to take on this gnarly case.

My esteemed colleague from my earliest A&M faculty days, Dr. Albert Casey, introduced me to a technological tool for treating enuresis known as Pants Alert. The device consists of an electronic noise (squawk) box and electrical lines that attach to leads inserted in the undergarments of the enuretic child. To get the Pants Alert operational, snap leads are strategically inserted on each side of the underwear at a place where the urinary flow is most likely to occur, then attached to the lines leading to the squawk box.

The Pants Alert is grounded in basic principles of conditioning and learning and assumes that the child has simply failed to properly acquire nocturnal bladder control. The typical adult has been conditioned over many years to respond to bladder pressure in the middle of the night, and simply gets up and goes to the bathroom when this signal occurs. The process usually plays out as follows in the case of the typical adult: The bladder signal is felt. The natural response is to assume it is time to get up anyway, so the person decides to grit his or her teeth for just a few more minutes of precious sleep. A few minutes later, the level of urgency has increased and there is no choice but to give in to the bladder pressure. To the sleepy person's dismay, a quick peek at the clock reveals that it is not time to get up at all, but rather three in the morning. The main point is that the person feels the pressure and responds to it appropriately, no matter how inconvenient the hour.

In the case of young bedwetters, they sleep so deeply that the signal from the bladder is missed, so the Pants Alert is designed to assist the conditioning process. When a few drops of urine pass between the snap leads, a signal is sent to the noise box and it emits a loud sound. This noise, in turn, prompts reflexive constriction of the bladder, thus limiting the amount of urine flow to a few drops. At this time, the child gets up, goes to the bathroom, changes underwear, and goes back to sleep in a dry condition.

In the process of getting background information on Henry, I learned that he and two male siblings had been adopted by the referring family. The mother was a housewife, the father a dentist, and they had raised two biological daughters, and when the older girls graduated and moved on, they decided to adopt these three wayward, troubled boys. Each of the boys had academic issues along with an assortment of behavioral difficulties, but only Henry had been referred so he was obviously the focus of my efforts.

When I tried to get permission to place Henry on Ritalin to facilitate the effectiveness of the Pants Alert device, the mother let me know in no uncertain terms, "You are not going to make a drug addict out of my son." She further explained that she had recently read somewhere that placing a child, such as Henry, on several cups of coffee a day would accomplish the same results as Ritalin, and she had done exactly that. The logic, of course, is that caffeine and Ritalin are both stimulants and should thus achieve the same calming results with children. I cannot speak for the reader, but I would hate to try to curtail my nocturnal urinary tendencies with a day-long regimen of strong, black coffee.

I also learned something even more critical to understanding Henry's situation while interviewing the mother. She was an evangelical, apocalyptic, hell-fire-and-damnation, Bible thumping, fire-breathing religious fanatic who spent her days proselytizing and passing out daily devotionals, religious tracts, and pamphlets. She truly believed to the core of her very existence in a punitive higher power that put us on earth to suffer on his behalf. She told me, "We were put on earth to suffer and it is my mission to see to it that my boys suffer. I can promise you they suffer in the name of that higher power." The boys went to church and begged for forgiveness (and deliverance from her, I suspect) every time the doors opened. They came home from school to do homework and chores, at which time they ate the evening meal, took baths, and went to bed. They were not allowed to have friends ("Friends teach children immoral, evil ways") and were prevented from getting involved in any of the school's extracurricular activities ("Sports and other activities are plots to subvert religious principles"). The children were put on earth to suffer, and she made it her mission to see that they did. She reassured the boys (and me) that the rewards were greatest in the after-life, and reserved mostly for those who suffered the most during their sin-filled, earthly stint. Is it any wonder that the boys had academic and behavioral problems?

Henry responded nicely to the Pants Alert regimen, and quickly experienced the requisite fourteen consecutive dry nights we set as a criterion for success. Then one day, Henry's mother reported he had lapsed back into his old ways, wetting the bed every night. In discussing this turn of events with Henry, he informed me that the Pants Alert system was actually working fine but he was intentionally unhooking the leads in the middle of the night, standing up, and urinating in the middle of his bed as a gesture of defiance directed at his mother. I could not help but feel that Henry had turned a big corner in his treatment. He had a grip on the enuresis issue and his defiance suggested to me a strength that might serve him well as he attempted to survive in such a pathologically hostile home environment.

I was able to get an unemployed (by choice) teacher to tutor Henry in his home on Mondays and he attended school the other four days of the week. His grades improved and the behavioral issues lessened in intensity but did not disappear entirely. The bedwetting had become pretty much a non-issue once I convinced him that continuing to defiantly urinate at inopportune or inappropriate times was not the best solution to his difficulties with his mother. The parents discontinued treatment at some point.

Tameka: Is There Such a Thing as a Zero IQ?

One mid-July day, our Director, Ed Wachholz, asked me to go over to the nearby Chapel Hill, maybe ten miles down Highway 290 in the direction of Houston, to certify a female child as mentally deficient. Once certified, she would thus be eligible for placement in a state school, most likely the facility in Brenham. Ed warned me before I left the office that the usual standard intelligence tests, the Wechsler Intelligence Scale for Children (WISC) or the Stanford-Binet, would not be necessary, and suggested I take along the Vineland Social Maturity Scale. The Vineland is used in circumstances where typical testing conditions do not apply, cases where the child is deaf, blind, paralyzed, or otherwise unable to respond for him- or herself. A loved one or knowledgeable caretaker assumes the role of respondent in these cases.

With Ed's friendly warning in mind, I jumped in my Nash Rambler Rogue (one of many mistakes I have made in my life) and headed for Chapel Hill. It took me a while to find the house as it was located in a rural area just outside the city. My problems locating it were compounded by suspicions among the locals that I might be a lawman or state or federal agent of some kind since I was wearing slacks, a dress shirt, and tie. Clearly, my motives were suspect in their eyes. In any case, I eventually found the house and immediately spotted children running hither, thither, and yon, spanning just about every age in one year increments from three to fourteen or fifteen. Some were on top of the house, others under it, and the remainder nearby. The home was a small frame structure, maybe five rooms, and adequate but looking a bit the worse for wear.

It was one of those July Texas scorchers, and the house had no air conditioning, so it was sweltering inside. After greeting and exchanging pleasantries with the woman of the house, I inquired about the whereabouts of the young lady I was to test and certify. The mother pointed to a room off the main living area, and when I entered it was obvious there was no need for an IQ test. The little girl was seven years old, weighed maybe seventeen pounds, and I later learned had been victimized by either meningitis or encephalitis, the mother could not remember which. The flies were so thick in the room they literally covered the child, and she could have been black, purple, or chartreuse and I would not have known the difference.

Tameka was so brain-damaged flies would crawl in one side of her mouth and out the other without response. Alternately (or concurrently), they would amble across her eyeballs without eliciting so much as a cursory blink on her part. It did not take a genius to figure out she was severely neurologically impaired but I did go through the motions of testing her, though I am not sure why. She could more or less accomplish two tasks on the Vineland. If your advocate or respondent says the person being tested can touch his or her thumb and forefinger together on command, he or she receives credit for that item. Also, if one can smile on command, there is a point for that act, too. The child could do both, though not on command, but I gave her credit anyway. This act of largesse, if you will, resulted in her having two-thirds of one IQ point. Her score was essentially zero and was by far the lowest I ever personally encountered.

In looking for the sources of the flies and various infectious diseases, it was noted the family disposed of their household garbage by opening the screen and dumping it outside whichever window was most receptive. Once the garbage became level with the window and no more could be accommodated, another window was chosen. Because the area adjacent to most windows was full, it was difficult to find a "friendly" place to dump the garbage. As you might guess, the flies absolutely adored this situation.

I am sure it depends on one's view of life, religion, morality, and so on, but I regard it as merciful that after enduring the endless intrusions related to obtaining the necessary medical, social work, and psychological certifications, the family decided not to institutionalize the child. Though I never heard, I suspect she probably died in six, twelve, maybe eighteen months, and that seemed merciful to me. Had she been institutionalized, the medical staff would have hyped her up on vitamins and nutritional supplements, possibly prolonging her life by years or even decades. I am not sure living a relatively long life in a vegetative state is life at all, so I applaud the family's decision to keep the child at home, irrespective of their reasons for doing so.

As I was leaving the premises, I asked the mother if she understood why several of her other children were also mentally deficient. She told me she was being punished by God for some unknown sins. I thought to myself that there might be a much more parsimonious and defensible explanation for the plight of her children; it is called flies, filth, germs, and high fever disease in infancy!

Travis the Troublemaker.

Travis was a most fascinating child but a client for only a brief time. He, like numerous other child clients, had been referred by a school principal, this time for misbehaving in the classroom and taking a lackadaisical approach to his school work. When he came into my office for the first time, I was immediately struck by his bright-eyed, handsome appearance, and amiable nature. He was quite intelligent, scoring in the mid-140's on the WISC. As a result of his considerable intellectual uptake, school represented no challenge and he was bored by it all, hence the acting out in class. In talking with Travis, I was able to piece together a portrait of his home life that was loving but fraught with inconsistent discipline. The mother supported the boy's take on things, stating that she and her husband started out when Travis was born with lax discipline they hoped would foster feelings of self-worth. After four years of very little discipline, the boy had become a hellion, so the parents switched to a draconian regimen of corporal punishment and other negative sanctions. This switch in reward and punishment regimen accomplished little, and the behaviors leading to the school referral were traceable to this inconsistent discipline. Travis the Terrible summed it up nicely for me when he said, "My parents are good people, they really are, but they do not have the slightest idea about how to raise children. They want to be successful but they don't know how to raise children like my brother and me." His assessment was right on target; they were good people who really did not have the foggiest notion about what it took to be effective parents.

He also told me that he resented his mother's attempts at discipline and would engage in rebellious behavior just to get back at her. He once said, "I know how to torture my mother. All I have to do is sucker punch my little brother in the stomach. He will scream and go running to her, and she will come running with belt in hand to teach me a lesson." He said another thing he did to greatly aggravate his mother was call her name when banished to his room for rule violations, both major and trivial. He said, "She thinks she punishes me by banishing me to my bedroom to do school homework. First of all, how much homework does a first grader really have, and secondly, how much time does it take a reasonably smart kid like me to do homework? I do it all at school."

"When she sends me to my room, I putter around for a few minutes, and then start this ritual where I call out to her with ever-increasing volume. I quietly and succinctly call out 'Mother.' The next time I call out 'Mother' I increase the length of the word as well as the volume. Each time I do this, the length and volume are raised. Finally, when the noise reaches its loudest level, she throws open the bedroom door and give me another spanking. It works every time, and she has never caught on to what I was doing. She is a good person and wants to be a good mother, but has no idea how to go about it."

Travis may seem to be a wise guy but I thought his analysis was spot on. The parents were good people in serious need of parenting skills training. I approached them about going in for counseling or training, but the father responded by pulling Travis from our clinic when he learned I was a psychologist. No kid of his was going to see a shrink!

Chareka, a Schizophrenic.

Chareka was a direct care staff member ("ward attendant" in the old days, I suppose), at the Brenham State School and was referred to us by the Superintendent of that facility, Dr. Jimmy Haskins, because she was wreaking havoc among her co-workers and administrators of the facility. In small Texas towns such as Brenham, there is often a black sub-community with its own distinct set of folkways, mores, and customs. It seems that Chareka would hang out at night in the drinking establishments in the black community, regaling her audiences with rumors of marital infidelity among her co-workers at the state school. These rumors led to several confrontations on the grounds of the facility, and Dr. Haskins had grown tired of men showing up and threatening to seek revenge on his staff for "crimes" they may or may not have committed.

When I met Chareka for the first time, she hallucinated actively, carrying on animated conversations with imaginary friends in a corner of my office. In the course of our initial interview, she told me she was the only female employee at the state school with an IQ over a hundred. As well, she claimed to be the only sexually straight woman working there. The latter assertion was apparently untrue as I later learned from reliable sources Chareka was an active bisexual who also had several illegitimate children. She also told me she fought a battle every Sunday trying to keep her minister from taking advantage of her sexually in his quarters after church. When I asked his age, she said, "Oh, he's eighty-six." Chareka was subsequently referred to the mental hospital in Austin and I never saw her again.

Miss Marlene: Borderline Personality Disorder.

Miss Marlene was a thrice-divorced woman in her early thirties, almost certainly a borderline personality. I only saw her maybe three times, and the third session ended up being our last. Marlene was attractive, sexy and seductive, justifiably proud of her shapely, toned figure, and well-aware of her effect on men. She was gazing pensively out the window of my office during that ill-fated third session, and I asked her what was going through her mind. Her response went pretty much as follows, "I want you to take me to a motel and I want you to take off all my clothes and put your hands all over my body. We can do whatever you want after that. I promise I will make you happy." I am no paragon of virtue but the counseling relationship is sacrosanct and should never be used as a forum for forming sexual liaisons. Given the new parameters she introduced into the counseling relationship, I thanked Marlene for her kind thoughts and politely suggested that perhaps it would be best if she started seeing our director, Ed Wachholz. Ed was much older than me, maybe sixty, and I thought she might be more likely to maintain a counseling relationship with him. She declined my referral and was never heard from again.

Jasmine: A Schizophrenic Prostitute.

Jasmine was in her late thirties and seen as an eccentric, town character by the locals. She walked the streets of Brenham almost every day wearing a World War II wool trench coat, genuflecting and engaging in religious crossing rituals each time she passed by city hall. Weather was no obstacle; it could be freezing or a hundred degrees in the shade, and she would still wear that old itchy, scratchy trench coat. I recommended to Ed Wachholz that we institutionalize her for a time, not so much for her mental condition but more in hopes she would get some dental care. Her teeth were rotting off at the gum level and she had to have been in considerable pain. When we finally got her to agree to go to the mental hospital in Austin, Jasmine got in the car wearing her ritual trench coat. She also brought a rubber snake along, wrapping it around her neck for security, I suppose, for the ninety-minute trip. Our client and her snake companion entertained each other all the way to Austin, engaging in animated conversation about who knows what.

Fred: An Epileptic.

Fred experienced a severe adverse reaction to the basic childhood vaccination against diphtheria, whooping cough, and tetanus, or the so-called DPT series, and became severely intellectually disabled and epileptic as a result. His seizures, the big ones, the *grand mal* variety, were never brought under control by the standard anti-convulsant medications (i.e., Dilantin, Phenobarbital, Valproate) and he seldom went an entire day without experiencing an epileptic episode. There were many days in which he would suffer endless seizures, as many as a dozen in a row on one occasion. Fred was dearly loved by his mother and sister who constantly doted on him throughout his short life. He died in his late twenties of complications from his seizures.

Edgar: A Chronic Schizophrenia.

Edgar was a barber by training, but could not hold a job for any length of time because of his auditory hallucinations. In an effort to block out the mysterious voices that haunted his every moment, he would put objects in his ears; match sticks, gum, gum wrappers, cigarette filters, you name it. It often appeared as if he had rat nests attached to each side of his head. Talk about an idiosyncrasy that stereotypes you as eccentric or worse!

Eleanor: A Case of Schizophrenia in Remission.

Eleanor would only agree to work in our sheltered workshop if one of my students would take her to a hairdresser to have her eyebrows plucked. She absolutely loved going to a salon once every two weeks, and the eyebrow plucking became a ritual for Eleanor and the student assigned to her that semester. She would do anything we asked if she could just get those brows plucked every so often.

Luke: My Lenny.

Luke was in his thirties, intellectually disabled and probably borderline psychotic. I only talked to him once, but he was memorable. He was a giant of a man borrowed from Steinbeck's novel *Of Mice and Men,* maybe six feet seven, a muscular 275 pounds or thereabouts, who carried a giant walking stick artfully carved from a large tree limb. He could have taken me out with one swing but fortunately was a docile, easy-going, gentle giant.

Interesting Clients from Other Venues

Brenham State School

I served as the consulting psychologist for the Brenham State School (BSS) for roughly the same five years that I worked for Ed Wachholz at the BWCCS. During that time, I had the distinct pleasure of getting to know a number of outstanding young BSS staff psychologists, all master's degree holders, and most of them Aggies. Their professionalism, collective ingenuity, and attention to subtle nuances in treating their clients were constant sources of joy and wonderment.

At that time, BSS was a treatment facility under the jurisdiction of the Texas Department of Mental Health and Mental Retardation (TDMHMR). In 2004, TDMHMR was dissolved and mental retardation treatment became the responsibility of the Texas Department of Aging and Disability Services (DADS). As a result of this change and subsequent deliberations, state schools no longer exist in name, and are now called State Supported Living Centers (SSLC'S). Thus, the Brenham facility is now abbreviated not as BSS but as BSSLC. Brenham was one of thirteen such schools in Texas when it opened its doors for the first clients in 1974, and was administered most capably by the aforementioned Dr. Jimmy Haskins and his able and affable Deputy Superintendent, Dr. Keith Stewart. Haskins and Stewart hired me to consult with the master's level psychologists, to ensure that there was no systematic abuse of clients taking place, and to sign off on psychological evaluations. The latter function required the presence of a licensed psychologist and they had no such person on staff other than me.

Self-Destructive Serena. Thanks to the ingenuity of the staff psychologists, I was able to witness a most interesting and successful treatment plan involving a thirteen-year old intellectually disabled female. The client had been under observation at John Sealy Hospital in Galveston for a month before being referred to BSS for follow-up treatment related to severe and unrelenting self-abuse. In this instance, the self-abuse consisted primarily of slaps to the face, and some of the blows were violent enough to send rivulets of saliva flying through the air.

To get a baseline on the extent of the self-abusive behavior, direct care staff members were equipped with clickers and instructed to record the number of times the client hit herself in the face. The staff worked three eight-hour shifts, so the client was followed literally around the clock for seventy-two consecutive hours. When the three-day observation period was concluded, the tally of self-abusive slaps to the face reached 7,200. This was 2,400 per day, or one hundred times per hour. To put it another way, she slapped herself silly almost twice per minute.

After the initial baseline phase, she was placed in soft ankle and wrist restraints which did not cut off circulation but were sufficiently restrictive to keep her confined to bed. Each time she pulled at the restraints, these acts were also counted as self-destructive incidents. Again, the three-day tally was 7,200. Thus, in the free environment as well as the restrained one, she was self-abusive to the tune of 2,400 acts per day.

The young staff psychologists decided to treat this case with as many positive features as they could find while relying as little as possible on aversive or punitive techniques. For a variety of reasons, some political and others philosophical, they wanted to demonstrate the efficacy of positive reinforcement in the treatment of a very serious, deeply entrenched behavior. Through a process of observation, trial and error, and some degree of serendipity, the psychologists determined that the client responded strongly to at least two rewards or reinforcers. One was country and western music; real country music, not the fluff that passes for C&W today. She perked up mightily at the sound of Bob Wills, Merle Haggard, Willie Nelson, George Jones, and the like. She also loved to have her head rubbed gently which seemed to induce a state of relaxation, and that became our second reinforcing procedure. Thus, the treatment consisted of little more than country music and gentle head-rubbing. Any time she relaxed and did not strain at her cuffs, an attendant flipped on the country music and commenced the gentle stroking. If she pulled at the cuffs, off went the music and the gentle stroking would stop.

At the end of every hour and forty-five minutes, she was released from her restraints for fifteen minutes to stretch her legs and use the bathroom if needed. It was assumed that letting her walk around and use the bathroom would also be reinforcing and supportive of the other positive incentives being used. During these brief walks, she was accompanied by two attendants, one on each side, who held on to her wrists. If she made a move toward her face with a hand or knee, the attendants were instructed to stop her with authority and put firm pressure on her wrist bones as a reminder that she was behaving unacceptably. If she relaxed, the walking would commence once again.

This simple regimen went on for six weeks or thereabouts, with a steady diminution in the frequency and the severity of the self-abusive acts, so much so that the restraints were removed and she was returned to the general population. Everything rocked along nicely for twenty-eight days or so, at which time she showed some minor agitation and a repeat of the abusive pattern to the tune of four hundred slaps per day. Even then, the slaps were much milder in intensity and seemed to be more stimulatory than abusive. After three days or so, the self-abuse stopped, only to be resurrected some twenty-eight days later. It continued for roughly three days and disappeared. The third recurrence a month later resulted in an epiphany for the male psychologists who had observed the pattern for about ninety days. They had inadvertently configured a predictable menstrual cycle that lasted for three days every twenty-eight days, though they were largely unaware of it until it slapped them in the face, if you will pardon the pun.

This treatment program was one of the simplest and most creative I had ever witnessed, and my role was totally that of interested bystander. The regimen was one hundred percent the creation of those imaginative young master's degree psychologists, and I have kicked myself for years for not writing up this piece of ingenuity for one of the psychology journals focusing on treatment. My hat still goes off to those sensitive and creative young professionals.

Central Brazos Valley MHMR Center

Several years before I began consulting with the two Brenham facilities, I worked with the Brazos Valley Mental Health-Mental Retardation Authority, primarily as the unpaid supervisor of my own students who were volunteering at the MHMR treatment facility in Bryan. As I watched the students work so diligently with their clients, it dawned on me that it should be possible for them to receive course credit at A&M for their efforts. This epiphany led me to create Psychology 484, Field Experiences, and thousands of students have received course credit for their involvement in a variety of activities and settings over the past five decades.

Lobotomized Larry. One of the students under my supervision was a Psychology major named Robbie Young. To protect Robbie's identity in the past, I always used an alias when referring to this case in my classes for fear someone might recognize his name. After maybe fifteen years of telling this story, I decided I could safely get away with using his name. The first time I did so, a coed came by after class to let me know that Robbie Young was her much older half-brother. So much for unfounded assumptions!

I always thought Robbie Young's efforts spoke well for his creativity and ingenuity though his failure to use time-honored or more orthodox treatment techniques could have been problematic. One of his assigned clients for the semester was a middle-aged man who had been lobotomized in the late 1940's or early 1950's at the height of the obsession on the part of some members of the medical community with psychosurgery. Perhaps 100,000 patients were lobotomized from the mid-1930's to the mid-1950's, though little if any good came from it. Considered by many to be a method of last resort to be used only in the worst cases, psychosurgery was often applied in situations where it was inappropriate and ethically indefensible. For example, one of my students of thirty-five years ago came by after a tour of the Austin State Hospital, wanting to know if I would help him track down his mother who he literally had never seen. He knew that she had been diagnosed with postpartum depression following his birth and subsequently committed to the Austin State Hospital for treatment. While postpartum depression is a serious disorder, performing a lobotomy on someone for a condition that typically responds well to far less invasive procedures is nothing less than a criminal act. I assured the student that he would not need my help to locate her but I did urge him to carefully consider the repercussions of his pursuit. To wit, I said to him: "She will not know you and you will not like what you see." I never heard whether or not he sought her out but I am guessing his curiosity about his ancestry ultimately won out. I must confess it would have been tempting to look her up if she had been my mother.

Let's get back to Robbie and his client who was forty-ish and living in the LaSalle, a "flophouse" hotel in downtown Bryan (which has since been nicely restored as part of the city's hugely successful downtown revitalization plan). The client could be seen at all hours of the day imitating television comedian Tim Conway's well-known senility shuffle, whiling away the hours and days putzing along at the pace of a soporific snail.

In one of two acts of creativity, Robbie ran a simple *in vivo* experiment to help determine if his client's slowness was due to brain damage or the result of environmental deprivation which lent itself to a "Why be in a hurry if there is nowhere to go" mentality. To test his hypothesis, Robbie pushed his client in front of an oncoming truck in downtown Bryan. He did it in such a way that retrieval could be made at the last second, though the client was not so sure. It turns out the guy could move like a gazelle, so the slowness due to brain damage hypothesis was rejected. Robbie then decided that if his client could move, he could get a job, a nice, middle-class American value. Eventually, Robbie found jobs for Larry at three small downtown restaurants where he washed dishes, swept the premises, ran errands, and the like. He was fed at two of the restaurants and made enough money each month from the third that he no longer needed his welfare check. Creative act number one accomplished! If the guy could run, the guy could work! If he could work, he could get off welfare!

A year after he graduated, Robbie passed through town and apprised me of "creative act" number two. It seems that around the mid-point of the semester Robbie was assigned to Larry, we experienced an unforeseen mini-crisis at the MHMR Center. Our problem was that Larry began making passes at the nurses, secretaries, and my female students to the point we had to temporarily restrict his accessibility to the women in the building. Larry had never been a problem before, so the suddenness and incongruity of his misbehavior were striking.

Robbie's year-old revelation yielded considerable after-the-fact insight into the genesis of the problem. It seems that Robbie and his buddies were sitting around the dormitory one night talking about this, that, and the other, and the topic of Larry and his lack of interest in women came up. It seemed to the younger, more hormonal college guys that this just was not right…they reasoned that a forty-year old guy should be interested in women. They decided his lack of interest in women, like his slowness afoot, was a function of psychosocial deprivation and/or lack of opportunity rather than brain damage, and proceeded to put that hypothesis to a test. The guys chipped in some money and arranged to transport Larry to the famous house of prostitution in LaGrange, the Chicken Ranch, which later became the focus of Larry McMurtry's famous play, *The Best Little Whorehouse in Texas*.

As noted elsewhere, there were few women at A&M until the mid- to late-1960's and sampling the wares at the Chicken Ranch at least once had become a tradition and was required if you wanted to call yourself a real Aggie. I suspect the Chicken Ranch sexual experience was more an urban legend than a real tradition, and obviously not enforceable, but it took on a life of its own as a part of campus folklore.

So the unholy alliance, Robbie, his friends, and Larry, motored to LaGrange. I do not know precisely what transpired at the Chicken Ranch but Larry certainly came back from the visit with a renewed fascination with females. Ah, Robbie, I never had a gray hair until I met you! However, based on some of the things he tried with Larry, I would predict that Robbie Young is a successful psychologist though hopefully more orthodox in the application of, "creative" treatment strategies.

The Community

Occasionally, those of us providing mental health services in the old days (The 1960's and 1970's) would be contacted by local citizens looking for help with a variety of problems. The following case of enuresis was an eye-opener for me because of the availability of new technology to treat the problem. This case is where I got the idea to try the technology a few years later with the aforementioned Henry the Bedwetter while working at the counseling service in Brenham.

Mimi, a Six-Year Old Bedwetter. I received a call late one evening from a single mother of three who was working as an assistant to a university administrator. She was upset because of her inability to get a handle on her oldest daughter's persistent bedwetting. The behavior occurred on an almost nightly basis and had not responded to any of the random interventions the mother had employed.

The precipitating factor that led to the call was a visit from a door-to-door salesman who was hawking an enuresis treatment that pretty much guaranteed success but at a relatively high price (around $500) for a single working mother. I was vaguely aware of the treatment system the salesman was promoting, and as near as I could tell from reading their promotional materials, it appeared to be based on solid psychological theory, research, and practice. I assured the mother that her visitor was probably not a charlatan, but I also told her that a colleague and I would do the same thing for one-third the price using the Pants Alert device mentioned earlier in the case of Henry. Because children typically sleep quite deeply, I asked the mother if we could temporarily put her daughter on a small dose of Ritalin, the drug most commonly prescribed for hyperactivity in children. Because of the stimulant properties of Ritalin, it energizes the child's nervous system, thus keeping the child from sleeping at such a deep level which, in turn, makes him or her more responsive to bladder pressure.

A male undergraduate Psychology major was assigned to the case for support. In order to get some practice in administering intelligence tests, he received permission from the mother to run a WISC on Mimi. She scored 140, a statistically rare level of intellectual functioning, in the upper one percent of the American population. This same student visited Mimi several times a week, talked to her about school and life, and generally served as a supportive big brother. He also rewarded her with small gifts for certain numbers of dry nights.

As was the case with Henry, we predetermined that fourteen dry nights would constitute successful treatment, and in six weeks or so, Mimi achieved that standard. Unfortunately, at least in terms of the treatment, the mother remarried about the same time the procedure was deemed successful. In a matter of moments, Mimi went from being the oldest child of three to the middle child of five. She had some temporary adjustment problems associated with these changes, and one was recurrence of the bedwetting pattern. To top things off, the family moved to New York before we were able to deal with the problem a second time. Hopefully, the mother gained valuable experience and insights about her daughter's enuresis and was able to find someone to treat Mimi in the reconfigured family structure and new home state.

I Meet Judy Webb LeUnes

"You give little when you give of your possessions.
It is when you give of yourself that you truly give."

Khalil Gibran (1883-1931), Lebanese philosopher, poet, and writer

"Women who seek to be equal with men lack ambition."

Timothy Leary, Professor

The 1970's were the most interesting of times and I probably enjoyed the decade from age thirty to forty the most of any in my entire life. They were exciting times; I was trying to help raise four children, I taught my classes with enthusiasm (and still do), gave the university's "publish or perish" mandate my best shot, and consulted here and there with various mental health and criminal justice agencies. I fished for bass, dabbled at golf, played thousands of softball games, and ran three miles a day Monday through Friday almost without fail for thirty-five years. In the midst of all this to-do and tumult, I met a young woman named Judy Kay Webb. That was back in the good old days when you could still have twenty-four students in a regular class instead of the current norm of several hundred. My daughter, Natalie, teaches in the Mays Business School, and typically has over four hundred students in each section of her introductory classes in Accounting. I cannot imagine such a situation in my wildest dreams, though I suppose teaching 450 is not much different than the 215 I sometimes am assigned to educate in the big lecture hall, Room 337, in the Psychology Building. We crank them out of A&M in a robotic, mechanical, cookie-cutter fashion and I sometime wonder if they are really getting an education. A degree? Yes! An education? Probably not, in a number of cases! I would estimate that as many as ninety percent of the students here at A&M get no individual attention from a professor in their entire four- or five-year stay.

Judy and I met quite by accident one day shortly after the semester started at the water fountain on the second floor of Nagle Hall. I held the button down while she drank, she thanked me, and we went our separate ways. Though I had no way of knowing it at the time, Judy had been in the Miss Texas Pageant when she was eighteen, and had the pretty face and lean body one might expect of a "beauty queen."

From this humble beginning, Judy and I developed a friendship that flourished over the next five years and culminated in us getting married in 1979.

JUDY AND ALL-TIME FAVORITE DOG, HEY DUDE!

School Marm

Judy got her teaching degree in 1976, the Centennial Class, paying for most of her education by waiting tables at TJ's and Pelican's Wharf, two extremely popular College Station bar/restaurants of the 1970's. After graduation, she took a teaching job in Hearne ISD, which I will talk about at some length later. She taught there for four unforgettable years, and then spent the next twenty-six with the College Station Independent School District, mostly teaching fifth graders. Judy was cited for outstanding teaching on several occasions, and with good reason. She was damn good at it!

She has always been a vocal force for teacher rights, and was able to put that advocacy into action as President of the College Station Education Association (CSEA) chapter which is as close as Texas gets to having a teacher's union. Judy was also appointed in the 1990's to serve on an important committee focusing on teacher preparation for the National Education Association (NEA) in Washington, DC. This appointment required her to be in DC four or five times a year during a five-year period, and the NEA experiences there dovetailed nicely with her long-term involvement in educational affairs in College Station and Austin.

For a couple of years after prematurely retiring in 2004 at the young age of fifty-one due to quirks in the Social Security law, she served as a Consultant on a federal grant program sponsored by the University of Texas. This consultancy eventually ran out and Judy formed her own educational consulting company known as Higher Expectations for All. She has since consulted with school districts in Caldwell, Calvert, Hearne, Kingsville, Snook, and Somerville. She also consulted with a faculty research group at A&M in need of someone external to the university with an understanding of public education, and she certainly is eminently qualified in that regard.

Community Servant

Judy has also served her community well. She acted as a volunteer counselor for the Rape Crisis Center, now known as the Sexual Assault Resource Center, and was a member of their Board of Directors for several years. She was President of the College Station Parks and Recreation Board for eight years, and served in the Board of Directors for the Aggieland Humane Society, the last few years of her term as President. She served a two-year term as President of the Pride Community Center Board, a local GLBTQ organization, a somewhat unique role for a heterosexual. As well, she served for several years as the only Anglo on the steering committee for the Bryan Blues Festival which is held every June.

In 2006, she started her signature event, Wiener Fest™, to raise money for homeless and unwanted animals. Wiener Fest™ is a celebration going into its twelfth year in 2018, and is built around dachshund races and what she calls "Wanna-Be-A-Wiener" races for any breed other than a dachshund. The event is held in October each year, and features a costume contest, races, raffles, fun runs for dogs, and other activities. Races are seventy feet in length and take place on $2,500 worth of carpet donated by the local Home Depot store. Wiener Fest™ was modeled after the immensely successful event in Buda, Texas, which typically attracts six hundred dogs (all Dachshunds). Wiener Fest™ is one of the largest races of its kind, with three to four hundred dogs, one hundred vendors, four hundred volunteers (mostly A&M students), and several thousand spectators.

DACHSHUNDS KICKING UP CHALK, WIENER FEST

In 2015, she served on the board of Health For All, a non-profit operation providing services to people without means to pay for medical care. Local physicians and nurses staff the operation on a volunteer basis. In an effort to bring in some money for the operation, Judy created an activity known as "Bra Art." The idea was that men and women would decorate bras, display them for a month at the Village Café in downtown Bryan, and ultimately auction them off at a gala celebration replete with food, live music, belly dancers, a silent auction, and the bra auction itself. Bra Art just completed its third year in 2017 and somewhere between $75,000 and $100,000 has been raised to support Health for All.

In 2016, she and a co-founder created Brazos Valley Fashion Week, with help from a local talent agent, and raised $40,000 for a local park, Fun For All Playground, which is being built to serve disabled children.

For all of the preceding and other activities too numerous to be mentioned in this humble little document, Judy was named The Eagle's Reader's Choice Volunteer of the Year as voted on by the readership. Volunteer of the year in 2015 and 2017, and she finished second in 2016. As additional recognition for her efforts on behalf of the community, she received the Jefferson Award in 2015, the highest honor one can receive in the US for community activism. That award led to her being sent to Washington, DC, for a three-day stay capped off at a gala recognition ceremony on the final night. Approximately five dozen community activists and volunteers were recognized in what the sponsors, in a moment of hyperbole, in DC call "the Nobel Prize for Community Service."

BRAZOS VALLEY FASHION WEEK, 2016

2015 JEFFERSON AWARD CEREMONY, WASHINGTON, DC

Judy as Politician

Judy's energy is boundless, and her passionate concern for the welfare of children, teachers, and animals is a thing to behold. She ran for the Texas House of Representatives, District 14, as a Democrat in 2011 to fill the unexpired term of Fred Brown, and was opposed by three Republican candidates, all of whom were local business owners, and a young, inexperienced, underfunded Libertarian. District 14 is small geographically, confined to the majority of Brazos County with a couple of small exceptions. It made for comparatively easy campaigning, travel-wise, particularly when compared with District 12 which contains small parts of Brazos County but extends north to Hearne, Mart, Marlin, and Waco and to the east in Groesbeck and Mexia.

We found a consensus among most astute political observers in Austin which suggested a Democrat cannot get elected in Brazos County because of the mindless, brain-dead, straight-ticket voting on the part of the ultra-right and ultra-light, ultra-conservative and ultra-religious inhabitants of Bryan and College Station. No Democrat has won a race in Brazos County at the state level since 1985, and that person was local attorney Neeley Lewis who got elected to the Texas House for one term. The only other successful Brazos County Democrat of any significance was the many-times elected and now retired District Attorney, Bill Turner. We believed that Judy was grounded and charismatic enough to transcend the prevailing conservative zeitgeist, but as things unfolded, it is clear we underestimated the mindless intransigency of the Republican voters. In retrospect, the voters of Brazos County opted for partisanship over real representation.

JUDY POLITICAL CAMPAIGN SLOGANS, 2011-2012

Due to an unanticipated quirk that took place the day of the elections, Judy was knocked out of the second place position, and this caused her to miss the runoff. It seems that a week before the election, early voting and straw polls conducted under the auspices of the Texas Farm Bureau had her running second to one of the Republican candidates. At about that time, the fourth place Republican, in a fit of desperation, initiated a vicious mail-out attack on the top candidate, and when Election Day rolled around, her support base shrunk by about fifty percent. Those voters who abandoned her sinking ship essentially voted for the third place candidate, also a Republican, because they were much opposed to voting for number one and they certainly were not going to vote for the Democrat. This switch in allegiances vaulted number three, John Raney, ahead of number two, Judy and into the runoff which he won handily. The original front-runner still to this day believes his runoff loss was a function of Judy getting her supporters to vote for the ultimate winner, the original third place candidate. In reality, I can honestly say she stayed above the fray and supported no one. I think the original number three was seen as a much safer, non-threatening candidate, and thus got the votes needed to win from his Republican friends and perhaps a few of Judy's original supporters.

Undaunted, she announced for the position again in the 2012 November election, and ran another busy, high profile campaign against staggering odds. She was able to get forty percent of the vote, a tribute to her campaign skills and local acceptance as a leader. It was more or less a moral victory to receive 15,000 votes in this district. It is a sad state of affairs knowing she was asked by many to run as a Republican which would have virtually guaranteed her election. That may or may not be true, but there is probably some validity there.

Shortly after that second failed attempt, Judy was talking after a meeting with the four of the most powerful administrators at A&M, and three went on record verbally about how disappointed they were that she was not representing the university in Austin. Ever the political animal, then President Bowen Loftin stayed above the fray, not giving any indication of his feelings about the issue.

Cancer Raises its Ugly Head

In November of 2015, Judy was operated on for squamous cell cancer of the head, a procedure she had been putting off for months due to her incredibly busy schedule and a certain feeling of invincibility, or the idea that bad things only happen to other people. That decision as it turns out was quite disastrous, for the cancer reemerged in October of 2016 and was diagnosed as squamous cell head and neck cancer. There was a spot on top of her head and cells had moved along the left side of her head and then settled in two lymph glands on the neck. Various exams and scans indicated the cancers had not metastasized and were confined to the head and neck, which of course was good news.

After much initial deliberation, an operation was deemed too problematic (dangerous) so she began chemotherapy and radiation to eradicate the cancerous cells. Five weeks and seven chemotherapies and thirty-seven radiation treatments later, she was pronounced in remission early in 2017. She actually had six chemotherapy treatments for the final one was cancelled for fear it would be fatal because she was in such a weakened condition from the other chemo and radiation sessions.

We had heard of the horrors of chemotherapy and radiation, but words cannot begin to convey just how horrific the treatment regimen would be. Judy was fine for about three weeks but the effects of the treatment set in during the fourth week and my daughter Katie and I had to drive her to the cancer clinic after that. Treatment ceased on December 6 and Judy had to fight for her life for the next several months due to the chemo and radiation side-effects.

She endured two fourteen-day hospitalizations, necessitated by vomiting and resultant starvation which, in turn, caused potentially fatal irregularities in a number of electrolytes that, among other things, regulate heartbeat. We lived with the specter of a heart attack for two weeks in December when she was hospitalized in the coronary critical care unit of St. Joseph's Hospital in Bryan. For the next eight weeks or so, she was not able to retain any food and eventually lost sixty pounds (She got down to ninety-eight pounds before being placed on an appetite stimulant by Dr. Scott Goble, her radiologist). That drug performed wonders and she has a healthy appetite and now weighs around one hundred twenty pounds.

Conservatively, I would say she took in about one cup of solid food in December and January. Most of what she was able to get down came right back up in most cases. After a time out of St. Joseph's, I had to take her back because of malnutrition. That resulted in a second fourteen-day stay. During those two weeks, she ate bananas, a small portion of chicken pot pie, a third cup of squash and zucchini, and a few other food items. She also had a few chocolate milk shakes and several small bottles of grape and cranberry juice. I could only see painfully slow progress and it was obvious we were in it for the long haul regarding nutrition and, ultimately, her life.

Eating is not much of a priority when you feel bad, have no appetite, lose your taste buds, have extremely limited ability to swallow due to the absence of saliva, and throw up whatever you do eat. I never knew the importance of salivary glands in helping to swallow food. I guess I never gave it much of a thought really.

While Judy was hospitalized those two times, twelve doctors of varying specialties weighed in on the vomiting and none had the foggiest notion about the source of the problem. The prevailing hypothesis was that Judy was a treatment outlier, that one to five percent of cancer patients for whom the effects of chemotherapy and radiation linger much, much longer than usual. I am reasonably positive that the outlier hypothesis is the best explanation, but we will never really know.

On a romantic note, Judy and I celebrated our thirty-eighth anniversary on January 13, 2017, in the oncology unit of the hospital by sharing broccoli and cheese soup from Panera Bread. Pretty hard to beat soup in a hospital for an anniversary celebration! On a less romantic note, Judy's hospital bill for the cardiac critical care treatment was $71,000 plus change and the second hospitalization was even more expensive than the first. Overall, her treatment bill was at least $200,000. Fortunately, our share of that medical bill is manageable (barely). It sure gives you pause when you think about what people do when they have no insurance. This situation only serves to reinforce my belief that our system of medical care is broken with no fix in sight. It also reinforces my feeling that little will get done about medical care by our folks in Washington who spend most of their time bitching about Obamacare while providing no viable alternative. Our elected representatives are far more preoccupied with solidifying their fiefdoms and raising money for their next re-election campaigns than they are with doing the right thing. This situation creates an environment of disenchantment that allows an emotionally unbalanced person like Donald Trump to become President. I am partially consoled by knowing in my heart of hearts that the man will quit the job due to boredom, be impeached for incompetence, or simply not be re-elected for a second term. I do not think there is any way his tenure will end well.

THE LEUNES'ES CAN DO IT!

Lucky Me

It has been my good fortune to have been Judy's husband. She is a good woman and a fun wife, and a fantastic mother to our two children. She is also very good to my four oldest children and is known affectionately as the "wicked stepmother." She became a grandmother for the first time on July 11, 2011, thanks to our daughter, Katie Elizabeth, and her husband Joel Cryer. The granddaughter's name is Ashlynn Grace Cryer. Ashlynn was joined on March 12, 2013, by little sister, Kendall Nicole.

LESLIE, NATALIE, CHAY, AMY, KATIE, LYNDON CIRCA 2010

The LeUnes Children

"Never raise your hand to your children—it leaves your midsection unprotected."

Robert Orben, Author, Humorist

I have been blessed to have six happy, healthy, and reasonably well-educated and accomplished children, and all have been or will be mentioned from time to time throughout this narrative. However, I would like to devote a little more space to each of them here and now. Our family doctor, the now-retired John Hall, once remarked that the files of my first four children were the thinnest in his practice, and what parent would not be pleased with that revelation. Those same four children are from my first marriage to Barbara, and Judy is the mother of the last two. Both wives always got along very well prior to Barbara's death, due no doubt to a bond forged from having a common enemy, and the six children are quite good friends. All in all, they were easy children to raise and a joy to be around as adults. Judy and I always look forward to family get-togethers for they are always fun-filled events.

I do not get together with the first four as much as I would like but we have a great time when we do meet up. I cannot argue with my fate at all; they have children, jobs, and full lives, and I would not have it any other way. I have been blessed to have those children and I thank them for the eternal kindness and respect they have accorded their father.

FIRST FAMILY-WIFE BARBARA AND CHILDREN, 1973

Leslie Katherine LeUnes Stiteler. Leslie turned fifty-five years of age on September 28, 2017. She has worked as waitress, restaurant manager, and real estate agent, and is married to Craig Stiteler, an Aggie, who owns his own building construction firm in the greater metropolitan Houston area. When Craig and Leslie met many years ago, he was dating his high school sweetheart and former *Dancing With the Stars* notable, Paula Abdul, and I guess Leslie stole him away. I once told Craig he made a good marital decision but probably would have been better off financially had he stuck with Ms. Abdul. Leslie and Craig have two boys, Dylan and Blake. Dylan had a good run as a soccer player, entered A&M in the fall of 2011, studied abroad in Costa Rica where he completed the requirements for his dual degrees in Political Science and Spanish, and graduated from A&M in August, 2015. He is currently employed in Houston in commercial real estate.

NATALIE WEDDING CIRCA 1985

LESLIE AND NATALIE, JUNIOR HIGH CHEERLEADERS

Child number two, Blake, is an interesting young man. As an infant, he was a bit of a mathematics whiz, doing calculations in his head that would boggle the "mind" of the best calculator. He moved on from mathematics to become a music guru of sorts, winning his school district's classical music competition in which contestants were required to identify selected passages and their composers in five seconds or less. Blake made a perfect score and ran away with the competition which included contestants from many schools within the Cypress-Fairbanks district.

Later, Blake decided to teach himself German but I am not sure about the ultimate fate of that sizable undertaking. Given the breadth and depth of his considerable intellect and dilettante-ish pattern of interests, it will be interesting to see what he ends up doing with his life; after a failed stint at the University of North Texas (he just did not like it there), Blake currently attends the University of Houston.

Leslie was the instigator of fun for her friends and family while an adolescent, and little has changed over the intervening four decades. Even today, she is an indefatigable extrovert and the life of the party wherever she goes. She started college at Southwest Texas State (now Texas State University), widely known among young people as a party school. Leslie fit in immediately, appointing herself *de facto* social chairperson for the entire university. Those self-appointed duties at SWT were considerable and took a predictable toll on her grades. If she were to start back to school today to complete the undergraduate degree, she probably would need a year and a half of course work.

Natalie Jean LeUnes Allen. Natalie is fifteen months younger than Leslie and has been a Lecturer in Accounting in A&M's Mays Business School for nearly thirty years. She was a cheerleader, homecoming princess, and named A&M Consolidated High School's Most Beautiful Girl her senior year. Natalie always had the best disposition of any of my children, and little has changed over the years. She was a wonderful daughter and remains so today. She is married to Jeff Allen, a self-taught technology guru, who until recently was Vice President and Division Manager of Technology for A&M's Twelfth Man Foundation, the well-known money raiser for A&M athletics. Jeff was deposed a couple of years ago in a change of leadership within the Foundation and now sells real estate locally.

Their oldest daughter, Kayla, is widely acknowledged as the "family brain" for having made a 1540 on the SAT and never making a grade below A from kindergarten through her master's degree in Accounting at A&M and two different PhD programs. Kayla was originally in the doctoral program in Accounting but dropped out after one semester because she was being groomed to be a professor at a Tier One research university, a role she did not covet. She then studied for and passed all parts of the Certified Public Accountant (CPA) examination, took an accounting job, and concurrently married another A&M graduate and fellow CPA, Mark Cline, on August 11, 2012. After a year of working as an accountant, Kayla resigned her job, talked Mark into moving back to College Station where she completed the PhD in Public Health in May 2017. For the time being at least, Kayla has followed in her mother's footsteps by taking a teaching position in the Department of Accounting in A&M's esteemed Mays Business School. It appears Kayla has finally found her calling. There has certainly never been any doubt about her academic ability.

The younger daughter, Lauren was an Education major, an outstanding student in her own right, and graduated from A&M in December, 2011. Lauren married Patrick Powell in the summer of 2012 while I was in Germany with my students. Lauren assumed her first teaching position in nearby Somerville in August of 2012 where she corralled the energies of first graders for two years. Lauren accepted a teaching position in the College Station ISD in the summer or 2015, and that move is most certainly CSISD's gain and Somerville ISD's loss. She has a reputation of being a wonderful teacher. Husband Patrick, a summer 2012 graduate of A&M, took a position as teacher and technology person for both College Station high schools, and he loves his job. Lauren and Patrick became the parents of Henry Declan Powell in late February, 2018.

Little brother Ryan Timothy Allen graduated from A&M Consolidated and had high hopes of attending his dream school, Colorado School of Mines, where he planned to combine computer science and engineering in some interdisciplinary manner. There were some initial and justifiable reservations about the School of Mines because it is so far away geographically and so much more expensive than his second choice, good old Texas A&M University. As is so often the case in life, money drives decision-making and A&M made it much more financially palatable for Ryan to attend school here. He chose to major in Chemical Engineering, and he finished the first year with a 3.80 grade point average. He entered his final year at A&M in the fall of 2017 after completing a summer internship at the University of Georgia in the lovely college town of Athens. Ryan is a tall, slim, handsome, personable, and polite young man with a fine mind who has, among other things, taken to hiking, running distances, and lifting a few weights in his spare time away from his studies. He is quite a fine young man with a bright future! He plans to attend graduate school with the goal of ultimately becoming a college professor, thus adding his name to a growing list of professors and teachers in the family.

Christopher Chay Blythe LeUnes. Chay turned fifty-one on December 22, 2017, is six feet tall, weighs 180 pounds, and is movie-star handsome in the view of his mostly unbiased father and prejudiced-beyond-belief-on-his-behalf stepmother. His academic accomplishments include graduating from A&M with a major in Spanish and subsequently earning a Juris Doctor (JD) degree from St. Mary's Law School in San Antonio. Chay currently combines the practice of law with a real estate business in the Cypress area of Houston and is the father of three kiddos. He is divorced from Jennifer (Watson) LeUnes who was one of my students in her undergraduate days. Chay is a wonderful father to his three children, Jackson, Julian, and Emma, and there is not much higher praise. I am convinced he went to school on how to be a good father by observing my far-too-numerous miscues.

Chay went through some turbulent times in high school and found himself lagging behind academically as a result. One day he called me on the phone, announcing he was in over his head and was dropping out of high school. I was not too pleased with the news but asked if he had a plan, and he said he did. To wit, he had signed up for the GED examination at A&M the following Thursday. I told him that sounded like a plan, and he went on to ace the exam. The absence of a high school diploma forced him to start college at Southwest Texas State like his sister, but he transferred into A&M for his last two years of studies.

Amy Kendall LeUnes Norland. My number four child, Amy, has a degree from A&M in Kinesiology and worked in the field of occupational therapy before moving on to pharmaceutical sales and, several years later, to her present position in pet insurance sales. Amy turned forty-six on May 9, 2017, and she and her husband, Kyle Norland, are childless. Amy and Kyle will continue to raise dogs (King Cavalier Spaniels)!

Amy was born on somewhat of a cloud on Mother's Day of 1971. Her mother had given birth to three children with little difficulty prior to her arrival, but there was something about this pregnancy that alarmed the family doctor almost from day one. He must have known things were not going to be easy, and sure enough, we woke up early in the morning on Mother's Day in a pool of blood maybe eighteen to twenty-four inches in circumference. You do not have to be a neonatologist to know blood in that situation is not a good thing. We rushed off to St. Joseph's Hospital and checked Barbara in for observation. The physician and nurses went into the delivery room, and shortly after their departure, a harried nurse came out, grabbed a phone, and called another doctor to join them. In her words, "You need to get down here immediately. We have one of those!" I stopped the nurse as she headed back into the room, asking her to tell me, "What in the hell is a those?" She proceeded to give me a sixty-second tutorial on placenta previa, a potentially life-threatening medical emergency in which the placenta, or after-birth, detaches prior to the delivery of the child, thus blocking the birth canal. The extent of the blockage varies from partial to total, but the treatment of choice is a Caesarian Section, which I signed off on immediately. Maybe fifteen minutes later, Amy was born and pronounced hale and hearty. Thank goodness for modern medicine! The placenta previa condition partially accounts for why so many prominent male historical figures had multiple wives. Another potential down side to placenta previa is that children born under these conditions often survived but were left with mental or physical handicaps due to pressure on the brain and/or the oxygen deprivation inherent in complicated deliveries.

Today, Amy is healthy and a devoted jogger who keeps herself in wonderful shape. She is four feet eleven inches tall, weighs maybe ninety-five pounds, and is the outward picture of health.

Are President Bill Clinton and the LeUnes Children Descendants of Thomas Jefferson? Before leaving the discussion of my first four children, there is a piece of interesting historical speculation possibly related to their ancestry, and it involves President Thomas Jefferson and one of his estimated two hundred slaves, a woman named Sally Hemings. Jefferson's relationship with Sally Hemings has been the subject of much historical curiosity, literary argumentation, and gnashing of teeth within and outside academic circles for quite some time. There is considerable evidence suggesting Thomas Jefferson fathered six children with Sally Hemings, one of whom died in infancy. All descendants of two of the children, Madison (1805) and Eston (1808), have been definitively identified. On the other hand, the descendants of the other three children, Harriet (1795), Beverly (1798), and, for whatever reason, a second Harriet (1801), have never been authoritatively ascertained. This lack of closure is where the plot thickens.

It has been suggested by some historians and a passel of writers that one of those three children with unknown descendants could easily have been the father of Thomas Jefferson Blythe (1829-1907). The first two names of Mr. Blythe do little to dispel the speculation surrounding the supposed Jefferson-Hemings relationship. Thomas Jefferson Blythe had a son, Henry Patton Foote Blythe (1851-1898) who, in turn, fathered two sons, William Jefferson Blythe, Sr. (1884-1935) (again the reference to Jefferson) and John Hardy Blythe (1880-1962). William Blythe, Sr. had a son who bore his name, and thus was known as William Jefferson Blythe Jr (1918-1946). John Hardy Blythe had several sons, one of whom was Homer Hardy Blythe, my first wife's wonderful father. William Jefferson Blythe, Jr. had a male child named William Jefferson Blythe III (1945-). Thus, William Jefferson Blythe III and my first wife, Barbara Laverne Blythe LeUnes Pearson were first cousins.

As the attentive reader may have noted, there was a close temporal relationship between the birth of William Jefferson Blythe III in 1945 and the death of his father in 1946. Blythe Junior was a traveling salesman and died in an automobile accident shortly after Blythe III's birth. Junior's wife remarried in 1950, and her new husband was named Roger Clinton. When William Jefferson Blythe III turned fourteen years of age, he formally took the name of his stepfather as his own, and William Jefferson "Bill" Clinton, later the forty-second President of the United States, took stage center for the first time. The rest is history, as they say.

I will go to my grave (urn?) eternally envious that Bill Clinton invited his cousin Barbara, my first wife, as well as my four oldest children to the White House for a Christmas celebration while he was President. He omitted his biggest Democratic supporter, me, from the guest list, and I will always be a bit perturbed about what in my heart of hearts I know was an accidental oversight on the part of the Commander-in-Chief. On the other hand, I am thrilled for my kiddos and their mother, and was elated to hear that Chay was among the last ones to leave the White House Christmas party, thus upholding an old family tradition put in place by his father when he was younger and possessed of more late-night staying power.

What conclusion can be drawn from all this speculation? I do not know and I suspect the relationship of Bill Clinton, my ex-wife, and four oldest children to Thomas Jefferson and Sally Hemings will remain nebulous and probably never completely understood. The situation makes for fun speculation, though!

While we are on the topic of Thomas Jefferson, it seems that our third President crafted his own version of the Bible in the early 1800's to make it more closely correspond with his own views. Jefferson's perspective on the Bible remained hidden for many years at his request, and the first publicly accessible version appeared for a short time in the 1940's. Interest in Jefferson's Bible was rekindled recently through two prominent exposures. One involved the publication of a new edition by Targer/Penguin and the other when it became the focus of a Smithsonian exhibit.

BROTHER-IN-LAW GUY WILLIAMS, NEPHEWS RYAN WILLIAMS, JONATHAN WILLIAMS, DAVID CROSSLEY, BROTHER BUB AND SON, JOHN THOMAS

SECOND FAMILY, JUDY, KATIE, LYNDON

The Editor-in-Chief of Targer/Penguin, Mitch Horowitz, wrote a blog for CNN on January 11, 2012, summarizing the history and current status of the Jefferson Bible. Apparently, struggling mightily with his faith, Jefferson crafted his own personal magnum opus in the first two decades of the 1800's using scissors and glue, literally cutting and pasting selected passages from the English, French, Greek, and Latin versions of Scriptures. Jefferson exorcised those portions of Scripture that dealt with what he believed were "superstitions, fanaticisms, and fabrications." By this, Jefferson meant the virgin birth, divine healings, exorcisms, and resurrection of the dead. The final product of this cut-and-paste exercise was, in the words of Horowitz, "…an exquisitely crafted, multilingual chronology of Christ's life." Horowitz felt that Jefferson had created a Bible free of fluff, poof, radicalism, and mysticism (my words, not his), a treatise that has as its focus Christ's moral code alone. Horowitz went on to say that had Jefferson's document been published in the early 1800's instead of seventy years after his death, it might well have served as the basis for a major religious movement known as "Jeffersonian Christianity", thus taking its place in history alongside such faiths as Mormonism, Universal Unitarianism, and Shakerism, among others. Interestingly, Jefferson had his Bible professionally bound and its discovery after his death came as a complete surprise to his family. It is also interesting to note that Jefferson's primary consultant in putting together his version of the Bible was none other than his predecessor in the White House, John Adams, who confessedly shared Jefferson's distrust of many aspects of religious orthodoxy. Quotes from Jefferson and Adams concerning religion can be found toward the end of this document.

One can only wonder how Jefferson, one of America's most profound thinkers, greatest Presidents, and widely respected statesmen would fare in today's politics with its rampant religious piety, pomposity, posturing, and out-and-out, running amok, mean-spirited venality. The majority of Republican political candidates at all levels of government spend a great deal of time posturing as the "True Christian Conservative", a label which would probably be appalling to Jefferson. I find the term more than appalling, and am sick and tired of these candidates who try to out-conservative, out-religion, out-parent, and out-family values each other during election speeches, particularly since many do little or nothing after getting elected but work on getting elected again so they can strengthen their fiefdoms and enjoy the perks of office.

Katie Elizabeth LeUnes Cryer. My last two children have provided me with many opportunities to indulge my fascination with sports, much more so than the first four. Katie, thirty-seven years of age on July 3, 2017, was interested in basketball and softball as a young child but settled on softball as her only sport by age fourteen. She played Little League ball, was on various touring tournament teams, and pitched and caught for her high school team at A&M Consolidated in College Station. Her pitching career ended after two years of junior varsity competition and she spent her last two years as the starting catcher for the varsity. Katie was a so-so, run-of-the-mill hitter but a solid defensive catcher with a fine glove and a passable but accurate arm. Her senior year, she had only one passed ball and saved her pitcher, Leah Gronberg, many a wild pitch with her agility and good glove work. Being five feet tall and maybe 110 pounds, she was probably the smallest club and high school catcher in the state of Texas.

KATIE SOFTBALL IMAGES, COACHES TIM GRONBERG AND ARNOLD LEUNES

    I coached her for four years, two in Little League and two with touring tournament teams. Little League was an eye-opening experience and taught me just how little I knew about coaching young females. I naively made an assumption that kids always played sports with the goal of improving their skills, but I found out that most of my Little League players were there to be with their friends. This point was hammered home at the start of my second season of Little League coaching. The girls were warming up the first day of practice and one young lady for whom I had held high hopes because of her foot speed was struggling with her glove work and throwing accuracy. I sauntered over to her and said: "It appears to me you have not picked up a ball since the end of last season. I was hoping you would work on your skills in the off-season." She quickly put me in my place, uttering politely but with a trace of contempt: "You don't understand, Coach. I have far more important things in my life than softball." She became a cheerleader in high school, no doubt a much higher calling. Speaking of cheerleading, I once asked Katie when she was an early teen if she would like to be a cheerleader like two of her older sisters. With controlled but obvious contempt in her voice, she said: "Daddy, why would you yell for other people when you can get them to yell for you?"

One of the more humorous occurrences during my Little League stint involved the All-Star playoffs which are reprehensible and indefensible as they are currently constructed. If we really cared about kids getting to play softball or baseball, there would long seasons and damn little All-Stars stuff (fluff?) instead of short seasons, weeks of twice-a-day All-Stars practice, and endless All-Star playoffs. I know I live in a dream world but I love despising the All-Stars concept (and parents who throw their political weight around so their kids who in no way, shape, or form deserve to be All-Stars can do so). My two youngest kiddos were All-Stars here and there, by the way, so do not try using the sour grapes argument on me.

The quasi-humorous event I was referring to before I went off on the preceding diatribe took place when Little League North (us) was getting ready for a playoff game to be played on our home field with Little League East. The opposing coaches fancied themselves to be quite a bunting team, employing what is sometimes known as "small ball" as an important part of their offensive strategy. Apparently, rumors circulated about suggesting the North coaching staff was going to counter East's bunting ability by shaving its baselines in such a manner that bunts would almost always roll into foul territory. I looked up one afternoon and saw the coaches from East wandering up and down the respective base lines looking for visible evidence of premeditated tampering. Seeing none, the East coach and a parent who is a local attorney (and A&M yell leader in his undergraduate days) whipped out a carpenter's level and starting assessing the slope of our baselines. The investigative team found no evidence of skullduggery and, frankly, our coaches were not capable of doctoring the base lines even if they had thought of it. However, the opposition left the field uncertain about whether or not our coaches had done some pretty egregious things in the name of winning a softball game. I still have vivid images of my attorney friend, dressed in suit and tie, down on his hands and knees, looking to see if that little green bubble on the level was off kilter anywhere.

Late in the league season and prior to the sacrosanct Little League playoffs, my girls were preparing to play the top team which was blessed with two of the best youth pitchers not just in Bryan but the entire US. Their names were Monica and Denise Briggs, and they were precocious pitching phenoms who had led their age-related tournament teams to national honors and would later lead the Bryan High School team to a Division 5-A state championship. As youth pitchers, they were both simply unhittable.

As we warmed up for the game, I wandered among my girls, hearing nothing but doom and gloom predictions about batting against the twins. I kept hearing words to the effect, "We can't hit Monica and we can't hit Denise. It does not matter which one pitches. Why are we even here?" I finally got fed up with all the pessimism, called my girls over, and asked them to replace their negative thoughts with positive ones, a common tool in the bag of tricks of the sport psychologist. I told them, "Do not say I can't hit Denise/Monica. Instead, tell yourself I will hit because I am a tough competitor. Furthermore, I have had the hitting instruction of the world's greatest hitting coach, Arnold LeUnes." Five innings and fifteen outs later, whichever twin pitched against us had racked up fourteen strikeouts and the other out was a pop foul to the catcher. The girl who hit the foul was absolutely ecstatic because she made contact with a pitch. Of course, I was well aware that the gibberish about me being the world's best hitting instructor was a crock. I also knew what the outcome was destined to be, but I wanted my team to think about facing their fate with a more positive frame of mind. Such is life in Little League softball.

The last year I coached softball, I carefully crafted a successful tournament team through the local Avengers organization composed of players from Brenham, Bryan, College Station, and Huntsville in roughly equal numbers. I liked all the girls but I became particularly fond of the ones from Huntsville as the season progressed. They were good players and likeable young ladies with positive attitudes about softball and life. And their parents were generally sane!

I was most ably assisted by one of the most interesting and finest people I know, Dr. Bob Biles of the Political Science faculty at Sam Houston State University. Bob's daughter, Katie, was one of our pitchers. I was not always sure how much softball Bob knew but he was a hard worker and served as a buffer between the players and their almost always peripatetic and sometimes ill-tempered head coach. Bob stayed with the sport after our daughters gave up the game a decade and more ago and has been a great role model for another generation of young female players. Bob is one of the good guys you just like to be around. He still sends out a family newsletter each Christmas and those things can run the gamut from boringly boastful to absolutely awful to occasionally interesting and informative. Bob's letters are always a nice amalgam of family information supplemented with a wonderful blend of wry, tongue-in-cheek humor. I always look forward to the annual Biles family update.

At our initial team meeting with the parents, the question arose as to how long the season would run. I responded, "The season ends when you can no longer stand to be around me. When I have worn out my welcome, we will hang it up." Three months later, I found out my half-joking, self-deprecating comment was prophetic. We were entered in a July tournament in Brenham and competing well with some of the best teams in the Houston area, warming up for an early evening game of considerable importance. The wind was blowing out quite strongly and visions of sugar plums danced in my head as I thought about what would happen if one of my hitters really got hold of a pitch and lofted it into the maelstrom. And I had exactly the player in mind to do that, a reserved player named Carrie who was a raw talent, big and strong, with a tendency to strike out often but who occasionally sprinkled in some magnificent, prodigious fly balls. Carrie was the youngest and final player selected for the team at the initial tryouts, primarily because her softball upside seemed substantial. As it turned out, I was prophetic in this assessment also, for Carrie received a scholarship to play softball at Texas State University after her high school career ended.

At the start of the season, I pulled the parents aside and explained that Carrie would be added to our roster as a project for the future because of her youth in comparison with the other girls and aforementioned potential. They were told straight out she would not play as much as some of the other girls but should profit from competing at a high level and being around older, more mature players. As an added extra, Bob Biles and I were beneficiaries of the invaluable assistance of the esteemed softball coach at A&M, Bob Brock (now at Sam Houston State University). At that time, Bob was the second winningest coach in the history of NCAA softball and his knowledge of and enthusiasm for the game knows no bounds. Carrie's parents were particularly pleased that she was going to be under his tutelage as a perk for being on our team. Finding enough playing time to keep all the girls and their parents happy is one of the banes of coaching, and Carrie's parents, as is almost perfectly predictable, conveniently forgot our earlier agreement and became increasingly agitated about her lesser visibility on the team.

The issue came to an ugly head as we were finishing our pre-game warm-ups that fateful July evening in Brenham. I told Carrie she was not going to be a starter because I had another role in mind for her (i.e., ideally coming in as a pinch hitter and launching a long, wind-blown home run at a critical juncture in the late innings). When she got the news she was not starting, Carrie strode angrily into the dugout, unceremoniously scattering bats and water coolers in her wake. At this point, Marshall, her father, said: "Carrie, get of the dugout. I don't want you anywhere near that sorry son-of-a-bitch." The mother, Pearl, then chimed in her two cents worth: "He's not a sorry son-of-a-bitch, Marshall, he's a no-good motherfucker." The parents continued their heated invective against me in front of Carrie and the rest of the players, each arguing fervently on behalf of their favorite assessment of my character. After a minute of venting, they collected their daughter and headed home. As I think back on the dispute between Carrie's parents, I could have solved the argument for them, for I am probably equal parts sorry son-of-a-bitch and no-good motherfucker!

We lost the game, were eliminated from the tournament, and my brief, ill-fated coaching career came to an abrupt conclusion. However, I had fulfilled my promise to the parents about when the season would end. The incident with Carrie, Pearl, and Marshall no doubt sped up the process for all of us.

My Katie ended her softball career in May of the senior year of high school and I did not watch so much as one live inning of softball in the next eighteen years. Enough was enough! I made it through eighty years without getting cussed out much except for those softball years where I alienated more people than I care to remember. I must confess the burden of being both a sorry son-of-a-bitch and a no-good motherfucker is quite a cross to bear.

LYNDON GOLF SWING

Lyndon Webb LeUnes. In terms of sheer athleticism, Lyndon, my youngest child, is another story. Katie was a grinder who learned by repetition and hard work in the trenches. Lyndon, on the other hand, was a natural. Life in athletics was always simple for him. Judy and I think we detected a ball in his hand when viewing his first sonogram, and I never saw him without one during the first fourteen years of his life. He kicked balls through the living room, bounced balls off of the fireplace as we watched television, shot baskets at each end of his shower, putted golf balls across our carpet, and played hours and hours of wall ball while his sister played softball. If there were scholarships awarded for wall ball, he would have had a free ride to college somewhere; the boy was wall ball whiz!

As he approached age six, I had a set of golf clubs cut down to size because, more than any other sport I know, golf absolutely demands an early start. Just ask Tiger Woods. I wanted more than anything else in sports for Lyndon to be a golfer, hopefully at the college level and beyond. We started out hitting golf balls in the yard, initially from the front of the house to midway to the barn, and then all the way to the barn maybe seventy yards hence, and finally over the barn which would inevitably scatter his mother's three horses. The prospect of bouncing a ball off the metal barn with a loud clang or spooking a horse with an errant shot was too much for Lyndon to pass up. Fortunately, I do not think he ever actually ever hit a horse, so go easy on us, animal lovers! Call off the PETA people!

When Lyndon turned seven, I joined Pebble Creek Country Club just across Highway 6 from our house so he would have a place to play golf. I envisioned him eventually living on the course, shooting a round or two every day, perhaps caddying for some old duffers to make a buck, generally honing his golfing skills, and becoming a total golf junkie. Unfortunately, my vision never took roots.

Lyndon and I eventually agreed he had made enough progress while spooking the horses to move on to bigger and better things, so we vacated the front yard in favor of the Pebble Creek Country Club golf course. Besides, the horses needed some respite from the fusillade of golf balls disrupting their leisurely grazing every day! Since he was seven and had never been on an actual golf course, I thought it would be a fair test for a novice like him to play from the women's tees. He started out hitting the ball well, used the one mulligan (extra shot) we agreed was allowable, and after six holes he was three over par. Not bad for a first time out, huh? Unfortunately, his game fell apart and he ended up five over par for the final three holes. Still, shooting an eight-over par forty-three the first time ever on a regulation golf course is nothing to sneeze at. I was elated, of course, with his overall play.

He continued to golf at Pebble Creek as time allowed, hitting balls from the driving range or on the putting green. I had two or three professionals look him over and in every case they told me to leave him alone as there was no weakness in his game that needed tweaking. Jeanne Southerland, then the coach of A&M women's golf team, suggested the best course of action was to just let him play until he was thirteen or so. It was her opinion if a promising golfer plays enough, he or she will work out most of the kinks in their game naturally, at which point instruction from a professional becomes advantageous. What she suggested made a lot of sense to me…establish the requisite muscle memory so that much of the game is second nature, and let the professional do the necessary tweaking of the stance, swing, grip, and the thousand other things it takes to be a good golfer.

One summer when Lyndon was eleven, he was playing in a Central Texas Junior Golf League (CTJGL) tournament on the A&M course, but I was not able to assume my customary place in the gallery because of a class that met at the same time. However, I was able to get there right after class let out to catch the finish of the tournament and as I walked up, Lyndon was playing the final hole. While I was standing there watching, a tanned, slightly weather-beaten, middle-aged gentleman approached me and asked if I was Lyndon's father. I allowed that I was, and the man said, "I have been walking the course with my grandson who is paired with your son. I just wanted to let you know that I am a teaching professional and I think your son has a magnificent future in this game. You need to get him out of all other sports so he can focus only on golf. Just looking at him, I can tell he is a good athlete who plays a number of sports, but he has the sweetest swing, finest touch, best temperament, and most creativity on a golf course of any youth golfer I have ever seen. Please, please get him to make golf his total focus." I thanked the pro for his kind assessment and words of wisdom but knew getting Lyndon to give up sports where being fleet of foot is at a premium would be difficult if not impossible. I went on to tell his new-found admirer, "Yeah, I wish golf was more important to him, but he loves baseball, basketball, soccer, and track. I am assuming that when he goes to junior high, football will also get factored into the equation. He is fleet afoot and if you are fast, all of those sports respond well to foot speed. He likes golf but the game is simply too slow." This was one time when I wished I was wrong, but I knew differently. He was fast afoot and loved the competition and exertion of team ball sports and track.

Lyndon dabbled with golf after that, and was the number two player on the junior high team behind their best player, Jordan Russell, who finished his senior year at A&M in 2012. Though Jordan was a pretty decent youth athlete, he gave up all other sports to concentrate on golf around age twelve. He played high school golf at A&M Consolidated and walked on at A&M where he worked hard to improve his game in hopes of eventually making the team. Over time, he improved to the point that he became an important team member, and as evidence of his progress, Jordan played in a tournament in Japan in 2010 in which he set an all-time A&M record for best single round by shooting a sixty-three. He also tied the A&M record in Japan for best three-round score of 203. By the 2011 season, Jordan was A&M's low scorer and the twenty-fourth ranked collegiate golfer in the country. Later, in the summer of 2011, he made the final four in the US Amateur tournament, but lost in the semis to the number one ranked amateur player in the world at the time, a UCLA sophomore named Patrick Cantlay. Cantlay finished as the top amateur in the 2011 US Open, one of the premier professional golf events in the world, and is now competing very successfully on the PGA tour. Currently, he is ranked number thirty-five in the world.

In mid-2015, Jordan earned a spot on the web.com tour, professional golf's second tier. He previously played in Central and South America, competing in tournaments in Mexico, Guatemala, Panama, and Colombia. To wrap up this little vignette, I am pleased to report that Jordan made his PGA debut in June of 2017 at the Saint Jude Open in Memphis, Tennessee. He shot 72 and 71 on the par 70 course and missed the cut by three strokes. However, he has arrived, his initial effort has to be encouraging to him, and I wish him the best. It is nice to see Aggies listed every week in the newspaper golf results, and Jordan has joined the likes Ryan Palmer, Shane Bertsch, Bronson Burgoon, Martin Piller, Bobby Gates, and Conrad Shindler in that regard. Another possible future star is Former A&M player, Cameron Champ, who was the second low amateur in a recent PGA tournament where much media attention was focused in his scores and powerful shots off the tee box. In the latter regard, his drives averaged a phenomenal 340 yards for the four days of the tournament.

Other locals of note are Jeff Maggert, a very successful competitor on both the PGA and Over-50 tours, and local high school graduate Casey Grice who competes on the LPGA circuit. Casey's mother played tennis at A&M and her father is a friend and colleague in the field of Kinesiology and one of the top badminton players in the world in his day. Clearly, Casey comes by her athletic prowess honestly.

Lyndon got to where he could swing a pretty wicked driver despite the fact that he only weighed 119 pounds in junior high (and not much more than that in high school). He occasionally drove some of the short par fours on the A&M course and was on or near the green in two shots on most of the par fives. His two longest drives not affected by wind and in which the fairway did not slope toward the green was 365 yards on number ten and 335 yards on number four on A&M's course prior to its renovation in 2013. On the old number three at A&M, a par four 304-yard hole, I once lined up three balls on the tee since there was no one else within striking distance of us on the course. Lyndon hit one ball just short of the green, one on the right frog hair pin high, and one pin high fifteen yards to the right of the hole. And all this power at 119 pounds! Clearly, club head speed trumps sheer size.

Lyndon quit playing golf for the most part in the 8th grade and seldom picks up the clubs any more. He played once in 2009 at A&M and shot a forty-one on the front nine on the A&M course. He picked up his clubs for the first time in 2010 and played the Pecan Lakes course in Navasota, which can be a pretty demanding at times. He was thirteen over on four of the holes and two under for the other fourteen, and ended up shooting a forty-two on the front nine and a forty-one on the back despite taking a triple bogey on eighteen. His 18-hole score was eighty-three. How good could he have been if the game were important to him? It is clear to me that we will never know.

When I looked at Jordan Russell's accomplishments at A&M, I could only wince. The worst thing that can happen to the Jordan's of the world and their fellow collegiate golfers is they get a free education for going to school in the morning. They then play golf every afternoon and spend their weekends, no doubt being forced at gun point to compete with golfers from other universities on beautiful courses in Japan, Hawaii, California, Arizona, Florida, and elsewhere. I suspect Lyndon could have been one of those guys; he was never as good as Jordan as a youth and may never have been as good as a collegian or professional, but he was competitive at one time with his talented classmate. If you catch a sense of regret on my part, you are right. It is classic case of wondering what could have been.

As a postscript to all this, Lyndon, now works at a golf shop on a part-time basis and gets to play a round whenever time allows. He went on to tell me he hit every par five on the course in two shots, hit a sixty-foot putt for eagle on one of them, drove the green on four of the short par fours, and ended up with an eighty-five for the round. Since all the speed sports are a thing of the past, perhaps he can work on developing his golf game and compete in some local tournaments as his life plays out.

A Soccer Dream. As for the other sports, he was a star from the first day in soccer, averaging five or six goals per game as six-year old. In baseball, he was quite good. The same could be said for basketball. Ditto for track where he competed in the AAU summer meets. He tried out for football in the seventh grade and was reasonably successful as a running back/defensive back on the B team. He hung up the cleats a year later, and I applauded that decision. Football is too violent for me, and Lyndon shared my misgivings about the game. He dropped baseball at age twelve and basketball went by the wayside at the start of his tenth grade soccer season.

LYNDON SOCCER

I love to watch basketball, and hoped he would like and excel at it. After his freshman year in high school, I got him involved in private lessons with a former A&M female All-American, Lisa Branch, at Lincoln Center in College Station. Under her incredibly astute tutelage, he developed into a very adept ball handler and a most promising free throw and three-point shooter. One day Lisa created a drill in which he had to take nine shots while moving from point to point in a semi-circle along the three-point line; he was nine for nine. He also hit seventy-two percent of his free throws in another drill. I thought it a stroke of genius that she only let him shoot free throws when he was exhausted and gasping for air. Lisa's rationale made a lot of sense though I had never given it any thought. Lisa said to me: "When do you shoot free throws in game? Almost always when you're so tired you can barely hang on, that's when! That's when you shoot in a game and that is when I have players shoot in practice." Wind sprint after wind sprint, shoot ten free throws, wind sprint after wind sprint, shoot ten free throws...that was the way it went down every practice. I was impressed with what Lyndon learned and came away with a lot of admiration for Lisa as a teacher and coach. Every roundballer should have someone like Lisa Branch teaching them the game.

A couple of weeks into the pre-season basketball practices, Lyndon told the high school coaches he was going to give up the game and devote his time exclusively to soccer. I was disappointed but said little. Ultimately, he has to live with his choices, not me. And there was no doubt about his soccer capabilities; he was an exceptional player.

He played soccer throughout high school and with the Houston Texans futbol club, touring most of Texas and much of Oklahoma, North Carolina, and Florida as a member of the club team. He was the leading scorer on his high school team as a sophomore, tore an Anterior Cruciate Ligament (ACL) in his knee early in the junior season, and set the all-time single season scoring record for A&M Consolidated High School during his senior campaign. He scored twenty-three goals and had thirteen assists in twenty-two games, made All-District and All-Region, and was one of ninety-six players considered for All-State honors. His club and high school successes led him to play a year at the University of Texas at Tyler where he was either first or second in minutes played among all players and was the only freshman starter. Unfortunately, he and the coach did not see eye to eye on a lot of things, most particularly Lyndon's role on the team for the last three years. Never the prima donna, Lyndon had accepted the fact that he was going to always be a defender on his college team, but wanted an expanded role where he got to move forward with the ball if circumstances dictated such a move, but the coach would not move on expanding his responsibilities. He did tell Lyndon he was aware of his accomplishments as a scorer, but needed his speed and quickness of recovery on the defensive side of the ball. It was his position that you never lost if the other team could not score, so you stack your defense with the best players. Also and unfortunately, Lyndon was not particularly fond of school, which is not altogether a good thing, and he left Tyler after one year.

Lyndon worked as a waitperson at Wings and More in College Station for the ensuing six years, sometimes going to Blinn College and sometimes taking off to seek his fame and fortune in Germany where he worked in the summer and fall of 2010 for Dr. Rainer Zaeck, the man who sponsored my annual Study Abroad trips for A&M students from 2003 to 2017. Lyndon had hoped to hook up with a semi-pro or low-level professional team in Germany, but those plans were derailed by a knee injury, his second. Four different orthopedic surgeons in Germany looked over his MRI's and could not come up with a consensus about the nature or the seriousness of his injury. All specialists did agree, however, that he had junk floating around in his kneecap, probably cartilage from an earlier injury.

He had surgery on that nettlesome knee in December, 2010, with Dr. J. P. Bramhall doing the repairs. J. P., a former Aggie and professional baseball player, performs surgeries for the A&M athletic department and has studied under Dr. James Andrews, arguably the most renowned orthopedic surgeon in the world. Lyndon's second surgery was mostly devoted to cleaning up junk that was floating around in the knee from the earlier anterior cruciate ligament (ACL) tear suffered his junior year in a high school tournament in Carrollton, near Dallas. Needless to say, his club coaches were furious with him (and the other club teammates for even playing high school soccer). Club trainers wear their intense dislike for high school soccer prominently displayed on their sleeves, so to speak. Because of the precarious knee situation, Lyndon's soccer dreams are pretty much, as our German friends would say, kaput.

LEUNES TRIBE-FIVE CHILDREN, EIGHT GRANDCHILDREN, ASSORTED OTHERS

JUDY, SIX CHILDREN, THREE GRANDCHILDREN, ASSORTED SPOUSES AND FRIENDS

While in Germany, Lyndon completed two months of intensive Germany language instruction and he followed that up with four semesters of German courses at nearby Blinn College. He moved from College Station to San Marcos to begin studies at Texas State University in the fall of 2014. He chose History as his major field of concentration and graduated in December of 2016. His current

Sentimental Journey Home I (1965-2018)

plans are to pursue the PhD in History and become a college professor like his father, sister Natalie, and niece Kayla. He got tired of pussy-footing around, and his mother and I are pleased that he has decided to get serious about his studies. He made between a 3.25 and 3.75 the last three semesters while working full-time at Hofbrau on the River, a German-theme restaurant in New Braunfels fifteen minutes down I-35 from San Marcos. For the first time in his life, he gets it about school. If you attend class regularly, listen intently, sit your butt in a chair at night, and develop a relationship with your professors, good things happen to your grades. As a youth and an avowed jock, he labored under the false assumption the only way to make good grades was to be born a genius like his niece, the aforementioned Dr. Kayla Allen Cline.

I am happy for Lyndon. He has pursued a dream that began at age seven when he announced all he ever hoped to be in life was a European soccer player. While being a professional soccer player is no longer in the cards, his life experiences in Germany, Italy, and other countries and cities in western Europe are priceless. Where all of it will lead, if anywhere, is anybody's guess.

Personal Heroes

It has been a curious situation having children at home from the time I was twenty-four up to ten years ago, or a total of forty-seven years. In the process of raising children, I have had a somewhat atypical relationship with the grandchildren. My youngest child is twenty-nine and the oldest grandchild thirty, a somewhat unusual though not unheard of situation. Simply put, I was too busy raising children to devote as much time to the grandchildren as I would have liked. I am neither proud nor happy about that but it will not change one iota if I get despondent and slash my wrists. Also, in every case, each of the grandchildren had wonderful relationships with one or both sets of grandparents, or in the case of my last two children, with their great-grandmother, Grace, and her second husband, Gene Kiser.

Because of their impact on the lives of many family members including the children and grandchildren, I would like to devote a few paragraphs to a couple of life heroes, my wife Judy's maternal grandmother, Grace Jones Kiser, and first wife Barbara's father, Homer Hardy Blythe.

Grace Jones Kiser. Grace Kiser was Judy's maternal grandmother and the great-grandmother of Katie and Lyndon, our last two children. I do not think there was ever a time when the children thought of Grace as a great-grandmother for she filled the role of grandmother in grand fashion from their perspective (which is pretty much the only opinion that counts, is it not?).

I thought the world of Grace and appreciated her forthrightness, warmth, and unconditional acceptance. For the first several years of my relationship with Judy, Grace was a beacon of light. Though I am fourteen-plus years older than Judy, Grace never seemed to regard that as a negative, which was not always the case with other relatives who viewed my relationship with Judy with a jaundiced eye.

GRACE JONES KISER

Grace grew up in the small Kansas town of Downs, married Roice Jones at an early age, and spent her life with him in Dallas until his death. Roice Jones did well financially with Ryder, the trucking company, and left Grace reasonably well-fixed financially when he died of cancer just a few months shy of their fiftieth wedding anniversary. For most of Judy's childhood, Grace and Roice Jones lived in a large home in North Dallas, and Judy's mother, Joyce, graduated from Highland Park High School located in the well-to-do section of Dallas. Judy always reminds me that, yes, her mother went to Highland Park High School but was among the least affluent students there. Joyce met her future husband, John Webb, who later graduated from Southern Methodist University, and they raised their three children, Judy, Randy (aka John for business purposes), and Sharon in Dallas for Judy's first fourteen years. The family then moved to Frisco, at the time a village of a thousand people because Judy's father wanted to raise quarter horses. The decision turned out to be very judicious, as all three children prospered in Frisco. Judy is always fond of telling current residents of that thriving city that she graduated in a class of fifty-eight. Today, the Frisco Independent School District has 56,000 students attending nine high schools, sixteen middle schools, forty elementary schools, and three special program centers. As well, there are several private and parochial schools in the "new" Frisco.

JUDY'S PARENTS, JOHN & JOYCE WEBB

Frisco was the home of the "Coons", as the school mascot was known, and Judy was a "Fightin' Coon" cheerleader, a leader of several high school clubs, participated in the Miss Texas Pageant (Miss Farmersville), and showed horses in her spare time. Randy played baseball and was the star quarterback on the football team. Sharon, five years younger Judy, was a star all-around athlete, and earned an athletic scholarship to East Texas State University (now Texas A&M-Commerce) from which she graduated. She also met her husband, Bob Curtis, at ETSU. Clearly, the plans the Webb's laid out for their children worked out well, and I think all have many fond memories of those days in Frisco in the 1960's and early 1970's.

As children, the Webb kids spent a lot of time with both sets of grandparents, the Webb's and the Jones'es, and were fortunate enough to be nurtured by people who loved them. It has always struck me as interesting, at a philosophical level, how young people feel about their grandparents. The students in my classes I have talked to about this issue seem to cherish their grandparents greatly on the one hand or hardly know them at all on the other; there does not appear to be much of a middle ground. In my own case, and as noted elsewhere, both grandmothers died nearly two decades before I was born and both grandfathers passed away before I was eleven, so my perspective on this topic is necessarily rather narrow.

In the mid-1970's, Roice Jones died, leaving Grace a grieving but reasonably well-to-do widow. After a mourning period of several years, Grace developed a fondness for a fellow widower, Eugene "Gene" Kiser, whose wife had died at about the same time as Roice Jones, also just before reaching their own fiftieth wedding anniversary. Interestingly, the Kisers and the Jones'es had known each other previously through their participation in a bowling league. Grace and Gene struck up a relationship that lasted twenty wonderful years before she died in 2000.

Slowly, surely, and inexorably, in a matter of a few years, most of Grace's Dallas friends died, developed terminal illnesses, or become infirm, so she and Gene decided to pull up stakes after all those many years in Dallas and move to Canyon Lake, near New Braunfels and San Antonio. Part of their rationale for moving to that area was that Gene's sister Peggy and her husband, Teddy, a career pilot for business executives and other dignitaries, had retired there. The Kiser's built a very comfortable home next door to Ted and "Peg", joined the country club where they played a lot of bridge with a wide assortment of new friends, and in no time were immersed in the social life of Canyon Lake.

Gene and Grace were fortunate to be in good health and have the financial wherewithal to travel throughout the US as well as internationally in the first fifteen years of their marriage. Gene had a son who was an architect on assignment in Paris, so they visited him and his family several times while he was working in the "City of Lights." In the process, they travelled around the countryside in France and other European countries. On one or two occasions, they flew to France on the supersonic SST before it was grounded for safety reasons.

In addition to several sojourns through mainland Europe and the United Kingdom, they also traveled to Alaska, Hawaii, the Panama Canal, and most of the continental United States. Gene was originally from Indiana so they also made quite a number of stateside trips to Indianapolis and the surrounding area to visit his friends and relatives.

Gene was never really warmly embraced by the other Webb family members, which is a shame for he brought indescribable joy to Grace's life for two decades. It is hard to put a price tag on what the two of them meant to each other and the wonderful years they had together. As a result, I find it disconcerting that anyone would begrudge Grace and Gene the happiness and joy they brought each other in those last twenty years of her life.

I think Gene was viewed by a segment of family members as financially predatory, for his modest retirement program was no match for the estate that Roice Jones left Grace. It is indeed fair to say that thanks to Grace (and the foresight of Roice Jones), Gene was able to live much more luxuriously than he would have with his own retirement package. For example, Gene was extravagant in his choice of cars, and always drove a late model, top-of-the-line Cadillac. I once asked Gene what kind of mileage he got on his vehicle and he told me that if you kept up with that kind of stuff, you should not own a Cadillac. I still do not know what kind of mileage a Cadillac gets (nor do I really care)! Gene also had a play toy, a Chrysler convertible, he brought out of hiding a few times a year, most particularly for the annual parade at Canyon Lake where he would put the top down and high-roll in his fancy car and trademark Shriner's hat. Gene also heaped extravagant gifts on Grace, especially jewelry, of which she was justifiably proud.

In reality, "Grandma Grace and Gene", as they were most affectionately known to Katie and Lyndon, were great-grandparents but were viewed as grandparents by the kids. For a variety of reasons not worthy of elaboration, this somewhat unusual arrangement arose in part because the kids had such limited relationships with both sets of actual grandparents. Grace and Gene often came to the kids' athletic and school events in the role of grandparents, and we visited with them fairly often at the lake. They were always gracious hosts who just so happened to absolutely dote on our children. And Grace clearly adored Judy and appeared to think I was passably acceptable, too!

For most of the twenty-five years I knew Grace, she was robust and healthy, though quite overweight. Her doctors were always somewhat reluctant to come down too hard on the weight issue because her overall health indicators were so highly positive. Over the years, however, her body began to break down, particularly her spinal column and rib cage. She became less willing and able to walk which made her more sedentary which, in turn, made her less prone to move about, and the vicious cycle of inactivity ultimately led to her demise. She and Gene traveled less, had fewer and fewer interactions with friends and relatives, and lived a mostly sedentary life those last few years. Grace's spinal column and rib cage deteriorated to the point that the pain became unbearable, leading her to talk obsessively of wanting to die. I am convinced Grace willed herself to death when the pain became unbearable and she could no longer enjoy life.

The night before Grace passed away, Judy and I were getting ready to retire around midnight when word came that her grandmother was hanging on to life by a thread at her home on the lake, a good three hours away from College Station. Judy immediately jumped in her car and, fortunately for her long-term mental well-being, arrived at the house in time to hold Grace's hand as she passed away early that fateful morning. My wife's grandmother and my dear, dear friend, Grace Ortel Jones Kiser, died in 2000 at the age of ninety-one. She and Judy shared a very special bond, and because of that relationship, I was fortunate enough to be included as one of Grace Jones Kiser's circle of close friends, and for that I am also eternally thankful.

In her will, Grace divided a portion of her estate between the three Webb children, leaving each of them with what I would estimate to be in excess of a quarter of a million dollars in money, stocks, and other assets. The other part of her estate, a million dollars or perhaps more, was left to Gene who lived another five years after Grace passed on. Prior to Grace's death, Gene started having speech difficulties and tremors, and was ultimately diagnosed with the dreaded Parkinson's disease. Gene died a slow death from Parkinson's while enduring its inexorable physical and psychological complications.

As might be expected, Gene went through a period of profound loneliness after Grace died and, as we were to find out, became terribly vulnerable to exploitation, and exploited he was. It seems that shortly after Grace passed away, Gene hired a mid-sixties nurse/housekeeper to look after him and the house. The caretaker's name was Doris, and it took her all of two weeks to wrap her mean-spirited, treasure-hunting tentacles around Gene's psyche and soul. Doris convinced Gene he was the man she had been looking for all her life, and in what I can only assume was desperation over Grace's death, he fell for her litany of unadulterated bullshit, hook, line, and sinker. As her stranglehold on Gene's emotions (and pocketbook) deepened, Doris asked her brother (brother-in-law?) who was supposedly a "minister" to come in and marry them, a ceremony that took place in what had been Gene and Grace's bedroom at something like 2:30 in the morning. Do any of you readers smell a rat?

Well, the bizarre wedding ceremony was just the tip of the iceberg. Immediately after Gene and Doris were joined in holy matrimony and wedded bliss, you know, the "love, honor, and obey in sickness and in health till death do us part" thing, the new bride proceeded to line up a number of exotic travel adventures for the two of them. They "honeymooned" for the very brief time Gene was still physically able to travel. At the same time, Doris spent money like it was going out of style, mostly on out-and-out junk. After Gene died, his daughter, also a Judy, told me that Doris had a thing for clothes, art, home decorations, jewelry, and assorted gewgaws and doodads that were outlandish and "trashy." From what Judy described, I would characterize Doris's taste in life's amenities as ostentatious, cheap, gaudy, and gauche.

As Doris's profligacy was unfolding in full force, Gene's condition worsened precipitously. He became largely unable to speak, and he could only get around with the help of a walker. We visited Gene a few times before his death, and it was painful to watch him trying to ambulate around the house. He teetered and tottered and lurched about, and we were told he had suffered some significant injuries from falls. There were strong suspicions on the part of Gene's two adult children that some of these injuries were not from falls but from physical abuse at the hands of his loving wife, none other than the adorable, doting Doris. As a result of these suspicions, social workers from Adult Protective Services visited the house on more than one occasion but were unable to turn up anything conclusive. How many times has that drama been re-enacted?

By the time Gene died in 2005, the once decent estate had pretty much been reduced to the value of the Canyon Lake home. Strangely enough, once the money and assets were spent, Doris hit the road, no doubt in search for the next "love of her life." Gene's children then put peace bonds and restraining orders in place, and Doris was not able to return to sell the house out from under the heirs. When Gene died, his children took over the house and kept it for a couple of years as a vacation or weekend retreat before being forced to sell it due to high taxes and mounting maintenance costs. As the Doris saga wound down, there were strong rumors about her being institutionalized with a diagnosis of bipolar illness. Poor Gene deserved better, once again affirming the old adages that life isn't fair and the "Golden Years" are not always golden. No one should meet his or her maker in the condition Gene found himself in at the end.

Though the story did not have a happy ending, Gene and Grace made an indelible impression on my "second family" for which I am eternally grateful. The relationship Grace shared with my wife and our two children plus the friendship and acceptance accorded me is still special. I cannot thank Grace Jones Kiser enough for her unending kindness and the many good and generous things she did for my family. She was a very special woman and a dear, dear friend who I have missed virtually every day since her death. Hardly a day goes by that I don't think of her. Grace reminds me of a saying emanating from the last episode of the iconic television comedy show, "Cheers", to the effect: "Time goes so fast, people go in and out of your life. You must never miss the opportunity to tell these people how much they meant to you." I tried to communicate my affection for her through words and actions, and I think Grace always knew how I felt!

A couple of concluding anecdotes represent personal cherished memories of Grace. The events are small in stature, the little things of which our lives are made, but they tell a great deal about Grace Jones as a person. One concerns her wonderful sense of humor and a joke she was so fond of telling about what she called the "With-It Grandmother." The joke was way beyond corny but Grace enjoyed it a great deal, as did I. It seems that the "With-It Grandmother" would gather her young grandchildren around the fireplace from time to time for a recitation of their favorite childhood stories. The "With-It Grandmother" would ask if they wanted to hear the story of "Goldilocks and the Three Bears", or maybe the saga of "Three Little Pigs." One of the more irreverent among the grandchildren piped up, "No, grandma we don't want to hear about 'Goldilocks' or 'Three Little Pigs'. We want to hear about the time you were whoring in Dallas." Grace told the joke ever so often and I enjoyed it the twentieth time as much as I did the first. The joke certainly bore no similarities to her actual life in Dallas but it did say something about the fun-loving and sometimes perverse spirit that was Grace Kiser.

Though it may strike the reader as a bit quirky (I think it is, too!), the second anecdote was about me using the restroom at Grace's house during a weekend visit when I was in my mid-thirties and first dating Judy. She happened to overhear the bathroom proceedings from a nearby den, and commented to Judy, in her own imitable way, "He has the stream of a much younger man, and that is good, Judy." I had never thought about a urinary stream as a measure of a man, but now that I am eighty, I am far more familiar than I would like to be with the insights inherent in Grace's perspicacious words of four decades ago. I have been held hostage, yea, even tortured, for over a decade, the unwitting victim of a cranky, pernicious prostate gland. Why did no one ever warn me? Where did I miss out on such important information? But, then again, what could I have done if I had known?

Homer Hardy Blythe (1919-1994). As meaningful as my own father was in my formative days, I probably had no bigger life hero as a young adult than Homer Hardy Blythe. Homer was the father of my first wife, Barbara, and the grandfather to my four oldest children. He was absolutely without question the nicest person I have ever met anywhere, anytime, anyplace, bar none. Homer was a small-town boy who never outgrew those roots, having been raised in Van Alstyne, a small city located between Dallas and Sherman, in a large family who made their living as farmers. As of 2014, there were 3,221 people residing there though I doubt it was half that size in Homer's day.

Homer was a star running back in high school and ended up going to school at Taft Junior College in California where he continued playing football for a while. Along the way, he met Verna Fawcett who, after a short courtship, became his wife. After his two-year stay in California, the two of them married, relocated to Texas, and raised their two daughters and son in Sherman, just south of the Oklahoma line near Lake Texoma. Homer owned and operated a used car business until his retirement, and did quite well financially. Though not rich by any means, he was able to provide a very comfortable living for his family.

All three children were accomplished and popular, and prospered in the small town environment that was Sherman. Barbara and her sister, Jerrianne, were cheerleaders and class officers, and their brother, Stanley, was an accomplished football player who played collegiately for four years at Texas Western College (TWC), now the University of Texas-El Paso. Stan actually was in school there during the Don Haskins and "Bad News" Barnes era of basketball. A major turning point in sport history occurred at TWC in 1966 when their essentially all-black basketball team won the NCAA championship 72-65 over an all-white Kentucky team led by the legendary player Pat Riley and coached by the acknowledged racist coaching icon, Adolph Rupp. Basketball was never again the same after the TWC win, and the sport was soon transformed from essentially an all-Anglo enterprise to one dominated today by black players, particularly at the professional and Olympic level.

Stanley was not a highly-prized recruit coming out of Sherman High School, having offers as I remember only from Dartmouth College and Texas Western. Though clearly an exaggeration, Sherman is almost as close to Hanover, New Hampshire (home of Dartmouth College) in terms of miles as it is El Paso, so it was obvious Stanley was going to end up a long way from home either way. Stan was an undersized offensive lineman, weighing perhaps 175 pounds coming out of high school, but he eventually bulked up to 215 while at Western. Even by standards of the 1960's, he was small but thanks to smarts, tenacity, and the weight room, Stan started for three years on the offensive line. The teams he played on were quite successful and a number of his more gifted teammates played professionally.

I was witness to one of Stan's most memorable football experiences, playing opposite the all-time North Texas State College (now UNT) great, Mean Joe Greene. Greene outweighed Stan by fifty to sixty pounds and nearly beat him to death, knocking him out early in the game with a slap to the ear holes on his helmet. Greene proceeded to knock Stan's replacement out with similar shots to the head, and when Stan recovered enough to return to action, Mean Joe went back to work on him for the rest of the game. As you hard-core football fans may recall, Mean Joe Greene was a legend in professional football, being named Most Valuable Player (MVP) twice and chosen for the Pro Bowl ten times while playing for the Pittsburgh Steelers in the 1960's and 1970's. Stan also got to play against another NFL star of that era, a fellow by the name of Dave Rowe from Utah State, who also outweighed him by sixty pounds. Stan's summation of his experiences with the two collegiate/professional stars suggested Dave Rowe, big and mean though he was, was a pussycat compared to Joe Greene. But most mortals were…

Stan eventually received his degree in Accounting at TWC and launched a highly successful carpet manufacturing business in Georgia and Texas. He is now retired and lives in the Dallas area. Thanks to weddings and occasional family funerals, I have seen Stan a number of times over the years, and it is an eerie experience because of his striking similarity to his father, Homer. I have to do a double-take every time I see Stan. Homer's nose was more prominent and his frame a bit larger than Stan's, but the visual effect is indeed surreal.

Homer Blythe was nearly six feet tall and probably weighed 190 pounds at his peak. He never put on the middle age paunch so endemic (epidemic) to middle-aged American males, and he was handsome up to the day he died. He had a prominent nose, and both his daughters thanked the grand geneticist in the great beyond daily and profusely for sparing them that fate. Homer also had huge hands and wore a size fourteen ring. But the thing that marked Homer Blythe most was his kind, gentle spirit. I can honestly say that I never once heard him curse, gossip, or say anything negative about anyone in the forty years I knew the man. He was a gentle giant, not so much in size but in spirit.

HOMER AND VERNA BLYTHE

I was fond of Verna Elaine Fawcett Blythe (1916-1989), his wife, but she could be pretty difficult, particularly when she was under stress such as that generated by having a house full of people during the holidays. Stress usually led to migraine headaches that would put her on bed rest for a day or two at a time, and we all came to accept the fact that her presence would be missing for part of our stay at the Blythe house. All things considered, I always liked Verna and thought we shared a reasonable relationship with each other.

Verna had an interesting shoe fetish that Homer indulged, and I think her closet at its peak held maybe four hundred pairs of assorted footwear. This shoe collection brings to mind a story involving the two of them. Verna was visiting me in College Station one time, and Homer had plans in place to join up with us a day or two later. Verna called him the evening before he was to leave Sherman for College Station, asking that he bring a pair of Pallizio shoes from her closet. Shortly after getting comfortable from the four-hour trip to College Station, Homer took the shoes from a bag, and it was obvious from the look on Verna's face they were not the correct ones. When she asked why he failed to bring the highly-prized Pallizio's, Homer remarked, "I'm sorry, Verna, but these shoes looked pretty Pallizio to me." That was Homer Blythe in a nutshell; not a pretentious bone in his body!

Even at his financial peak, he spent little money on clothes or cars and other frills, and purchased his shoes from Walmart when they had a two-for-the-price-of-one sale till the day he died. Maybe a year or so after Verna passed away, a widower phoned Homer, indicating she had been eyeing him for quite a while. The two of them eventually agreed to go out and eat together, and in true Homer Blythe style, he treated her to an elegant meal at McDonald's which was largely underwritten by a two-for-one coupon he had received in the mail. It is this charming, almost boyish lack of pretense and guile that made Homer so special to me.

Even after Barbara and I got divorced, I would see Homer at family occasions, weddings, and occasional funerals, and he remained friendly and cordial. He could have easily been standoffish or vindictive to a man who had, perhaps in his eyes, mistreated his daughter, but he remained true to form until his death. When I heard that he had terminal cancer, I asked several of my children or their spouses to let me know when I should say my goodbyes. Unfortunately, I found out from my son-in-law, Craig Stiteler, who in the course of normal conversation while attempting to lure bass from my front-yard pond, happened to mention Homer's upcoming funeral. I was quite nonplussed with my kids for not informing me of the fatal downturn in Homer's health situation, but nothing could have kept me from attending his funeral service in Sherman. I would never have missed the last chance to remember and offer praise to perhaps the finest man I have ever known, and it was indeed a high honor to be a pall bearer at his funeral. His guidance, kindness, and example have been huge forces in my life. However, I have given up hopes of ever becoming even an approximation of Homer as a human being. Cancer did him in and the world is a lesser place because of his death. If there were more gentle, kind, soulful spirits like Homer Hardy Blythe among us, this would be an infinitely better world in which to live.

Aberrant Aggies:
An Axe Murderer and a Pedophile

I have been involved in different ways and to varying degrees with two very interesting local criminal cases, one a student who murdered his wife with a hatchet in 1978 and the other an A&M administrator who was arrested in 2007 because of his pervasive penchant for pedophilia and possession of child and adult pornography. In the hatchet murder case, I provided expert testimony at the request of two local defense attorneys. In the pedophilia/pornography case, I was simply a bystander though I had worked very closely with the perpetrator for several years and had absolutely no inkling he was such a Jekyll and Hyde character. The situation is reminiscent of accounts of Ted Bundy in the book, *This Stranger Beside Me*, in which the author, Anne Rule, writes about working for eighteen months on a crisis hotline in Seattle with the infamous serial killer. Ms. Rule was totally unaware of what her partner was doing, had done, and would continue to do, namely terrorize young women in at least four states! I was caught completely off guard in this case, much like Anne Rule. As will be seen shortly, Dr. Ronald Smith, Ted Bundy's undergraduate research mentor at the University of Washington, was also taken in, hook, line, and sinker, by his one-time protégé.

Mike R., Axe Murderer

In the axe murder case, I was sitting around the office one afternoon when the phone rang. I picked it up and answered with my customary, "LeUnes." The caller identified himself as Fred Davis, a local attorney and personal friend. Fred said, "Arnold, my dad and I are representing a young man, an Aggie, who has murdered his wife. You may have read about it in *The Eagle* some time ago. He was the guy who hit his wife in the head with the axe last March. His name is Michael Loren Reynolds, or Mike, and his wife was Pamela Sue Reynolds, or Pam. Pop and I are his attorneys and we want a psychological workup on him if you can fit it into your schedule, say in the next week. We are primarily interested in your assessment of how dangerous he might be if the court allows him back on the street. We want to hit the judge and jury with this information at some point if you think he represents minimal or no risk to the public."

The other attorney in the case was Fred's father, the now-deceased A. W. "Head" Davis, a well-known and highly respected figure in local legal circles. He also served for a time as President of the A&M Association of Former Students. With his incisive mind and folksy courtroom demeanor, watching "Head" Davis work a case was reminiscent of Atticus Finch in Harper Lee's Pulitzer prizewinning novel, *To Kill a Mockingbird* (thought his resemblance to the esteemed actor and portrayer of Atticus Finch, Gregory Peck, was marginal at best).

Dr. Death Number Two. Fred went on to say, "Mike has already been interviewed extensively by a top forensic psychiatrist, a fellow by the name of Holbrook; Dr. John Holbrook of Dallas. He is perhaps the top person in the country on expert psychiatric testimony." In fact, Holbrook and Dr. John Grigson were two of the ten psychiatrists who interviewed Jack Ruby shortly after he killed Lee Harvey Oswald, President John Kennedy's assassin, in Dallas in 1963. Holbrook and Grigson were expert witnesses for the prosecution, and Holbrook's court testimony in the case earned him considerable public notoriety. Holbrook testified that Ruby was not insane at the time of the Oswald shooting. In response, the defense attorneys contended that Ruby suffered from psychomotor epilepsy which led him to shoot Oswald.

Fred went on to say, "As for his collaborator, Grigson, he is widely known as "Dr. Death" because his testimony can be so damning and often results in the defendant receiving the death penalty. Also, his unwavering support of the ultimate punishment does nothing to detract from his legendary status as "Dr. Death." Because of the association with Grigson, Holbrook is dubbed "Dr. Death Number Two" by some authorities and legal experts. We feel lucky to have Holbrook on our side but we would like to beef up what he is doing with a thorough psychological workup, and we think you are the man for the task."

I told Fred, "You could not have called at a better time. I have discontinued my consulting jobs with the two treatment facilities in Brenham, and I'm looking for something to fill that void. Things are relatively quiet around the department also, and I can see Mike as soon as you can make the necessary arrangements with the sheriff. I'll give it my best shot." "Thanks, my man", Fred said. "I really appreciate it. I'll be back in touch soon." The phone then went dead.

A few days later, I got the expected call from Fred and I agreed to meet with Mr. Reynolds, the young axe murderer, the next afternoon. At 1400 hours, I pulled up to the county jail, entered the facility, and was immediately escorted to a private area to meet with our client. Mike Reynolds walked in to the room a few minutes after my arrival, and I was struck by his physical presence; he was handsome, clean-cut, and, at least on the surface, quite self-confident. I don't know what I expected, but he looked more like a pleasant choir boy than a heinous axe murderer. Mike stuck out his hand and I extended mine. He had large hands and a firm grip. He was twenty-five years old, maybe six feet tall, weighed around 185 or 190 pounds, muscular though not chiseled, and immaculately groomed. He had neatly combed short brown hair, sparkling blue eyes, unblemished skin, and looked every bit the Boy Scout he had been in his youth.

After exchanging pleasantries, we went to work. I asked him to give me a brief personal history and he offered the following summary: "I was a National Honors Society graduate of Lamar Consolidated in Rosenberg, Texas, graduating fifteenth out of a class of 420. I have since graduated Magna Cum Laude from A&M where I later received a master's degree. I am also a certified Emergency Medical Technician (EMT)." He went on to tell me that, despite the academic accomplishments and honors, he was hardly perfect: "I was part of a big misunderstanding in 1975 where it was alleged I had shoplifted a couple of fishing weights and a ladle spoon from a sporting goods store in Rosenberg. I accidentally put the items in one of my pockets while waiting in line to pay, and fully intended to take them out to pay for them, but a store security person apprehended me before I could complete the transaction. The local police were notified and in order to get the whole issue over with in an expeditious fashion, I agreed to pay a fifty dollar fine."

That brief run-in with the law was the extent of his "criminal activity", though he did tell me he had once received a citation for running a red light and was cited on three occasions for driving with excessive speed. In each of the three speeding cases, he was caught driving ten miles over the posted limit. As he related these minor misdeeds, all I could think was this is hardly the stuff of which axe murderers are made.

From there, I went right to the heart of the matter: "Mike, tell me about the day of the murder. What went on that got you into this mess?" I am not sure asking a guy to talk about the day he murdered his wife is the way to proceed, but it seemed like a straightforward way to get things moving. Also, it was not like I was the first person to ask him about the murder. He had been over it many times with the police, his attorneys, and Dr. Holbrook. Mike told me, "I killed Pam because she was having an affair with her archery coach, a fellow by the name of Ferris, and I could not get her to call it off. I knew about it for over a year, but I always kinda' figured it would run its course and she would end it. Or Ferris would."

As I was to find out through our subsequent discussions, this attitude captured the essence of Mike Reynolds. He truly believed in a just, orderly, orthogonal world, one in which thinking pure thoughts, doing the right thing, not confronting troublesome issues head-on, and just being an all-around nice person were sufficient to guarantee a good, orderly life. However, Pam never gave up her relationship with the coach and that sin of omission was to play a big role in her death that fateful March night. I think in some ways it was this bursting of the perfect, just-world bubble he had created in his mind that sent Mike over the edge and into a homicidal state.

Mike went on to tell me in a reserved tone, "I bit my lip and bided my time for almost eighteen months, knowing my wife was having this affair. She traveled a lot with the team, often came home on weekdays as late as midnight and some weekends at two or three in the morning. Quite often, she would wake me up, wanting to have sex, which is okay but I often had to be up early the next day to go to work, and that made the whole situation a hassle. When I would bring up the late hours she was keeping, Pam would vehemently deny anything was going on other than the typical above-board coach-athlete relationship. I knew better and so did our friends, but I tried to be positive and upbeat about it all."

One friend, a laboratory technician by the name of Dave Hassler, was particularly close to both Mike and Pam, and in fact lived with them for a time at their small home in College Station, on the east side of the campus. At the trial, Hassler testified the two were an easy-going couple at the outset of their marriage but increasingly argued about money issues, and the specter of the affair lingered over their relationship like an ominous dark cloud. During subsequent testimony, Hassler indicated to the twelve-person jury that Pam's belated confirmation of the affair became a major source of friction during the latter stages of the marriage and leading up to the night of her murder. Mike himself indicated in his interview with Dr. Holbrook that Pam put a lot of pressure on him to keep his job as a car salesman because he made good money, even though she knew he intensely disliked it. She wanted Mike to continue selling cars so they could move from their modest College Station home into a new one in a nice sub-division on the outskirts of town.

Mike was held in high regard at the car dealership and it was frankly unlikely that he could make more money elsewhere, at least in the short run. Thus, Mike stayed on in a job he detested to make ends meet financially and to please Pam. This situation was understandably stressful and played a significant role in pushing Mike over the edge the night he killed Pam.

Mike further stated, "What really did me in were events of the day I killed her. My boss at the car dealership, Ted Wilkinson, had given me four days off when I threatened to quit. He told me that I was the second best car salesman he had ever seen; I guess we both know who was number one. In any case, the boss told me to get my marriage straightened out over the weekend and come in rested and ready on the following Monday."

"Things must have gone downhill that Monday, huh?" I conjectured.

"You don't know the half of it," Mike said. "I got up, ate some cereal, and went to work. I called Pam at home around nine am and got no answer; then again at ten and eleven; still no response. Finally at noon, she answered the phone. I asked where she had been and she said, 'I have been practicing archery all morning with Ferris and a male friend of his." Mike went on to say, "The three of them apparently were at Ferris' trailer home in the Oak Forest Mobile Home Park on Krenek Tap Road. If you drive by the mobile home park, you can see the archery range Ferris created so his team would have a place to practice."

Mike continued on with his story: "I pretty much let it go at that, talked of events of the day at work, and hung up. At one I called again. Guess what? No answer; I called every hour or so for the rest of the afternoon. Again silence as I let the phone ring ten or twelve times. Finally, I got a response from her around five. I kept my anger under wraps as best I could by engaging in small talk. I eventually asked if she wanted to go out and eat around seven. She did, and we agreed to meet at Sambo's on Texas Avenue."

He went on to lay out the details of the evening: "We met around 7:30 instead of 7:00 because things were hopping at the dealership. We had a decent meal at Sambo's, nothing out of the ordinary, just some soup and sandwiches, I guess. Though the food was decent enough, the restaurant motif depicting black people being chased around in the jungle by lions and tiger was distracting. I am not a wild-eyed liberal or big human rights activist or anything, but the out-and-out racism in those wall scenes bothered me a lot."

Rapidly changing societal attitudes about race and the burgeoning Civil Rights Movement would soon ring the death knell for the Sambo's restaurant chain. Originating in 1957 and named after segments of the names of the co-founders, Sam Battistone and Newell Bohnett, the chain somehow became associated with *The Story of Little Black Sambo*, the children's book published in 1899. The plot of the story has a young boy encountering four hungry tigers and he avoids being eaten by giving his nice clothes to them. The tigers, in an attempt to outdo each other with their sartorial splendor, chase each other around and around until they turn into melted butter. The boy then retrieves his clothes, goes home, and his mother uses the butter for the pancakes she is feeding her family. Harmless enough at the outset, the book became controversial and eventually the word Sambo became a pejorative term for blacks, or a racial slur.

The chain was immensely popular and there were nearly 1200 Sambo's operating in forty-seven states as of 1979. The Civil Rights Act of 1964 and the racial unrest of the 1970's pretty much put an end to the Sambo's chain, and the only one still operating today is in Santa Barbara, California. Chad Stevens, the grandson of one of the founders, Sam Battistone, is the owner of that shop

Beginning of the End for Pam. Mike told me he and Pam drove home, arriving there around 8:30. Mike went on to tell me, "We goofed around for thirty minutes or so after getting home. At some point, Pam did something I thought was sexy and it turned me on. I really wanted to have sex with her, so I put my arms around her, kissed her a few times, and suggested that we go back to the bedroom. Pam said that she could not engage in sex with me at that moment because she had to work on a term paper for one of her courses. She said there was something she wanted to watch on TV later, too." I inquired of Mike: "What was your response to being rejected like that? What was going on in your head?"

His eyes narrowed, his breathing became shallower, and his face flushed ever so slightly as he related his feelings at that life-changing, transformative moment. "I didn't say this out loud, but I looked at her with my best poker face and thought to myself: 'You are dead! All you have ever done since we got married is lie around on the couch in your coveralls with your dirty, stringy hair and watch TV. The rest of the time you are out screwing your coach's eyeballs out. And don't give me this nonsense about writing a term paper. I have made notes on every book you have ever read and written every theme and term paper you have ever turned in. You are dead! You are one dead bitch!"

He told me he went to the kitchen, picked up a pencil and pad, and wrote down how he was going to carry out the death sentence he had silently conferred on Pam a few moments earlier. He told me, "I wrote down a few notes and then went across the kitchen to the silverware drawer and retrieved a sharp knife. My original intent was to somehow render her unconscious, stab her, and cut her throat. However, I had some misgivings about that plan because I was afraid that she might not die immediately. I also envisioned a scenario in which she would retaliate and somehow survive the knife attack."

"My next thought was to go a hallway closet where I kept an axe. I grabbed the axe and told Pam I was leaving to run an errand and would be back shortly. I walked outside to my pickup, carrying two murder weapons and a makeshift blindfold crafted from a ragged t-shirt. I then drove out east of College Station to the Fed Mart store. It was pretty quiet out there because there aren't all that many businesses on University Avenue."

Mike went on to say, "I called Pam from a store pay phone, suggesting that she meet me at Fed Mart in thirty minutes as I had a big surprise in store for her. She had no idea!"

He continued his tale, "When she got to Fed Mart, I told her I wanted to show her the lot I had purchased for our new home which was in the early planning stages. In order to make it a real surprise, I asked her if she would put on a blindfold. I told her I wanted this to be a real surprise right up to the second we got to our lot. She agreed to my request, and the two of us went searching for what I knew was essentially a never-to-be home site."

Mike further told me, "I kept going east from Fed Mart in the direction of Steep Hollow Road outside of Bryan. I eventually stopped the car on a country road off the main highway. Before she could remove the blindfold, I took out my axe and hit her on top of the head. She reflexively put her arm out to protect herself, and the second blow nearly severed her arm. I then hit her six more times in the head, three times in the neck, and though I had no idea at the time, a total of two more wounds were found on her right hand. I dumped her body at the intersection of Farm to Market Road 1179 and Grassbur Road, returned home and placed the incriminating evidence in a bag for the garbage pickup the next morning. I then developed some doubts about this plan so I placed the bag with all the evidence inside several other garbage bags and headed back to Fed Mart to dispose of everything in a dumpster there."

The Case Begins to Come Apart. He continued, "After a sleepless night, I called the police the next morning and reported my wife was missing. I then went to work and informed the sales manager at Ted Wilkinson's that Pam had not come home the previous night and I was concerned about her well-being. I later made phone calls to a friend of Pam's by the name of Elaine but got no answer. I made yet another call to an ambulance service to see if there had been any reports of accidents overnight. Later that morning, I thought about calling Pam's parents, the Dotson's, to see if she had gone home overnight to visit them, but I never made that call because I obviously knew for sure she had not contacted them."

On the morning of March 15, 1978, some oil field workers discovered the body of Pamela Reynolds lying at the bottom of a ditch. With the body were her university identification card, Texas driver's license, and Aggie ring. Shortly after Pam was identified, Detective Bobby Yeager of the College Station Police Department informed Mike of the location of her body. Yeager later testified at the trial, "I found it odd that Mike's grief at the news lasted about a minute and at no time did he inquire about what had happened to her or where she was at that time." Bob Connell, a Texas Ranger who also interviewed Mike, testified in court that, "...he was shocked at how calm Mike had been at the news of his wife's death."

Four days later, Mike agreed to undergo a polygraph examination and was transported to Waco where the test was administered. In his own words, Mike said, "I went to Waco, took the polygraph test and I lied on the polygraph test. I knew it and they knew it. The needles jumped all over." He pretty much came apart at the seams after the polygraph session and signed a detailed four-page confession that sealed his fate as an axe murderer and Pam's as a victim of spousal violence.

Detective Bobby Yeager later became the Sheriff of Brazos County, and the incarceration of Mike Reynolds eventually ended up being his responsibility. In the twenty-one months between Mike's arrest and the trial, Mike became a legendary figure around the county jail. For all intents and purposes he had become the *de facto* Deputy Sheriff of Brazos County. In his role as would-be Deputy Sheriff, he transported work teams from the jail into the community, appointed himself the chief mechanic in the motor pool, had his own vehicle to drive whenever he needed to leave the jail, and rode with Emergency Medical Teams at night throughout Brazos County. Can you imagine the public outcry and brouhaha if they had known a heinous, cold-blooded, axe-murdering wife-killer was free from dawn to dusk and again at night to do pretty much as he wished within our peaceful little county? Adding to Mike's stature as *de facto* Deputy Sheriff was his heroic response to a fire in the jail in which he was given credit for saving the lives of several of his incarcerated peers. I heard through the grapevine that Sheriff Yeager once described Mike Reynolds "...as the second best lawman he had ever met." Anyone want to bet who the best lawman was? Mike's credentials as second-best were starting to pile up, thanks to Ted Wilkinson at the auto dealership and Sheriff Yeager at the county jail.

My Psychological Workup on Mike. After the initial interview, I administered a battery of psychological tests to Mike in hopes of gaining some additional insights into what made him tick and whether he would be a threat to society should a jury set him free at the trial. Because I was not pressed for time and Mike was not going anywhere for the foreseeable future, I was able to administer a broader battery of tests than would be the norm in a "typical" felony murder case. The tests used and the dates of their administration were:

October 31, 1978
    Bender Visual Motor Gestalt Test (Bender)
    Edwards Personal Preference Schedule (EPPS)
    Eysenck Personality Inventory (EPI)
    Rorschach Inkblot Test (Rorschach)

November 7, 1978
    Attitude Statement Survey (Locus of Control Scale)
    Minnesota Multiphasic Personality Inventory (MMPI)
    State-Trait Anxiety Inventory (STAI)
    Wechsler Adult Intelligence Scale (WAIS)

The WAIS, a valid and reliable measure of individual adult intelligence, the Rorschach, a projective test of personality, the MMPI, the so-called "grand-daddy" of all objective personality measures, and the Bender, a global screening device for detection of possible brain damage, were the four critical components of the battery. All other tests were ancillary and used in support of the major assessment instruments. Mike's IQ as determined by results on the WAIS was 120, a score that put him in the upper fourteen percent of the American adult population; he was clearly a bright enough guy. With regard to the two major personality measures, the Rorschach and the MMPI, nothing particularly remarkable showed up. As for the Bender, it was included, as I said, because it is a brief and easily administered global assessment tool for detecting possible brain pathology. I knew going in the likelihood of finding brain impairment in this case was minimal at best, but since the Bender yields so much information in such a short time, I went ahead with it. The test consists of pictures of eight geometric drawings and the subject is asked to reproduce each of them as accurately as possible on a blank sheet of typing paper. When the test was over, Mike's replications were so precise, it is not much of an exaggeration to say I could have taken scissors to the sheet of paper, cut up his responses, and used them as a back-up set.

After all was said and done, I wrote up the following summation for the attorneys and the court:

"Based on the results of the eight tests that were administered, the most likely conclusion to be drawn is that the subject, Michael Loren Reynolds, is sound in terms of mental health. The overwhelming bulk of the evidence is in favor of this interpretation.

In terms of understanding this client, a number of salient points emerge. First of all, in cases such as this, it would seem useful to examine the possibility of brain damage or related neurological impairment as a possible contributing factor. Based on results of the Bender Gestalt and the WAIS Block Design subtest, this eventuality can be ruled out. Too, the fact that his IQ falls in the upper 14% of the population adds depth to this preceding conclusion.

A second point of concern is the existence or absence of amoral or psychopathic tendencies. All evidence points to the client being in possession of considerable conscience, honesty, or morality. He is aware of the rules of society, generally acts in accordance with those rules, and generally comes across as honest and reliable. His Psychopathic Deviate score in the MMPI was quite within the desirable range, and his honesty scores on the EPI, the EPPS, and the MMPI were most acceptable. Every piece of psychometric evidence points to the absence of psychopathic or amoral tendencies in this case.

A third feature, anxiety, deserves mention in that it is such a pervasive aspect of a number of psychopathological states. All indicators point to the presence of sufficient but not crippling anxiety. The neuroticism score on the EPI was in the lower half of the distribution, and state and trait anxiety scores on the STAI were quite low. There is little likelihood of neuroses or other anxiety-related states here.

A fourth consideration has to do with organization and control. This subject is highly organized and methodical, sees himself at the center of the determination of his own fate, and is generally a self-contained person. His locus of control is decidedly internal, his need for order (EPPS) is quite high, and his approach to the Rorschach is indicative of the same general personality traits of orderliness, organization, and self-governance or self-regulation.

Finally, in terms of his pattern of needs as assessed by the EPPS, he shows a clear need to persevere and endure, to be nurturing and helpful to others, to have order in his life, and a pronounced need for abasement. This last need may be a manifestation or an outgrowth of a need for punishment related to his alleged crime of several months ago. If, on the other hand, it represents a more pervasive and deeply-rooted need for punishment, it may be viewed as a negative.

All things considered, Michael Loren Reynolds appears to be emotionally stable without any pronounced signs of neurosis, psychosis, or psychopathic behavior. These things should be considered when determining guilt and assigning punishment."

Request for a Change of Venue. The two defense attorneys, "Head" and Fred Davis, petitioned a plea bargain agreement that would have resulted in Mike receiving a twenty-year sentence. However, the magistrate presiding over the case, the Honorable Tom McDonald, was not receptive to this proposal. A request for a change of venue was subsequently lodged with and granted by the court, and the case was moved to the Criminal Justice Center on the campus of Sam Houston State University in Huntsville, Texas, some sixty miles east of Bryan-College Station.

At the onset of the proceedings in Huntsville, I walked in the front door of the Criminal Justice Center and was immediately greeted by a couple of young Assistant District Attorneys, one of whom was Jim James. Jim had taken my class in Abnormal Psychology during the fall semester of 1975, so he knew something was up when he spotted me coming into the center. Once he figured out my purpose for being there, Jim and his associates immediately got on the phone and summoned an expert psychiatric witness from the University of Texas Medical Branch in Galveston to come to Huntsville to testify on behalf of the prosecution.

The psychiatrist who was brought in on short notice read the relevant documents related to the case including my psychological assessment, and she testified, "...Mike Reynolds is a cold-blooded killer who will undoubtedly kill again within twenty-four hours if allowed back on the streets." Her interpretation and testimony were diametrically opposite of mine and a potential source of embarrassment for our respective professions. There is always room for disagreements about test interpretation, but it is a stretch to interpret the same data so differently.

A decade or so earlier, I had heard a talk at the same Criminal Justice Center delivered by the famous Kansas psychiatrist, Karl Menninger of Menninger Clinic fame, in which he, in no uncertain terms, said psychologists and psychiatrists had no place in the courtroom. In every case, he said, they end up embarrassing themselves and their respective professions. Such was the case here; the psychology/psychiatry professions were given a real black eye in terms of public perception and confidence by the substantial gap between her testimony and mine. I spent many hours with Mike and the witness for the prosecution spent none and yet offered up dire and draconian predictions about his future behavior.

This incident reminds me of a local case in which a young Iraq veteran was found guilty of murdering his girlfriend and her brother, both A&M students. During the trial, a psychologist for the defense testified that the perpetrator did not mean to shoot the two victims, one of whom had been shot three times. I cannot wrap my mind around shooting someone three times and not meaning to do it. Heavens to Betsy, what were you thinking, Mr. Psychologist!

Prior to and during jury selection for the case, Fred, "Head", Dr. Holbrook, and I sat around telling war stories, speculating about the jury selection process, and estimating where we stood in defending our client. It is interesting to note that the jury panel ended up with eight women and four men, and we four so-called experts agreed that the men might end up being the most lenient with our client. Our collective reasoning was that several worked for the prison system and would know our client was not your typical poorly educated, low intelligence, lowbrow, recidivistic, petty criminal. On the other hand, we believed the women would be predisposed to hang our client from the highest scaffold for the grisly, brutal slaying of one of their own kind.

Because the case was not a capital offense and the death penalty was thus not an issue, the jury was charged with punishment parameters ranging from probation to ninety-nine years in prison. The men on the panel, counter to our predictions, took the most punitive stances on sentencing while one or two of the women actually held out for probation. After the dust settled, the presiding judge sentenced Mike to thirty-eight years in the prison. Once there, Mike was assigned to work in the infirmary at the Walls unit in Huntsville, no doubt a function of his previous EMT training and experience. He worked in the infirmary for the duration of his sentence and was eventually paroled after thirteen years for good behavior. He disappeared at that point except as a most interesting memory.

I often thought of visiting Mike because of the cordial relationship we had established prior to his trial but decided not to intrude on his prison privacy. I certainly have thought about him many times over the years. He was a bright, capable, likeable, and conscientious young man who made a horrible mistake just once in his life, a miscue that cost him in ways that only he can fully understand.

I am reminded of similar sentiments expressed by the original FBI profiler, John Douglas, when he interviewed the heinous serial killer, Edmund Kemper. Kemper was a giant of a man physically, being six feet nine inches tall and weighing in at three hundred pounds. He was also bright, scoring 145 on an IQ test. Kemper was as mean and sadistic as he was big and bright, and was linked to murders of his grandmother, grandfather, mother, two coeds from Fresno State University in California, a fifteen-year-old female hitchhiker, a student from Santa Cruz, a friend of his mother, and two women from the San Francisco area. Of the murder of his grandmother, Kemper was quoted as follows: "I just wondered how it would feel to shoot grandma." In the case of his mother, he beat her to death with a claw hammer, sliced off her head, cut out her larynx, and raped her. Of the "surgery" to remove the larynx, he said, "It seemed appropriate as much as she bitched, and screamed and yelled at me over the years." In the case of the student from Santa Cruz, he shot her, dissected the body, and threw it in the Pacific Ocean. He retained her severed head which he buried in his back yard with the head tilted toward his mother's bedroom. His explanation for this senseless sadism: "My mother had always wanted people to look up to her." Ed Kemper was eventually arrested and Douglas was called in to interview him several times as part of the police work-up. In his book, *Mindhunter*, Douglas summed up his relationship with Kemper as follows: "I would be less than honest if I did not admit that I liked Ed. He was friendly, open, sensitive, and had a good sense of humor. As much as you can say such a thing in this setting, I enjoyed being around him. Many of these guys are quite charming, highly articulate, and glib." Though the personalities and the criminal acts varied greatly in our respective cases, John Douglas and I share similar positive feelings about encounters with two men who inflicted horrible suffering and pain on other human beings.

The Unfortunate Demise of Dr. Death Number Two. As a postscript to the Reynolds case, Dr. Holbrook, the defense psychiatrist, was on cloud nine during the entire trial. He was engaged to be married (his second) to a nurse named Azalea Bankston, had recently obtained a pilot's license, and generally appeared to be on top of the world. Holbrook held forth at great length during breaks in the trial about how good life was, particularly the existential high he experienced as a new pilot piloting his plane in the skies above the metropolitan Dallas area.

Unfortunately, in the third week of June, 1980, or roughly eighteen months after the Reynolds trial, Dr. Holbrook was found dead in his room at the Boots and Saddle motel in Mexia, Texas, halfway between College Station and Dallas. The cause of death was determined to be a massive heart attack though suspicions of a possible suicide were hard to rule out. Word was he had become disenchanted with his practice in Dallas, suspicious notes were found in both the Mexia motel and his Dallas home, and there were empty containers of liquor and Valium on the nightstand beside the motel bed. He apparently intentionally or unintentionally overdosed which may, in turn, have triggered the coronary event that killed him. Dr. John Holbrook was fifty-six years of age at the time of his death. An interesting take on Dr. Holbrook's death was spun by Kennedy conspiracy theorists who intimated that the sudden and somewhat mysterious demise of our psychiatrist friend was part of a plot to get rid of all important figures in the Lee Harvey Oswald/Jack Ruby cases. No such link was ever established.

Brian Lancaster: Pornographer and Pedophile

Most of us take pride in our ability to accurately size up others we meet, and some people are so smug and complacent they actually think their powers of judgment are infallible. However, it has been proven time and time again that even the best judges of human behavior can be fooled from time to time. Yours truly has been duped with the best of them. To wit:

One morning in 2007, I was eating breakfast at McDonald's on Rock Prairie Road in south College Station, clogging some arteries with an Egg McMuffin and greasy tater tots while engaging in a typical morning ritual, reading my local and regional newspapers, *The Bryan-College Station*

Eagle and *Houston Chronicle*. One of the front page *Eagle* headlines featured a provocative entry that caught my attention. It went "A&M Administrator Charged with Sex Crimes" or something to that effect. My first thought was A&M is big and impersonal, almost a mid-sized city in its own right, with 50,000 students and thousands of faculty and support staff. In addition, the combined population of Bryan, College Station, and Texas A&M University is greater than that of the Gulf Coast city of Galveston. Given this caveat, I thought to myself, "What is the likelihood I would recognize a person from a random story about a sex crime involving an administrator at A&M?" However, mild curiosity got the best of me so I took a peek.

The headline of interest was placed just above the fold in the upper half of the paper and the actual story was imbedded just below. Thus, I had to lift the paper up and unfold it to see if I might know the alleged miscreant. Lo and behold, there was a picture of one of my most admired, respected, and trusted colleagues, a man I thought the world of, someone I would have bet my last dollar on when the genuinely nice guy accolades are handed out. I never thought of this man as anything but squeaky clean but, like Ann Rule and Dr. Ron Smith and their experiences with Ted Bundy, I could have not been more wrong!

The article indicated that pedophilia and child pornography charges had been leveled against my friend and colleague, Dr. Brian Lancaster, Acting Director of the Study Abroad activities sponsored by A&M's Office of International Programs. In his capacity as overseer of large segments of the substantial Study Abroad operation, Brian had become a trusted ally and a major facilitator and promoter of my programs in Germany discussed in some detail elsewhere. When dealing with the Study Abroad office, I always knew who to go for help when it was needed. And more importantly, I knew where the buck stopped. Simply stated, I could not have had a better working relationship with a more helpful, facilitative, cordial, and collegial colleague than Brian Lancaster.

Brian Visits My Study Abroad Program in Germany. In the summer of 2005, Brian made a trip to Europe to look in on programs in Germany and Italy operating under his jurisdiction, one of which was mine. As part of his overseas junket, he spent a day with my students while we basked in the sun during a boat cruise on the Rhine River just south of Bonn, the main base of operations during my summer stays in Germany. We also spent some time that day touring the Marksburg Castle, one of many such structures along the Rhine and, later, took part in a wine-tasting at a small, family-owned Rhineland winery. My students and associates in Germany found Brian to be forthcoming and delightful, just one of the guys, really. He had an uncanny way of making people feel at ease, and this trait did not go unnoticed by my students. He was, simply put, a great fit!

Jekyll and Hyde Personality. Physically, Brian was pretty unremarkable, average looking, most certainly no Cary Grant or Brad Pitt (who I always somehow mentally confuse with Sean Penn)....just a normal looking guy. The word "thin" aptly described Brian; thin in facial structure, thin in body build, with thinning light brown hair. He was perhaps six feet in height and weighed maybe one hundred-sixty pounds, tops. He was not imposing at all physically but his interpersonal skills were considerable. He was cordial, open, friendly, facilitating, organized, and professional in his work habits, just a good guy in the best sense of the word. There was nothing whatsoever in his daily demeanor to suggest that he was anything but a thirty-six year old, newly-anointed PhD with a bright future in university administration.

Despite the clean-cut veneer, there was clearly a dark side to this man that none of us could have possibly foreseen. I know from conversations with people who worked with Brian that all were absolutely blown away when the depth of his depravity surfaced in newspaper accounts following his arrest in January, 2007. More gory revelations came out later that year during his trial in November and December. His wife testified that Brian Lancaster was a Jekyll and Hyde character, wonderfully straight during the day and a full-blown threat to society by night.

When his arrest was announced, it was apparent that the authorities knew things about Dr. Brian Lancaster we outsiders could not imagine even in our wildest dreams. To put an exclamation point on this statement, Brian's bail was set at slightly over thirteen million dollars. Yes, you read the figure correctly! Thirteen million smackeroos for a pedophile and pornographer! By way of comparison, the highest bail ever put up by the notorious serial killer Ted Bundy was $15,000 and that was for a 1975 kidnapping charge. The authorities must have known a lot about Brian Lancaster and his criminal history to justify what appears on the surface to be an outrageous bail figure in a sex case.

Brian was arrested at his office on the campus in January of 2007 after two sisters, both younger than ten, reported that he had sexually abused them. It seems the two girls were at the Lancaster home taking piano lessons from Brian's wife when the abuse occurred. Subsequent searches of his home computer revealed videos of the molestation of the two sisters as well as incriminating videos involving several other young females. Also, more than twenty-thousand child pornography images were stored on his computer.

It turns out that the above offenses were only part of a criminal history that began in adolescence and intensified shortly after Brian received his bachelor's degree in Biblical Studies from Abilene Christian University (ACU) where he also received a master's degree. He and his wife met at ACU, and upon graduation, Brian took an intern position as youth minister at the Church of Christ in Lampasas, Texas. Brian began his internship there one week after their honeymoon in 1994, and was soon arrested for felony indecency with a fourteen-year old female who he had offered a ride home after evening church services. Brian said that the relationship with the teen was consensual but the young girl insisted that she fell asleep in his car and he forced himself on her while she slept. In either case, what he had done was a criminal act, given the age of the victim. Eventually, a plea bargain was reached in which Brian agreed to plead guilty to a misdemeanor charge of public lewdness. It was also a part of the plea agreement that he take part in six months of sex offender counseling. Brian conveniently "forgot" to mention this Lampasas indiscretion when he accepted the Study Abroad position with A&M. Apparently, a criminal history check failed to turn up anything because his name was never entered into any sex offender registry due to the plea-bargained misdemeanor lewdness charges. Coincidentally, it was about the time he took the position at A&M that his appetite for child pornography intensified.

In terms of trying to understand the origins of Brian's fascination with child pornography and pedophilia, it is instructive to know he grew up in a family with at least three generations of convicted pedophiles. His grandfather, father, and an older brother all served time in prison for crimes against children. There was also a family history of drug abuse, and Brian had been arrested with his older brothers at age nineteen for dealing cocaine. It also came out at the time of the arrest that Brian was a regular user of marijuana, cocaine, and methamphetamines. On the day of his arrest at A&M, a bag of marijuana was found in his briefcase.

As further evidence of the deviance and depravity of his sexual appetites, Brian possessed videotapes of a female college student who lived near his home in Bryan. Testimony presented at the trial indicated he had secretly videotaped the student in her bedroom fourteen times during a six-week voyeuristic spree. It is interesting that throughout his repeated taping of the female college student, no one apparently noticed nor reported him lurking about outside her home.

Trial and Sentencing. His trial ended on Monday, November 19, 2007, and Brian was assessed a penalty of one hundred years in prison. Three weeks later, a new jury and the presiding magistrate in the case, Judge Rick Davis of the 272nd District Court, assessed a more severe penalty of 540 years and a fine of one million dollars. Among the charges brought against Brian that led to these penalties were one hundred counts of possession of child pornography, two counts of promotion of child pornography, five counts of child molestation by contact, one count of molestation by exposure, and one count of solicitation of a minor. He declined to plead guilty to over one hundred other felony charges, mostly for possession of child pornography. The fact that two of the abused girls were his own nieces further suggests that there were no boundaries on how wide a net he would cast to satisfy his deviant sexual appetites.

Though it is a topic for another time, the disparity in sentences handed down in criminal cases has always been a mystery. Back in the late 1960's, my colleague, Dr. Larry Christensen, and I conducted a study of criminals incarcerated in the Texas prison system. I remember being awestruck by the sentencing disparities among the two hundred prisoners we tested. The most egregious example was one in which a nineteen-year old Hispanic male from the Rio Grande Valley of Texas was sentenced to forty years in prison for possession of one marijuana cigarette while a thirty-three-year old murderer, a black man, was sentenced to nineteen years for his crime. The outrageous sentence handed out to the Hispanic youth was in stark contrast to that of the murderer and serves to underscore the archaic and punitive nature of our marijuana laws in those days. Fortunately, injustices such as this led to the decriminalization of marijuana a few years later. Even today, however, our jails and prisons are full of minor drug users and pushers who need treatment far more than they need incarceration. And at what cost financially?

It also came out during the trial that Brian had been engaging in explicit online conversations for some time with a Church of Christ minister in Corpus Christi. Brian dismissed the conversations as nothing more than online role-playing whereby the minister would indulge Brian's fantasies of pedophilia while he, in turn, would entertain the minister's gay wishes and ruminations.

Brian's wife filed for divorce the same month he was arrested. She did state that Brian had been kind to their three children, ranging in age from two to nine years, but hoped they would have no further contact with him after the trial and subsequent incarceration. A question that ran through my mind as this saga unfolded was whether or not he abused his own children. It appears that he did not but it came out in court testimony that he used them on occasion to distract his victims. Apparently, he would get his own children to tickle his young victims to divert their attention away from sex acts he was perpetrating. Brian also filmed the episodes for later sexual gratification.

I still wonder to this day why his wife was having young girls in her home for piano lessons when she must have known of her husband's perverse pedophilic propensities. I guess an even greater question is raised if she did not know! Other questions that kept coming up in my mind included: Was she left out of the loop? Was she stupid? Did she overtly or covertly enable her husband's sexual appetites? Was she herself a victim of some kind?

This Stranger Beside Me. One of the lessons I learned from this episode is that we may never really know about other people, even good friends, acquaintances, and close work associates. We may think we know, but all of us harbor a huge capacity for being fooled by people closest to us. Most of the time, our assessments of others are validated by subsequent behavior, but there are times when even the most cynical among us can be taken in by a wily con man. The same thing goes for trained mental health professionals who bring a lot of training and experience to the assessment of human behavior. They, too, get bamboozled and flimflammed by their clients from time to time.

A most interesting example of being taken in by an antisocial personality or psychopath, one with personal overtones, is that of the notorious serial killer Ted Bundy and his aforementioned mentor at the University of Washington, my esteemed colleague Dr. Ronald Smith. Though I do not know Ron well, what I do know of him is highly positive; he is an experienced clinical psychologist, a good scientist, and in my brief interactions with him a very nice man. In addition to being mentored by Ron Smith, it seems that Ted Bundy was also a favorite undergraduate student of another member of the University of Washington Psychology faculty in Seattle, Dr. Patricia Lunneborg.

As can be seen in the letter below, Bundy developed an interest in the law and as his graduation date neared, he asked Ron Smith to write him a letter of recommendation to the University of Utah Law School. Ron Smith, of course, agreed to write a letter for one of his most respected undergraduates, and it read:

> "Mr. Bundy is undoubtedly one of the top undergraduate students in our department. Indeed, I would place him in the top 1% of undergraduate students with whom I have interacted both here at the University of Washington and at Purdue University. He is exceedingly bright, personable, highly motivated, and conscientious.
>
> He conducts himself more like a young professional than like a student. He has the capacity for hard work and because of his intellectual curiosity is a pleasure to

interact with....As a result of his undergraduate psychology major, Mr. Bundy has become intensely interested in studying psychological variables which influence jury decisions. He and I are currently engaged in a research project in which we are attempting to study experimentally some of the variables which influence jury decisions.

I must admit that I regret Mr. Bundy's decision to pursue a career in law rather than to continue his professional training in psychology. Our loss is your gain.

I have no doubt that Mr. Bundy will distinguish himself as a law student and as a professional and I recommend him to you without qualification."

Ron Smith's laudatory comments concerning the academic acumen and character of Ted Bundy is a poignant reminder that even the best psychologist can be fooled by a crafty psychopathic liar! In the case of yours truly, my Ted Bundy was Brian Lancaster.

Slow-Pitch Softball, 1974-2007

From Bad News Bears To Bullies on the Block

One of the more interesting and, in some ways, pathological phases of my adult life was my three-decade addiction to slow-pitch softball. As noted elsewhere in some detail, I was a passably decent baseball player through Little League, Teenage League, American Legion, and high school. However, the old bat and glove were buried in the deepest recesses of various personal closets from the time I graduated from good old Dewey High School in 1956 until I was in my mid-thirties. The hiatus came to an end in the mid-1970's when Leslie Denton, a mailman for the university postal service, asked around during one of his stops in the department to see if anyone would be interested in playing on a team for which he would serve as organizer and nominal coach. Leslie and I had developed a cordial relationship based on mailroom chats and old family ties. Leslie was the son of a respected colleague, Allen "Buddy" Denton and the brother of one of my favorite students who went on to become a physician, Allen Denton. In addition, his mother, Alice, was one of wife Judy's teacher colleagues in the local public schools.

Two facts emerged from the first practice Leslie threw together on one of the local softball diamonds. For one thing, the team was awful and, secondly, I was perhaps more awful, and both were in need of serious triage. I offer four of many possible examples in support of my triage hypothesis: (1) Tony Bourgeois, a very experienced baseball and softball player, struck out his first at bat; Cless Jay, our department head, tore a hamstring that hemorrhaged badly, and the off-color, bloody internal wound made a gravity-dictated downward journey, taking weeks to descend from high on the hamstring near the buttocks to low on the calf; (3) Jeff Kern, a Clinical Psychology faculty member, asked Tony, who had a rifle for an arm, to take it easy on him during pregame warm-ups, wailing "Tony, please don't throw so hard. You are hurting my hand"; (4) Jeff Kramer, one of our graduate students, camped under a softly hit routine fly ball, yelling appropriately enough for all to hear, "I've got it. I've got it" only to see the ball drop three feet behind and four feet to his left. And these were highlights of the first few practices, not low points. The sad thing was Tony, Cless, and I, were among the best players, not the worst!

Predictably, the team struggled and died a richly deserved death at the end of the first disastrous season. In the process, however, some of us improved enough to catch the softball bug. Tony and I joined a local fastpitch team the following summer, one doomed to the league cellar because we had no pitcher which is certain death in that sport. It was impossible to even have a meaningful batting practice when your pitchers were incapable of throwing strikes, and it was even harder to win league games with that glaring deficiency.

There was one bright light in that collection of ragamuffins, an undergraduate student named Tommy Royder who had magic hands and a lightning bat. He also showed glimmers of talent as a pitcher though he was raw and a work in progress at that time. Tommy did little pitching the one season we played together, but he worked on his delivery and went on to become a top pitcher and all-around player. After graduating from A&M, Tommy took a job in Seattle, Washington, where he played serious softball in his spare time. For a few years after he left College Station, we were able to briefly renew our friendship because his team made the long trek to College Station to play in the men's national fastpitch tournament held at Central Park. Tommy had become a respectable thrower around the Seattle leagues but regarded himself as only so-so as a pitcher on a team good enough to play at the national tournament level. He was far more than respectable as a fielder and hitter, however, and it was always good to see him come back to town as an all-star player and all-around good guy.

> **Tom's Barbecue wins again**
>
> For the second straight year, Tom's Barbecue has captured the Texas A&M intramural slowpitch softball championship for both summer semesters.
>
> Tom's defeated perennial rival, the Roughnecks, 14-2, in the latest championship game. Prior tournament victories were taken over the Big Sticks, 17-3; X-300's, 15-2; and the Summer Cutters, 8-3.
>
> In addition to the four summer first place finishes, Tom's has won both annual Penberthy tournaments and owns a second place finish in the All-University playoffs this past spring.
>
> Team members include: Tony Bourgeois, Marshall Collins, Jim Emig, Mike Goodenough, Dave Griffin, Rick Hall, Bruce Henry, Tim Jamieson, Scott Lee, Arnold LeUnes, Chip Murphey, Gary O'Neal, Brent Rice, Joe Schultz, Steve Schultz and Val Joe Walker. O'Neal and Murphey are the coaches.

TOM'S BBQ WINS TOURNAMENT, CIRCA 1980

Tony Takes One For the Team. One of the more humorous events of that brief foray into fastpitch softball involved my friend and many years teammate, Tony Bourgeois, who was our catcher that evening. It seems that one of our invariably wild and erratic throwers launched a pitch that bounced a few feet in front of home plate, skipping under Tony's glove and hitting him squarely in the crotch.

Fortunately, the force of the pitch was partially absorbed by his protective cup, but the sound of the collision of ball and cup echoed around the diamond like a rifle shot. The ball then trickled slowly back along the line from whence it came, finally assuming a resting position halfway between home plate and the pitcher who had launched the errant missile. Our league games were played with a time limit and we were rapidly running out of clock that night, so our manager, Jim Bevers, started yelling at Tony: "Come on Tony. Quit stalling, man. Time's running out and we're behind. Pick up the ball and get it back to the pitcher." Jim and I were sitting next to each other on the bench and I said to him, "Jim, if you look closely, you will see that Tony is turning green and walking on egg shells, and the reason is he just took a shot to the nuts. That loud noise you heard was the ball ricocheting off his cup!" Jim then understood the gravity of the situation as only another male could, and he let up as Tony gingerly retrieved the ball and returned it to our "pitcher."

In retrospect, the incident involving Tony and the wild pitch was a metaphor for our failed venture into fastpitch softball. I gave up the game after that one season and Tony did so a year later. And I well should have hung up the cleats, based on my performance. I was far removed from being a competitive player at that time. My skills had eroded from disuse over the years and much reclamation work was needed if I was to function at a competitive level. On the whole, however, I am convinced if Tony and I had stayed with fastpitch we would have become good, solid, contributing players, but not without a lot of hard work.

Our Slow-Pitch Fortunes Take A Turn For the Better. When the next season rolled around, Tony and I agreed to give slow-pitch a second shot, and we played in both the city league and university intramurals programs. Thanks to Spanish lessons from my friend Sandra Campos Semper down in the Rio Grande Valley city of McAllen, we were known for that one season as Guajalote (Spanish for turkey). She later gave us another team title, Cloche, which she defined for us as Spanish for "your pants are caught in the crack of your ass." We subsequently settled for several subsequent seasons on the highly imaginative name of Psychology. After that, a local restaurant sponsored us and we then became Tom's Barbecue. After a successful run as Tom's, we were able to wheedle a sponsorship from the popular student hangout at North Gate, Duddley's Draw, and they were our sponsor for many years. Among the incentives to play for Duddley's was the promise of three free pitchers of beer after each game. The three pitchers almost always became five or ten or even fifteen, thanks to the ability of our wives and girlfriends to cadge free pitchers from the female-vulnerable male bartenders.

Initially, we were accustomed to getting our asses handed to us on a platter by the good teams from Bay City, Brenham, Huntsville, Pasadena, and Temple, but the tables eventually turned. We became the bullies on the block, and rightfully took our place with the big boys after 1980.

Richard Benning, Duddley's Draw, and the "Bar Team." Richard Benning came to College Station in 1973 from Lubbock where he was part owner of a bar called the Town Draw. He arrived in town just in time to help introduce alcoholic beverages to North Gate, the student hangout area separated from the north edge of the campus by University Drive. Richard's main competition for the North Gate beer market was the iconic hangout, The Dixie Chicken, founded by an ex-student of mine, Donnie Anz, and his curmudgeonly, crabby, and sometimes scary partner, Don Ganter. Ganter, by reputation, was known to carry a scarcely concealed weapon which he was not reluctant to brandish for effect if he thought a customer or employee was out of line.

Shortly after starting his business in College Station, Richard met an Aggie sorority girl by the name of Letty Bujanos, and they eventually married and had two children. Richard was an astute businessman and a gentle and inordinately kind soul to his innumerable friends and acquaintances. Duddley's became a meeting place and second home for a generation of softball players and other athletes who played on the myriad teams Richard sponsored in soccer, basketball, volleyball, and who knows what else. Richard Benning was a man among men who died far too young of cancer. I still miss him; Richard and I were not close friends, but we got along well and I held him in high esteem. As I said earlier in my discussion of my former father-in-law, Homer Blythe, the world would be a better place if there were more people like Richard Benning in it.

Duddley's was an instant success with the students and locals, and Richard subsequently poured some of his profits into supporting numerous male, female, and mixed teams sporting the Duddley's logo, including the one I managed and played for which came to be known as the "A Team." Richard also sponsored and played on a second team known as the Duddley's Brewers, aka "The Bar Team." Thus Duddley's had an "A Team" and a "Bar Team" for a decade or more.

The Brewers were not nearly the team we were, talent-wise, but they made up for any shortcomings on the diamond with a spirit of camaraderie that was unparalleled in my softball experience. Benny DeWitt, Glen Highfill, Guy Denoux, Ken Bob (the only name I ever knew him by), Ken Poenisch, Kevin Morgan, John Hinton, Rodney Hurt, Mike Walsh, the boss man himself, too many others to mention were the key players in that beer drinking fraternity. Those guys enjoyed each other's company immensely and drank unfathomable quantities of beer to cement their friendships. Quite a few of the Bar team members have stayed in touch with each other in the intervening decades since the team folded.

Fate has not been kind to the Bar Team guys. One unfortunate case was Benny DeWitt, a defensive lineman on the A&M football team in his undergraduate days. Benny was a giant of a man, maybe six feet five and 280 solid pounds, with a full beard and thinning hair which he combed straight back. Benny was a menacing figure, seemingly as surly as he was big. I knew Benny for quite a number of years and really never decided if he was as surly and ill-natured as he appeared or if he just wanted to project that gruff persona to everyone. He became a legend among the regulars at the bar and served as the inspiration for a sandwich known as the "Big Benny", a staple on the Duddley's Draw menu even today. Benny was an oceanographer by training but his career was curtailed by kidney disease that prematurely took his life in his early fifties. Benny was on kidney dialysis for those last few years but not even death could diminish his status as a legendary member of "The Bar Team."

Our generous benefactor, Richard Benning, also met an early demise. He had a rare form of bone cancer that cut his life short at the age of fifty-five. Cancer also prematurely claimed the life of Guy Denoux, a proud Catholic Cajun and self-proclaimed chef who spent most of his professional life, like Big Benny, as an oceanographer who specialized in polar expeditions. From the first time I met him in the 1970's to the day of his untimely death in 2007 at the age of fifty-seven, Guy sported a full, black beard that was central to his identity. No one who knew Guy Denoux could imagine seeing him without that trademark beard. He was married to Jane who played on one of the women's teams sponsored by Duddley's, and they had two children, Elise and Henry, both of whom were good athletes, much better than their father who was at best a passable softball player.

DUDDLEY'S DRAW SOFTBALL, CIRCA 1980

Another unfortunate case is that of Glen Highfill, but he has at least survived to see another day. Glen was muscular, athletic-looking, blue-eyed blonde, movie-star handsome, a brooding and seemingly volatile personality. I always thought he was just one misadventure away from some kind of explosive physical eruption though I must confess I never saw one.

In 2007, Glen volunteered to drive a friend's motorcycle back to College Station from somewhere north and east of Texas, maybe Ohio or some other midwestern state. While motoring along on Interstate 40 in Mississippi, minding his own business, Glen got caught up in a driving rainstorm which led him to seek protection under an overpass. As he parked his motorcycle, a couple of strangers who had also sought refuge from the deluge invited Glen over to chat and ride out the storm. In a freaky set of events I cannot recapture in precise detail, a teenager driving entirely too fast for the conditions came speeding along the Interstate, lost control of his vehicle, and the next thing Glen knew, his left leg was severed by a guard rail that had somehow become detached in the collision between the out-of-control automobile and the protective barrier. Glen would have probably died of blood loss on the spot except for the life-saving efforts of a Good Samaritan who witnessed the entire ordeal from her automobile while following the reckless, unthinking teenager. The Good Samaritan turned out to be a nurse who had a first aid kit in her vehicle, and she expertly attended to Glen's grievous injury by applying a tourniquet which no doubt kept him from bleeding to death. After much expense, many surgeries, and incredible mental and physical suffering, Glen is now able to walk thanks to advances in prostheses technology. He is back at work and occasionally can be seen having a beer at Duddley's with the remnants of "The Bar Team" and other friends and work associates. It is good to see Glen up and around again.

As for some of the other members mentioned earlier, they are alive and well insofar as I know. Ken Poenisch received his PhD in Counseling Psychology and presently serves as Associate Vice Chancellor for Academic Affairs at A&M. John Hinton is a technology specialist for the Department of Recreational Sports on campus. Rodney Hurt and Mike Walsh are local businessmen and can be seen quaffing an occasional brew at Duddley's. As for Kevin Morgan and Ken Bob and the numerous unnamed members of "The Bar Team", their whereabouts are unknown to me. From time to time, there is talk of having a Duddley's reunion involving members of both teams though so far nothing has come of it, at least for me.

Duddley's Brewers, aka "The Bar Team", were an important part of this chapter of my life. To a man, they were good guys, well-educated, and successful in their work and family lives, and yet there was a maverick quality to them, both individually and as a team. It is too bad that those who have passed on cannot gather one more time at Duddley's. Perhaps Richard has started another Duddley's in the "great perhaps" to go with those he established in Lubbock, College Station, Austin, Blacksburg (VA), Knoxville (TN), and a number of other college towns.

Over the years, I put together some outstanding teams for Duddley's. In the process, our team kept getting better and better and my own modest skills improved, and I was eventually thrown together with the best softball players in the area for maybe two decades. My teammates and opponents came from every walk of local life including undergraduate, graduate, and veterinary medicine students, professors, attorneys, accountants, businessmen and women (in the case of coed softball), high school and A&M coaches, laboratory technicians, plumbers, practicing psychologists, and who knows what else.

I played on both men's and mixed (coed or co-rec) teams, and my primary position was pitcher. If one were to combine the statistics from intramurals, city league, and tournaments, I probably played in somewhere between five- and seven-thousand games and was on the winning side of the ledger in probably ninety percent of them. Because of my age and longevity as a player, my long-time friend and immensely gifted shortstop, Doug Williams, used to call me "Nolie" in honor of a famous baseball player from nearby Alvin, Texas. Some of you know him as Nolan Ryan.

During our peak years, we probably won maybe a hundred city and intramural championships. During one decade long run, we won twenty-two of twenty-five intramural co-rec championships, finishing second, fourth, and out of the running the other three times. We also won six of nine men's championships during one run, competing at the highest level in the intramural system.

I played for over thirty years and retired pretty much from competitive ball at the age of sixty-five. I did not really retire out of boredom or noticeably diminished skills, but more because my younger male friends no longer played. The last season I played co-rec, I showed up for the games and none of my male friends were there. Yes, the women were there; many were gay, and thus not tied down with children, Little League, Peewee Football, soccer, and all the other activities that occupy the off-hours of the more traditional parent. As for the guys, they had reached their late thirties and early forties and had become deeply involved in their marriages, work, the lives of their children and, in several cases, officiating sports themselves. I would show up for games, the women would be there, and the guys would send mostly younger surrogates, all of whom were strangers to me. The air went out of co-rec balloon and I hung up my spikes at that point. In addition to fun going out of the game socially, others factors leading to my retirement were the intensity of the games and the fact that the gorillas I faced on the mound were bulked up on weights and hyped up on creatine and assorted dietary supplements (or steroids), making the game dangerous for pitchers.

I was brought out of retirement for a season or two of departmental co-rec play, a far cry from the intensity and talent level I had grown accustomed to for so many years. At the first game, one of the graduate students took notice of me during warm-ups, and said, "You obviously have done this before." I responded that I had thrown a ball or two in my day. After the game, which went exceedingly well for me at bat and on first base, several of the younger players came up, asking me how many years of professional ball I had played. None, of course, was my answer. At the same time, I knew they thought I was a ball player, but they should have seen the real talented ones I played with all those years, guys like Doug Williams, Rick Hall, Rick Fuentes, Steve Schultz, Rick Majewski and far too many others to mention here. As of this writing, the retirement is permanent this time. I occasionally think of seeking out an over-70 team in Houston but there is a time for all good things to end. I could still play a bit but there is little joy left. Without joy, what remains?

My fascination with the competition and the camaraderie of softball was all-consuming, perhaps to the point of being an addiction. Upon reflection, it is amazing that any of my family members still speak to me considering my neglectful ways. I was a member of three and four teams at a time, playing 150-250 games a year for thirty years. During one memorable stretch, I played one game or more each night for sixty-two consecutive nights. I also umpired the sport for several years at the local, regional, and state level. There was even one rather bizarre occasion in which I umpired or played in thirty-six games in one three-day weekend. Juggling the two masters was difficult but I managed to get it done. Yes, I was tired. Yes, I was stiff. And, yes, I recuperated in time for a game the following Tuesday. And, yes, I almost forgot that I had a family and children who needed me to be a husband and father.

I made a few all-tournament teams in my forties, and once even received the Most Valuable Player (MVP) award in a small, local tournament at the age of forty-five. And in my own hopefully unbiased assessment, the best decade I had as a player was from age fifty to sixty. I had worked out all the kinks from those years of inactivity, learned to truly enjoy playing for the sake of playing, and was surrounded by truly exceptional players and, most importantly, even finer human beings.

During the 1980's, 1990's, and into the early 2000's, there were individuals that you could count on to find sponsors and field teams. Scott Burns, David Hicks, Jerry Eden, "Bubba" Moore, and yours truly were five "managers" who hung in there for years, recruiting and managing players and taking this stuff far more seriously than was warranted. In retrospect, our rivalries were undoubtedly fought with such intensity because the stakes were so abysmally low.

"Bubba's Briefs"

I really enjoyed the rivalries with Burns, Hicks, and Eden but of the group, "Bubba" Moore stood out as a most unique and interesting character. He was a more than passable pitcher on several teams, a tenacious competitor, and the publisher of *The Press*, a local newspaper devoted primarily to business advertisements of various kinds. Reflecting "Bubba's" interest in the game, *The Press* included a column entitled "Bubba's Briefs" and another devoted to slow-pitch softball which he wrote for a while before handing the reins over to a colleague named Greg Huchingson. "Bubba" was a loud, gregarious, extrovert who was the life of the party wherever he went. He died a few years ago of cancer at quite a young age, mid- to late fifties as I recall, and he went to his grave denying the following story though several reliable sources are convinced of its veracity.

It seems that after a long weekend of softball, a number of the regulars were hanging around at Sue Haswell Park about midnight on a Sunday, resting comfortably on their bat bags, folding chairs, or pickup tailgates in close proximity to the portable toilets placed here and there the preceding Friday. By the time the tournament was over at midnight on Sunday, the Porta-Pots, those homely, foul-smelling collectors of human waste, had had seventy-two hours for their contents to age, ferment, and ripen.

The guys were kibitzing about the ebb and flow of the tournament, bitching as always about real or imagined bad calls from the Blind Tom umpires, and drinking the customary copious quantities of mostly really bad beer (i.e., Lone Star, Pearl, Miller Lite) when "Bubba" decided to take a turn in one of the Porta-Pots. Once inside, several of his devious "friends" ran over to the pot, threw a rope around it, tipped it over, and rolled it from side to side several times. After much protest, both loud and profane, the restraints were loosened and "Bubba" emerged from the refuse. To say that he was a mess was an understatement. Can you imagine what it would be like to be rolled around in human waste that has been festering in a portable toilet in the hot July Texas sun for three days? I once asked "Bubba" whether this episode was apocryphal or actual, and he vehemently denied that it ever took place. His "friends" insist that it occurred as reported. If the tale is true, one has to ask: With friends like "Bubba's", who needs enemies?

Prior to his death, "Bubba" came up with a unique fundraiser for Habitat for Humanity in which he raised $150,000 for that most worthy cause by isolating himself in a glass cage at the Post Oak Mall in Bryan for a month. A final contribution of $10,000 by local jewelers David and Julia Gardner got him to his lofty goal and freed him to rejoin his family and the city he loved so much. There is a still a strong "Bubba" Moore support group in town that raises money in his name for an assortment of worthy humanitarian causes.

"Bubba" has been dead for over a decade, Jerry Eden moved away twenty years ago, but I still see Hicks and Burns around town from time to time. Hicks is in the fund-raising business at A&M, Burns is retired from a local energy provider, and we locked horns many a time in those days of yore. We had a lot of fun and met some fascinating characters, and I look back on the experience as if it had taken place both yesterday and eons ago.

My All-Time All-Star Slowpitch Team

The at-large readership is asked to have patience as I take a brief two-page detour to honor what I remember to be the best slowpitch softball players in town during my playing time. I have often thought over the years about the softball players I competed with and against, and in that connection, have thrown together my All-Time Team composed of my teammates and opponents. I have confined my list to those pioneers from the 1970's up to the year 2000, players who were pivotal in getting slowpitch softball off the ground when the sport locally was pretty primitive. No doubt, I have forgotten a major player or two. Also, no slight is intended for those guys who came along later who would belong on any all-time list, particularly those players on the nationally competitive Budweiser teams of the 2000's. However, I want to pay special tribute to these top players from the 1970's, 1980's and 1990's who were instrumental in making the game such a delight during my tenure as a player. I have my top player at each position listed first and all others are unranked.

P	<u>Robert Eaton</u>, Bubba Moore, David Hicks, Scott Burns, Wayne Watson, Jerry Eden, Joe Brewster, Bud Nelson, Gary O'Neal, "Bubba" Moore, Arnold LeUnes (of course)
C	<u>Jerry O'Banion</u>, Tim Corder, Leonard Millsap, Tony Bourgeois
1B	<u>Jimmy Salazar</u>, Reggie Washington, Fred Wilganowski, Glen Barrett, Bob Coen, Brady Brown, Clay Bibb
2B	<u>Rick Hall</u>, Steve Beasley
SS	<u>Curtis Kaiser</u>, <u>Paul Rieger</u>, <u>Doug Williams</u>, Cliff Stewart, Cisco McKenty
3B	<u>Lee Bason</u>, Tommy Barrett, Greg Schmidt
OF	<u>David Hudspeth</u>, <u>Dell "Tuna" Thompson</u>, <u>Randy Martell</u>, "Hoot" Gibson, Rick Majewski, Rick Fuentes, Lester Beaird, Steve Schultz, Joe Schultz, Dwayne Vann, Donnie Wilganowski, Richard Hubacek, Bruce Henry, Brett Henry, Robert Cessna, Bernie Huckabee

My All-Time Favorite Umpires

Without good umpires, there would be no games, and we were blessed to have many good ones during my time. They were outstanding umpires and, almost to a man, super guys. They are:

Tony Bourgeois, Raymond Bradley, Tim Corder, Jerry Eden, Andy Ezell, David Fain, Dennis Fink, Rick Hall, Bruce Henry, Henry Hoermann (deceased), Arnold LeUnes (of course!), Albert Macias, Junior Murdoch, Gary O'Neal, Larry Parker (deceased), Randall Pitcock, Steve Pursley (deceased), Tony (The Godfather) Scazzero, Matt Stellges, James Welford, and Chris White. Of the group, Rick Hall and Matt Stellges went on to officiate baseball at the college level and James Welford achieved luminary status in women's college softball before he retired.

TONY BOURGEOIS AND YOURS TRULY, JOGGING, KYLE FIELD, 1975

Hearne, Texas 1968-2017

I have a begrudging soft spot in my heart for the city of Hearne, as it has played a major role in the professional life of my wife and, by proxy, mine. The city is remarkable in so many ways I feel compelled to give it some space in this modest document. More importantly, the city and school system occupy a cherished recess in my wife's heart, and I cannot and would not ignore that fact. For the most part, she was an outsider with no great investment in the city and its schools, but she gave several pints of blood, untold gallons of sweat, and more than few tears into making Hearne a better place to live, work, and obtain an education.

A Brief History

My own familiarity with the city began shortly after I joined the A&M faculty in 1966, eight years before I met Judy. One morning, I was reading the local rag, *The Eagle*, over breakfast and noticed a blurb indicating that Robertson County, Texas had the lowest per capita income of any county in the United States. Today, Hearne, the Sunflower Capital of Texas, is the largest city in Robertson County though it is not the county seat; that honor belongs to Franklin. The 2010 census showed Hearne to have a population of 4,690 and a median household income of $19,556. Hearne is home to twenty-seven churches, and claims two professional football stars as famous local citizens, John Randle, a many-times honored defensive lineman who played with the Minnesota Vikings, and Steve O'Neal of the New York Jets who holds the record for the longest punt in NFL history, ninety-nine yards. Interestingly, unlike most records in sports, Steve O'Neal's can never be broken because the maximum distance a punt can travel under the existing NFL rules is that same ninety-nine yards. Steve O'Neal was an honors student at A&M (and made a solid A in my class), and had a dental practice in Bryan for many years. His brother, Gary, was an accountant at A&M for years in addition to being a softball teammate, opponent, and fellow umpire. Gary was mentioned a bit earlier with my all-time softball selections, for he was a good player and excellent umpire.

It is hard for me to think of Hearne without harking back to one of my former students, Anthony Ware, who provided me with an interesting anecdote about the city. Anthony grew up dirt-poor without a penny in his pocket in the projects of Chicago and through a long, circuitous set of events ended up at A&M where he played basketball for the Aggies his last two years. When Anthony graduated, his first teaching position was in nearby Caldwell where he also served as varsity basketball coach.

I ran into Anthony and his new bride one evening shortly after he had taken his Caldwell basketball team to Hearne for the first time. The chance meeting took place in Wings and More, a popular eatery in College Station owned by former A&M and Miami Dolphins football star, Mark Dennard. In the course of our brief conversation, Anthony told me, "Doc, it was *deja vu* all over again for me. I have been in the Fifth Ward in Houston, the South Oak Cliff area in Dallas, the barrios of San Antonio, and the people, the city, and the social environment of Hearne, Texas, reminded me more of the projects in Chicago than any other place I have ever been." That was quite a commentary from someone with such a unique perspective on growing up in a big-city high poverty, high crime environment.

Judy graduated from A&M in 1976 and landed her first teaching job in Hearne where she spent four demanding but unbelievably rewarding years. The Hearne teaching faculty consisted of essentially two groups, one of which was a mix of young Anglo females, most of whom were A&M graduates who commuted to Hearne from College Station. In almost every case, they were first- or second-year graduates of A&M, usually hanging around until their boyfriends or husbands graduated. The second contingent was made up of locals who had obtained their degrees, in many cases from then all-black Prairie View University, prior to moving back to teach in their home town. This latter group was the backbone of the school system. Most have retired by now and the citizens are worse off for it for these locals anchored that school district and gave it focus. They knew the Hearne zeitgeist backward and forward, and exerted much leadership for the school and community.

Judy commuted from College Station for those four years and developed close friendships with several teachers and their husbands including Tom and Fleurette Rehak, David and Debbie Walls, Chuck and Ruth Anderson, and Janice Williamson. Janice did a lot of the driving during the latter stages of the fourth year due to Judy's late stage pregnancy with our first child, Katie Elizabeth, who was born five weeks after the school year ended. Janice was a softball teammate who later became a highly successful softball coach at Bryan High School. One of the major highlights of her coaching career took place at the end of the 2002 season when the Vikings won the 5A championship, beating San Antonio O'Connor 1-0 in the title game.

Poverty and Despondency. Teaching in Hearne was rife with nuances and idiosyncrasies that were never addressed in any of Judy's classes in Elementary Education at A&M. In listening to Judy and her peers talk about their training, it sounded a bit on the Pollyanna-ish side to me. The operative training model seemed to emphasize that, as teachers, they would have only wealthy, highly-motivated, lily-white, eager learners in their classes. Judy quickly found out most of her Hearne students were just the opposite, black or brown, desperately poor, and largely uninspired.

The grinding poverty and resultant despondency were so thick in Hearne you could cut them with a knife. These problems, of course, carry over into the schools which mirror the mores and folkways of the community. As one example of poverty and community norms, Judy noticed a tendency for her class attendance to be low on Mondays. When she asked some of the older teachers, the locals, why this occurred, she was told that Monday was the day children scavenged Highway 6 north and south of town to collect aluminum cans thrown from passing cars. Another index of poverty involved two brothers she had in class who showed up every other day because they shared one pair of blue jeans. Sounds far-fetched? Yes! True? Yes! Life, as they say, can be stranger than fiction.

Another eye-opener about poverty and lower class values was having eleven- and twelve-year-old girls in her class who were already expecting their first baby, often with a father half again or twice their age. I do not recall a time in her four years in Hearne in which this pre-teen pregnancy scenario was not re-enacted, and it was not at all unusual for it to happen to more than one child a year.

A most interesting story involved one of Judy's second graders, an intellectually challenged black girl named Katie who came to school one day so proud she was bursting at the seams over the birth of a new baby brother. She asked Judy to come over to the house to greet the new arrival who was maybe a week old. At Judy's request, I agreed to go along for moral support. We arrived at Katie's house late in the day. It was a ramshackle affair with no indoor plumbing. The new arrival was swaddled in a baby crib fashioned from the lower unit of a beat-up old chest of drawers. Katie told us the baby went unnamed for a couple of days before her mother settled on the given name, Killer, for the little tyke. All I could think of was: "What a legacy to live up to. If you believe in self-fulfilling prophecy, Killer's mother had mapped out a future for him, literally from day three." Katie has siblings named Princess, Prince Albert, Peaches, and others, but naming a baby Killer boggles the imagination. To my knowledge, Killer has not lived up to his birth legacy, and he would be in his forties by now.

Despite obvious intellectual limitations, Katie eventually graduated from high school. The *Hearne Democrat*, the local newspaper, reported that Katie had the distinction of being the first Hearne High School student to graduate from the twelfth grade at the same time her oldest child graduated from kindergarten. Geez, Louise!

Mr. Norris McDaniel, Mentor and Friend.

Judy's tenure in that district gave her a wonderfully serendipitous opportunity to work for a black administrator, Mr. Norris McDaniel, himself a lifelong resident of Hearne. He provided Judy with astute counsel and guidance and was the most pivotal person in her early professional life. They came to know each other well and shared a deep, abiding mutual admiration. Judy has always called him "Mr. McDaniel" and has never once wavered from that gesture of respect; he is and always will be, pure and simple, "Mr. McDaniel!" He was Judy's first principal and helped her form a positive, accepting perspective concerning the issue of race and poverty, most particularly the plight of poor black people who make up almost fifty percent of Hearne's population. One third of the locals live below the poverty line, and that figure is fifty percent among those under age eighteen. By way of contrast, Judy grew up in the predominantly white areas of Dallas, graduated from predominantly white Frisco High School, and attended A&M at a time when black students were a novelty. She sorely needed some grounding in race and poverty issues to deal with a city like Hearne, and Mr. McDaniel and several of the older, more knowledgeable, experienced black teachers were instrumental in bringing her up to speed.

Judy LeUnes Rejoins Hearne ISD. In a most interesting and fortuitous postscript to our collective lessons in the sociology of rural poverty and racial inequality, Judy ended up thirty years later working in Hearne as an educational consultant. After teaching four years in Hearne, she was hired by the College Station ISD where she taught an assortment of subjects to fifth graders for twenty-six years. She, like several hundred other experienced and often great teachers in Bryan and College Station, was forced to retire prematurely due a complicated provision in the Social Security laws that prevented teachers who were not contributing to the system themselves from being eligible to receive their spouse's benefits should they precede their spouses in going on to the great heavenly hoopla. Only a handful of school districts in Texas contribute to Social Security so the loophole had widespread repercussions not only for Bryan and College Station but the entire state. Many, many wonderful teachers with incredible institutional memories were forced to retire long before their time. Yes, a few deadheads went out in the purge but the overall quality of teaching and educational leadership in the two cities, as well as most of Texas, took a significant hit when those experienced teachers retired.

Judy's retirement was short-lived thanks to a tip from Chrissy Hester, herself a retired teacher, counselor, and high school principal at A&M Consolidated. It seems that a research group at the University of Texas had a grant program with a slot for a half-time employee to work with high-poverty, low-performing school districts with the goal of improving teacher performance, effectiveness, and morale. Hearne ISD fit the low-performing and poverty-stricken descriptors and then some, and Judy was assigned there as a consultant, or what they called an External Coach, under the aegis of that UT grant program.

As fate would have it, the person representing Hearne in the negotiations with UT to administer the program was none other than the irrepressible Mr. Norris McDaniel, Judy's first and foremost mentor. Mr. McDaniel had been at various times a teacher, coach, principal, and superintendent with the district, and had retired only to be called back into the high school principal's job to restore order to the chaos created by having six high school principals in a period of three years. Mr. McDaniel and Judy meshed immediately, as if there had never been a break in their relationship. Judy worked with the UT grant program for two years and when it ran out, she stayed on in Hearne at Superintendent David Deaver's request as a consultant with her own newly-formed educational consultancy which she named Higher Expectations for All. Under Judy's leadership of culture and change, the high school went from a state rating of "Unacceptable" to "Recognized" in three years. An improvement of this magnitude typically takes three or five years.

When the UT grant ran out, Judy asked me what she should charge Hearne ISD in the way of a fee, and I suggested she start the negotiations at a figure twice what the University of Texas had been paying. No one so much as blinked an eye at her request, and she spent five rewarding if sometimes perplexing years with the Hearne schools. As well, she expanded her consulting efforts to include the Somerville ISD, with briefer stints in Calvert, Snook, Caldwell, and Kingsville in south Texas.

Unfortunately, the aforementioned and most influential Mr. Norris McDaniel once again went into retirement a couple of years ago, and we suspected it was permanent this time. However, as fate would have it, the Hearne School Board relieved the superintendent, Dr. Jackie Kowalski, of her duties in 2011 and the ever-present Norris McDaniel took over once again as the district's chief administrator, but only in an acting capacity. Mr. McDaniel is deeply religious, a good man, and an outstanding administrator, and the school district will miss his firm but gentle hand when he finally retires for good. As for Judy, she remains eternally grateful for his warm friendship and kind mentoring.

A scholarship fund has been set up in Mr. McDaniel's name, and there is an awards ceremony each spring to reward some of Hearne's finest young people with financial assistance for college. It is both reassuring and, at times, heartbreaking to look into those youthful, hopeful, and almost-always black faces and think about how many obstacles they have overcome and how many more they will have to face down in their pursuit of something other than a life of low income and despair. Mr. McDaniel, Judy, and a handful of dedicated teachers have done everything they can to make sure these young people, despite staggering odds, have a shot at realizing the so-called American dream.

Camp Hearne: A German Prisoner of War (POW) Camp.

Judy and I celebrated Memorial Day 2009 in Hearne, attending the dedication of the Camp Hearne Historical Site so designated by the State Historical Commission. It seems that Hearne was one of a number of cities in Texas that petitioned the U.S. Government in 1942 to become a German Prisoner of War (POW) camp site. This action was prompted by a growing awareness on the part of both our military leaders and legislators in Washington that Allied forces were capturing hundreds of thousands of Germans and had no satisfactory place(s) to incarcerate them in Europe. The Hearne petition was granted and construction began in late 1942 at a site a mile northwest of the city. The first POW's began arriving early in 1943, and were unloaded from trains at the Southern Pacific Railroad station near the present intersection of Highways 6 and 190 on the south side of town. As the POW's were unloaded, the roadways throughout the city were lined with cars and spectators who were curious about their new guests.

At its peak, the camp population of 4,800 was greater than that of the city with its 3,600 citizens. Most of these POW's were troops in General Erwin Rommel's Afrika Korps and had been captured in North Africa. Many arrived at the camp in the clothes they were wearing when they surrendered, and some of the wounded among them were still sporting blood stains from their injuries. They were marched under heavy guard from the rail station to the camp, given an opportunity to bathe, and issued their POW uniforms. They were then separated into two groups based on the estimated strength of their endorsement of Nazi ideology. Prisoners were also allowed to work if they wanted to, mostly in nearby agricultural operations, and they were paid the equivalent of eighty cents per day. To put the pay scale in perspective, one captured soldier put it this way: "…80 cents will get you 8 beers or 8 packs of cigarettes at the canteen."

The Hearne detention camp was part of a national POW incarceration program that culminated in the creation of 511 camps in 45 of the lower 48 states housing over 425,000 prisoners by war's end. Only Nevada, North Dakota, and Vermont of the lower 48 had no camps. As warfare wound down in the Pacific Theater, more and more Japanese POW's were brought to the US, and Hearne actually moved a group of Germans from one barracks to another so that 323 soldiers captured at the Battle of Iwo Jima could be accommodated.

Overall, life was pretty comfortable for the POW's, their days being filled with soccer, music, theater, college correspondence courses, and artisan work. Speaking of music at Camp Hearne, members of an exquisite German military orchestra or ensemble were captured *in toto* in Tunisia and assigned to Hearne where they performed many Bach, Beethoven, and Mozart concerts over the next two years for their fellow POW's and the area citizenry. What a delight that must have been for classical music aficionados.

My friend Dr. Arnold Krammer, Professor of History at A&M and an expert on Nazi Germany and the Holocaust, has written extensively about the various POW camps in Texas and the US. He had a book published in 1979 entitled, *Nazi Prisoners of War in America*, in which he included humorous accounts of attempts to escape from the various camps. Dr. Krammer places the total number of escapees at two dozen, mostly from the sister camp in Mexia and the one in Hearne. One Mexia POW fled the camp but his quest for freedom was cut short when an angry bull chased him up a tree as he tried to cross a nearby pasture. A group of three POW's from Hearne were captured in a boat on the nearby Brazos River, apparently believing they could make the seven thousand mile voyage back to Germany in their home-made dinghy. Yet another Hearne escapee was picked up along Highway 79 near Franklin, some ten miles east of Hearne, singing German army march songs. Such was life for the typical escapee and those charged with their detainment.

With the end of World War II in August, 1945, the U.S. Government started returning the POW's to their respective countries at the rate of 50,000 per month. The soldiers were eventually all sent home and Camp Hearne ceased to exist by 1947. Over a period of the next six decades, the camp fell victim to neglect and the ravages of the elements and essentially disappeared. It was not until the early 2000's that a reawakening of interest in the camp as a historical site emerged, thanks to an anthropologist from A&M, Dr. Michael Waters, a team of assistants, and some interested parties from Hearne who began digging around in the ruins. Their efforts led to restoration of some of the camps' architecture and grounds as a memorial to the war effort. The Camp Hearne Historical site is now a tourist attraction for the city of Hearne.

A major step in putting the camp's best foot forward was the dedication of the site on Memorial Day 2009. At the dedication ceremony, World War II veterans whose numbers are rapidly dwindling were recognized for their efforts, and the featured speaker was then Texas Congressman and fellow Aggie Chet Edwards, a Democrat and true beacon of light in a predominantly conservative Republican district. Somehow Congressman Edwards withstood the onslaught of the well-funded Republicans who cherished his congressional seat for two decades, but his luck ran out in 2010 when he was defeated by another Aggie, Bill Flores, who still holds the position thanks to the conservative climate in his district.

In circumstances such as those surrounding the Camp Hearne dedication, it is hard to restrain one's pride at having served in the same Army as the proud veterans of World War II, Korea, Vietnam, Iraq, and Afghanistan who showed up for the dedication. I never saw combat duty during my three-year stint but I am prouder every day of being afforded the privilege of serving, no matter how insignificant my contribution may have been. In no way, form, or fashion was I a hero; I merely served. It seems a bit of a stretch for me to believe that each and every GI is a hero simply because some politician or bleeding heart says so.

Judy had been a volunteer in several of Chet Edward's election campaigns and had visited with him in Washington, DC, on occasion, so they were more than speaking acquaintances. Prior to the formal dedication ceremony, Congressman Edwards and Judy greeted each other with big smiles and a warm mutual hug. I observed this interaction from maybe fifty yards away alongside the aforementioned and now-deposed Hearne Superintendent of Schools, Dr. Jackie Kowalski, and her chief lieutenant, a female administrator whose name will go unmentioned to protect the innocent. The sincerity of the warm greeting Judy received from the Congressman was palpable and, as it was taking place, I noted the immense hostility coming from the eyes of the obviously jealous female administrator. Of course, Judy had no way of knowing what was going on, so I told her later about the incident and what I had observed. I predicted on the way home from the ceremony that the obviously envious and insecure administrator would get back at Judy professionally sooner or later. It took two years, but she eventually succeeded in her quest, apparently convincing Superintendent Kowalski not to renew Judy's consulting contract with the Hearne district. The reasons given for the non-renewal were, of course couched in "administrator-ese" and bureaucrat-generated verbiage about funding shortages, "a need to go another direction", and an assortment of other horseshit school administrator excuses.

Prior to her demise as the Hearne ISD consultant, a telling incident occurred when Judy and the professionally jealous lieutenant were walking across one of the school campuses late in the afternoon. In the course of a casual discussion, the woman asked Judy, "Why do all the teachers love you and all hate me?" I cannot imagine asking such a damning or self-incriminating question in the first place, nor can I come to grips with feeling that way about myself and my job. Nor can I wrap my mind around going after the job of a person who by your own admittance was "loved", effective, and greatly admired by the teachers. Politics mixed with pettiness are wonderful, are they not? It is gratifying to know that the lieutenant has since "retired" from Hearne ISD. Dr. Kowalski later resigned, and was replaced by the once again resurrected from the ranks of the retired, Mr. Norris McDaniel who had more lives than a cat.

A Dedicated Teacher.

A final lingering memory of Hearne predates Judy's days with the district by a few years and has to do with an elementary school teacher by the name of Rhonda Baze, an A&M graduate in Secondary Education, who was teaching at Hearne High School around 1970. Rhonda now has a PhD in Psychology from the University of Southern California and operates a private practice in Arab, Alabama. She also teaches at a satellite of the University of Alabama at Birmingham and has re-established a relationship with my friend, Tony Bourgeois, with whom she was close to in the late 1960's while a student at A&M. Several divorces and four decades later, coupled with the recent death of Rhonda's husband, Tony and Rhonda have reconnected via the social media.

But let us return to Hearne, circa 1970. Rhonda rang me up one day and asked if I would come to Hearne and visit a first grade class taught by one of her colleagues who was in need of help or, at the very least, some moral support. I spent the day in that classroom, and got a fast lesson in the sociology of poverty. The poor teacher was in her third year, the first two years of which were spent teaching children of local undocumented workers (euphemistically referred to as "illegal aliens") who worked the area agricultural operations. Most of the families spoke little or no English and the teacher spoke no Spanish when her first year started. She became passably fluent in Tex-Mex, that Texas hybrid blend of the languages of the two cultures, and was able to communicate reasonably effectively with her students throughout the second year. For her third year, she was asked to take over a first grade class composed of kiddos who had flunked the first grade the year before. Needless to say, it was to be a challenging, sometimes daunting task.

My primary observational target that day was an exceedingly emotionally disturbed black male. He was violent with teachers and peers alike, and threw monumental tantrums that sometimes lasted for a half-hour or more. He once took an errant swat at a teacher and fell forehead first onto the metal rail that runs along the front of blackboard. This misadventure opened up a gash requiring several stitches, and he went home and told his mother the cut was inflicted by an angry teacher who ripped off her belt and hit him repeatedly across the forehead with a big metal buckle.

Most of his day was spent in time out which allowed the poor, downtrodden teacher to devote instructional time to the other children. As her young charges toiled away on a coloring assignment, the teacher pointed out different children in the room accompanied by a torrent of tales of woe about their lives. There were twins who had been removed from their home several times by the Department of Child Protective Services for neglect and malnutrition; their IQ's were in the fifties, no doubt a byproduct of nutritional deprivation. One boy had been the subject of a death threat and was under police surveillance; it seems that his older sister jilted her high school boyfriend and he threatened to exact retribution by killing the little brother. Another boy was partially deaf due to repeated parental beatings about the head. Another girl slept outside all or parts of many nights because her mother needed the trailer to conduct her prostitution business. Another child had an older sibling who set himself on fire to protest racial discrimination. The teacher added a postscript to the soliloquy, indicating the two worst kids got off the bus and headed for who knows where to spend the day. She never offered any elaboration about what "worst kids" meant and I never got around to asking. I am not sure I want to know...

There was one very special girl in the class who was not mentally deficient, abused, or starved. The best way I know to describe her situation was she was simply unappreciated. The teacher admitted that she felt guilty at having the child in her room because she should have been in a regular class. However, the poor, bedraggled, overworked teacher needed help with the roll book, the teaching machines, and other various and sundry administrative tasks, and the little girl literally served as her *de facto* teacher's aide; thus her presence in the class. The child was absolutely beautiful and took an immediate liking to me. Everywhere I went, she followed, and in moments of quietness, would lay her head on the side of my knee just to have physical contact which I am sure was in short supply elsewhere in her life. She was an absolute doll and I would have been honored to have her in my own family which, of course, was not feasible. Your heart goes out to unfortunate kids like her who have the deck stacked against them, almost from day one.

At the end of that extremely exhausting day, I asked the teacher if anyone had ever been to the home of the emotionally disturbed boy, and the answer, not unexpectedly, was no. I decided I would round up our mentally ill, malevolent miscreant and go visit the family. He said he would be glad to take me to his home but wanted to know if it was alright if his little sister rode with us. Little sister was a year younger but only slightly less emotionally disturbed than her older brother. After thirty or forty minutes traveling over roads that must have been uploaded and transported from Baja California, we ended up at his house some two miles south of town and maybe a half mile off of Highway 6. Had I known what I know now, I could have taken the highway and been at his home in a few minutes without tearing the bottom out from under my vehicle. Rather than admit I may have been duped by an emotionally disturbed seven-year old, I have placated myself all these years with the thought that he simply took me home via his bus route. I do not know that interpretation of events to be true, but is preserves my sense of emotional well-being to continue to think so.

I asked the mother if her boy was a problem at home and she assured me he was not. I then asked what a typical day at home was like and was told he spent almost every waking hour after school and on weekends with his grandfather, doing chores, fishing, walking in the woods, picking pecans, or just hanging out. No wonder he was never a problem at home....he was seldom there!

I came away from my Sociology 101 lesson that day with a new appreciation for public school teachers and what they are often asked to endure. I was absolutely exhausted by the events I had witnessed; I fell into bed right after the evening meal and slept for twelve hours. I was physically spent and psychologically drained!

American Life in the 1980's

U. S. Population is 227 million
Average Annual Salary is $15,800
Minimum Wage was $3.10
A BMW Automobile Cost $12,000, a Mercedes 280-E $14,800
This Period Is Known as the Me! Me! Me! Generation
"Shop Till You Drop" Was the Popular Catch Phrase Summarizing This Era
The Reverend Jesse Jackson Was the First Black Presidential Candidate
Thirteen Books Sold One Million Copies; S. King, T. Clancy, D. Steele Wrote Ten of Them
Ironweed, Bonfire of the Vanities, and 1984 Were Bestselling Books
New York Libraries ban *Huckleberry Finn, Catcher in the Rye, Grapes of Wrath*
Constitutional Amendment to Allow School Prayer is Defeated in Congress
Children Loved Sweetarts, Skittles, Nerds, Hubba Bubba Chewing Gum
Video Games like Nintendo, Pac Man, Game Boy Very Popular
Slam Dancing, Break Dancing, and Lambada Popular Dances Learned from MTV
Berlin Wall Comes Down, Setting Stage for German Reunification
Tabloid Television Filled With Geraldo, Dr. Phil, Sally Jessie Raphael, Oprah
60 Minutes, 20/20, and *Nightline* Popular News Shows
Rain Man, ET: The Extraterrestrial, Platoon, The Big Chill Popular Movies
Women's Sport Thrive due to Passage of Title IX Legislation in the 1970's

Anecdotes and Remembrances From the 1980's

For me personally, the decade of the 1980's stands out as most noteworthy. Judy and I married on January 13, 1979, thus setting the table for the next four decades. At that time, I was in my early forties and Judy was in her mid-twenties. Softball and jogging dominated my free time, we met many unforgettable people, and interesting stories and anecdotes mounted up and were stockpiled for later retelling. With some help from my friends, I was able to induce catatonia in an adolescent busboy in Mississippi, teach and mentor a local wet tee-shirt contest legend, be mistaken in O'Hare Airport for country singer Merle Haggard, run a coaching workshop with professional basketball luminary John Lucas and legendary soccer star Kyle Rote, monitor the psychological mood state and performance progress of a top female collegiate distance runner, share some moments with the exceedingly eccentric musician and mystery writer Kinky Friedman, and hear a brilliant, transformative talk by the President of Yale University/Commissioner of Major League Baseball, A. Bartlett "Bart" Giammati. Life was good.

Two Psychologists Induce Catatonia in an Adolescent Bus Boy in Mississippi

Late in the spring of 1980, Tony Bourgeois, another good friend named Don Meck, and yours truly set out one afternoon headed for the Biofeedback Society of American Convention in Orlando, Florida. Don, then a doctoral student in Counseling Psychology at A&M, volunteered to drive his camper to Florida, and our plans were to camp out among the oranges and the alligators somewhere near Orlando for the duration of the convention where Don was presenting a paper. Glen Beecher, a graduate student friend and softball teammate, set us up with a bass fishing expedition, courtesy of his family who had made the retirement move from New York to Orlando. For bass fisherman, landing a Florida hybrid bass is the ultimate experience in that sport, and we looked forward with great anticipation to a few hours on a Florida lake, thanks to the largesse of the Beecher family.

Tony is a native of Lafayette, Louisiana, deep in the heart of Cajun country, and it was our intent to drop in on his mother, Eleanor, for a brief visit and a good cup of strong Cajun coffee as we passed through. Lafayette is on Interstate 10 which took us from Houston all the way to Tallahassee, so a visit with Tony's mother was not at all inconvenient. Once we downed our coffee and paid our respects to Mrs. Bourgeois, we hit the road, stupidly thinking we could make it all the way to Tallahassee without stopping. However, it was only a short time before we ran out of steam near the Mississippi border in far eastern Louisiana, so we decided to take a catnap in the camper. Once the impromptu and all-too-brief early morning siesta was over, we moved on along the Interstate to a small town in western Mississippi where we stopped for a quick breakfast.

We were joined at our table by a "Moonie", one of the legions of misguided disciples of the enormously wealthy religious flimflam artist of the period, Reverend Sun Myung Moon (1920-2012) of South Korea who founded the Unification Church and subsequently proclaimed himself Messiah. At its peak, his empire was said to be a multi-billion dollar global enterprise. Disciples were everywhere on the streets of America during the 1970's and 1980's, raising money in service of the unbelievably wealthy, Machiavellian, and Messianic Reverend Moon. The "Moonie" provided some comic relief while we ate, offering up tidbits of information about how we could become good soldiers like her, living the life of a pauper while filling Reverend Moon's coffers with untold amounts of money. We eventually finished our memorable breakfast, paid our modest tab, and bid our "Moonie" friend adieu.

Tony and I decided it would be judicious if we made a pit stop given the copious amounts of water, orange juice, and coffee we had ingested. He and I, in unison, walked up to separate urinals and conducted our business. In the process, Tony noticed a pair of blue shoes framed in the lower part of the lone bathroom stall. Knowing that Don Meck was wearing blue running shoes and feeling confident the pair we had spotted were attached to his feet, we began to heap as much abuse on him as possible while he was in a temporary state of immobilization. Tony and I directed barbs at Don along the lines of, "Did you hear about the constipated mathematician who worked in out with a slide rule?", or "Did you hear about the constipated secretary who worked it out with a pencil?", or "Did you hear a moose roar, Tony? Who let a moose in this place?' or "Wish I had brought my gas mask. The smell is deadly." or "The smell is so bad that something must have had to crawl up Meck's rectum and died."

To support the verbal flak, we launched a joint aerial bombardment. Tony hastily crafted a couple of paper airplanes while I simultaneously constructed paper helicopters to catapult over the top of the stall. The bombardment must have been reminiscent, though on a smaller and safer scale, of the Nazi Blitzkrieg of London in World War II. We launched plane after plane and chopper after chopper at our blue-shoed target, strangely hearing nary a peep. We figured the silence was Meck's way of telling us to go to hell; he was not going to dignify our stupid-ass foolishness with a verbal rejoinder. He was not going to give us the satisfaction of any kind of reaction. Finally, in a tone of total exasperation, Tony said, "Let's get out of here before we die." With that, Tony put his recently acquired karate skills to use, delivering a ferocious kick to the stall that shook its walls mightily.

Justifiably proud of our efforts at bad comedy, Tony and I waited in the lobby for Don to emerge from the mayhem. All of a sudden, Tony looked at me quizzically and said, "Arnie. Meck's in the truck. Who in the hell was in that stall?" I looked at Tony, he looked at me, and we simultaneously broke into uncontrollable laughter. We sprinted to the van and when Meck saw us coming, he opened the van's side doors to expedite our entry. Tony and I tumbled in, pulled the door shut, all the while pleading with Meck to get the hell out of Dodge before some irate guy comes looking for us. We laughed so hard we could not catch our breath long enough to tell Meck what was going on. Eventually, we were able to compose ourselves sufficiently to urge him to step on it in case we were being followed by an unknown assailant in blue shoes. We laughed pretty much uncontrollably off and on until reaching Tallahassee many hours later, and periodically for days after that when memories of the event intruded on our consciousness.

All we could figure was the person in the stall was a young busboy or something. However, you would think he would have told us to bug out or can it or go to hell or something. But no protest came from within that besieged stall. To this day, when we recant this story, Tony and I have this lasting vision of a teen-age busboy spending the rest of his life in a permanent catatonic stupor in a bathroom stall in rural Mississippi. But what are psychologists for if they can't create a little business for themselves?

"The Body"

At the start of the spring semester of 1982, a sophomore Education major named Megan, aka "The Body", showed up in my Psychology 305 (Psychology of Adjustment) class which met in Room 402 of the Academic Building. Other students in that particular section for whom I have fond remembrances include Karen Price, Robbin Robertson, and Julie Troy.

Megan "The Body" was one of those students you could not miss. She was tall, flashy, and abundantly aware of her absolutely stunning physique that would probably cause a few Playboy models to abandon their bikinis. "The Body" made a grand entrance every Monday, Wednesday, and Friday shortly before 10 am, striding confidently down the center aisle to take her seat in the middle of the section on my right. There were sixteen guys in the class who I am sure noticed her, and I suspect more than one of the thirty-nine females also sneaked an occasional peek at that terrific torso.

But "The Body's" real claim to fame, as I came to find out in casual office conversations, was an impressive winning streak at several wet t-shirt contests held in pubs, bars, chili cook-offs, and other venues in the local area. One day she came by the office to visit about this, that, or the other, and started reminiscing about her experiences with wet t-shirt competitions. I was in the midst of developing my expertise in sport and exercise psychology about that time and the more she talked, the more I became aware of a real competitive streak that seemed to rival what you would find in high visibility, big-time athletes. Wet t-shirt contests were clearly serious business to her! I once asked if she had a boyfriend and, if so, what he thought about all this showmanship, if you will. She said he typically sat front row and center at each contest, cheering her on and taking great pride in her competitive achievements.

"The Body" won a couple of local contests and several hundred dollars but went into a self-imposed retirement after some of her sorority sisters inadvertently caught her titillating act. The sisters, no doubt driven by the purest of emotions and acting in what could only be construed as the best interests of "The Body", turned her in to the Panhellenic Council where she was summarily excommunicated from the sorority sisterhood following a brief hearing.

I think my favorite interlude with "The Body", however, centered on her supposed retirement from competition. She told me she had gone into what she thought at the time was permanent retirement after a nice string of successes, but the old competitive juices started flowing again while watching a contest won by what she considered to be a collection of seriously inferior rivals. "The Body" expressed her thoughts as follows "I knew my rack was better than any of theirs and I felt I had no choice at that point but to rejoin the wet t-shirt circuit." I heard through the grapevine that she had apparently resumed her winning ways without missing a beat. Megan made a nice solid, comfortable C with me that semester and I never saw or heard of her again.

"The Body" would be in her mid-fifties by now, and it would be interesting to know how her life has played out. One cannot help but wonder what happens to old wet t-shirt competitors as they go through the various phases of adult life, fighting off the inexorable effects of gravity and its partner in crime, wrinkles.

As an addendum, I also had a student in class about that same time who had compiled a most impressive record in "Legs Contests" in local bars, festivals, chili cook-offs, and other local competitive venues. I must admit that I agree with the judges about her legs, as they were nicely sculpted. She was slightly above five feet in height, and ordinarily one would think of tall, leggy women winning those kinds of competitions.

In any case, it was nice, as an avid sportsman and budding young sport psychologist, to be able to monitor at a distance their accomplishments in what might be called atypical competitive arenas.

A Merle Haggard Sighting in Chicago's O'Hare Airport

Tony Bourgeois and I were flying back to Texas in 1980 after attending the American Psychological Association (APA) convention in the lovely city of Montreal, and had an early evening layover at O'Hare Airport in Chicago. I was sitting on a bench, killing time people-watching, when I noticed a rather unremarkable guy about my age (forty-two at the time) pacing back and forth, sneaking occasional surreptitious glances in my direction. After a while, curiosity began to kill the proverbial cat and the curious fellow worked up the courage to walk over for a visit. Nervously, almost apologetically, he uttered, "Could I ask you a question?" I responded to his overture with, "Sure. No problem. What's up?" He replied with a second question: "Are you Merle Haggard?" I assured him that I was not Merle Haggard, but I could tell by the look on his face he was not satisfied with my answer. I guess he thought I was just another unfriendly celebrity trying to maintain public anonymity. He asked once again, "Are you sure you're not Merle Haggard? You look just like him." Again, I assured him I was not Merle Haggard. He asked me a third time to fess up, but to no avail. It was hard to admit to being someone I was not!

After a while, he drifted away, all the while muttering to himself that I just had to be Merle Haggard. I can just hear the conversation he had with his wife when he got home: "Mable I just saw Merle Haggard out at O'Hare and the son-of-a-bitch refused to give me his autograph. It would not have taken much for him to sign my baseball cap, but, no! He wouldn't give me the time of day. I guess he thinks he is too important for Average Joe's like me."

As I gave the matter some additional thought, it dawned on me that I could have gotten out of the situation by agreeing that I was Merle Haggard, engaged my new friend with some good-natured banter, joke-telling, and backslapping, and gone ahead and autographed the cap for him. It further occurred to me I should have told him my lead guitar player, Tony Bourgeois, was with me and if he liked, I would get Tony to come over and add his John Henry. My anonymous friend from Chicago would have sung a very different tune, maybe something along the lines of, "Mable. I ran into Merle Haggard out at the airport and he was a heck of a nice guy. He gave me his autograph and got his lead guitar man, Tony something-or-other, to give me his, too!" It is not often that you get an opportunity to make someone's day and I blew the chance big-time. I had it in my grasp and let it get away. And Merle Haggard may have lost a fan!

IMAGES OF PURPORTED LOOK-ALIKE, C&W LEGEND
MERLE HAGGARD

Speaking of Tony and Chicago, he and I were in Chicago again a few years later for the American Psychological Association Convention which was held at the storied Palmer House. Trying to eke by on a meager travel budget, we decided to stay outside the Chicago Loop and take the elevated train back and forth to the convention center each day. We wandered around looking for a place to stay and ended up somehow in the old 1920's Mafia hotspot of Cicero where we rented a cheap but passably decent hotel room. As we walked the streets near our accommodations, we heard numerous foreign dialects attesting to the blue collar, melting-pot European mix of the Chicago suburb.

Cicero was officially incorporated as a city in 1869, and in line with our 1980's observations, its earliest settlers were immigrants from Eastern Europe countries such as Bohemia, Czechoslovakia, and Poland. In the 1920's, Cicero was the headquarters for the notorious Mafia chieftain, Al Capone, and his henchmen. Capone elected to set up shop in Cicero because he thought it would be easier to conduct his nefarious business dealings outside the jurisdiction of the Chicago law enforcement authorities.

For a number of reasons, not the least of which was the Mafia presence, Cicero has never been known as a place that coddled racial minorities. We had heard Cicero was not a friendly place for black people, and we noticed there were few to be seen anywhere. Even as late as 1960, only four black people were counted in the Cicero census, and it was known widely among blacks in the Chicago area as a place to be avoided. The accepted mantra seemed to be: "Nigger, you may pass through here on the way to the race track, but don't let the sun set on your black ass." The Cicero reputation for violence against blacks was such that even the usually unshakeable Reverend Martin Luther King chose not to lead marches there, opting instead for other less dangerous Chicago-area locales to spread his message of peace and racial equality. By the year 2000, out of a total population of 86,000 people, there were still fewer than a thousand blacks living in Cicero. The city was named for Marcus Tullius Cicero, the Roman orator of old, and I have wondered from time to time what he would think about his namesake today.

We found a neighborhood bar near our hotel and stopped in each day for a couple of beers after hanging around the convention site. We were told that the establishment was a "breather bar", a local term applied to bars and pubs where frazzled, ragged-out commuters could wind down from the stresses and strains of big city Chicago life, throwing back a few stiff shots of their favorite scotch or bourbon before heading home for the evening.

As we made our way to the bar that first evening, we noticed the front entrance featured a one way mirror and entry could only be gained by ringing a buzzer. Upon hearing the buzzer, the bartender would make a decision about whether or not you were worthy of admittance. If the answer was affirmative, there would be a loud click as the bartender disengaged the door lock. We further noticed as we sipped our beers that when black delivery boys rang up, they were admitted but seemed uncomfortable and apologetic about being there, intruding on the good will of the bartenders and their hard drinking patrons. There was a noticeable shuffling of feet with eyes averted, giving the place a real Steppin Fetchit feeling.

Toward the end the third day of our brief stay, we asked our female bartender to explain the one-way mirror and buzzer system. Without so much of as a blink of an eye, she bellowed, "Niggers!!! You don't want to drink with niggers, do you? We make sure the only ones that get in this bar are delivery boys. The rest are not welcome here. No one here wants to drink with a nigger!" The whole episode with the one way mirrors and door locks made a lot more sense once the bartender clued us Texas country bumpkins in on the purpose of the system.

Our last morning in Cicero/Chicago, a Sunday, was spent seeking a decent place to eat breakfast. It was not an easy search for few businesses were open and there was an eerie quietness in the air. We finally settled on a seamy, hole-in-the-wall place which was full of bleary-eyed, toothless, leering druggies who looked at us as if we might be the sources of their next fix. As if those guys were not disconcerting enough, when my breakfast arrived, I noticed a long, six-inch brown hair traversing the entire length of my plate, weaving its way among the yolks and whites of my three eggs like some kind of emaciated, needle-thin eel. That visual effect, coupled with the presence of our leering druggie friends, did it for me. I put down a few dollars to cover my meal, walked out to the street, and window-shopped until Tony finished eating. Tony had his back to the druggies and thus was spared their drooling and snickering. How Tony did it I don't know to this day, but he somehow was able to eat both his breakfast and mine. Clear evidence once again, I think, that he is simply a better man than me!

LeUnes Look-A-Likes

Speaking of Merle Haggard, what do actors Marlon Brando (1924-2004), Paul Newman (1925-2006), McLean Stevenson (1927-1996), James Dean (1931-1955), Clint Eastwood (1930 to present), Dean Stockwell (1936 to present), and Jack Nicholson (1937 to present) and yours truly have in common? However dubious the comparisons, numerous friends and acquaintances throughout my life have commented at one time or another how much I look like one or more of these celebrities. Whether I do or not is of no consequence to me at this point in my life, but it was sort of heady stuff as a 1950's adolescent and 1960's young adult to be compared with the likes of James Dean, Paul Newman, and the less famous but nevertheless consummately handsome Dean Stockwell.

In this connection, a few years ago I discovered a letter in an old file folder dated June, 1968, written by a woman named Pat to a friend named Irene. I remember finding it on the floor after class one day but was not aware that I had buried it in my files for more than forty years. I opened the letter and the first paragraph started off, "I told you to come to A&M. In Personality Adjustment I have this doll for a prof....Almost a Paul Newman." I thought to myself: "Almost Paul Newman is plenty good enough!" It is interesting in the context of the present discussion that a middle-aged female colleague not of my acquaintance came up to me at a faculty social in May of 2012 and breathlessly blurted out: "I just figured it out. I just figured it out! It has finally come to me! You are Paul Newman." I hate to admit it, but it was heady stuff. Perhaps one never gets too old to enjoy heady comparisons.

OTHER PURPORTED LOOK-ALIKES
TOP L TO R ACTOR DEAN STOCKWELL
MIDDLE L TO R ACTOR JAMES DEAN
LOWER L TO R ACTORS PAUL NEWMAN AND MARLON BRANDO

The most flattering comparison I have gotten lately, though we both have grayed and grizzled a bit, is Clint Eastwood, thanks to my colleague, Jotsnya Vaid. As for McLean Stevenson or Jack Nicholson? But my latest brush with celebrity took place at the Omni Hotel in Dallas a couple of years ago. When I emerged from my room one morning, a cleaning woman jumped at least a foot in the air, exclaiming, "Pardon me, but I thought you were President Kennedy!" Yikes! Where did those come from? Surely left field!

John Lucas, Kyle Rote, Jr., and Dexter Manley

I once worked a weekend conference in the early 1980's generated by my brother-in-law, John "Randy" Webb. The program was set up for coaches in the Plano (TX) Independent School District, and the key presenters included John Lucas, the former NBA basketball star and erstwhile drug counselor, his protégé Dexter Manley (who did not show because he had relapsed and been arrested for cocaine-related violations), and soccer great Kyle Rote, Jr.

A personal highlight of the conference came at the end when the eternally gregarious and ever-ebullient Lucas introduced our keynote speaker, Kyle Rote, Jr. The introduction was flowery and long and laudatory with regard to the Rote family athletic history, legendary stuff in Dallas because of Junior's prowess as a soccer player and that of his even more famous football-playing father, Kyle Senior. Soccer thirty-five years ago was in its infancy in this country and stars were few and far between, but Junior was definitely among the elite. Lucas ended his long, eloquent introduction by saying: "Kyle Rote Jr. is without doubt the best soccer player in America." Kyle Rote Jr. took over the microphone, allowed the considerable applause to slowly subside, and countered the Lucas introduction as follows: "I would like to thank John profusely for his kind introduction. However, being designated as the best soccer player in America is sort of like being named the best third baseman in Italy." Rote's quick-witted response brought the house down!

After the conference was over, we adjourned to a nearby restaurant where Lucas held forth at his effervescent best, regaling us with stories from his extensive background in collegiate and professional basketball as well as collegiate tennis where he was also an All-American. On a more serious note, we talked extensively about his work with Dexter Manley and others with cocaine addictions who were Lucas clients at his treatment center in Houston.

Dexter Manley represents a real failure of a system that is prone to coddle athletes while looking the other way when they misbehave, show character flaws, and repeatedly demonstrate poor judgment. Dexter stood six feet three and weighed two hundred seventy pounds, and was a collegiate and professional superstar with the Oklahoma State Cowboys and the NFL Washington Redskins. Coming out of college, he was viewed by professional scouts as somewhat of a long shot, and ended up being selected 119th in the 1981 draft. Dexter played eleven years in the NFL, nine of them with the Redskins, made the Pro Bowl once, was on two Super Bowl championship teams, and ranks twenty-sixth all-time for tackling the quarterback behind the line of scrimmage, or what is popularly known among the football literate as a "sack."

Dexter spent four years at Oklahoma State University, and left there functionally illiterate. He was barely able to read, unable to calculate even the most rudimentary of arithmetic problems, and essentially unprepared to do anything other than play football. Once his NFL glory days were over, the cheering stopped. Dexter was left to face the fact he had almost no survival skills, due in great part to the coddling he received from his paternalistic high school, college, and professional coaches.

In 1995, Dexter was imprisoned in the Texas Department of Criminal Justice (TDCJ), the state-run prison system headquartered in Huntsville, where he served two years of a four-year sentence for cocaine possession. Of his prison stay, he once commented that as big, tough, and mean as he was, he never turned his back to the other inmates when taking a shower. If someone like Dexter is afraid of homosexual gang rape, what is the regular little guy with few protective skills going to do? In the eloquent words of G. Gordon Liddy, one of President Richard Nixon's aides who himself spent some time in prison, to survive you quickly learn to avoid the prison predators by "fighting, fucking, or hitting the fence." Another Liddy anecdote is related to the "hit list" of prominent political enemies Nixon had prepared. In an office conversation, the President reportedly said he would like to get rid of, with TV newsman Dan Rather who supposedly was number one on his list, and Liddy said something to the effect: "Mr. President, you want the son-of-a-bitch killed? Give me the okay and he's history!"

In 2006, Dexter collapsed in a department store in the Washington D. C. area, due to a brain problem. He subsequently underwent ten hours of surgery to remove a cyst. He recovered from that surgery, somehow exorcised the drug demons, and now lives in suburban Washington with his wife and family. At last report, Dexter was the director of a community outreach program for drug addicts in the DC area. It is also noteworthy that Dexter finally learned to read as an older adult and became a spokesperson for illiteracy causes.

The Loneliness of the Long Distance Runner Redux

A student-athlete (a distance runner), Barbara C., came by my office one mid-March day in the early 1980's upset about being unable to improve on her time in her specialty, the 10,000-meter run. It was Barbara's opinion she had reached a mental block that needed to be overcome if she were going to improve her future performance. Though I did not say anything at the time, I knew Barbara was a big-time overachiever and hypothesized silently to myself that she had simply reached her physiological limit. Simply put, I felt she was as good as she was ever going to be, and her limitations were physical not psychological. On the other hand, I knew whether or not she could improve was an empirical question, and my job as someone possessed of a modicum of expertise in sport psychology was to help her make progress if possible.

Barbara graduated from high school in New York but lacked the financial backing necessary to attend college, so she joined the Army. Eventually, she was assigned to my old base, Fort Hood, in Killeen where she continually improved as a runner and was able to attract the attention of the A&M coaching staff. Upon being released from active duty, she moved to College Station, enrolled in school, and joined the university track and field and cross country teams.

Based on our discussions about her performance issues, I suggested we undertake a regimen for the remainder of the spring season in which she was to come by my office at a set time every Wednesday to fill out a brief mood questionnaire I thought to be relevant to sport performance. I also asked her to follow up the psychological testing with a visit to the Student Counseling Service for treatment sessions with a colleague, Dr. Nick Dobrovolsky, a Vietnam veteran, counseling psychologist, and all-around good guy. I felt that if anyone could help Barbara, it would be Nick. Dr. Dobrovolsky focused his efforts on helping Barbara make more efficient use of performance enhancement techniques such as visualization, attentional focus, mind and muscle relaxation, and anxiety reduction, all essential ingredients of behavioral intervention with athletes.

At the end of the season, I dug into my files and retrieved the tests she had filled out each week, scored them, and compared them with her times in the 10,000 meters for the season. The scale used is known as the Profile of Mood States (POMS), and it assesses tension, depression, anger, vigor, fatigue, and confusion. As is obvious, five of the assessed dimensions are negative in connotation, with vigor being the lone positive mood state. Once the inventory is scored, a global assessment of mood can be calculated by summing the scores on the five negative states and subtracting the positive vigor score from that total. This computation yields what is known as a Total Mood Disturbance (TMD) score. The authors of the scale suggest that the TMD score be used with caution but do believe it gives you a broad, global look at overall mood state. Barbara's scores were as follows:

	Tension	Depression	Anger	Vigor	Fatigue	Confusion	TMD
March 17	6	7	5	21	2	9	+8
March 24	12	12	19	13	1	12	+43
March 31	10	1	8	15	0	6	+10
April 7	1	0	2	23	3	5	-12
April 14	3	0	5	21	4	6	-3
April 21	7	4	6	14	2	7	+12
April 28	8	0	1	17	0	6	-2

A couple of observations are warranted concerning these scores. One, it is important to remember that I knew none of this information until early May though the various measures were administered in March and April. Thus the scales taken each Wednesday sat in my files untouched for over six weeks. Secondly, there was a substantial change in week two with a high TMD of +43. In investigating the reasons for this spike, I found out that Barbara had been raised by her "auntie" who unfortunately had died that second week of testing and treatment. As might be expected, this loss of a loved one sent Barbara into a temporary mood-related tailspin, though her recovery by the third week was substantial.

A significant event took place after the last test administration and the final counseling session with her psychologist. Barbara set a personal best in her event at the Southwest Conference meet, a time of ten minutes and fifteen seconds. Was the old expert ever wrong! I completely missed this one! As Barbara had rightly suggested at our initial interaction, she really had developed a mental block and Nick Dobrovolsky helped her get past it.

I published an article based on these data and observations, suggesting an athlete could be monitored weekly or periodically with the POMS, looking for mood alterations that might affect performance. Also, if mood changes were noted that might interfere with performance, then perhaps a counseling or sport psychologist could be brought in to employ some of the techniques used with Barbara by my friend and colleague, Nick Dobrovolsky.

Speaking of Dr. Dobrovolsky, he and one of my former students, Carl Englemann, both Vietnam veterans, were sitting around my office one day in the 1970's talking of their experiences in that ugly Asian War. Nick was a helicopter pilot who during one of his tours was assigned to fly body bags from combat areas to the nearest graves registration site. He made a comment in passing that from time to time there would be lulls in the action, and the troops would want to kick around the old soccer ball. In the absence of a real ball, the remains of a North Vietnamese soldier would be retrieved from a body bag, the head would be removed with a sharp knife, and Voila!, the boys had a soccer ball. Let the games begin! Such vignettes as these serve as poignant reminders of the man's inhumanity to man and the sheer, unvarnished ugliness of war. They also probably help explain why Carl Englemann never completely recovered psychologically from his experiences as an artillery forward observer in Vietnam.

Life Can Get Pretty Kinky

On December 5, 1985, I attended a faculty soiree at the home of our department chair, Dr. Steve Worchel, and his spouse (later ex-wife) Frances, also a PhD and a member of the School Psychology faculty in the College of Education. One of Steve's fraternity brothers from his undergraduate days at the University of Texas was the guest of honor, and his name was none other than "Kinky" Friedman. The ever-quirky Kinky was fond of introducing himself as follows, "Hi. My name is Richard Kinky Big Dick Friedman."

Kinky and Steve had been members of the same Jewish fraternity at UT and had remained friends, though their lives and careers after college took very divergent paths. Steve went off to graduate school, earned the PhD, developed a reputation as an outstanding scholar as evidenced by his numerous books and journal articles, and became our department head at A&M in the late 1980's. As for Kinky, he did a stint in the Peace Corps in Borneo (now Brunei), had a brief and mildly successful run in Austin and elsewhere as a musician and songwriter, and later became a critically acclaimed writer of numerous mysteries featuring a fictional detective known only as "The Kinkster."

Kinky originated his musical group in 1971, composed most of their songs, and was the lead singer for the band known as Kinky Friedman and the Texas Jewboys. Some of his signature tunes included "They Ain't Making Jews Like Jesus Anymore", "Get Your Biscuits in the Oven and Your Buns in the Bed", "The Ballad of Joseph Charles Whitman" (The 1966 University of Texas Tower sniper), and a parody of the immensely popular "Okie from Muskogee" entitled "Asshole from El Paso." The latter title speaks volumes about the intent and ability of Mr. Friedman to shock the establishment, or the politically correct crowd. His most recent shocker has achieved some popularity and is entitled "My Shit's all Fucked Up."

It also speaks loudly, if you will pardon the pun, of the man that his musical CD's are produced by Sphincter Records. His latest CD was recorded in a venue in Sydney, Australia, and of the two CD set Kinky says, "The CD's are great. Sphincter is the best at putting out live sounds." His colleague, Little Jewford, who is also President and CEO of Sphincter, says he himself is, "Proud of this latest Sphincter release."

In 2005, Kinky announced his candidacy for Governor of Texas, with campaign slogans reading "How Hard Can It Be?" and "Why the Hell Not?" In 2010, he ran for Agriculture Commissioner where he received one-eighth of the total vote, and rejoined the political trail in late 2013 announcing his candidacy for Agricultural Commissioner once again. A major plank in his platform was the legalization of marijuana, something that is long overdue in Texas. I have never used marijuana and am not an apologist but criminalizing young people for marijuana use is criminal in itself. I have had the distinct honor of voting for Kinky in at least two of those races, and perhaps all three.

During the party hosted by his old frat-rat buddy, Steve Worchel, I spent a fair amount of time picking Kinky's brain to see what makes the man tick. I was particularly interested in hearing what he had to say about music and, perhaps most of all, hear his thoughts on being a successful writer, the latter a pinnacle to which I have always aspired. In a typical Kinky twist, he held forth at length about a topic near and dear to his heart, at least for that evening. It was Kinky's hypothesis that few of us really get to do what we want in life, so we accept compromises. For example, in his own case, he always wanted to be a musician and only a musician but ended up being a writer. I told him that all I had ever wanted once I found out I was not going to be the point guard for the Rockets or centerfielder for the Astros was to be a fiction writer. He used that statement as ammunition to substantiate his theory. He said, "See. I rest my case. You wanted to be a fiction writer but settled for being a professor and writer of erudite academic articles. I wanted to be a musician and ended up writing detective novels. You and I are proof positive that no one really gets to do what they want to do."

Even more interesting was the on-going, all-night pissing contest between the Kinkster himself and the lovely Mrs. LeUnes who has been known to be cantankerous in her own right. While chatting casually with "The Kinkster", she asked if he would come to her fifth grade class the next time he was in College Station to talk about creative writing. He said he would be happy to do so if she would pay his asking price of $500. Judy assumed he was kidding, but he held his position…500 bucks per pop, he reiterated. She let him have it verbally at that point, and they spent the rest of the evening in an uneasy *détente* broken only by occasional plaintive pleas from Kinky asking me to keep her away from him. He told me on more than one occasion to call her off, or as he put it, "Arnold, get your wife under control, man. The woman is up my sleeve. She's up my sleeve, man!" On at least three or four occasions that night I got the "Up my sleeve" plea, so I guess Judy must have done a good job of making him miserable, a talent at which she excels once she fixates her tenacious bulldog-like energies on someone she regards as a deserving target.

Kinky left much later that evening in the company of one of our administrative staff (a female), thus capping off a most interesting evening. Kinky Friedman may be, as Paul Williams puts it, "...a Stetson-wearing, cigar-smoking, cat-loving, Jewish Texas songwriter turned mystery writer." I fully agree with that assessment and would add that Kinky is also one of the most creative people that I have ever met when it comes to turning a phrase. I have read most of his mystery titles and find them to be fast reading, irreverent, clever, and funny. I'm glad I met Kinky up close and personal. And, given his sexist tendencies, maybe he needs a woman to "get up his sleeve" every once in a while! A woman's touch might make him a better person.

As a postscript, Kinky held a concert at the Village Cafe in downtown Bryan in early 2012 as part of a promotional tour to tout his music and a recent book about his favorite Texas heroes. Judy and I ponied up the necessary sixty dollars per person to hear him sing and ad lib for about ninety minutes. We enjoyed his renditions of his old standby songs mentioned earlier, and his reflections on modern life and Texas politics were vintage Kinky. I particularly liked his observation about our governor and erstwhile 2012 candidate for President of the United States, Governor Goodhair himself, none other than Rick Perry. Of his misadventures and malapropos, Kinky said, "Rick Perry makes George W. Bush look like Thomas "Freaking" Jefferson." He also suggested that our Governor turned failed Presidential candidate had changed the political landscape in Texas to the point that "blondes and Aggies are now telling Rick Perry jokes."

Prior to his evening musical program, I bought a copy of his book and reminded him of the 1985 get-together at Steve Worchel's. Thirty-three years is a long time, and a lot of sometimes turbulent water had floated under both our bridges, and I didn't expect him to necessarily remember our previous encounter. He certainly did not mention anything about Judy being "up his sleeve", though she was visibly present that evening.

As soon as I looked at the table of contents of his book on Texas heroes, it was clear to me I had read it several months earlier. A week later, I dug up the old copy and gave it to a friend of Judy's named Judy McCoy (recently deceased) while keeping the newly-autographed one for myself.

My last sighting of Kinky was when he was on our campus in the spring of 2014 as part of his most recent (and now unsuccessful) political campaign in which he was running for Agriculture Commissioner. I visited with him briefly after his talk, and in the course of our conversation, someone took our picture together. I could not pass up telling Kinky I had been captured on camera months earlier with Texas Democrat gubernatorial candidate, Wendy Davis, and, of the two of them, she was far better looking. He smiled but I could not tell from his response if he thought my perhaps feeble attempt at humor was funny to him.

Words of wisdom from the Kinkster

(1) "Beauty is in the eye of the beerholder."
(2) "I support gay marriage. I believe they have a right to be as miserable as the rest of us."
(3) "How can you look at the Texas Legislature and still believe in Intelligent design?"

(4) "We're first in executions. We're 47ᵗʰ in funding public education. We're in the race with Mississippi for the bottom and we're winning."
(5) "The folks in Mississippi are saying 'Thank God for Texas.'"
(6) "Well, I just said that Jesus and I are both Jewish and that neither of us ever had a job, we never had a home, we never married and we traveled around the countryside irritating people."

Angelo Bartlett "Bart" Giammati

One of the most compelling lectures I have ever attended was delivered thirty years ago by Angelo Bartlett (Bart) Giammati, then the President of Yale University. Dr. Giammati assumed the Presidency of Yale in 1978 at the unprecedented age of forty, making him the youngest person in the history of that storied institution to hold such a lofty position. He served in that capacity until 1986, at which time a new and exciting job offer arose which was simply too good to pass up. I will have more on that topic soon.

His presentation took place in one of the meeting rooms in A&M's Cushing Library. Giammati, a Comparative British and Italian literature scholar of the first order, eloquently traced the history of sports, which was his topic for the occasion, all the while lamenting the loss of amateurism in collegiate athletics. Giammati held forth at length about the "Ivy Group" (what the hoi polloi among us call the "Ivy League"), and the views of his fellow university presidential colleagues about big-time sports. Essentially, Giammati felt that financial need rather than intellectual giftedness or athletic prowess should determine how much financial support a university should provide to any given student. In his scheme, the gifted trombone player in the band who could demonstrate financial need would get more institutional support than the best football player who happened to be born into a wealthy family.

Giammati also proposed a system for taking the professionalism out of collegiate football. To wit, he said an announcement should be made the first day of classes each fall heralding the beginning of the football season. As part of his proposal, notes would be posted prominently on all campus bulletin boards and kiosks, calling for all young men who aspire to play football to show up at an announced date, time, and place. In Giammati's view, this idyllic approach would create a level playing field level for everyone. At the same time, it would help curb the well-documented excesses associated with the insane recruiting process now in place by essentially eliminating it altogether. Ever the realist, Giammati admitted that the entrenched system, admittedly outlandish and corrupt, would prevail and the professionalization of college sports would continue unabated.

In the course of his lecture, Giammati admitted that he had been a life-long baseball fan, and mentioned in passing that as a small child all he had ever hoped to be when he grew up was President of the Boston Red Sox. Most popular attributions along this line have Giammati saying his childhood goal was to achieve the Presidency of the American League, no doubt a function of his life-long love affair with the beloved Red Sox. In any event, those of us in attendance at his talk that day caught a glimpse of just how prophetic Giammati's musings were concerning baseball and his role in the game.

In 1986, Bart Giammati was named President of the National League, and three years later, he became commissioner of Major League Baseball, a position he held for only 154 days, cut short due to his most unfortunate, untimely death from a heart attack. Giammati was fifty-one-years old at the time of his death.

Giammati was an ardent supporter of the lifetime ban imposed on Pete Rose, the great Cincinnati Reds (and later Philadelphia Phillies) outfielder and hitter *par excellence*. There are many conflicting points of view concerning Rose and his gambling indiscretions, but there is little debate about his greatness as a player. None of that mattered much to the Commissioner; for as far as he was concerned, Rose had sullied the reputation of the sport he loved. Commissioner forgiveness was thus not an option. Not much has changed concerning Rose's status in the Hall of Fame in the intervening three decades.

Needless to say, I was most disheartened at the news of Giammati's demise; we never officially met but I came away from that momentous, at-a-distance encounter feeling like I had just listened to an old friend hold forth on a subject near and dear to both of us. A statement issued through the auspices of the George Bush Presidential Library and Museum by former President George Herbert Walker Bush (Bush '41) on the day of Giammati's death captures nicely the essence of the man. The tribute dated September 1, 1986 reads as follows:

"I am shocked and deeply saddened by the tragic death of Bart Giammati. He had an abiding love of baseball and an enduring zest for life. Author, teacher, college president, Commissioner – Bart Giammati was a man of many talents and a man who lived by the highest standards of excellence and ethics. He was my friend of longstanding. I will miss him very much. He was a strong, gentle, and generous man; and his loss is the nation's. Barbara joins me in mourning the death of this remarkable human being."

I came away from my brief exposure to Bart Giammati with many of the emotions expressed so eloquently by our former President and aging elder statesman. Bart Giammati was indeed a brilliant human being with a zest for life and baseball, and his presentation was that of a remarkable, insightful, and thoughtful man. Looking back on those two hours in Cushing Library, I regret that I did not bring along a tape recorder to capture his words. What he related was incredibly eloquent and it is truly a shame that his talk was not preserved for baseball fans and social and sport historians.

American Life in the 1990's

U. S. Population is 281 Million
Average Annual Salary is $13.97 Per Hour
Average Annual Teacher Salary is $39,300
Life Expectancy for Men is Seventy-three Years, Seventy-nine for Women
Minimum Wage is Five Dollars and Fifteen Cents
U. S. Fights Gulf War in Kuwait and Iraq
For Different Reasons, Bill Clinton and O. J. Simpson Monopolize TV Coverage
Martha Stewart is Guru of Home Crafts and Design
Fads Include Tae-Bo, Beanie Babies, and Tickle Me Elmo
Americans With Disabilities Act Passed
The World of Technology Dominated by Steven Jobs and Bill Gates
Hootie and the Blowfish, Spice Girls, Madonna, Celine Dion Dominate Music Scene
Cheers, 60 Minutes, Home Improvement, and *Seinfeld* Top Four TV Shows of Decade
Average American Spends Seven Hours per Day Watching Television
Foul Language, Sexual Innuendos, Crude Behavior, Violence Typical TV Fare
Dances With Wolves, Schindler's List, and *Forrest Gump* Among Oscar Winners
Author John Grisham's Books Sold over Forty Million Copies
Best-Sellers include *Seven Habits of Highly Successful People* and *Into Thin Air*

The 1990's: Australia, New Zealand, and the Fiji Islands

A major highlight of the decade of the 1990's was having the good fortune to spend ten weeks in Australia and New Zealand and two days in the Fiji Islands, thanks to Texas A&M University and the University of Wollongong in Australia where I was sponsored by Dr. Mark Anshel, a Wollongong faculty member who was born and educated in North America.

LIGHTHOUSE, WOLLONGONG, AUSTRALIA, 1991

Australia, 1991

In 1991, I was granted a Faculty Development Leave (aka Sabbatical at other universities) which I spent in Australia, or more specifically the city of Wollongong, maybe 150 kilometers south of Sydney. Wollongong had 300,000 residents, was home to the university bearing its name, and was my host city for the duration of the so-called developmental leave. The city was lovely and I really enjoyed my stay there. I met some nice people and spent most of the last four weeks in the company of a British graduate student named Graeme Maw, an Australian undergraduate student named Allison Hass, and an Aussie female of German descent who had also lived in Germany and the United States, Monika Berndt. The three of us were inseparable for a short time and it made the last month there an extremely delightful blur. Interestingly, Monika is married and now lives in Colorado. I do not know the fate of my other two companions.

AUSSIE MATES ALLISON HASS, GRAEME MAW, MONIKA BERNDT

Late in November of that year, Allison, Graeme, and yours truly took off for Melbourne to attend the Asian-South Pacific Association for Sport Psychology (ASPASP) Conference where I presented a paper on a pain scale developed by Tony Bourgeois, my esteemed colleague and good friend, Dr. Michael Meyers, yours truly, and an undergraduate research assistant named Stacey Stewart. Sometime later, I was able to visit the Australian Institute for Sport (AIS), the Olympic training site in Canberra, where I presented a version of the same paper and met the sport psychology section director Geoff Bond, an Aussie, and his American sidekick, Clark Perry, a PhD graduate of Temple University. Geoff and Clark were great guys and a joy to be around.

Geoff told me of an interesting incident involving one of his Olympians, an elite pistol shooter. It seems that the marksperson, a female, came by his office requesting an impromptu appointment, only to be frustrated by his completely full schedule. She repeatedly asked to see him anyway, and after turning her away several times Geoff finally relented by rescheduling one of his late-in-the day appointments. When the shooter walked into his office, she shut the door, pulled out a pistol, pointed it right between his eyes, and held Geoff hostage for several hours. She was eventually talked down by Geoff and the police, at which point she was taken into custody; only then, Geoff reported, did he draw a deep breath. As he told me, "She was our top shooter and if she had wanted to she could have easily put out both of my eyes before I blinked twice." For her terror tactics, the judge in the case fined our distraught shooter a small amount of money and ordered her to stay away from Geoff in the future. Geoff said he was not convinced the penalty fit the crime, given the potential consequences of her hostile, threatening actions.

SPORT PSYCHOLOGIST, GEOFF BOND, AUSTRALIAN INSTITUTE OF SPORT, 1991

One day I was eating lunch in the AIS dining hall with my new colleagues, enjoying the boundless, athletic energy of groups of high-spirited young athletes. The joy was short-lived and the moment broken, however, when the robots, the automatons, aka the little female gymnasts, silently and solemnly strode into the dining hall. I asked Geoff to give me his most secret and honest opinion of the gymnasts, and he said: "If you quote me, I'll deny I said it, but they are the only athletes here that we genuinely feel sorry for. They have no life except gymnastics. We brought their coach in from China to do something about our standing in gymnastics, and she has taken us from nineteenth to sixth in the world, but at what price?" Interestingly and perhaps predictably, that same coach was fired several years later amid allegations of athlete abuse.

Events of late involving Dr. Larry Nassar, the US Gymnastics Federation, and Michigan State University have shaken the gymnastics world.

FRIENDLY CRIMSON ROSELLAS, MOMMA KANGAROO AND BABY JOEY

Rob de Castella and Plantar Fasciitis. At one point, Geoff and Craig introduced me to the AIS Director, Rob de Castella, who also happened to be the premier marathon runner in the world at the time. As testimony to his status as a marathoner, he set the world record in the event at two hours and six minutes shortly before our chance meeting. For those of you who are arithmetically challenged or just not familiar with the sport, Rob's time required that he run twenty-six consecutive miles at a five-minute pace per mile. How many of us have ever run one five-minute mile? I can think of few achievements in athletics that are more mind-boggling than the statistic I just quoted. How does one string that many five-minute miles together for two hours?

In the course of our brief conversation, I learned Rob and I shared a common affliction, the much-dreaded foot problem known as plantar fasciitis, an overuse syndrome common among athletes. This shared awareness provided Rob and I with an immediate bond, and we proceeded to "regale" each other with assorted tales of woe about the condition. We also agreed that about the only thing you could do to treat it was "run through it", which is easier said than done.

Plantar fasciitis is the result of inflamed connective tissue running along the underside of the instep and is most painful, particularly when you are inactive and suddenly have to use your feet. The pain can be excruciating, debilitating, chronic, and is often unresponsive to conventional treatments. The good thing about plantar fasciitis is that it bothers you little when you actually compete; it is in periods of rest where it really exerts its effects. Getting up in the morning and taking those first steps or sitting at a desk for extended periods of time and then having to move about are two prominent examples of where the condition is most likely to manifest itself. Explaining the condition to those who have never experienced it is difficult, but if you have ever had plantar fasciitis, you know it!

After twenty minutes or so, de Castella bid us farewell to attend a meeting, so Geoff, Clark, and I departed. A short time later, we decided to take a three-mile recreational run. To liven up the mix a bit, my sport psychologist friends invited the coaches of the Australian Olympic swimming team along. The five of us soon found ourselves on "Deke's Course", a trail cut through a wooded area near the AIS and named in honor of de Castella because he did most of his own training there. As we were going through our paces, I asked the two coaches if there really were sinkers, people who could not be taught to swim even by experts like themselves. They both agreed that some people probably can never learn to swim. I assured them they were in the presence of a true sinker, one of those unfortunate few who apparently cannot swim despite repeated attempts to learn that important recreational and life-saving skill. But I suppose it was nice to know that there are other sinkers out there besides me. I know that my still muscular sixty-ish colleague, Dr. Steve Smith, and the boxing great Mike Tyson are also sinkers. Perhaps Steve Smith, Mike Tyson, and I could form three legs of a freestyle sprint relay team composed totally of sinkers. If any of you readers are sinkers, let us know. We need an anchor leg!

At the aforementioned sports medicine conference in Melbourne, I found some shoe inserts at one of the vendor displays that did wonders for my plantar fasciitis. After a three-year siege which affected each foot for approximately eighteen months, the pain subsided and I was cured several months after returning home from Australia. I hope Rob de Castella somehow fared as well.

JIMMY WALKABOUT, AUSTRALIAN ABORIGINAL, 1991

New Zealand

I left Wollongong via Sydney in late November, bound for Christchurch, New Zealand. Though it was the first day of summer, the temperature when I arrived in that consummately lovely city, was forty-two degrees, accompanied by a light rain. For the seven days I spent there, I do not think the temperature ever reached sixty. After departing the airport, I checked into a youth hostel in the middle of Christchurch, and got myself set up for a stay of several days. It was not long before I heard a knock on my door, and it turned out the person hailing me was a twenty-eight-year old woman from Austin, Texas (I am appalled at the memory deficit that prevents me from retrieving her name). She had gotten my room number and name from the hostel registry, thus the rap on my door to inquire about my plans for the next day or two. She and I, along with a couple of young Brits, a mid-twenties female ski instructor from Austria, and a middle-aged Kiwi (person, not bird) became traveling companions for the next week.

It seems that my new friend from Austin had received her degree in accounting and worked for several years auditing financial ledgers at various universities, including A&M. Six years of looking at endless numbers led her to give up the accounting profession, and she then spent a year backpacking in Australia and New Zealand. That hiatus from the work-a-day world provided a good cooling down period to let get her head together concerning the future. She set out to intentionally deplete her life savings (which she did), return to Austin by Christmas (which she did), and start a whole new career by enrolling in nursing school (which she did). No more account ledgers for this girl, she said!

Words cannot capture the beauty of New Zealand, as anyone who has visited that unbelievably gorgeous country can attest, and you can never run out of scintillating scenery to stimulate your senses. Due to time and other limitations, I spent my entire week in the South Island with its magnificent mountains, bluebonnets the size of sunflowers, and endless vistas beyond comprehension and description. I was later able in 2004, as part of a Study Abroad program, to spend ten days on both islands, and though they are vastly different, they each have beauty to spare. I do not think I have ever been anywhere where the people are more likeable. They seem happy, love their country, and seem fond enough of Americans. My memories of those two trips to New Zealand are rich with transcendent images of the people and the countryside.

Nadi, Fiji Islands

On my return trip from "Down Under" just before Christmas of 1991, I stopped over for two nights in Nadi, the second largest city in Fiji, with a population of almost 45,000. I had located my accommodations from a travel brochure which I later learned was the antithesis of truth in advertising. My room was shown to be near an enticing beach, and appeared to be quite luxurious. In reality, if Rob de Castella had been a traveling companion and looking to run a practice marathon, we probably could have found some sand in maybe two hours. My room was luxurious if you think a large puddle of water standing in one corner providing sustenance for thirsty tarantula-sized spiders defines luxury! I was told by the management not to worry; my arachnid roommates were largely docile and seldom if ever dined on Americans.

After unpacking my belongings, I decided to take leave of my spider friends and headed to the streets to look for signs of Fijian life. I quickly located a small bar that looked reasonably inviting. I peeked in to get a feel for the place, found it acceptable, sat down, and asked the dark-skinned, dark-eyed bartender for his beer menu. He said, "We have only one beer, Fiji. That's it. One beer! Fiji." Being a decisive sort, I said, "Why don't you give me a Fiji?" After a couple of mellow Fiji's, I fell in with some folks who were members of the house band. I hung around with them for the next two nights, drinking beer and tapping my toes to their excellent music. My stay there was made even more enjoyable by Lucy Madden, the affable sister of the band leader. Lucy was a half-Irish, half-Fiji woman in her mid-twenties, dark-skinned (much Fiji, little Irish) and buxom, who took it on herself to make sure I was treated like some sort of visiting royalty.

On my final day in Fiji, I decided to do the tourist thing so I hired a guide to show me around the area and introduce me to the cultural dances and feasts of the native people. My guide was dressed in a brightly colored shirt and a blue denim skirt which I noticed was commonly worn by Fijian males. It was rather strange to see a hairy-legged dark man with the build of a college football linebacker wearing a denim skirt, but that was the custom.

Before we left Nadi, the guide asked if it would be okay if his eighteen-year old daughter came along on our trip, which of course was fine with me. The daughter was tall, attractive, lean and athletic, and we hit it off immediately. She was a member of the Fijian national netball team which gave us a common ground for some conversation and male-female bonding.

For the uninitiated, netball is played mostly in Oceania and is pretty much basketball minus dribbling and backboards. Thus, the ball must be passed from person to person sans dribbling and when a player takes a shot, there is no backboard to help guide the ball into the basket. In any case, it was nice to get to know my first and only netballer!

The three of us rode for maybe two hours, and ended up in a Fijian village where I watched a ceremonial dance. We adjourned to a nearby wooded area to dine on a native lunch which has been prepared by the guide. After lunch, he dropped his daughter off with some relatives and we headed back to Nadi in what was to become my most up close and personal near-death experience ever. On the trip down with the athletic daughter in tow, the guide was a model driver. Once she was safely in the hands of her relatives, however, the guy declared open season on everything that moved on or off the highway. This guy made Hamed el-Feky of Austin field trip fame look like a driver's education teacher. He drove at maniacal, breakneck speed, indiscriminately ran stop signs and red lights, passed repeatedly on blind curves and hills, and literally forced several oncoming cars off the road in what I assume were inadvertent games of chicken. I have truly never been so scared for such a long period of time at any point in my life. We all experience occasional fleeting moments of fear, but ninety minutes of sheer terror cannot be captured in words. Some say as you near death, your life briefly flashes before your eyes; mine did so at least a dozen times. And all this wackiness took place in an open air Jeep with seat belts that long ago had ceased to be functional! My man the maniac never once manifested any misgivings about the peril our lives were in, but he did offer an apology a couple of times for the absence of proper body restraints in case we did collide with something. I doubt seriously if it mattered much because at the speed he drove, there would have been only bits and pieces of both of us left anyway. My best guess was that only a few teeth would be found at the scene of our demise, thus placing our identification in the hands of a team of forensic dentists!

I breathed a huge sigh of relief when we finally reached Nadi. I was ready to put some distance between me and "The Fiji Flyer." However, because our sightseeing and lunch had taken so long, I was in danger of missing my flight to the states by way of Honolulu. Thus, I did not have time to find an alternate means of transportation to the airport so the wild man quickly became my only option. I figured since I had made it this far, maybe, just maybe, I could make a few more miles. Fortunately, the traffic was heavy in the vicinity of the airport and my rusty, trusty guide was never really free to get up any meaningful speed and otherwise wax maniacal. We were virtually bumper-to-bumper all the way, and gridlock has never looked so good. Anything keeping this guy sane was fine with me. Upon our arrival at the airport, I thanked him for the tour and the ride to the airport, and entered the terminal a happy if much older, grayer, and beaten shell of a man.

Sentimental Journey Home I (1965-2018)

FIJI FRIENDS, 1991

American Life in the 2000's:
The "Naughtie Aughties", aka "The Uh-Ohs"

World Population is Six-and-a-half Billion, North American Population 332 Million
The Year 2000 Was Expected to Be Disastrous Due to Y2K Concerns
India's Billionth Person is Born
Hillary Clinton Becomes First Lady to be Elected to U. S. Senate
Terrorists Strike World Trade Center in New York, Killing 3,000 People
Civil Wars and Coups Break Out All Over World
War Begins in Afghanistan in 2001, Iraq in 2003
Largest Anti-War Rally in World History at the News of Iraq Invasion
President Bush Signs Patriot Act into Law
European Union (EU) Continues to Expand Influence Throughout Europe
2004 Tsunami Kills 230,000 People in Southeast Asia
Era of Google, Yahoo, Amazon, Wikipedia, MySpace, Twitter, YouTube
Mobile Phones in Use in Australia Outnumber Countries' Population
Rapper Eminem Sells Thirty-two Million Albums, Barely Outdistancing Beatles
Decade's Most Watched TV Shows are Friends, ER, Joe Millionaire, American Idol
American Swimmer Michael Phelps Wins Eighteen Olympic Gold Medals, 2004, 2008, 2012
Jamaican Usain Bolt Breaks World Record at 100 and 200 Meters in 2008 Olympics
Golf Legend Eldrick "Tiger" Woods Sullies His Reputation with Serial Infidelity

SCENES FROM SANTA CHIARA CAMPUS IN CASTIGLION FIORENTINO, ITALY, 2001

Study Abroad in Italy, Germany, and Oceania

"There is wisdom in turning as often as possible from the familiar to the unfamiliar; it keeps the mind nimble, it kills prejudice, it fosters humor."

George Santayana, Philosopher (1863-1952)

"Travel is fatal to prejudice, bigotry, and narrow-mindedness."

Mark Twain (1835-1910)

"Heaven is where the police are British, the chefs Italian, the mechanics German, the lovers French, and it is all organized by the Swiss.
Hell is where the police are German, the chefs British, the mechanics French, the lovers Swiss, and it is all organized by the Italians."

Unknown Source

Italy, 2001

One of the more rewarding things I have done during my teaching career is becoming involved in the university Study Abroad program. My first exposure to this experience was in 2000 when I spent a week visiting my colleague, Tony Bourgeois, at A&M's Santa Chiara campus in Castiglion Fiorentino, Italy. Tony taught at Santa Chiara all spring so I arranged to drop in for his final week there. During those seven days, I was able to accompany Tony and his students to Rome and Florence, among other sites. When the semester ended and the students departed Castiglion Fiorentino, Tony was free to go so he and I caught a train to Venice where we spent a couple of days. We camped out in Lido, an island near Venice, endured the endless pigeons on the Piazza San Marco, walked the winding and watery streets, visited the Guggenheim Collection of Modern Art, and took full advantage of the sites to be seen riding the vaporettas, or water taxis. After two days of sightseeing in Venezia, we made the incredibly scenic nine-hour train ride to Munich where we spent another two nights. We then rented a car and headed for Strasbourg, thus beginning a ten-day, 2,100-mile trip around the perimeter of France. The overriding reason for the caper in France was for Tony to touch base with his French ancestral roots while concurrently indulging his fascination with oysters. He had thoroughly studied relevant sources of tourist and culinary information, and was able to isolate different French cities famous for either a particular type of oyster or a special type of preparation. Each of our stops in France was thus orchestrated to cater to his oyster addiction, as it were. Interestingly, at the end of the trip, Tony surmised that his favorite oysters were still those from the Gulf Coast of Texas and Louisiana. I agree, and no one of recent memory prepares them better than Amico Nave on Villa Maria in good old Bryan, Texas. Wade and Mary Beckman, the proprietors, have also created the best salmon dish I have ever eaten, and I have eaten that delicacy all over the US, Canada, Australia, and many countries in Europe. As well, they serve an outstanding Caesar salad embellished with the most delightfully tasteful anchovies one can imagine (if one can imagine anchovies ever being delightful).

During that week at the Santa Chiara campus, I met the staff as well as professors from several universities and generally got a feel for how things were done there. Upon returning to campus after the journey across France, I wrote a proposal to teach a Study Abroad course in Italy for the summer of 2001. My part of the program was approved and we ended up with a total of seventy-four students, fifty-seven females and seventeen males. I had the good fortune to have forty-one of them in my section of sport psychology. In retrospect, sport psychology is perhaps an odd offering for Italy where sports other than soccer receive little attention.

Castiglion Fiorentino. The city of Castiglion Fiorentino has around 13,000 citizens, the majority of whom speak little or no English, with no being far more common than little. Learning some adaptive, survival Italian thus becomes more or less mandatory, which is good for students and professors alike. The city is in the heart of Tuscany and is charming beyond description. Vineyards and olive trees dot the horizon in every direction, and a magnificent castle, the Castello de Montecchio Vesponi, towers over the entire area. I made it a mission to see that everyone made the trek up to the castle, and I think I initiated almost every single student and the majority of the faculty to the experience at one time or another. It is scary to contemplate what good physical shape I was in then and how different things are now since I have quit running three miles a day, playing softball, and working out almost every day with the last two children, Katie and Lyndon, on football, basketball, baseball, softball, soccer, and golf. The kids ran me ragged and there were many times when I didn't feel up to playing "HORSE" in basketball or throwing a softball or baseball around, but I miss those days now.

There was a central meeting point in Castiglion Fiorentino called the Piazza Garibaldi, populated with a couple of quaint bars, a handful of restaurants, and several outdoor fruit and vegetable markets. It was a steep, laborious climb from the A&M center to the piazza, and it was not unusual to have to stop several times to catch one's breath on the way up. You quickly learned that there is no such thing as flat terrain in Tuscany; everything is either up or down (up seemed far prevalent than down, in my memory).

There was an elderly signora who sold fruits and vegetables from a small store in the piazza and she took it on herself to indoctrinate us into the ways of Italy, with a mix of vocal admonitions and hand slaps if we dared touch her produce. It was also charming to try to figure out the nuances of using the lira which at that time was the prevailing currency. At its peak that summer, the exchange rate on the lira was something like twenty-three hundred to one US dollar.

I was in charge of the Working Fund, a money source set aside as part of every Study Abroad program to be used to cover miscellaneous expenditures and group activities considered beneficial to the students that might arise serendipitously. In reality, because our schedule was so highly organized from the outset, most of the funds ended up being used to buy gifts for the chefs, the kitchen staff and the cleaning crew, assorted bus drivers, an end of program reception, and a highly-popular redistribution of money to the students. At one time, I was in possession of over thirteen million lira, or 6,000 US dollars. I was, for a very short time, an Italian millionaire! Of the thirteen million lira, two million went for gifts and gratuities, and the remaining eleven million was redistributed to the students throughout the duration of the program. I was a very popular man on lira distribution day!

The Staff and the Fabulous Chefs. It is impossible to talk about Santa Chiara without mentioning the staff members who made the center run so efficiently. Santa Chiara Director Paolo Barucchieri and his brother, Giovanni, were the driving forces behind the creation of the program which began in 1989. However, the lion's share of the credit for making things work on a day-to-day basis, at least on the two occasions I was there, was attributable to their respective wives, Sharon Jones and Garnette Gott. These two lovely women were graduates of the University of Northern Colorado, met their husbands there, and eventually moved to Italy when their spouses returned to their homeland. I was most impressed with their hospitality, generosity, diligence, attentiveness, and general stewardship of the various programs sponsored through the Santa Chiara center. A final but ever-present piece of the puzzle was Alessandro Benatti who served as the cultural liaison attaché for Castiglion Fiorentino. His duties included connecting the students and faculty at Santa Chiara with activities and events taking place in the city.

Unfortunately, Paolo Barucchieri passed away in Rome in April of 2012 after a bout with cancer. Paolo taught art history courses at A&M prior to becoming the first director of the Santa Chiara campus when it opened in 1989. There were some who felt that the center might not survive the death of the man who was its heart and soul for so many years, but it seems to be thriving under the leadership of Sharon Jones with able assistance from Paolo's brother, Giovanni, and his wife, Garnette Gott.

In terms of memories of an enduring nature, it is hard to compete with the culinary creations of the two chefs at Santa Chiara, Lidia and Giuliana. There are no words at my disposal that can remotely begin to capture the elegance of the meals those women created; each and every Italian delicacy they put before us was simply magnificent. I have never eaten better food on a consistent basis in my life. Each meal started with a wonderful salad made from fresh vegetables grown nearby, followed by an array of soups that were indescribably elegant, followed yet again by a variety of vegetable and pasta dishes that should have been entered in a gourmet magazine cooking contest. Fortunately, the lifestyle in Italy is such that I was able to cancel out the effects of the substantial increase in caloric intake with lots of walking, hiking, and abstaining from eating snacks. As a result, rather than gaining weight, I actually lost six or eight pounds during that summer in Italy.

Evening meals were always delightful, with the A&M faculty and several members of the University of Texas delegation dining, talking, and drinking beer or wine for at least two and sometimes three hours. Once my "early to bed, early to rise" A&M colleagues and their wives headed in for the evening, I would go into the bar and consume a Moretti or five with the students. I guess I must have had more than several for one of the student bartenders hung the nickname "Dr. Moretti" on me, a title that stayed with me throughout the remainder of the summer. And I am proud to say that I came by that sobriquet quite honestly. I earned it the hard way, but someone had to do it!

Excursions. As part of the program, we went on many excursions to such places as Firenze (Florence), Venezia (Venice), and Roma, and the castles, cathedrals, museums, and works of art were staggering in their beauty and magnificent in their conceptualization, creation, and expression. One of the less glamorous but most challenging parts of our excursions dealt with the toileting logistics; getting fifty-seven women in and out of rest stop bagno's was a daunting task. I often commandeered the men's facilities and "warned" the male patrons women would be coming through in large numbers. Most of the men paid no attention to the female intruders, thus adding a whole new dimension to the term "unisex bagno."

The Faculty: Joe, Gary, and Howie. A most precious and unforgettable aspect of the trip was the comradeship I forged with two faculty colleagues, Dr. Joe Hutchinson and Dr. Gary Halter. Joe Hutchinson was a charming man in his mid-sixties, a painter and artist from our College of Architecture. He was accompanied by his wife Debbie who was emerging as an artistic talent in her own right. Joe had taught art history at Santa Chiara many times and his academic and "street" knowledge of the cities, Italian art, architecture, and history was immense. Joe has since retired from the University and he and Debbie now live in Santa Fe, New Mexico, where they are immersed in the fabric of that well-known artist colony.

Another colleague in Italy was the sometimes curmudgeonly and often confrontational but eminently likeable (for me, at least) Professor of Political Science, Dr. Gary Halter. I had known Gary not so much as Professor but as Mayor of our little village prior to that summer in Italy, but greatly enjoyed getting to know him and his wife, Linda. Gary taught a political science course there, focusing on similarities and differences in city governance in Italy and the US.

The third member of our group was not so charming, to put it mildly. He was a music professor by the name of Howard F., or "Howie", as Gary preferred to call him in the most derisive fashion imaginable. "Howie" struck me as a classic, textbook case of Asperger's Syndrome, a psychiatric diagnostic label attached to people who are often highly intelligent but invariably socially maladroit.

Our encounters with "Howie" prior to our departure from the US should have told us there was trouble brewing. It seemed clear from our earliest random conversations and casual interactions that "Howie" was different and his agenda was at odds with that of Joe, Gary, and me. I honestly think

"Howie" believed he would transport his summer course in music to Italy *in toto*, with no concessions to the many differences associated with holding forth on the home campus versus teaching abroad. One huge difference is that the foreign learning experience is very much a learn-by-doing, hands-on mix of cultural and educational experiences whereas the emphasis on campus is more with traditional didactic procedures such as lectures, presentations, examinations, and term papers sans the cultural component.

At one of our pre-departure orientation meetings, "Howie" grew confrontational at the idea of releasing students for a scheduled free weekend because he wanted those who were taking his course in music to attend an Italian opera instead. In discussing this matter, "Howie" made a statement that went roughly as follows: "Listening to one of my lectures or attending an opera of my choice is far more valuable to the students than spending three days in Munich, Paris, or London." I countered what I regarded as a pitiful piece of professorial pomposity with an amiable rejoinder along the lines of, "Howard, you are full of shit." "Howie" stomped out of the room, slamming the door so hard it reverberated like a rifle shot throughout the "short" Harrington Building (we have two Harrington Buildings adjacent to each other on campus, one eight stories tall and the other three).

"Howie" was accompanied to Italy by his wife, Lori, who was a diva with the Houston Opera, and the two of them succeeded almost instantaneously in alienating the other faculty, their wives, the Santa Chiara staff, and many of the students. For one thing, "Howie" and Lori often chose not to travel with the faculty and students during scheduled excursions. We would arrive by either bus or train at a preset destination, all seventy-four students plus entourage, and maybe an hour or two later, "Howie" and the diva would show up. It became the norm that they would travel separately from the group, making their own arrangements for buses, trains, or automobiles. They would often go off on their own while we toured as a group, and it was not unheard of for them to return to Santa Chiara long before our excursions ended.

"Howie" seemed to have a dim view of young people, and he struck me as one of those professors who loved exercising power and otherwise derived perverse pleasure in harassing students with capricious assignments and unfair grading. The problem eventually reached such proportions that Dr. Suzanne Droleskey, the Director of International Programs at A&M, got wind of a looming mutiny and flew from College Station to Castiglion Fiorentino to interview selected students and faculty to see if she could get a handle on the nature and extent of the problem. I talked with her for perhaps two hours about my take on the situation, and I was most certainly not on "Howie's" side. I thought his interactions with the students were hostile, mean-spirited, abusive, reprehensible, and unforgiveable.

I suppose everyone is familiar with what is known widely as "plumber's butt", that visually repugnant stereotypical image associated with people who fix sinks, repair leaky toilets, and install new garbage disposal units, i.e., the plumber. "Howie" had one of the most pronounced cases of "plumber's butt" I have ever had the displeasure of viewing. If the reader will pardon a really bad pun, "Howie" quickly became the butt of many jokes among students, staff, and faculty alike for the gross displays of his derriere. Watching him squat down with his back to an audience was frightening but unfortunately not always avoidable.

"Howie" and Professor Halter got into a major league tiff one night after dinner because the music man and Lori continually abused the guidelines for sharing the one computer set aside exclusively for faculty use. The spat was kindling and on the verge of going full-tilt when I happened to turn a corner in the hallway, and I caught "Howie" and Gary engaging in a shoving match in the computer room. It was a veritable rooster fight if you will, with Gary unleashing a staccato string of the most colorful expletives I have ever heard, and all were directed at "Howie." Gary is a pugnacious sort by nature anyway, and "Howie" brought out this trait in the worst way. The computer room confrontation ended with no real blows being struck, but the already fragile relations between the two antagonists in this drama were damaged beyond repair.

Just before the program ended in early July, the Santa Chiara staff put out a call for clothing and other items the faculty and students might want to donate to the citizens of Castiglion Fiorentino or the center itself. "Howie", ever the humanitarian, donated three or four pairs of his old, raggedy-ass, beat up boxer shorts, a gesture in some ways even more frightening and reprehensible than "plumber's butt." Though it has been seventeen years since the Italy excursion, the thought of "Howie's" "plumber's butt", and old underwear still gives me cold sweats.

Sometime after we got back to the states, "Howie" harangued Gary in a variety of public and professional forums, accusing him of being anti-Semitic. "Howie" alleged, in a California magazine article, that he had been a victim of anti-Semitism at A&M and had even been assaulted by a fellow faculty member (I am assuming this was the infamous Santa Chiara computer room confrontation with Professor Halter). This led a reporter with the local newspaper, *The Eagle*, to launch an investigation into Dr. Halter's role in this brouhaha, though nothing of substance was unearthed.

Later on, Gary contacted me with his response to the whole affair, sending a tersely worded email concerning the groundless assertions about ethnocentrism that read as follows: "He {"Howie"} cannot distinguish between anti-Semitism and anti-assholeism." Interestingly, the day Gary first heard about the anti-Semitism charges, he and Linda had Dr. Abraham (Abe) Clearfield, a Chemistry Professor, and his wife, Ruth, over as guests for the evening. Having the Clearfield's, both prominent Jewish community leaders and activists, over for dinner strikes me as strange behavior for an anti-Semite. "Howie" also sent an accusatory email or two to Joe Hutchinson but failed to implicate me in any way. I never knew quite why, but am offended that he failed to find me offensive. For reasons I can only guess but am not privy to, "Howie" F. and Texas A&M University went their separate ways in the academic year after the fiasco in Italy. I do see his name from time to time in the credits for the popular outdoor show, *Texas Parks and Wildlife*, where he is listed as the musical director. There is no doubt that "Howie" was both bright and creative, but he was a poor fit in Italy (and apparently in academia in general). I never had the feeling he understood what the Study Abroad experience is all about.

Sentimental Journey Home I (1965-2018)

DOLOMITI ALPS CLIMB WITH STUDENTS, 2001

A Climb in the Alps. Another peak experience in every sense of the word of that summer (one "Howie" chose not to attend, by the way), was a climb in the Dolomiti Alps orchestrated by Paolo Barucchieri, himself an experienced climber. Paolo listed scaling some of the more prominent faces of the Alps (including three trips over the summit at the Matterhorn) among his mountaineering accomplishments. As a safety precaution for our climb, Paolo arranged to have four experienced Alpine climbers in tow, and while the novices among us were breathlessly attaching ourselves to the side of the mountain with pitons, the guides effortlessly scurried about piton-free like mountain goats. The guides were in their thirties and forties, slim, wiry, muscular, and, paradoxically, all puffed on cigarettes throughout the entire climb.

We hiked for the better part of two hours to reach our jumping off point, followed by an arduous but exhilarating climb of several thousand feet to our final destination atop an Alpine peak. Once we reached our pre-determined destination, everyone sat around, ate and drank, talked, and took pictures. Two of my favorite students, Nichole Loup and Sarah Spector, celebrated our ascent to the top of the aforementioned Alpine peak by mugging for a picture which I still display in my office and elsewhere in this modest little treatise. And my friendly piton hangs from an office file cabinet in remembrance of a true, again pardon the pun, peak experience.

The group consensus concerning the Alpine adventure, in retrospect, went pretty much as follows: "If I had known what I was getting myself into, I would have never made the climb." On the other hand, all parties enthusiastically agreed they had mastered a daunting task without incident and were thrilled beyond words that they had done it. One of the students, Julie Wilson, eloquently summed up the experience for both herself and many others in the group in a note she penned after we returned to the states: "I greatly enjoyed the Dolomite excursion and I thank you for pushing for that to happen. I was terrified but I am so glad I did it. It was a big accomplishment for me. Thanks for not letting us know what we were in for. I really think it added a spiritual aspect to the whole trip, as well as team building. I had to rely on lots of others for help. I think it was great!"

When words and pictures of this adventure filtered back in bits and pieces to the administrators in charge of Study Abroad experiences, mountain climbs in future programs under their auspices were unceremoniously given the axe. Saber-toothed tigers, pterodactyls, dodos, and diplodoci may be spotted on our campus (or in the Alps) before another A&M student takes part in an Alpine climb under the Study Abroad banner!

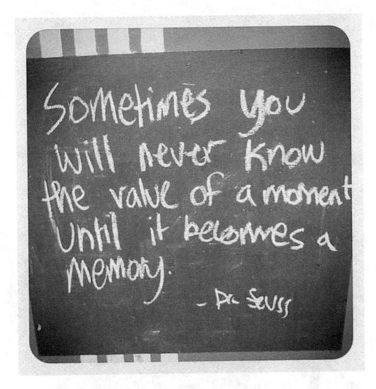

DR. SEUSS WEIGHS IN ON STUDYING ABROAD

Our Twelve-Year-Old Has the Time of His Life. Another highlight of the trip for Judy and me was the response of the A&M students and the local Italians to our then twelve-year old son, Lyndon. We essentially saw him only on fleeting occasions for five weeks; he played, ate, slept, and completely immersed himself in the student experience. We tried to put some limits on his socializing with the students if no other reason than their protection, but they insisted that he be a part of virtually everything they did. Every time we demurred, they would lodge a protest on his behalf, and off he would go. In addition to hanging out with the students, Lyndon played soccer with the locals, mostly late adolescents, and he picked up a working Italian street vocabulary before the summer session was over. Of course, the words have all vanished now, unfortunate victims of disuse.

A major daily group activity for the students, of which Lyndon was always a part, was visits to Castiglion Fiorentino's wonderful gelato shops that have made Italy famous anywhere ice cream is eaten or discussed. The students also insisted that while we were in Venice that Lyndon go on a gondola ride with them, and at their expense. He also accompanied them on the vaporetta trip to the famous glass factories on the island of Murano.

NICHOLE LOUP, SARA SPECTOR, YOURS TRULY TOP OF THE DOLOMITI ALPS, 2001

Lyndon was particularly befriended by a tall, blond, athletic guy by the name of Joe McCabe, a Computer Science major from San Marcos. Joe had played four sports in high school of which basketball was his favorite. He was lean and toned and blessed with the graceful gait and cool confidence often engendered by success in the competitive arena. Joe and Lyndon were virtually inseparable friends for five weeks, and they put an exclamation point on their relationship just before the program ended by jogging several miles to Castello de Montecchio Vesponi just to talk and watch the sun rise over beautiful Castiglion Fiorentino for their last time. Talk about a spiritual experience!

Memorable Students. As noted earlier in the aftermath of the Alpine climb and photo session, Nichole Loup, a Management Information Systems major from Missouri City, and Sarah Spector, a Psychology major from Dallas, were two of my favorite students. I was most impressed with the independence and daring of Nichole; she could be a great group member but was equally capable of vanishing for a few hours or even a day to explore cities and sites on her own.

Nichole brought me back down to earth toward the end of our stay in Castiglion Fiorentino, poignantly demonstrating the fallibility of my ability to make accurate interpersonal assessments. As we were preparing to leave Castiglion Fiorentino, I told Nichole my wife and six or eight of the students had agreed to go our separate ways and then get back together when everyone arrived in Paris a few days hence. I inquired as to her interest in joining the group in Gay Paree, and her response was so uncharacteristic of anything I had previously seen it almost left me speechless. She essentially said, "I am not interested in going to Paris. My friends tell me there is nothing to do there." There was nothing I could say, of course, that would properly address the absurdity of her comment, borne no doubt of youthful naiveté. I am sure her "friends" would tell her there is probably nothing to do in New York or London or Rio de Janeiro either.

I think Nichole's observation about Paris is easily trumped by one reported to me by one of my 2011 participants, Jenny Johnson. It seems that Jenny overheard a student from another Study Abroad program (thank goodness!) commenting to a friend in the US via Skype: "You would not believe Germany! These people are so primitive. Germany is a third-world country, no doubt about it. People here do not even have refrigerators. They are so backward they buy their food on the way home in the evening." Yikes and God Save the Queen! If the misguided woman thinks Germany is primitive, how would she describe a true third-world country?

I had a somewhat similar experience with one of my young charges from the 2011 group who stayed over in Europe for two weeks (London one week, Paris one week) at the conclusion of our program. I saw the student in the hall of our building after her return to the US and to make conversation, I asked: "How was Paris?" To this seemingly innocuous question, she lamented that the food in Paris was terrible and she was not able to find anything good to eat the whole time she was there. My now-retired colleague, world traveler, and resident gourmand, Ludy Benjamin, overheard her comment and almost had a coronary on the spot. It was all Ludy, a giant of a man who had traveled extensively and dined in some of the most elegant restaurants in the world, could do to restrain himself from making a comment…out of the mouth of babes, once again. In all fairness to the student, she and I have maintained relatively constant contact over the past seven years, and I have enjoyed getting to know her.

But back to the Italy experience. Sarah Spector was a dark-haired woman with a lean, well-proportioned body that was absolutely perfect for the low hip hugger look so popular at the time. Unfortunately, some of Sarah's leanness might have been attributable to her nicotine habit. I watched her light up many a cigarette in the Santa Chiara courtyard, and I always thought there is something incongruous about seeing a really pretty woman firing up an incredibly ugly cigarette. I found out in February of 2009 through an inadvertent email that Sarah has earned a master's degree in Psychology and is a Licensed Professional Counselor (LPC). I am hoping she has slain the nicotine monster.

Yet another memorable student in the Italy group was Aaron Stephen, a ruggedly handsome guy who had been an outstanding high school football and track star from the small east Texas town of Mabank. Those of us fortunate enough (some would say dumb enough) to sponsor these Study Abroad ventures repeatedly urge our students to pack as light as they possibly can. Aaron took us at our word, ingeniously cramming everything he needed for five weeks in Italy into one normal-sized backpack. He washed and dried clothes almost every day and, through grit and determination, never had to wear dirty underwear, shorts, or jeans. He took the admonition to pack light to a dimension unparalleled in any of my seventeen Study Abroad programs. Aaron graduated from A&M as well as chiropractic school, and married a daughter of some old friends in Bryan, Sam and Jan Wooderson. Jan, from Crystal City, or what she simply called "Crystal", was a student in my Abnormal Psychology class in the fall of 1973 and I played some softball with and against Sam for several years. Aaron and his wife, Amy, are both chiropractors and reside in Gun Barrel City which is in the Mabank ISD. Thus, Aaron has returned to his roots in east Texas.

Another memorable person was Ellen Bray who made the trip despite losing both parents in the preceding three years. I forget the order of the parental deaths, but the second passing occurred only three weeks before our departure to Italy, so all of us were naturally concerned about Ellen's mental state. However, she sailed through the summer abroad with only a few discernible down moments and garnered the symbolic LeUnes Trooper Award, an informal accolade given each year, and silently at that, to students who make the absolute most out of the experience while complaining the least.

I would be remiss if I did not make mention one of the more impressive duos on the trip, Brett Owens and Heather Howbert, high school and college sweethearts (though they broke up shortly after the Italy experience, once again suggesting too much togetherness is not always a good thing). Brett had been the starting center on offense and linebacker on defense for the state champion football team at Midland Lee High School where Heather was, as fate would have it, a cheerleader. It seems only appropriate that the handsome star from the state powerhouse football program would date the bright, beautiful, and charming cheerleader.

Brett was nice looking, ambitious and business-like, with future success written all over him. I sensed that being successful, respected, and perhaps even being seen as a bit intimidating meant a lot to Brett. It is my understanding that he received his law degree in 2006 from the prestigious University of Texas Law School and is a practicing attorney in Houston.

The last time I saw Brett was maybe a decade ago and occurred one weekend when Judy and I were at the Greyhound Dog Track in LaMarque, Texas. We were actually at the track not so much to watch the greyhounds run but rather to race our dachshunds who were participating in the fun-run wiener dog races. After the races, we ran into Brett and a girlfriend at a nearby restaurant where we shared a nice visit. The two of them seemed quite taken by each other, which is a good thing!

As for Heather, she was as bright as she was attractive. Upon graduation, Heather took a job with a corporation that offered an astronomical beginning salary for a liberal arts graduate, due in part and in no particular order to her strong science background, intelligence, ambition, appearance, and social skills. As recently as 2009, Heather was living in Round Rock and working as a Sales Associate for Saint Jude's Medical.

Sentimental Journey Home I (1965-2018)

MAP OF GERMANY

Another couple that stood out, in a relationship that did not make it much beyond that summer either, was Neal and Christine. It was obvious early on that Neal had a major drinking problem; he was generally tipsy by noon each day and stayed that way until sleep overtook him in the evening. Christina had ambitions of going to law school (I think she graduated from the Southern Methodist University School of Law) and seemed to spend most of her time in Italy ministering to Neal's considerable need for succor and support. It was difficult under the circumstances to see the attraction to Neal, given that Christina seemed sober and ambitious and he drunk and scattered.

Several years after the summer in Italy, I ran into Neal on campus and he said he quit school after the Italy trip to deal with his alcohol demons, and had not had a drink in quite some time. It was great to see that he was back in school and had kicked the habit; if anyone needed to, it was Neal. I applaud him for dealing with a tough issue at such a young age, and hope the effect has been a lasting one.

Other students who were memorable from that summer include the boisterous Italian-American Cari Cesaro, the serious Katti Doescher of St. Louis with medical school ambitions, James Orengo who was fluent in Italian by way of ancestry, the aforementioned Julie Wilson who later returned to the Italy campus as part of the wait staff after a couple of years working for Starbucks in San Francisco, Catherine Harris who later worked with me on an ill-fated, unpublished paper, and Suzanne Specht whose boyfriend flew over during our long weekend to offer a proposal of marriage in Rome, no less. At one time, I had a name and a face for all seventy-four of the Italy students but the passage of time has exacted a terrible toll on my memory.

Two letters sent to me shortly after the trip sum up the feelings of many of the students who were privileged to have been a part of the Italy trip. One who saw things in what I view as the proper spirit was the outgoing, oft-raucous Cari Cesaro who wrote:

"I really don't think that this letter is sufficient enough for what I owe to you all, but I would like to express my thanks. This experience helped me realize who I am and who I can strive to be. This trip has also revealed to me the important things in life: My faith, family, and my personal journey of discovery."

Another letter, this one from a more serene Lacey Barranco, captured other thoughts: "The trip was so amazing and I learned more than I ever dreamed of. I never imagined the trip would be as rewarding as it was."

After such an exhilarating first experience, the allure of returning to Italy simply would not go away. It is hard to get past the rolling terrain, lush vineyards, and opulent olive groves of Tuscany, the delicious meals prepared by Lidia and Giuliana at the center, the grand gelato in the city center, the treasures of Rome, the museums in Florence, the canals and vaporettas of Venice and the nearby island of Lido, and most of all the people of Italy. I cannot say enough about my two trips to that historical, colorful, and amazing country.

I applied to go back to Italy with a Study Abroad group in 2002 but the A&M authorities did not approve my proposal, and I suspect my chances of going back to Italy are scant unless I go as a tourist. However, one good thing came about as a result of the rejection of the ill-fated 2002 Italy proposal. An addendum to the rejection letter asked if I would consider taking my Italy proposal and conduct essentially the same program in Bonn, Germany. At that time, in my half-vast ignorance, I had never heard of Bonn, but what a fortuitous turn of events that suggestion has become.

Germany 2003, 2004, 2005, 2007, 2008, 2009, 2010, 2011, 2012, 2013, 2014, 2015, 2016, 2017

After being asked to think about moving my program from Italy to Germany, I began the retooling process by finding out as much as I could about the city of Bonn and the country of Germany. I knew a lot more about the latter than the former, but soon learned Bonn was the capital of Germany prior to its relocation to Berlin in 1991 after the fall of the Berlin Wall two years earlier. Bonn is an upscale city of 310,000, pretty much crime-free except for some white-collar action, and a fun and safe venue for students. Its location near Amsterdam, Brussels, Cologne, and Frankfurt, plus its rail system and the nearby Cologne-Bonn airport make it a great jumping off point to visit major cities in Europe, with exotic destinations such as London, Munich, Paris, Prague, Rome, and Vienna. One can be in any of those cities in three hours or less, with most an hour away by plane.

Dr. Rainer Zaeck. My program is hosted by the Akademie fuer Internationale Bildung (AIB), or Academy for International Education, an operation begun in 1993 and headed by Dr. Rainer Zaeck. Rainer has a PhD in History and has become a younger brother of sorts (he turned sixty-five in 2015). His AIB operation hosts programs from Texas A&M University in architecture, film, landscape architecture, language (German), history of medicine, psychology, and sports business. They also play host to various programs for Loyola Marymount from Los Angeles as well as several other universities in the US. Rainer Zaeck leaves no stone unturned to ensure that his sponsored programs are the best, and it would be hard to find a more pleasant, generous, and accommodating host.

I tried to keep my requests to Rainer at a minimum but was never told "No." He does not get excited about my fascination with the Hofbrauhaus in Munich and the concentration camp in Dachau, but he puts up with my personal peccadilloes with mild, passive resistance. In previous visits to the Hofbrauhaus, that beyond-touristy Munich biergarten, the students were exposed to a buffet meal and a three-hour dance, music, and culture program that were both educational and just plain fun. For whatever reason, the Hofbrauhaus management scaled back the cultural program, and we opted for similar experiences in venues with a less touristy feel to them. As for Dachau, of course it is a grim, sobering experience, and serves as a somber reminder of the Holocaust and man's continuing and seemingly endless inhumanity to man.

AIB FRIENDS KRISTIN VOSBECK, MIRA (SOMMERHAUSER) ARBEITER, TURE PETERSENN, UNKNOWN, GERMANY 2015

Dachau and Georg Elser. I visited Dachau on half a dozen occasions, but learned something new each time. The camp was originally created in the mid-1930's to incarcerate enemies of the Nazi movement, namely Communists, Catholic priests, labor union organizers, homosexuals, Roma's (i.e., gypsies) and others seen as unsympathetic or antagonistic to the cause. Only later on did imprisoning Jews take place, culminating in Dachau becoming an extermination camp toward the end of the war.

Perhaps the most fascinating of all my Dachau experiences took place during the 2008 visit. As our guide talked, he mentioned in passing the gripping story of a would-be Hitler assassin by the name of Johann Georg Elser. It seems that Georg Elser hatched a plot to kill der Fuhrer ("leader") by planting a bomb in one of Hitler's favorite Munich hangouts, the Burgerbraukeller. On that fateful night, November 8, 1939, the Nazi leader departed from his usual routine and went home early due to threatening weather. Thirteen minutes after Hitler vacated the Burgerbraukeller, the bomb detonated, killing eight people and seriously wounding thirteen others. Had he been there, Hitler almost certainly would have perished in the explosion.

Elser was arrested almost immediately and sentenced to serve time in Dachau. His crime normally would have led to immediate execution, but Hitler decreed that he be kept alive for future propaganda purposes. As a younger man, Elser had joined an organization affiliated with the Communist Party so abhorrent to Hitler but was not enthralled with their message, and his level of involvement and dedication to the Communist cause diminished early on. However, that brief association gave Hitler the ammunition he needed to spin the Burgerbraukeller bombing into a Communist plot against his life, thus further discrediting the Bolshevik movement.

Hitler's long range plan was to keep Elser alive until Nazi Germany prevailed in World War II, at which time he would try him publicly for crimes against the state and parade him before the German people as a poignant symbol of the evils of Communism. Unfortunately, when it became obvious that the Germans were not going to win the war, Hitler ordered Elser's execution. Johann Georg Elser died by gunshot on April 9, 1945, at the age of forty-two, three short weeks before the Allied forces liberated the camp. A small square, the Georg-Elser-Platz, and a concert hall, the Georg Elser Halle, have since been dedicated in his honor in the city of Munich.

Hitler was without any doubt the embodiment of the Nazi movement, but many believe if Elser had been successful in his 1939 assassination attempt, Nazism would have taken a highly unpredictable turn. Without the Fuhrer's charismatic and consummately evil leadership, the movement at a minimum would have been different. At the extreme, Nazism might well have lost momentum and died had Hitler not survived Elser's assassination plot.

Cities and Sites Visited. As part of my near-annual pilgrimage to Germany, the students and I visited the cities of Amsterdam, Berlin, Bratislava in Slovakia, Brussels, Budapest, Cologne, Dusseldorf, Frankfurt, Heidelberg, Leuven, Ljubljana in Slovenia, Munich, Nuremberg, Garmisch-Partenkirchen, Oberammergau, and Scheidegg in the Bavarian Alps, Paris, Prague, Pula and Zagreb in Croatia, and Salzburg and Vienna in Austria. In the process, we were exposed to innumerable cultural, work, and sport sites as well as the concentration or extermination camps in Dachau, Mauthausen in Austria, and Sachsenhausen near Berlin.

JUDY AND BEAR, "BEARLIN" (BERLIN), GERMANY, CIRCA 2005

Speaking of Mauthausen, it featured a quarry from which stones were harvested to build, among other things, giant stadia holding up to 250,000 people in cities such as Nuremberg so Hitler could dispense his message of hate out to large groups. It is said that each day the camp guards would march two Jews up to the top of the quarry and make one push his compadre to certain death in the quarry floor. If one refused, both were shot and kicked into the quarry. Other atrocities were elucidated in the fall of 2014 when I had a Jewish Holocaust survivor come talk to my students who were preparing to go to Germany in 2015. The man was named Bill Marks and he was from Houston. Marks spent ten months as a fourteen-year-old incarcerated in camps at Belk and Mauthausen. In the course of his talk, it was clear that he still harbored extreme animosity toward the Camp Commander, though he never said so in words. He talked at length about reports of unusual cruelty at the camp, and I asked him at the conclusion of his discussion if he personally had witnessed cruelty on the part to the commander. He cited an instance in which the commander decided for whatever reason to hang an eleven-year-old boy. It seems that the noose did not break the boy's neck and he dangled for minutes at the end of the rope, clawing and clutching and kicking his legs. After a minute or two of this, the commander ordered young Mr. Marks to go over and hold the boy's legs until he stopped kicking. A few minutes later, the legs stopped moving, signaling that the poor boy had finally died.

Marks also related another inhumanity inflicted on the Jewish prisoners involving carrying rocks up a flight of steps leading from the bottom of the deep quarry to the top. Essentially, prisoners who carried small rocks had the best chance of surviving the ordeal, and those with large ones typically perished under the strain. By the end of each week, a sizable collection of rocks would be amassed on the top edge of the quarry. Each Monday, a bulldozer would then push all the accumulated rocks back into the quarry, at which time the charade would begin anew. The cruelty of this act needs no elaboration. Watching others die while transporting the rocks is one thing, but to see the fruits of your labor have no meaning whatsoever is quite another. A prisoner might somehow find small consolation in knowing that the rocks would be put to some good use, but to see them pushed back into the quarry every Monday shows there were no limits to the cruelty of the Nazi's. Such was daily life at Mauthausen.

During each Study Abroad experience, the students were free to travel before or after the program as well as on a designated free weekend during our five weeks in Germany. This led them to explore cities such as Florence, London, Paris, Rome, and Venice, and countries such as Croatia, Ireland, Norway, Scotland, and Switzerland. Several have returned to Europe the summer following the Study Abroad experience and backpacked on their own.

One success story of which I am quite fond even if I can claim little credit involves Jennifer Kalinec, a student in my summer 2005 group. Jenny came back to A&M and graduated in 2006, spent two years in the Teach for America Program in inner city Philadelphia, and then moved to Prague where she completed six years teaching English and music. In 2014, I learned Jennifer had moved to Doha in Qatar, and later to Bangkok, Thailand, making her at the minimum my most adventurous former Study Abroad student.

Counting the 2017 program, 281 students had the good fortune to take part in the Germany experience, 236 of them female and forty-five male. The majority were Psychology or Sport Management majors with a smattering of people from other disciplines such as Business, Communications, Pre-Medicine, and Sociology. None caused me any legal problems, though there were some challenging moments involving accidents, illness, disrespect of the German culture, and a few bouts of out-and-out drunkenness. Of late, a new sickness pervaded my program, and it is known as technology. Thanks to cell phones, computers, texting, iPads, Skype, and the like, far too many students seem more interested in chatting with their parents and sorority sisters back in the states than soaking up German and European culture. It is truly a modern American malady, a serious addiction, for which I have no solution. It is sad that technology has become such a corruptive force, perhaps on par with alcohol, in the Study Abroad experience. I am convinced beyond any doubt that if I had taken up all of those devices the first day in Germany and returned them as we boarded a plane for home five weeks later, almost every single one of the students would have thanked me profusely for freeing them from their self-imposed techno-tyranny. But can you imagine the initial response to what would undoubtedly be viewed as a draconian, mean-spirited invasion of their privacy and their right to inflict pain on themselves? I would guess having me hanged, pilloried, or impaled on a sarcophagus would be seen as too mild a punishment for such a draconian measure.

Group Characters, Characteristics, and Idiosyncrasies. The Germany group in 2003 was pretty tame and easy to manage. They were cordial to each other, and quickly located a favorite hangout in which to express their conviviality for the rest of the summer. It was a bar called "Che" Guevara's, named after the anti-American revolutionary and Fidel Castro sympathizer. Being of another generation, not one of the students had the foggiest notion of who Ernesto "Che" Guevara was and that for which he stood. I burst their bubble a bit by asking them, more or less rhetorically, if they would frequent a bar that was named after and glorified the recently deceased modern day megalomaniacal monster from the middle-east, Osama bin-Laden. They agreed they would not but this realization did not stop them from assuming their regular stool at "Che" Guevara's the following night. One of the students, a tall, outgoing young woman named Allison Mohundro was popular with the bartenders there, so much so that they named a drink after her. If you were in Bonn tonight, you could walk into "Che" Guevara's, request an "Allison", and they would serve it right up. I emailed her recently to let her know the Mohundro legend lives on at "Che" Guevara's. Allison completed her PhD in Psychology at the University of North Texas in the summer of 2015.

Our Program Director for the first three summers was a chap named Pablo Valqui, a dual citizen of Germany and Peru, and a truly unforgettable personality. Meine freunde Pablo was fluent in German, English, Spanish, and possessed street smarts in several other languages.

During one of my annual visits to Germany, Pablo, the students, and I embarked on a bike trip down the Rhine River from Bonn to some point south of Remagen, the site of a major battle in World War II that added luster to the battle exploits of the legendary General, George S. Patton. After passing Remagen, we secured a ferry and went over to the other side of the Rhine for the return trip. In all, the bicycle trek was around seventy kilometers, or roughly forty-five miles. Though saddle-weary and worn out, we all made it and none were more proud of that accomplishment than two of my most froufrou persons, Jessica Frazier, and the diminutive Tonya Sulak. Jessica and Tonya were typical of most of my students in the sense they had not ridden a bicycle since they were eleven or twelve years old.

I ran into Jessica Frazier in 2012 at a local eatery, eight years after the fact, and she still talks about how proud she was of herself for completing what most college students would regard as an arduous and daunting challenge. Jessica has a master's degree and is a history teacher in the College Station ISD. The last I knew, Tonya had a master's degree and was a special education teacher somewhere in the Austin area.

One of the more interesting incidents involved a 2004 student, Hailey (not her real name), who was a nice-looking blond with an absolutely overpowering personality. From the time the group got off the plane in Germany until we headed home five-plus weeks later, she was the alpha female, dominating the other women who viewed her with what seemed to me to be a highly palpable love-hate mixture. The students were at once intimidated by and almost fearful of Hailey and yet constantly sought her approval. As evidence of their need for her validation, I overheard students on more than one occasion ask Hailey if she thought friends or family members back home would like the souvenirs they were thinking of purchasing. To wit, "Hailey, do you think this trinket would be okay for my mother?" For Pete's sakes! How in the world would Hailey know what someone else's mother would like in the way of a gift?

I was told by several of the students that our blond friend began her summer abroad by going to a bar the very first evening where she met an Irishman with whom she spent the night. The second night, her chosen playmate was an American she met on a train coming back from Cologne. When I got wind of these dalliances through the student grapevine, I thought to myself, "This is going to be a long summer keeping up with Hailey's sexual peccadilloes." Fortunately, she ended up living with the American for the rest of the program, and though none of us were thrilled with this arrangement, it appeared to be the lesser of two evils. I have no particular moral problems with her approach to heterosexuality but there are obvious physical safety and sexual health concerns to be considered if one is not selective (and lucky?). Her parents never did figure out why she was not available when they phoned the student residence, and her absence at these times was the source of much mirth among the other students.

Upon returning to the states at the end of the program, our female friend laid out of school for a year or two. I was not aware of this development until 2009 when I accidentally ran into her at Luigi's, an Italian restaurant in south College Station, where she was working as a bartender. She eventually did graduate and moved on, leaving me with some mixed but interesting memories.

Another interesting incident involving that group was a romance between one of my students, a redhead named Sarah, and Pablo, our AIB program coordinator. Pablo was assigned to our program in 2003, 2004, and 2005 and did an outstanding job of arranging activities for the group, both formally during the day and informally at night. Pablo was a night owl, irretrievably outgoing and extroverted, manic, narcissistic, self-absorbed, egotistical, sexist beyond pig, and fluent in at least three languages and passable in several others. Despite his innumerable interpersonal idiosyncrasies (liabilities?), I liked Pablo, enjoyed his company, and particularly admired his work ethic which bordered most of the time on manic. There was nothing he would not do to make the program more informative and enjoyable for everyone. He was not universally liked, and my wife had her issues with him, particularly his egotism flavored liberally with male chauvinism, which is another story, but most everyone agreed he was a hard worker who did his job well.

One night in 2004, Pablo, Sarah, and I were what remained of an earlier group of partiers, just hanging out together at his apartment when I suddenly sensed I was the odd man out, the proverbial third (fifth?) wheel. By one in the morning, it was obvious even to this slow learner the two of them were brewing up an agenda that did not include *moi*, so I left them to their own devices and made the fifteen-minute walk to my apartment. Shortly after that fateful evening, Sarah started spending nights with Pablo. In an attempt to put up a good front of decorum and professionalism, Pablo would return Sarah to the student residence early enough in the morning to hopefully convince her peers when they woke up she had been there all night, blissfully counting sheep. After ten days of the thinly disguised charade, Pablo and Sarah dropped all pretenses, and their now out-in-the-open public displays of affection sent minor shock waves through the group. Some of the students were intrigued by it all, others thought Pablo was incredibly unprofessional, and the remainder seemed to regard the whole affair as inconsequential.

Two years later, in 2006, Pablo and Sarah were married in the Houston suburb of Richmond. I attended the wedding which was nicely done, but the crowd was such that I could never get near Pablo, so I left the reception quite early. Four years later, in March of 2010, I received word from Pablo that the two of them had called it quits. He provided no details and I asked for none, which is probably just as well. I have since heard that Pablo has a girlfriend and Sarah a new husband.

Three young ladies, undoubtedly the more liberal among the 2004 group, decided to go to Nice, France, for a short weekend. They ended up going to the beach where it was soon apparent they were outliers, the only females wearing swimsuit tops (and bottoms). This observation led them to decide when in Nice, do as the people in Nice do….thus, off came the tops. When news (pictures?) of their breast-baring behavior got circulated among the group back in Bonn, one of the guys, a professed born-again, Bible-thumping Christian with a real need to pillory the unrepentant, told the girls it was his fondest hope God would punish them by burning their nipples off if they ever behaved so disgracefully again.

I had two overly pious people in the group, one male and one female, and their sermonizing and moralizing wore thin with the troops. This virulence spreads and is deadly to a program where some degree of hedonism is not uncommon. Before the summer was over, I really think all sixteen in this group hated each other. I have never sponsored a program with such pronounced enmity and division, and the evangelical fervor of the two proselytizers had quite a bit to do with the pervasive rancor.

The 2005 experience was among the best of my Study Abroad life. The kids, twenty-eight in number, were fabulous; they treated each other with respect, did not form impenetrable cliques, and the summer ended up being sort of a platonic (I think) love fest. The group was cohesive long before we left Texas, partied long and hard, and knew each other well by the time we got to Germany. In one notable case, too well might be the operative phrase. It seems that one of the guys apparently ended up in bed with a couple of the girls after a night of hard partying at one of their pre-departure socials, and things must have gotten a little out of hand, so to speak. I do not know the full story but in the process of analyzing the fragments I have been able to piece together, I think there may have been some excessive body contact, perhaps some breast and/or genital fondling involving one or more of the females and the male perp. I never got the full story, but hanky-panky of some magnitude must have taken place. The end result was the guy in question was relegated to pariah status with most if not all the girls before we ever left the cozy confines of College Station. I liked the guy myself but he had apparently committed an unforgivable faux pas, for the females barely acknowledged his existence the whole time we were in Europe. It took me a while to figure out he was being isolated from the group and a little more time to ascertain why.

One of the 2005 girls, Katie Dunn, was working on her suntan in April prior to our departure, soaking up some rays in her yard. Unbeknownst to both parties at the time, the roommate drove her automobile into the yard and ran Katie over, fracturing several vertebrae in the process. We were concerned about losing Katie to her injuries but she recovered sufficiently to make the trip. I still do not quite understand how one can be run over in one's yard by one's roommate but it can obviously happen. Katie outlined the scenario for me but I never quite got it down pat.

One of the most interesting events that summer, and one with potentially far-reaching consequences, involved a charming if naïve student named Jennifer. She was out on the town in Bonn one night and ran into an American guy with a long tale of woe and unadulterated line of bull, and she apparently fell for it, hook, line, and sinker. As near as I could piece the story together, it seems this guy, maybe a worldly twenty-five years old, had flown from the US to Cologne to supposedly meet his fiancée' at the airport. Shortly after deplaning, his dearly beloved told him the engagement was off and the relationship kaput. In an effort to recover from what reportedly was a devastating blow, our budding Romeo rented a BMW and headed for Bonn, totally at loose ends and with nowhere to stay. With his fancy car, genuine or fake Rolex watch, reasonably good looks, and polished line of bull, he charmed Jennifer into proffering an invitation to stay in the dorm with her nineteen female peers. Romeo spent the next three days hanging out, doing his laundry, and generally enjoying having a free place to sleep with a bevy of females for company. It did not take the other girls long to hang a nickname on their newly acquired roommate! The nickname, you ask? Try "Ted Bundy", of all things. Yikes and egad!

Somehow I got wind of this arrangement three or four days after it all started, and immediately set up a meeting with Jennifer. I was, in a word, perturbed about Jennifer putting herself and the other girls in such a potentially perilous predicament. After shedding oceans of crocodile tears, Jennifer convinced me she was genuinely remorseful for having pulled such a dumb stunt. To make sure there was no room for a misunderstanding of my intentions with regard to Romeo (aka "Ted Bundy"), I told Jennifer arrangements had been made with the local polizei to have him arrested for criminal trespass if he was still in the dorm by 1700 that afternoon. She passed the warning on and Romeo/Ted Bundy vanished from our lives. Jennifer never heard from him again despite his earlier vows of eternal love and devotion.

Jennifer and I visited on quite a few occasions during the next two years and I came to hold her in high regard as both a student and friend. She received her master's degree in the summer of 2009 from James Madison University, a national leader in training Industrial/Organizational (I/O) psychologists. Little brother, Brian, followed in Jennifer's footsteps by going with me to Germany in 2012. He is now a successful insurance agent in the Dallas area after a stint as a behavioral therapist for autistic children.

My son Lyndon, then sixteen, developed a close relationship with Jennifer and two other students during the trip, and the four of them were pretty much inseparable; if you saw one of them, you saw all four. The third member of their group was a wonderful guy named Marcus Galle from the small west Texas town of Lyford, and one of my all-time favorite males among the forty-five who have gone to Germany with my program. Bright, inquisitive, attentive, and personable....all of those descriptors fit Marcus to a tee. As near as I can tell from a brief foray into the social media, Marcus was in the doctoral program in Developmental Psychology at the University of Iowa from 2006 to 2014, but I cannot tell if he ever received his PhD. He is married, has a baby girl, and works for the university in some capacity. Marcus was a fine student, a great guy, and I continue to wish him the best!

The final member of their foursome was Elizabeth Atteberry who has her master's degree in Accounting and at last report was working for one of the nation's top accounting firms. As was the case with the students in Italy who several years earlier had taken our baby boy under their wings, I really appreciate the friendship and camaraderie the three of them provided Lyndon that summer.

Another interesting character from that group who caused some moments of concern was an openly gay guy named Eric. Everyone knew from day one that Eric was gay and he offered no pretenses to the contrary.

A problem of sorts developed one evening during the early stages of our stay in Europe when Eric went looking for "friends" on the streets of Cologne. Though Cologne is a relatively safe city in quite a safe country, there are still skinheads and neo-Nazis who would have liked nothing better than to punish a gay guy just for being gay, and a gay Amerikanisch at that!

Our director, Dr. Zaeck, got a call one evening from an unknown source, wanting to know why he had not shown up in a particular hotel restroom for their "meeting." Dr. Zaeck had no idea what the caller meant, of course. It seems that Eric had set up a tryst with a new friend earlier in the day but gave him Dr. Zaeck's phone number by mistake. You can imagine Rainer's thought processes when the guy asked why he had stood him up. Needless to say, Rainer, Pablo, and I had a counseling session with Eric about being safe and discreet and not letting himself get in harm's way. Eric was a great guy to have on the trip and we had no further incidents of any kind.

By way of an update, Eric came by my table at the local Cheddar's in 2011 and spent a few minutes filling Judy and I in on his life. He graduated from A&M, taught elementary school in Austin for a brief time (across the hall from his mother's classroom). I still see regular Facebook posts from Eric, and he appears to be doing well.

There were five women in that 2005 group who became inseparable and have remained pretty much so in the intervening nine years. They are the aforementioned Jennifer, Katie Dunn, and Jennifer Kalinec, as well as Brooke Hathaway and Tori Walters. None were acquainted before they signed up for the summer excursion, yet Jennifer, Brooke, Katie, and Jennifer all attended Tori's wedding in Austin in 2007, with three serving as bridesmaids. In July, 2009, Tori and Katie visited

Jennifer Kalinec in Prague, and they graciously invited me to come over from Bonn to be a part of their reunion. I was not able to go due to program obligations with the 2009 students, but I was able to arrange for Jennifer to meet up with us when we toured Prague as part of that year's program. This mini-reunion fell through at the last minute when Jennifer's parents sent her a plane ticket from Prague to Texas and back; it just so happened the dates coincided with our visit to Prague. Jennifer is now an I/O Psychologist in DC, Jenny Kalinec lives in Bangkok, Katie Dunn taught for a while but is a Licensed Professional Counselor (LPC) with two master's degrees, and Tori Walters was a public school teacher for several years but recently changed career paths after receiving a nursing degree from A&M. Brooke Hathaway also taught for a while but is now a Child Advocacy Specialist for a social agency in Austin.

Tori got in touch in 2013, indicating she was going to be in College Station in March to be a part of a mock disaster preparedness exercise. We planned to meet for a drink or two the night before, but she had to cancel due to some disruptions in the mock exercise schedule. Brooke also contacted me a couple of months ago, wanting a letter of recommendation for a Licensed Professional Counselor (LPC) graduate program at St. Edwards in Austin.

In 2007 and 2008, I tried a different approach to Germany programming by joining up with Paul Batista, an attorney and A&M professor in Sports Management, who proved to be a marvelous associate. The 2007 group was twenty-eight in number, and especially memorable because of the personal and group dynamics that emerged over the summer. They were the loudest, most raucous, hard-drinking group of human beings I have ever taken abroad. If they were not out drinking and partying, they were talking about drinking and partying. They tried to drink Germany dry, which admittedly is a daunting task. They gave it a hell of a shot, though, and no one can accuse them of failing for lack of effort.

The informal, self-appointed group leader was an extroverted guy named Drew. Unfortunately, Drew's leadership was not always in the direction Dr. Batista and I would have liked. He was a party animal and hell-raiser who was getting married when he returned home to Texas, and most of his leadership skills were used to promote his "no-holds-barred", "let it all hang out", "drink Germany dry" pre-nuptial agenda. Drew now practices law in the Dallas-Fort Worth area after completing his legal studies at Texas Tech.

Despite their situational wantonness, these characters make up my third most favorite group. There are individuals from other summers for whom I have very fond memories but this group was fascinating to watch and, even today, exhausting to contemplate.

Guido, Team T-Mobile, and the "Tour de Farce"

One of our more interesting field trips that summer was a last-minute, serendipitous visit to the T-Mobile cycling training facility in Bonn. The team was preparing to compete in the Tour de France, or what others have called the "Tour de Farce" due to the repeated abuses of performance-enhancing substances and methods. Of particular relevance in terms of cheating are blood doping and the use of Erythropoietin (EPO), a synthetic performance enhancing compound popular among world cyclists.

In 2006, just prior to our visit, Team T-Mobile named an American, Bob Stapleton, as its new manager. As part of the deal, Stapleton pledged to clean up the team's act and make them a model for the sport. Our guide that day was a professional cyclist by the name of Guido Eickelbeck, a fortyish veteran who rode in many top cycling events as a member of Team Telekom (forerunner of Team T-Mobile) in the 1990's. He was an excellent host, showed the students the ins and outs of the training site, and talked extensively of the new ownership and the owner's dream of running a clean, first-class operation. As we were concluding the tour, I was walking alongside Guido, chatting about the past sins of the Tour de France and T-Mobile's efforts to take the high road. In a cynical moment, I asked our host: "Guido, you don't really believe you're going to clean this shit up, do you?" He responded with a wistful, "Probably not, but we are going to try." Shortly after that, two T-Mobile cyclists admitted in a tearful news conference to doping.

As an interesting side note, Guido was telling me about the trials and tribulations of being a world class cyclist, not the least of which are injuries from falls. He said, "If you are a cyclist, you fall from time to time and break arms, wrists, collar bones, or legs, but at least those things heal up and you can still walk when you retire. None of my retired friends from Bundesliga (the top professional futbol league in Germany) can walk because of their injuries. They are literally forty-year old cripples." If you take a look at the list of elite players who missed the 2010 Soccer World Cup in South Africa and the 2014 event in Brazil due to injuries as just one example, it is scary. In line with Guido's point about forty-year-old cripples, most serious soccer injuries involve the knee, ankle, or other parts of the lower leg.

Trouble in Vienna

In 2008, the Germany program took a sizable hit on enrollment. I do not know if it was a promotional problem or the effects of the economic downturn or something cosmic and incomprehensible, but we ended up getting only eleven participants. And it was like pulling teeth the whole time to get that paltry number. About the only incident of note with that group involved a guy named Kevin and his girlfriend Erin. I was not aware they were a duo until the first day we arrived in Bonn. After clearing the Cologne-Bonn airport and making the short thirty-minute bus ride to the student housing facility, we gave our charges a couple of hours to clean up, rest, and get ready to tackle the program in full force. When the time came to depart student housing, there was no Kevin and no Erin. I went to Kevin's room and found them passed out with Erin asleep on top of him. Kevin played football at A&M and probably weighed nearly 275 pounds, so he had ample girth to support the much smaller Erin. Being a well-trained psychologist with finely-honed and astute insights into human behavior, I immediately deduced that the two of them were friends prior to our departure from the US or had developed a hell of an intense relationship on the flight over to Bonn. It turned out to be the former, which I suspected all along.

At the midpoint of the program, the students had a scheduled free weekend, and most of them headed off to Paris. For whatever reason, Kevin and Erin selected Vienna as their destination of choice. At midnight that Friday, I was alternately playing my guitar and reading occasional emails when I received a cryptic message from Erin that read: "Trouble in Vienna." One never wants a midnight email that speaks of trouble anywhere, and my first thought was that someone was hurt. Fortunately that turned out to be untrue. I subsequently learned Kevin had lost virtually every major possession during a subway ride from the Vienna airport to their hotel. It seems that a Good Samaritan offered to help them decipher the city map, and while listening to her advice and subsequently unloading their luggage from the subway, Kevin failed to take his backpack with him. Gone were his passport, computer, cell phone, and most of his money. The subway lost and found was closed from Friday until Monday so there was nothing he could do to locate the backpack for sixty hours or so. Kevin waited all that time to find out nothing fitting the description of his backpack had been turned in to lost and found. He and Erin spent the next two days getting him a new passport and making travel arrangements to get them back to Bonn. They rejoined us mid-day Tuesday, intact but a bit worse for wear.

The 2009 trip was marred by ugliness associated with one of the thorniest issues Study Abroad program sponsors face, abuse of alcohol. As the program entered its fifth week, four students, two male and two female, increasingly acted out against the rules, mores, and folkways of the group governing alcohol use, and perhaps other illegal substances. I say the latter because one of the four players in this drama made several trips to Amsterdam, that well-known hotbed of marijuana use, while in Europe.

Two incidents that took place one evening some nine or ten hours apart led us to decide to take action against the four students. One of these incidents centered on events surrounding attendance at a professional soccer game in Cologne. It seems that through some good fortune, we were able to get tickets for a friendly game between two Bundesliga futbol teams. As we prepared to entrain for Cologne, the fab four showed up in what can most aptly be described as an advanced state of inebriation, fueled in great part by the fact they had been drinking since noon that day. Given their obvious state of drunkenness, we should have never let them go with us to Cologne. However, in a moment of collective weakness, my Program Coordinator, a wonderful German woman named Miriam Hippchen, and I gave in. During the soccer game, the misbehavior of the four miscreants continued unabated and, from all subsequent reports, unashamedly. Because I wanted to be close to the soccer action, I sat near the pitch and thus was oblivious to the things transpiring behind me. Later on, some students told me it was just as well that I had my back to the non-soccer action, for I would have been embarrassed beyond belief and mad beyond redemption. Whatever it was the problem children were doing, and a number of students described their behavior as "shameful" and "embarrassing", it unfolded in all of its glory in front of 50,000 Germans, no doubt adding to our occasional ugly American image.

A second major event of the evening that finally led to the meeting of the minds, the straw that broke the camel's back, was a phone call I received at 0300 hours from one of the females telling me she had been yelled at, cussed out, and thrown up against the wall by her roommate who was a foot taller and at least fifty pounds heavier. In the process of investigating this early morning ruckus, I learned that several of the other girls locked their rooms when the brouhaha started, fearing that they would be the target of the drunken attacker's ill will.

The misbehavior finally reached such proportions that my German colleagues and I met with the foursome, threatening them with expulsion from the program with slightly over a week remaining. Dismissal would earn them an early flight home and loss of all course credit. In addition, if the powers in the A&M administration so chose, they could impose additional conduct sanctions upon their return from Germany. We met with the students for four hours, first as individuals by gender, then as twosomes by gender, and finally as a foursome, and they seemed to accurately process the message we were trying to impart. The problem behaviors changed ever so slightly in a positive manner for the last eight or nine days we were in Europe. However, in a final gesture of defiance that serves as a summary of the whole incident, the two male offenders of propriety showed up fifteen minutes late as we were catching a bus to Frankfort that last morning for our flight home. They just had to let everyone know one last time they were not intimidated by our threats.

One of the two males never really repented, always making himself out to be a victim. When the four were called on the carpet, I asked this particular fellow if he thought his mother would be proud of his drunkenness, open rebellion, and obvious resentment of authority. In the meeting with my German colleagues and me, he indicated he did not really know how his mother would feel but he later told his peers that she would approve of everything he did. If that is the case, I can only conclude that his mother has no standards and no shame. Her son was a disgrace to both the concept of studying abroad and to plain old common human decency. His demeanor and words were that of the classic amoral psychopath, and I do not use those words and that diagnostic label often or lightly.

Four years later in the fall of 2012, the other male perp in this episode dropped by my office to visit. He was accompanied by his father, and in the process of catching up, he indicated he had joined the Marines and was on his way to Afghanistan. We relived some of the moments in Germany, and as we talked I was struck by his still salient hero-worship admiration for his unrepentant pal and how little remorse he felt for his basically unforgiveable behavior.

As for 2010, I felt like I deserved a break after the events of the previous summer, and I got one. There were fourteen females and two males in the group and they behaved wonderfully. I am aware of only one incidence of indiscriminate drinking, and that instance involved a young lady who seldom consumed alcohol but seriously over-imbibed to celebrate her twenty-first birthday. The only negative in the whole trip was invested in the falsely entitled insolence, selfishness, rudeness, out-and-out disrespectfulness, and paranoia of one student who had a chip on her shoulder about life, I guess. She was rude to me, my wonderful AIB program coordinator, Olaf Broderson, waitpersons, hotel staff, and any other human being who got in her way as she did as she damn well pleased.

When her self-centered wishes were not met or she was inconvenienced in some way, Miss Congeniality would lapse into a temporary, stony silence accompanied by the wickedest, most withering stare I have ever witnessed. Though circumstances did not let us test the proposition scientifically, I am convinced even the strongest tungsten would wither under her gaze when things were not going her way. Miss Congeniality sported a large, maybe one inch high tattoo on the back of her neck that was usually visible above her shirt collar, announcing to the world she was "The Chosen One." I suppose someone thus anointed is granted dispensation from abiding by the rules of everyday human decency.

Other than the one outlier, the group was congenial, considerate, prompt, reliable, generally interested in virtually everything we did, and a delight to be around. They loved the days in the Bavarian Alps where we stayed in a nice hostel in the isolated, postage-stamp sized village of Scheidegg, hiking and climbing and just hanging out. It has been an endless source of amazement to know these kids almost always hail from large metropolitan areas in Texas and the majority plan to return to a large city when they graduate, yet they absolutely adored the quiet solitude of the Alps experience, the antithesis of the big city rat race. Perhaps there is something about listening to cow bells, visually processing the beauty of the Alps, communing with nature, and getting back to our roots that captivates the imagination of even the most devoted (jaded?) city-dweller.

There were many good things to be said for the 2011 and 2012 groups as they were generally well-behaved and engaged in the schedule of activities with a few minor exceptions. One of the biggest downers I encountered in all my trips involved a student, Catherine Hensley, who was diagnosed with Type One Diabetes at the end of the first week of the 2012 excursion. After flying into Munich, we spent three exhausting days in the Alps, engaging in arduous hikes, tackling a wall-climbing course, and trying to master the sometimes daunting task, at least for novices, of keeping a kayak on a straight path in the water. After a few days in the Alps, we headed for Bonn where all the students met their German host families. As that first evening in Bonn progressed, Catherine noticed swelling and discomfort in her legs, attributable in her mind to the strenuous physical regimen we had recently experienced. At around 0230 in the morning, the host family took her to the emergency room. After days of testing, the doctors confirmed that Catherine had Type One Diabetes. She remained in the hospital for twelve days, at which time she was placed in the care of a medical escort for the long trip back to the US. Catherine settled in to her new life as a diabetic and returned to school for the final year. Catherine has since graduated and I heard through the grapevine that her graduation present was a return trip, hopefully more enjoyable this time, to Europe.

One of the worst features of Catherine's hospital stay was she felt fine for most of the time. It is hard enough to imagine being in a hospital for two weeks if one felt absolutely rotten, but I cannot conceive what it would be like if you felt good the entire time. On top of feeling okay throughout her stay, she heard only broken or no English. To her credit, Catherine handled the twelve days in the hospital well for someone who was 7,000 miles from home and surrounded by people, however nice and accommodating, who spoke little or no English. She easily gets my All-Time Trooper Award!

Thanks to the requirement introduced five or six years ago requiring students to live with host families instead of a dormitory environment, my alcohol-related and other disciplinary issues have pretty much abated. About the most memorable thing that happened, alas, was Barbara Mora breaking her leg during a hike in the mountains near a famous castle ruin in the Bonn area, Schloss Drachenfels. Barbara, ever the Spartan, spent a week in the hospital in Bonn, and we shipped her home with two weeks left in the program.

The 2013 group was one of the smallest I have sponsored, but they were the best behaved collection of students in my experience. Imbedded in that outstanding group was one of the best, if not the best, participants I have ever encountered in all my trips abroad, a student named Brooke Emery. Brooke was bright, engaged in all aspects of the program, and asked the best questions and made the most astute observations of any student I have ever had in my many years of studying abroad. Brooke Emery has since graduated from A&M's School of Nursing and moved on with her life.

The 2014 and 2015 groups were my largest, with thirty students in each. Of the sixty students in the latter two groups, only five were male. My 2016 group, twenty-one in number, and the 2017 group, nineteen in number, were entirely female, firsts for me insofar as study abroad groups go. This gender imbalance is reasonably reflective of the composition of Psychology majors and minors in our department at A&M where eighty percent are female. I have, over the years, grown quite accustomed to the annual infusion of both adrenalin and estrogen into the European culture for five weeks. Quite a number of these students have been in my classes before or after the trip to Europe. Others have served as student research associates and at least half of them report in for a visit on occasion after our return. Three of them have also served as undergraduate teaching assistants (TA's) prior to or after Germany. I am pleased to call many of them friends, and some of the most delightful students I have met were in those last three groups.

I manage to maintain contact with many of these students from the past, but particularly those from 2005, 2007, 2013, 2014, and 2015, and their email and text messages, occasional phone calls, and almost daily appearances on the social media are constant reminders of some great times with some wonderful, thoughtful, and loyal students in Germany. A sizeable number of past participants are now in their late twenties and early thirties, well-educated, gainfully employed, and married and becoming parents of small children. I am convinced they are better informed world citizens because they studied abroad, and my thanks and congratulations go out to each and every one of them.

Sadly, in many ways, the 2017 excursion was my final one. Seventeen study abroad programs in fifteen years is enough. Fortunately, the Germany Study Abroad mantle has been picked up by a colleague in Psychology, Dr. Sherecce Fields, and it is my fondest hope that she enjoys the experience enough to host as many programs as I did. All good things must come to an end, and the Germany experience is no exception. It has been a wonderful ride and I will miss my German colleagues but do hope to visit from time to time as a "civilian."

Packing Light and Traveling Easy

I could go on and on with stories of other wonderful, interesting personalities and experiences from those trips but I have said enough. Words are always inadequate when attempting to summarize summers with wonderful students and interesting colleagues while basking in the breath-taking beauty and countless charms of Europe.

A final note: One of the major challenges I faced each year was getting the students to understand the wisdom of packing light for the trip. We traveled a lot, got on and off buses, trains, and planes, and sometimes are forced to lug suitcases up two or three or even four flights of stairs due to the absence of elevators in some of the older European hotels. The famous travel guru Rick Steves preaches the same "pack light" sermons, and accentuates his message with the admonition that no one ever packs more things the second time they go to Europe. To stress my point, I often signed off messages to the students prior to our departure as Arnold "Pack Light" LeUnes. Despite my efforts, there are always a few students who unloaded their closets and neighborhood clothing stores, afraid, I guess, their peers might see them wearing an outfit twice.

From time to time, I sent out tips to make the trip go just a little smoother, and I tried to combine wisdom gained from quite a number of trips abroad with some tongue-in-cheek humor. Here is a sample of a memo on packing I first sent out to the students in 2010 and used thereafter:

"Of particular importance is packing light and smart. We are not going to Europe to be runway models or win any fashion contests. Absolutely NO ONE cares if you wear the same outfit for thirty-five consecutive days if you intermittently wash it. Plus, most of you will pick up souvenir clothing as you go along and that is a good way to supplement your wardrobe and give yourself a different look.

We have two excursions and you are going to lug suitcases on and off buses, planes, and trains and in and out of hotels. Heavy suitcases are a real pain. Remember a LeUnes rule: If you bring it, you carry it…not your friends, not the bus drivers, not our program coordinator, not your strong-armed professor. YOU!!!

Books are heavy and you can buy them in Bonn if you are a reader.

Hiking boots would probably be used once. Why bother? Ditto swim suits and tennis rackets. And I'll bet you would be shocked at how nice it is to be unshackled from the tyranny of the cell phone for five weeks.

Heavy sweaters and coats are totally unnecessary. Long sleeves and a light wind breaker, preferably with a hood for the occasional drizzle, will get you by nicely. We might encounter some cool weather in the Alps early on but when is the last time you heard of a Study Abroad student freezing to death in Europe in the summer?

I had a woman once bring nine pairs of flip flops. Could she have made it for five weeks with one or two? Of course, if it were up to me, there would be NO flip flops allowed as part of my European beautification program.

Pack clothes that are sheer and dry easily if hung out overnight. Jeans are great but they are a pain to care for. They are heavy and hard to dry, so pack jeans with caution. Also, it is much cooler in Europe than the US and Europeans do not share our cleanliness fetish that drives us to wear clothes only once before laundering them. Some articles of clothing can easily be worn twice or even three times without you alienating your peers. And as my wife will attest, I am pretty much anosmic and most smells do not register with me. It is therefore unlikely you will offend me if you wear only one outfit for the entire summer.

You will have access to clothes dryers but they are more inefficient over there than here. Europeans hang their clothes out to dry in the summer for efficiency and to save energy. As a point of information, I hand wash and dry ALL my clothes for the five weeks and such a regimen is not unusual at all in Europe.

Women would be best advised to chip in and buy a hair dryer over there. Past students have been unbelievably adept at frying their American counterparts." viele Gruesse, Arnold "Pack Light" LeUnes

MY BEST ZEUS IMITATION, BAVARIAN ALPS, 2013

Christmas Down Under, 2004-2005.

As noted elsewhere, I took a Faculty Development Leave in Australia in 1991, and that experience laid the groundwork for a return in 2004, this time with students. Tony Bourgeois and I took twenty-eight eager students to New Zealand and Australia for three weeks over the 2004-2005 Christmas holidays. The trip was, of course, unforgettable, what with the transcendent beauty of both islands of New Zealand and the rugged, sometimes barren but always charming terrain of southeastern Australia. As a cultural experience, however, the trip does not come close to Italy or Germany. The Aussies and Kiwis act a lot like Americans, speak pretty much the same language (though it is not always obvious), the cities look pretty similar to ours, and few if any of us are their descendants. The food was an experience, though not always in the positive direction, and the two countries are quite expensive. On the surface, the US dollar looked pretty good but the exchange rate advantage was offset by higher costs of basic things like food, drinks, and so on. All in all, however, I would not trade the experiences "Down Under" for any amount of money. Well, maybe, there is a sum for which I would sell my soul; we all have our price on most things in life.

Tiffany Tracy is our First (and Only) Casualty. When we flew into the north island city of Auckland that December, a few days before Christmas, it took maybe an hour to clear customs. As we vacated the terminal and boarded our bus, the driver suggested we motor up to a nearby overlook to get a scenic view of the city from on high. As we neared the top of the promontory, a light drizzle forced us to abandon the bus and walk a few hundred meters to the suggested lookout point. In the process, a young woman named Tiffany Tracy slipped and fell on a wet, grassy incline. My first response to seeing her sitting on the ground holding her leg was that she had sprained an ankle, which in itself is bad enough on an active agenda such as ours. She quickly defused my relative optimism, suggesting instead she had most likely broken both the tibia and fibula in one of her legs (I forget whether she broke the right of the left). Sure enough, when we got her to the hospital in Auckland, the physicians x-rayed her leg and confirmed the diagnosis. It seems that Tiffany had shadowed an orthopedic surgeon the preceding summer, so her diagnostic skills in that medical specialty were quite advanced for a rank amateur. Tony Bourgeois spent a great deal of time in the hospital with her over the next twenty-four hours but it was obvious the trip had ended for Tiffany that fateful fifteen minutes up there on the overlook. The parents were contacted, met Tiffany in Los Angeles, and took her home to Houston for the holidays. Tiffany remains my second worst Study Abroad casualty (behind Catherine Hensley) and I hope it stays that way. To this day, I do not know if she able to recoup any of her trip expenses, but I suspect it was not much. By the time her injury occurred, the monies allocated to flights and the program were pretty much encumbered and thus not refundable.

Sites to Behold. During our three-week stay, the students took part in the traditional Maori feast known as the Hangi, bungee jumped in Queenstown (some students did three in one day!), rode a gondola to a high point overlooking Queenstown where we had Christmas dinner, took in visual images of the luxurious lupins, or bluebonnets as we call them in Texas (our driver promised to stop so people could take pictures but never did), viewed the scenery where "Lord of the Rings" was filmed, spent New Year's Eve on Sydney Harbor, toured the Sydney Opera House, walked the streets of Canberra, spent a day at the Australian Institute of Sports, and endured an extremely cold hike to the top of Mount Kosciuszko, the tallest mountain in Australia.

I thought the weather was most unfriendly in New Zealand, and local newspapers reported it was both the second coldest and second wettest spring in recorded history. Things were not greatly better in Australia. In fact, when we ascended Mount Kosciuszko toward the end of our stay in Australia, the temperature during our four-hour walk hovered near the freezing mark. Unfortunately, once we got off the bus, our driver immediately moved on to pick us up at the end of our trek which was maybe a dozen miles away by bus and four or five hours away by foot. Thus, there simply was no turning back once the trek started. To a person, the students were unprepared for cold weather, wearing mostly shorts and t-shirts. I felt bad for not anticipating problems with the cold but what would you expect from a bunch of Texas flatlanders? Anyone who has been in the mountains in spring or summer knows it can be chillingly cold at times, and I was one of the very few who took that fact into account when dressing for the hike. We finally completed the adventure with no casualties and no one suffered frostbite or froze to death. Despite the occasional ups and downs, the students learned a lot about life Down Under during our three-week stay.

Iran: A Texas Yankee in King Khomenei's Court

Mohammad Comes to the Mountain (Or, at Least, a Molehill)

At the relatively advanced age of seventy-one, I had pretty much given up on visiting any of the countries in the Middle East. As documented elsewhere, I have more than passing familiarity with Canada, Western Europe, Mexico, and Oceania, but not so with Africa, Asia, and South America. Insofar as the Middle East is concerned, things changed dramatically in one fell swoop in late August of 2009 when Dr. Mohammad Khabiri of the University of Tehran in Iran showed up at my office door. Mohammad presently serves as Associate Professor of Sport Management at his university, but was in the states in 2009 visiting his daughter and son-in-law who were at the time doctoral students in different engineering programs at A&M.

IRANIAN FRIENDS MOHAMMAD KHABIRI & MARYAM ABARGOUEINEJAD, 2009

Prior to accepting the faculty appointment in Tehran, Mohammad served as Vice President of the Iranian Soccer Association. Even earlier, while in his early- to mid-twenties, Mohammad had been a member of the Iranian national soccer team as had his younger brother, Habib. To be named to the national team in soccer obviously means you are one of the top twenty to twenty-five soccer players in your country which, of course, is quite an accolade. It is perhaps even more remarkable that two brothers from the same country were so honored? And in a country of seventy million people, at that. Talk about lottery odds!

Mohammad was also a spokesman for the International Conference on Science and Futbol and he was seeking my services as a keynote speaker at a gathering of sport scientists in Tehran in November of 2009. Professionals with expertise in physiology, psychology, nutrition, biomechanics, and other scientific disciplines presented an assortment of papers, colloquia, and workshops, all with a focus on the world's greatest game, soccer. Mohammad had tried to contact me by email on several occasions but I kept deleting his messages without so much as an acknowledgment. The reason for this lapse in etiquette probably is related to those nagging emails we all receive from time to time, notifying us we are the winners of huge sums of money in the Dutch lottery or affording us the opportunity of a lifetime to cash in on a lucrative financial deal in darkest Africa with only a modest investment of personal capital, and so on. Because of his middle-Eastern name and perhaps some latent ethnocentrism lurking in the darkest, most primeval recesses of my subconscious, I may have falsely associated Mohammad's name with those scams, hence the perfunctory deletion of his emails.

Mohammad had gotten my name from a colleague in A&M's Department of Kinesiology, done some homework on me via the Internet, and decided that I would be a good choice to address our colleagues at the Tehran conference. I was and am, of course, thrilled that he followed through with his quest. There is something to be said for good old dogged determination on his part for it resulted in an "Even a blind hog sometimes finds an acorn" experience for me. I can now look back in retrospect and realize how much I would have missed if the two of us had not crossed paths.

Mohammad and I met on August 24, 2009. He arrived at my office door tastefully attired in sport coat, slacks and a knit shirt. He was mid-fifties, handsome, short in stature, fit and athletic for his age, looking as if he could still suit up and play a bit of soccer. He later told me he often worked out with his soccer classes at the university to stay in shape and also to give his students a challenge.

As stated earlier, Mohammad was a member of the Iranian national soccer team (1973-1976) but, in his mid-twenties, made a decision to forsake his beloved futbol in favor of finishing his undergraduate degree at the university. This choice of education over athletics meant he had to essentially turn his back on the sport that had dominated his life for two decades. He completed his bachelor's degree in Psychology at the University of Tehran in 1976, and an opportunity then arose that allowed him to come to the US to pursue graduate school. At that time, relations between the US and Iran were far better than they are now for reasons to be discussed soon.

Mohammad received his Master's degree from Texas Southern University in Houston in 1980, and a bit later in 1984, the PhD degree in Higher Education from my old graduate alma mater, UNT, in Denton. Because of his educational and other experiences in the US, Mohammad has become quite knowledgeable about our culture and its mores and folkways.

Mohammad, Hassan, and Fari. Mohammad has two friends with an assortment of ties to Texas Southern University, the University of North Texas, and Texas Women's University, and I met one in Iran and the other upon my return to College Station from that historical and cultural mecca. The friend I met in Iran was Hassan Ghaffari, and it turns out that Hassan had recently returned to the country of his birth after spending twenty-nine years in the US. While in the states, Hassan became a collegiate basketball referee and, ironically enough, officiated Aggie games in the 1990's. Though I obviously did not know Hassan at the time, I had seen him officiate several times in G. Rollie White Coliseum because I never missed a men's home game during that decade and have probably missed no more than one hundred home contests in the past fifty-plus years.

In the course of our conversations, Hassan told me the character that stood out most in his officiating memories was Tom Penders, at that time the coach at the University of Texas, and who later occupied the same position at the University of Houston until resigning under pressure in March, 2010. Of course, I remembered the Penders era at Texas well, and Hassan and I shared some memories of those days.

Shortly before my arrival in Tehran, Hassan had moved his family back to Iran with an understanding that if the children did not like it there, they would pick up their belongings and return to the states. His children apparently adjusted well to their new surroundings and at last report the family planned to stay there indefinitely. Hassan was one of the most likeable people I met in Iran (or anywhere else for that matter)…full of life, energetic, animated, an eternal extrovert, one of those people for whom there is no such thing as a stranger. The three decades he spent in the US was very much in evidence from his English language facility and American mannerisms; he was by far the most "American" of the dozens of Iranians with ties to the US I met while in Tehran, including Mohammad.

Mohammad, Hassan, and I were walking through the Olympic Hotel lobby in Tehran one evening and I was lamenting the difficulties of establishing phone contact with my wife due in part to an unusually cumbersome Iranian calling card system. Hassan immediately drew his cell phone from its holster, asked for my home phone number, and in a matter of seconds, I was talking to Judy in College Station. When he handed me the phone, he asked to have it back before Judy got off the line. His intentions were to tell her that the government had decided to detain me for an unspecified period for questioning for my alleged misbehavior while in Iran. I forgot to give him back the phone before hanging up, so he was not able to pull off his ruse. I probably saved Judy from a fatal heart attack, for she had earlier expressed concerns I would get detained for committing a stupid breach of etiquette or the law while in Tehran.

Mohammad and Hassan jointly urged me to get in touch with their mutual friend in College Station, Fariborz (Fari) Estakhri, when I returned home. Fari is the owner of Fatburger's, a local bar and grill on Wellborn Road in College Station, and a former college roommate and life-long friend of both Hassan and Mohammad. I have since eaten at Fatburger's several times and have met Fari's wife, Cindy, a Research Engineer with the Texas Transportation Institute on campus, and both of his daughters. The oldest daughter, Ryann, graduated from A&M with a BA degree in Classics and the last I knew was attending graduate school at Columbia University in New York. The youngest daughter is Lisa, and she graduated in 2013 from A&M Consolidated in College Station.

Fari has lived in the states for forty years, but roomed with Hassan when they went to school in Denton. Hassan, Mohammad, and Fari had been students at either Texas Women's University (Hassan) or North Texas (Mohammad and Fari). They also had jobs typical of struggling college students, serving up pizzas or delivering newspapers such as the *Houston Chronicle*, the *Denton Record-Chronicle* and the *Dallas Morning News*. Collectively, Hassan, Mohammad, and I shared a "Gee, it's a small world" moment concerning our experiences in Houston, Denton, and College Station. It is surreal to be seven thousand miles from Texas, swapping anecdotes and stories with Iranians who are familiar with the Denton newspaper, Texas A&M basketball, Coach Tom Penders, Jersey Street (now George Bush Drive), Wellborn Road, and Fatburger!

While working on his master's degree in Houston, Mohammad helped make ends meet by delivering the *Chronicle*, and part of his service area was in a high crime neighborhood in the southeastern section of the city. It seems that early one morning, Mohammad made a run to collect money from a newspaper dispenser, and quickly found himself on the business end of a pistol pointed squarely at his temple. Without a second of deliberation and with no resistance whatsoever, he gave up the money and, luckily, the armed robber quickly fled the scene. Mohammad told me he fully believed he was getting ready to get better acquainted with Allah at any time.

During his ninety-minute stay in my office, Mohammad and I talked at length about life, A&M, soccer, and so on, and I found him to be low-key, extremely polite, soft-spoken, and a bright and engaging conversationalist. He was in College Station at the time visiting his daughter, Elham (Eli), and her husband, Rozbeh Daneshvar. Eli holds dual citizenship in Iran and the US, having been born in this country, and a few years ago completed the PhD program in Information Sciences while Rozbeh pursued a doctorate in some sort of hybridized program in the College of Engineering. Mohammad's wife, Masi was a student at UNT while he worked on his PhD there, and she earned a degree in Chemistry. Masi has been back and forth between Iran and the US with and without Mohammad on several occasions, and at last report they are talking about the possibility of staying in the US permanently so they can be near Eli and Rozbeh (and a grandson born in 2014). Their plans became more complicated when, upon graduation, Eli took a position in New York City with ConocoPhillips, if my memory serves me right. Over the years, Mohammad and Masi grew quite fond of College Station and were not enamored with the idea of living in or near the Big Apple. As of mid-2014, they were living in Houston, but I have not had a chance to visit with them about their newest choice of residence. Perhaps Eli has been transferred to Houston, which would account for the move to that city.

Brothers Mohammad and Habib. Eventually, Mohammad and I got around to talking about the International Conference on Science and Futbol (ICSF) which was created to bring together sport specialists from many disciplines to reflect on scientific aspects of the most popular sport in the world, futbol. Before we ended our conversation, I had agreed to come to Iran and present a keynote address and several presentations on the mental side of soccer.

After he left my office, I Googled Mohammad's name to learn more about him and, in the process, found out, as noted earlier, that he was quite an accomplished soccer player in his day as was his younger brother, Habib. Little brother was thought by many to be a better and more exciting player, perhaps because he was more outgoing and charismatic than the cerebral and reserved, maybe even guarded, Mohammad. Manook Khodabakhshian, an Iranian soccer announcer, went so far as to call Habib the "Iranian Kobe Bryant" because of his talent and charisma. Though Habib and Kobe Bryant played their respective sports two decades apart, it was this comparison that Khodabakhshian felt best captured the essence of the Iranian soccer hero from the past.

Toward the end of the decade of the 1970's, Habib unfortunately aligned himself politically with dissident factions and, despite his fame and notoriety, found himself at odds with the government and its Islamic fundamentalist leader, the Ayatollah Ruhollah Khomeini. Khomeini overthrew the previous dictatorship of Shah Reza Pahlavi, popularly known as "The Shah", in 1979. The Shah was widely regarded as a brutal despot who was propped up and supported for several decades by the American government, and so long as the man provided unlimited access to oil and other Iranian treasures, the US was perfectly happy to let him rule his people with a tyrannical iron fist. Our leaders willfully turned a blind eye to the brutal treatment of the Iranian citizenry that transpired during The Shah's regime. The despotic dictator was ably assisted in his reign of terror by his secret police, the SAVAK. The 1979 revolution was fomented to overthrow The Shah and, at the same time, rid the country of foreign imperialists who had exploited Iran for its oil and other riches. The US quickly became the chief target for the enmity of the new regime, along with the British and the Russians who had also plundered Iranian resources for decades.

Habib's dissident political views and actions eventually led to his arrest and incarceration in the early 1980's. Four years or so after his imprisonment, a contingent of Iranian government officials came to his cell to let him know his release was imminent. On the morning of his supposed release, June 21, 1984, Habib was awakened, escorted to the Wall of Allah Akhbar (Arabic for "God is great"), and along with forty other supposed enemies of the state, placed in front of a firing squad, and summarily executed. The Iranian government has never confirmed the execution of Habib Khabiri nor have details of charges against him and the supposed "trial" been divulged. No doubt, that information would make for some extremely fascinating reading.

What a shocking touch of irony in my search to learn more about the esteemed Iranian brothers! The Habib incident is, in many ways, symbolic of the perception that many westerners have of the system of justice in Iran. Even today, the Khabiri brothers are legends in the minds of their countrymen, and Habib's name surfaces every once in a while as an example of how far totalitarian governments will go to force their will on the people. As an additional index of the reverence accorded Habib in Iranian lore, I mentioned his name aloud in a conversation one evening at the conference, and was quickly hushed by Mohammad and others. Apparently, Habib's name and memory are not proper subjects for open discussion in Iran even though his execution took place over thirty years ago.

Preparing to Visit Tehran

As part of our negotiations, Mohammad assured me all trip expenses would be borne by the conference sponsors, so money was never an issue in the decision-making process. In return for his largesse, he asked that I serve as a keynote speaker, deliver several other papers at the conference, and repeat one or more of those talks with his Sport Management students at the University of Tehran. The schedule promised to be full and challenging, and an opportunity to visit a country with the mystique of Iran was simply too much to pass up. I must admit to one fleeting period of doubt about going to Tehran, but that moment of hesitancy passed rather rapidly.

My reservations about the trip were minimal and what few I had were undoubtedly misplaced, and centered primarily on the on-going tensions between the Iranians and their mortal enemies, the Israelis. My misgivings took on a new life two weeks prior to my departure while watching two political pundits on MSNBC talking about the constant tensions between the two countries. The essence of their combined messages was that Israel had to launch an attack in the upcoming two or three weeks in order to prevent the Iranians from completing the construction of a protective shield designed to ward off enemy missile or aircraft attacks. The two political analysts did not talk in tentative terms, but rather in scary, definitive ones. Essentially, they predicted that Israel would attack Iran sometime between the fifteenth of October and early November, or roughly the time frame of the futbol conference. These observers of world geo-politics were so certain in their assertions that I felt obligated to contact Mohammad and get his take on things. He assured me that he had lived most of his fifty-plus years with never-ending threats of annihilation from hostile forces and has never allowed these warnings to force him into paralyzed inaction. I took him at his word, for what he had to say made good sense. I then relaxed and continued with my plans to visit Iran. It has now been almost nine years since my visit to Iran and no Israeli missiles have rained down on the country yet.

I agreed to Mohammad's request pending permission from the upper administration at A&M and resolution of minutiae associated with obtaining a visa, setting up flight arrangements, and making hotel reservations. As things turned out, the visa and flight arrangements were nagging points right up to the penultimate travel day. Literally, the nitty-gritty details associated with obtaining a visa and reserving a flight were resolved at noon on Wednesday, October 28, with my flight scheduled to leave Houston some twenty-eight hours later on Thursday, October 29, at 1630 hours.

Postscript to my wife and most of my American friends: 1630 hours is 4:30 pm to you. Despite many trips to Europe, Judy has never tried to figure out military time which has been put to good use by most of the world. I actually like that system because it is the most parsimonious way to communicate time, and all my time-pieces are set accordingly. As well, I used that system daily during my three years in the U.S. Army.

The man in Iran responsible for my travel arrangements for the conference was named Mehrdad Beyaati and somewhere along the line, he or Emirates Airlines (or both) butchered my name, resulting in all calls from both Iran and the US to confirm my flight reservations falling on deaf ears. "We have no record of anyone booking a flight for anyone named Arnold LeUnes" was the mantra from the reservations desk at Emirates Airline. I am accustomed to having my name butchered in this country (i.e., Loowaynis, Leunesse, Loonis, Loons), so having the Iranians or the Emirates Airlines people struggle mightily with it came as no great surprise. Finally, Mr. Beyaati was able to untangle the mess with Emirates and my ticket and boarding pass were issued electronically and for the first time since Mohammad's original visit in August, I realized in late October I was actually going to Iran!

Problems in obtaining A&M's approval for the trip proved to be minimal. A request to visit countries deemed unsafe by the U.S. Government and Texas A&M University required the signatures of my department head, the Dean of the College of Liberal Arts, the Dean of Faculties, and, ultimately, the university President at that time, Dr. R. Bowen Loftin. The process took a couple of weeks but the permission was granted with nary a peep from anyone along the way.

My wife confessed to minor apprehensions about the trip, fearing that my tendency to wake up in a new world each day would lead me to make some kind of a bonehead move, thus causing the theocratic, thuggish, militaristic, and dogmatic Iranian government to detain me. I assured her I would be on my best behavior and studiously avoid doing something stupid. My number four daughter, Katie, probably the most politically and personally conservative of my six children, was adamantly opposed to the whole idea. When I told Laura Cook, one of our departmental staff members, I was going to Iran, she requested that I come by for a hug the day before leaving because, as she put it, "We will never get to see you again." My fondest hopes were that Laura was mistaken, of course!

Interestingly, I talked with Mohammad and Masi during one of their return trips to the US in February of 2012, and they expressed great concern about the severe deterioration in relations between their country and Israel. As well, they talked of renewed fears of a nuclear holocaust. Mohammad said he would not be inviting any westerners to Iran until tensions between the two countries thaw. I had never seen him so pessimistic about developments in his country, the ominous threats of attack by the Israeli's, and the effects of the economic embargo imposed by the US and several allies. I have always wondered if embargos work, and Mohammad said the one imposed by the US was having a most severe effect on the quality of life in Iran. My guess is the man on the street was greatly affected by the embargo but somehow I have the suspicion the daily life of the Iranian higher-ups, the poobahs, changed minimally if at all.

After innumerable emails and phone calls concerning the errant flight arrangements and to a lesser extent, the visa, I drove to Houston, stashed my Toyota Tundra in a remote parking area, caught a shuttle, and headed for the international terminal at George Bush Airport. When asked by the shuttle driver what airline I was flying with, I said "Emirates." In response, she said, "Hmmm. Never heard of it. How do you say it? Emirants? Amerits?" This was not a confidence-building exchange, to say the least, and I could visualize the two of us circling the various IAH terminals in the shuttle bus, vainly searching for an airline that did not exist, at least in the mind of the shuttle driver. The temporarily confused driver at least had the good sense to make a quick call to the shuttle service office where she received explicit instructions on how to get to the appropriate stop for Emirates Airlines. Crisis avoided!

A Welcome Layover in Dubai

My flight left Houston almost two hours late, with a scheduled six-hour layover in Dubai that became four thanks to the delayed departure from George Bush International. The fifteen-hour flight to Dubai was an interesting one made only slightly more tolerable by the fact that I sat in the last row of the rearmost section of the plane with an unoccupied seat next to me.

The first half of the flight was a payback for all the numerous uneventful flights I had experienced during other domestic and international junkets. The plane bounced up and down and from side to side almost non-stop for eight or nine hours, bucking and sashaying through the turbulence all the way from Houston to the western edge of the European mainland. How people who are prone to motion sickness made it, I will never know. Maybe they did not and I just never noticed. Since I sat in the rear of the plane, I got to hear the kitchen utensils and other items in the galley bang around freely for nine hours. Fortunately, the last portion of the flight from Germany to Dubai and on to Iran was the inverse of the first half, as smooth as the proverbial baby's butt. We white-knuckled passengers deserved a break after that long, bucking-bronco, rodeo ride.

The view as we approached the airport in Dubai at night was spectacular, due in large part to a carefully orchestrated, colorful panache of orange street lights. Though the tallest building in the world, the Burj Khalifa, is in Dubai, I was unaware of its existence at the time and thus unable to pick it out as we descended. The imposing edifice, all 2,717 feet of it, officially opened four months after my arrival in Dubai, having been completed after nearly six years at a cost of one and a half billion dollars. The tower is the focal point of an overall urban development known as Downtown Burj Khalifa which bore a juicy price tag of twenty billion USD. I entertain hopes of going back to Dubai some time to soak up the sights, sounds, and scenery in that great city.

Even more spectacular than the approach was the Dubai terminal itself. It looked more like a well-lighted, ornately-decorated castle than an airport and may well be the most glamorous and user-friendly facility of its kind I have seen. I was told there are plans to build an even newer and improved airport, either as an addition to the current one or as a replacement. The financial crisis that plagued The United Emirates and Dubai for some time threw a monkey wrench into those plans and I do not know if they have ever been resurrected.

My flight arrived around 2100 hours and I spent the next four hours wandering around the terminal, taking in the many sights and excesses of the beautiful airport, and doing some serious people-watching while waiting on my connecting flight to Tehran scheduled for around 0100 hours. Though located in the heart of Islamic culture, the Dubai airport was a cacophonous collection of humanity from every part of the world, and there were fascinating people speaking innumerable languages everywhere, running hither, thither, and yon.

However, after an hour of looking in stores and walking about, I decided to seek out a place to have a beer, though I was not totally sure there would be such a thing in an airport situated in the heart of Islamic-dominated Middle Eastern culture. As it turned out, and consistent with expectancy, it was not easy to locate a pub. This situation was in stark contrast to the people and cultures with which I was more familiar in previous travels, namely the Germans, Belgians, Czechs, and Dutch and their abiding fascination with and unfettered openness about beer.

In Search of a $12 Bottle of Guinness. I had done some earlier homework on alcohol consumption in Iran, and figured if I had a couple of beers in Dubai, they might be my last ones for several days. Was I ever right on target on that one! I had read just days before that the Iranian government was considering instituting a policy to deal with alcohol consumption I thought a bit draconian. To wit, punishment commenced with seventy-four lashes with a whip, followed by jail time and a hefty fine for making or selling alcoholic beverages. There is no question about the existence of an alcohol underground in Iran and it is well-known that creative Iranian imbibers brew their own at home. I suspect where there are people, there is alcohol. Such has been the case since time immemorial, and is likely to remain so in even the most authoritarian, restrictive, punitive cultures. The same can be said for other illegal drugs, and Iran reportedly has over one million drug addicts, or nearly two percent of its seventy million people.

Feeling for a while like Diogenes futilely searching for an honest man, I finally located a watering hole called The Hub tucked back in an out-of-the-way recess. I did not have any dirhams, the United Arab Emirates (UAE) currency, so I asked the waiter if he would take US dollars, and if so, how much the tomato soup on the menu would cost. It was twenty-one dirhams, or roughly seven US dollars, so I decided to have a bowl. Over a period of the next hour and a half, I also put down three glasses of one of my favorite beers in the entire world, Guinness Stout. Eventually, the time for the hour and forty-five minute flight from Dubai to Tehran neared, so I asked the waiter for my ticket. When he handed me a tab for forty-three US dollars, I was a bit flummoxed but assumed that I had misunderstood the exchange rate or I had been taken in by an avaricious waitperson. I paid up, reluctantly but without argument.

On the return trip from Tehran to Dubai, I once again visited The Hub as I had learned from my initial visit that it stayed opened around the clock. Though it was early in the morning, maybe 0700 hours, when I arrived in Dubai, I decided to have a celebratory Guinness as an expression of my elation at being back in the midst of a civilized environment where beer was actually served minus the soon-to-be-mandated six dozen lashes. I more or less chugalugged my lone beer and was handed a bill for twelve US dollars. I knew then the forty-three dollars I owed on the initial trip was not a misunderstanding about currency differences or an artifact of being in the clutches of a greedy waiter. Simply put, a glass of Guinness in the Dubai airport was twelve US dollars! Multiply that tidy little sum by three, throw in a seven-dollar bowl of tomato soup, and you have a forty-three dollar tab! Twelve dollars for a bottle of beer seems a bit steep, even for an airport, but I was thrilled to have one. Welcome to the oil-rich Middle East, I guess.

Wonderful Experiences in Iran

I arrived in Tehran around 0400 hours and was met immediately by my trip planner, Mehrdad Beyaati and some young assistants. Finally, I came face-to-face with the heretofore invisible man I had spent so much time with electronically over the past week concerning the visa and travel arrangements. Beyaati looked to be in his thirties, maybe six feet tall, of moderate build, dark, swarthy and handsome, and possessed of a wry grin that seemed to be hiding a deep, dark, "cat that ate the canary" secret to which only he were privy. Beyaati immediately whisked me into a VIP waiting room decorated with two oversized pictures located on either side, one of Ayatollah Khomeini, the aforementioned cleric who was instrumental in overthrowing the regime of The Shah in 1979, and the other the country's present ruling cleric, Ayatollah Ali Hoseyni Khomein'i.

TWO AYATOLLAHS

Wherever one goes in Iran, it is difficult to avoid the ominous visages of those two authoritarian figures who have exerted so much influence on Iranian politics, religious expression, and daily life for the past nearly forty years. Their pictures were poignant reminders that I had just landed in a foreign country governed by a real honest-to-goodness dictatorial theocracy. My most immediate thought after seeing the two pictures was that we could have a similar totalitarian form of government right here in the good old US of A if the zealots from the religious right had their way. Fortunately, we are blessed by a wonderful system of checks and balances provided, first of all, by an abiding belief on the part of our founding fathers in the separation of church and state, and secondly by a free press. Unfortunately in Iran, church and state are one and the same and the media is totally controlled by the theocracy.

Many observers of Iranian affairs agree the government is indeed a theocracy, but there are well-informed analysts who argue that the real locus of power lies with the Guardians of the Islamic Revolution, officially known as the Islamic Revolutionary Army Corps (IRGC) and often referred to in the American press as the Islamic Revolutionary Guard. One person sharing this belief is Richard Haass, President of the Council on Foreign Relations. In an article written for *Financial Times,* Haass called Iran a "thugocracy." It is his contention that their domination of the military and possession of vast financial holdings throughout the country has catapulted the Guard past the Islamic clerics in terms of influencing matters of importance to that country. Michael Slackman, a writer for the *New York Times* took a position similar to that of Haass, suggesting that many Iranians fear their country has become more of a military dictatorship controlled by the IRGC (i.e., the aforementioned "thugocracy") than one controlled by the Islamic clerics (i.e., a theocracy). In either case, it is clearly a controlled society with limited freedoms.

Any discussion of Iranian politics is incomplete without mentioning its past President, Mahmoud Ahmadenijad, himself an ex-Guardian. For quite a number of years, he was the face of the Iranian government to the rest of the world, and I find it fascinating that, to my knowledge, he was never photographed or interviewed wearing that dreaded symbol of western exploitation and oppression, the necktie. Suit? Yes. Open-collared shirt? Yes. Necktie? Not a chance!

But I digress. After a short time in the Tehran airport, I was asked to step out of the VIP lounge long enough to be fingerprinted while Mr. Beyaati's assistants were picking up my visa and tracking down my luggage. Around 0500 hours, we started the half hour drive to the Olympic Hotel in Tehran where I stayed during my four days in Iran. For a good part of the trip from the airport to the hotel I talked with a nice-looking, twenty-something savant who told me he had little talent for anything else in this world but language acquisition. He professed to total fluency in Farsi, Arabic, English, German, French, and Spanish, and indicated he was making good progress toward command of Italian. I took him at his word with some reservations, but had the opportunity over the next several days to overhear him pretty much validate his claims through random but flawlessly fluent conversations with conference participants in several of those languages.

Due to the hurry and hubbub surrounding my long-awaited arrival and subsequent rapid departure from the airport, I never got a chance to go through my usual ritual of protecting my passport. Typically, I treat my passport with an obsessive-compulsive fanaticism and once I am through using the document, it goes in a device I wear around my neck on a string which is designed to carry my wallet, important papers, and cash. The failure to follow my ritual for one of the few times in my travel life came back to scarily haunt me for a brief time. As we left the airport, I literally was grabbed, however politely, by both arms and inserted with a firm Iranian hand placed on the back of my head into a waiting vehicle. Everything was done with great haste and urgency, in a manner similar to that of dignitaries or celebrities you see on television who are rushed through crowds of clamoring admirers, potential adversaries, or the paparazzi. Thirty minutes later, we arrived at the hotel where I walked into the lobby, once again to be greeted by large, strategically placed, bigger-than-life pictures of the two Ayatollahs, Khomeini and Khomene'i, sternly gazing down at me and the rest of the world with cold, steely, accusatory, and suspicious, paranoid, eyes.

As part of the ritual of getting checked into the hotel, the night clerk requested my passport. A quick search of all possible pockets, backpack compartments, and suitcase nooks and crannies revealed that the document was nowhere to be found. My first thought was, "Losing a passport is pretty much a disaster anywhere but there might not be many places more ominous and foreboding to misplace one than in Iran."

I was told by the desk clerk that the vehicle transporting us to the hotel was still on the premises and maybe a look-see there might be prudent. It took only three or four minutes to track down the car, and fortunately my passport rested quite comfortably in the middle of the back seat. I had either laid it there during the considerable commotion surrounding my exit from the airport or it had slipped out of my pants pocket. Either way, the potential crisis was averted and I checked into my room around 0600 (or 6 am). Sleep came slowly and in fits and spells, but I eventually logged about six hours of fitful rest. I woke up slightly after noon, shaved and washed away the grit and grime of the flight, and left my room to wander the halls of the hotel so I could stretch my legs, remove the travel-induced cobwebs from my head, and get a feel for my surroundings.

Meeting Mostafa. One of my first missions was to try to establish phone contact with Judy back in the states, and the desk clerk recommended an international calling card rather than the ultra-expensive room phone. I was directed to the business office where I fell into the gracious and helpful hands of a young clerk named Mostafa Nasiri. Mostafa had a master's degree, clerked at the hotel, and taught English to Iranian adults and children in his spare time. He expressed a strong desire to come to the states to work on a PhD in the field of tourism, which in and of itself is interesting given the virtual absence of tourists in Iran, at least at that time. Perhaps Mostafa knew something about the future of Iran he was not sharing with the rest of us. Or maybe he was an optimist with a gift for wishful thinking.

My man Mostafa sold me an international phone card and, in trying to make a call home, I kept plugging the country code "49" into the numbers sequence with no success. It took a few minutes for the two of us to realize that "49" was the country code of Germany, not the US. We are all creatures of habit and spending eight of the previous nine summers in Germany led me to think of "49" when Mostafa had asked for my country code number. Miraculously enough, when we plugged in the correct country code, 001, the international calling card came alive.

At one point, Mostafa asked me if I knew why the country code for the US was 001 and I replied that I did not. He offered up the following response: "Your country code is 001 because you come from the greatest country in the world. It is number one." It was this sort of admiration for and fascination with the US that I encountered repeatedly during my stay. Incidentally, in order to call Judy, the number sequence I had to use each time with that Iranian calling card was 9-23333000-32040759430593-979-492-3438#! The potential for Murphy's Law to intrude while dialing that many numbers is immense, but I handled the challenge pretty well most of the time. Pretty doggone good for someone with happy fingers, if I do say so myself!

Mostafa asked me a question about our language that turned out to be gnarly despite its seeming simplicity. It seems Mostafa had recently encountered a new English term, "smart aleck", and was perplexed about its meaning. It was his assumption that the term was essentially positive because of the presence of the word "smart." I told him that being called a smart aleck was not really positive but for the life of me I could not satisfactorily tell him why not….maybe I was brain dead from fatigue or jet lag. Smart aleck is one of those terms I clearly knew the meaning of but when asked by someone unfamiliar with the many idiosyncrasies of our language, I was hard pressed to come up with a very good explanation. I wanted to say that a smart aleck is a know-it-all, a wise guy, or even a smart-ass, but I knew those descriptors were too similar to the semantic trap from which I was trying to extricate myself.

I never really came up with a really good synonym for smart aleck, so after a while we moved on to other English language nuances. Mostafa picked my brain for about an hour concerning the English language, but I finally had to excuse myself to go prepare for my upcoming conference talks the next day. As I departed the hotel business office, Mostafa, three other staff members, and I had a good laugh about his hoodwinking me into conducting an impromptu sixty-minute English tutorial. I, of course, was happy to do so, and Mostafa seemed most appreciative.

Westerners in the Olympic Hotel. The Olympic Hotel was one of three options for conference visitors, and it often housed Olympic dignitaries, athletes, and visitors such as yours truly. It was clean, modern, attractive, bare bones but comfortable, not at all glitzy, blessed with a decent restaurant, and had perhaps the single most uncomfortable bed onto which I have ever placed this old, increasingly ossified skeletal system. I might as well have slept in the hotel parking lot or on the floor of the hotel lobby. To compound my sleeping difficulties, the management had turned off the air conditioning for the season, and my room was hot and humid, sort of Galveston-like really, and residents of that city and area will tell you that is not a good thing. To further complicate my sleep misadventures, the pavement-caliber mattress and the tropical, circulation-deprived room forced me to open a window to get some air circulation. That move was ill-advised for it gave the kamikaze Iranian mosquitoes just the excuse they needed to declare war on the succulent pores of a newly-arrived, died-in-the-wool Westerner. I ended up sleeping a grand total of perhaps thirty hours from the Thursday morning I left the US to the following Wednesday evening when I got home. I could have complained to Mohammad and perhaps been transferred to one of the other two hotels, but I did not want to take advantage of his hospitality nor was I interested in packing up and moving once I got settled in, such as it was. Other than the bed, I liked the hotel and my newly-found friends very much.

Speaking of Westerners, I encountered scant few of us once I left Dubai. I think I was the lone occidental on the flight from Dubai to Tehran and one of only three such people in the hotel. The others of Anglo persuasion were a young attorney from Zurich by the name of Vitus Derungs and a British bloke in his late twenties, Matthew Pearson, who was working as the Biomechanics Officer at Aspire, an elite soccer developmental operation in Qatar. I got to know both Vitus and Matthew pretty well and we had a good time together, just hanging out, visiting, and sharing life experiences for those few days we were in Tehran together.

The only other westerners I met in Tehran were participants in the convention, one being a German soccer official from Cologne, Herr Erish Rote Muller, who had been at one time an assistant coach for the Iranian national team, and a British bloke named Craig Simmons, a Player Development Advisor to the Football Association (FA) group at Wembley Stadium in London. It is FA's mission to make sure futbol flourishes at every level in England. I have since learned that Herr Rote Muller is highly placed in the Deutscher Fussball Bund (DFB), or the German Soccer Committee, and widely regarded as one of the premier talent scouts and trainers of elite soccer players in all of Germany.

Around 1600 on that first day, Mohammad arrived at the hotel and we sat and visited until it came time to adjourn for what was to be a most interesting social event. It seems a new sport facility was being dedicated at the nearby Olympic complex which was within easy walking distance of the hotel. It also turned out that the guest of honor for that ceremony as well as for the International Science and Futbol Conference was the President of the Asian Football Confederation (AFC), Mohamed bin Hammam from Qatar.

Qatar's Mohammed bin Hammam of the Asian Futbol Confederation

As Mohammad and I neared the ceremony site, we were witness to a veritable explosion of lights, cameras, commotion, and people scurrying about like good old Texas fire ants. It was clear that something significant was taking place and we were about to miss out. As we drew closer to the center of the hubbub, we could see that Hammam had arrived and was the focus of considerable media attention. Professional and amateur photographers were busy taking still photos while the video cameras from the local media were working overtime to document the arrival of the AFC President. Hammam was around six feet tall, sixty years of age, a light skinned Qatari with a white beard, wearing the thobe, ghutra, and agal so common to people from his country. For the uninitiated among us, including me, the thobe is a white, long-sleeved, ankle-length, loose-fitting garment worn over white trousers, the ghutra is a square all-white or red and white scarf folded in a triangle and held in place by a braided black cord, or agal.

The President had an understated charismatic aura about him, and his presence was accentuated by a light beard and the long, flowing Middle Eastern garb. It was obvious we were in the presence of a luminary, someone of the stature of a major religious or political icon. As the entourage accompanied Hammam through the new facility, people bowed in deference as he passed, and the video and still cameras continued non-stop. I was convinced President Obama or the Pope would not have been accorded a warmer and more deferential reception in their world travels. We were clearly in the presence of an iconic, almost god-like figure, though the religion in this case was futbol. The AFC and Hammam maintained jurisdiction over soccer programs in forty-seven countries embracing sixty percent of the world's population. Hammam was a major compelling figure in a sport that often transcends politics and religion in much of the world.

MOHAMED BIN HAMMAM, IRAN, 2009

As a measure of his status in the soccer world, Hammam was one of two finalists in 2011 for the Presidency of FIFA, the world governing body for that sport. Allegations of wrongdoing plagued his candidacy, mostly surrounding the awarding of the 2022 Soccer World Cup to his home country, Qatar. In response to the allegations and attendant hoopla, Hammam withdrew from the race in May, 2011, leaving the seventy-five-year old incumbent, Sepp Blatter, to continue running the organization. Countercharges were lodged, asserting Blatter created the furor to discredit Hammam in the name of retaining his grip on FIFA. In 2011, Hammam was banned for life by FIFA for bribing officials to vote for his failed run at the Presidency of that organization. Hammam has since been charged with using millions of dollars to bribe and influence officials having a say-so about where the 2022 World Cup would be held (Qatar).

As if the Hamman saga was not enough, the informed follower of soccer knows the brouhaha surrounding the selection of Russia to host the World Cup in 2018 and Qatar in 2022 is the source of much negative publicity. Bribes in the millions of dollars are alleged, Sepp Blatter has resigned the Presidency of FIFA, and the scandal surrounding the organization widens in scope and complexity with the arrest and indictment by the U.S. Department of Justice of nine senior FIFA officials and five sports marketing executives on charges of corruption, wire fraud, racketeering, and money-laundering. Hopefully, FIFA, or what one television reporter recently called "Thiefa", will be a less corrupt and more open, accountable, transparent, and efficient organization now that the despotic Blatter is gone.

Talk of taking the World Cup away from Qatar continues despite the fact that expensive soccer venues are being constructed all over the country. Much of the furor centers on the bribery scandal that led to the selection of Qatar, but a potential catastrophe is causing FIFA to have second thoughts. The most recent brouhaha is focused on migrant worker deaths since the aforementioned soccer venue construction began in 2010, with the fatalities already at an unprecedented 1,800. Projections are that 4,000 will die by the time the 2022 Games open. By way of contrast, there were two worker deaths in South Africa and ten in Brazil as those two countries hosted World Cups in 2010 and 2014 respectively. The human toll in the case of Qatar is potentially staggering and most certainly indefensible. Furthermore, the bad publicity generated by these abuses could not have come at a worse time for the increasingly embattled FIFA.

But let us return to Iran in 2009. Mr. Hammam was accompanied that night and throughout the conference by two highly placed AFC figures, Hasan al Sabah, the Deputy Secretary General for Education, and Dr. Gurcharan Singh, Deputy Secretary General for Sports Medicine. Hasan al Sabah was a fortyish, good-natured, amiable, likeable type with a boyish grin that flashed with little prompting or provocation. He always seemed to be enjoying the moment and having a good time. I found al Sabah to be most pleasant and we talked of collaborating on some future projects. It is difficult to know if any of those "Let's get together soon and see what we can work out" conversations at conferences actually ever come to fruition. As for Dr. Singh, he was fiftyish, distinguished looking, originally from India, and trained as a physician in his home country. He was pleasant enough but a bit more reserved than his fellow Deputy Secretary General, Mr. al Sabah.

Once the dedication of the new sports facility was over, we adjourned to a large tent for a sumptuous Iranian-inspired feast and welcoming ceremony in honor of the dignitaries and conference participants. I sat at the table with Hammam, al Sabah, Dr. Singh, Mohammad, and my friends from Switzerland and Qatar, Vitus Derungs and Matthew Pearson. As a result of our physical proximity to Hammam, we received a lot of attention from the media, and individuals brought personal cameras over to have their pictures taken with Hammam and, as an afterthought I suppose, us.

Finally, the evening ended around 2100 hours and I gladly headed back to the hotel in search of a good night's sleep. Sleep, for reasons mentioned earlier, unfortunately was fitful at best; the torturous triumvirate, my rock-hard bed, the stuffy room, and kamikaze mosquitoes with an insatiable blood lust for at least one American, me, ruled the night.

Gridlock to End All Gridlock

Bright and early the second day, Vitus Derungs, Matthew Pearson, yours truly, and an assortment of persons unknown to me loaded into the VIP shuttle and headed for the conference, a trip that turned out to be a fascinating slice of everyday Iranian life. I thought I had seen it all in terms of traffic while in Rome in 2000 and 2001, but the city of Romulus and Remus is minor league compared to Tehran. Tehran has twelve to fourteen million people, give or take, and it seemed as if every single one of them drove the freeways at the same time. All motorists there are blessed with a dog-eat-dog, every-man-for-himself, Orwellian approach to driving, and Charles Darwin would have been proud.

For starters, there were four lanes painted on the freeway but for all intents and purposes there were six. Our driver had literally straddled the lane marker, forcing the car on our left over against the rail, thus creating a fifth lane. At the same time, someone was doing the same thing on the far right so the five lanes thus became six. Drivers wishing to make a left turn through the traffic circle had to work their way through six lanes of oncoming traffic to do so. Those trying to navigate from right to left or left to right across the six lanes also faced a daunting task. After much haranguing, arm waving, and yelling of epithets, every car somehow made its way through the gauntlet and ended up at its pre-determined destination.

Each time someone slowed down, another car would pull in sideways from another lane to get ahead. The net effect was that some cars were pointed straight ahead and others jackknifed at forty-five degree (more or less) angles on both the left and the right. I am positive if one were viewing the traffic snarl from a helicopter, it would look like a series of mobile twenty-car pileups. What I was witnessing was not a pretty sight to behold but as Mohammad told me later, "Yes, it may look strange to an outsider but it works for us." And I must say that he seemed to be correct. I probably saw a thousand near-wrecks, with misses measured in nano-seconds and fractions of inches, but I never witnessed an actual out-and-out collision. And seldom did I see a dented car, either. I suspect that visitors to Jakarta, Lima, Mexico City, or Mumbai probably witness pretty much the same thing every day but I had never seen anything like it, not even in wild and crazy Italy. Tehran puts Rome to shame for traffic noise and confusion, and I never thought I would say that.

ICSF Opening Ceremonies

We arrived at the conference location after thirty minutes of fighting traffic and were promptly escorted into the building via a length of red carpet, with cameras flashing and video cameras whirring. I had never been given the VIP treatment before, but I want you to understand in no uncertain terms I could get accustomed to it if necessary. Being a VIP is a nasty job but I could do it if forced to do so! We were met at the entrance to the conference center and promptly escorted to the VIP dining area where Hammam and other dignitaries were eating a light breakfast prior to adjourning to the main hall for the opening ceremonies.

Following the recitation of the Holy Quran, or Koran, the playing of the national anthem of the Islamic Republic of Iran, brief speeches by several conference dignitaries, and the comments from the Secretary General, the time arrived for my brief keynote address focusing on the current status of sport psychology in the United States. Of course, my talk was in English and for those who did not speak that language the information was provided in Farsi, the first language of Iran, via translators speaking into ear phones. Though I was nervous as my time to talk arrived, I calmed upon reaching the podium and was reasonably pleased by my delivery and content.

After I finished my presentation, the dignitaries were entertained for perhaps a half hour by a five-man group playing traditional Iranian music. The musicians were quite proficient and the lead vocalist had a nice, pleasing voice, but what I was most impressed with were solos and duets done by two men playing the traditional Iranian percussion instruments, the daf and the tombak. The daf is a cymbal-like instrument with far more range of sounds than its American counterpart, and the tombak is a one-headed drum carved of a single piece of wood and covered with a sheepskin membrane. The sounds those two musicians coaxed out of those instruments, both solo and together, were simultaneously remarkable and enchanting.

This merger of the daf and the tombak also afforded me the impromptu opportunity to meet a young Iranian graduate student, Maryam Abargoueinejad. Maryam sat directly behind me during the opening ceremonies, though I was unaware of her presence until she tapped me on the shoulder to share some comments about her enjoyment of the musicians. Once the group finished playing and the opening ceremonies officially concluded, Maryam sought me out and we talked for a few minutes. She departed with assurances we would meet up later at one of the convention sessions.

Shortly before delivering my opening keynote address, I learned that old Ish, yours truly, was scheduled to give another presentation at 1330 that same day. I had not seen a copy of the conference program and misunderstood what I had been told about my speaking schedule. I thought the only talk scheduled that first day was the keynote, and upon finding out that was not true, I informed Mohammad my power point presentation was on a flash drive back in the hotel. That meant we had to once again make the tedious trip to the hotel to pick up my materials. I arrived back from the hotel with a few minutes to spare, and mistakenly grabbed a CD instead of the DVD that was to be an important part of my afternoon presentation on "Mental Toughness in Soccer." The mistake was not fatal; I winged it and the presentation went reasonably well.

Later that afternoon, I found out I was scheduled to give a workshop entitled "Mental Skills in Soccer" at 1830 hours that same evening. At this point, rather than go back to the hotel, I decided to really wing it this time. Again, things went well enough and I survived without embarrassing myself. The thing that made these communication gaffes more bearable is that I had a day of rest the second day of the conference. This break in the action allowed me to pretty much relax and enjoy the conference and get to know my new associates and friends.

Maryam Abargoueinejad. Maryam was in her early twenties and had completed her master's degree in Sport Management at the Islamic Azad University in her hometown of Isfahan, some 400 kilometers south of Tehran. As was the case with every Iranian woman I saw or met at the conference, she was wearing the appropriate required headdress, the hijab, in her case a black one, and the required manteau (pronounced montoo), also black, that came down to just above her knees, covering her neck, upper torso, and arms. Long pants covered the lower part of her legs, so that all one could see as required by Islamic convention were her hands and most of her face.

After our brief initial encounter at the opening ceremony, I ran into Maryam at a poster session where she presented her research on injuries among female soccer players. Her proud father was among the on-lookers and we met and talked briefly. Mohammad indicated as part of the introduction that Maryam's father was the top soccer official in the state in which Isfahan is located, and thus exerted considerable influence over that sport both there and in Iran in general.

The poster session gave me a chance to visit with Maryam about her research, and in the course of our discussion, she mentioned a desire to come to the states to work on a PhD. I asked her if she had any part of the US in mind, or any particular program, and she said emphatically, "I want to come to the US to be your student. I want to be yours for the next three or four years." She also indicated that she and her father were departing the convention that afternoon for Isfahan, and they would not be in attendance for its final two days. Her impending absence was not good news as I would have liked to have had more time to talk about graduate school, find out more about her goals, and generally get to know her. As she prepared to depart, she stuck out her hand for a handshake, something that is done with some frequency by younger females in Iran but is verboten with older ones.

I found out about that cultural custom the hard way when I was introduced to a middle-aged female faculty member from the University of Tehran the first night in Iran. As we were introduced, I reflexively stuck out my hand as I would to any woman in the US, and was met with no hand in return, followed by an admonition from Mohammad and several others in the vicinity that, "We don't do that sort of thing here." I smiled and said, "I just found that out. Pardon me for violating your customs." So far as I know, that was my only violation of Iranian social norms during the entire visit. So far as I know….

Maryam's hopes of coming to the US to study was repeated over and over during my stay in Tehran. At least six young women approached me, expressing a desire to come to the US to study under my supervision. Several dozen more talked to me at times about coming to other universities in this country. It was interesting to note that every one of the students who talked to me at the conference about coming to the US was female. The Iranian males were more interested in receiving assistance with their research and related educational issues within their respective universities. The preceding vignette says something significant about life satisfaction among males and females in a decidedly male-dominated culture.

IRANIAN FEMALES IN SOCCER GEAR. THEY COMPETE AT A HUGE
DISADVANTAGE DUE TO WEIGHT OF UNIFORMS
WHICH ARE WORN THROUGHOUT ALL MATCHES

In explaining my seeming popularity with the students, it would be a mistake to think I was a household name in Iranian sport science circles. Rather, part of the attraction was probably a function of marketing on the part of my newly-found public relations guru, Mohammad Khabiri. Also, there was a certain aura of authenticity and expertise associated with being an outsider, and an American outsider at that.

This desire to study in America was in some ways depressing because it seemed unlikely that Maryam or any of the others would ever get the opportunity to study here. US and Iranian immigration policies, the continuing enmity between the two governments, language barriers, our fascination with standardized testing scores, and difficulties in matching transcripts and degrees of a university in the US with those in Iran are just a few of the impediments facing those students. I have done what I can but their belief that all I had to do was snap my fingers and miracles automatically happen has no basis in reality. The students imputed far more significance to my powers to move academic mountains than the facts of the case would merit. I was pessimistic that any of them would end up studying in the US, unless it would be Gilda Khalaj because of her language familiarity and dual citizenship.

Gilda Khalaj. I had occasion to meet Gilda Khalaj, and we developed a cordial relationship in a short time. She was attractive but in a very different way from the dark-skinned, dark-eyed, and more exotic Maryam. Gilda was actually born in the US to an Irani father and non-Iranian mother which no doubt accounts for her noticeably different, less than full Iranian appearance.

Gilda finished her master's degree in Sport Management in the summer of 2010 under the supervision of my friend and colleague, Mohammad. She also co-authored a couple of publications in sports management journals and showed considerable promise for additional graduate work, particularly in light of her relatively advanced command of English.

On the third day of the conference, I attended several presentations in a totally relaxed frame of mind, thinking that my responsibilities were completed other than a trip Mohammad had scheduled to the University of Tehran. I assumed for some reason that the trip to the university was set up so I could meet some professors and administrators of Mohammad's choosing. However, Gilda burst that bubble for me. I ran into her after lunch, and she commented that she was excited about going to the university to listen to my talk to Mohammad's Sports Management students. I inquired of her, "Talk? What talk" She said in return, "Dr. Khabiri has you scheduled to talk with a large group of his students for an hour or so." As was the case with my other presentations, all didactic materials were safely ensconced back in my hotel room. As we made the thirty-minute drive to the university, I hastily scribbled notes on a piece of scratch paper in an effort to reconstruct my previous presentation on mental skills in soccer.

The presentation to the students turned out to be the best of all the ones I made in Tehran, and I think it was because I was back in the element I know best and am most comfortable with, the college classroom with its bright, enthusiastic young people. As Mohammad and I walked into the lecture hall prior to my presentation, the students rose in unison and bowed on our behalf, a practice I hope to eventually initiate in my classrooms at A&M. Yeah, right! Lots of luck! You are lucky here if they don't lynch you!

An Iranian Runway Model. Mohammad translated as I talked since maybe half of the students spoke only Farsi. Speaking thirty or forty words and then having them translated was a new experience for me, but the ever-facile Mohammad handled the challenge beautifully and I became quite comfortable with that format. As I talked, I saw many bright, intelligent looking faces in the audience but was particularly struck by one young woman whose penetrating, laser-like gaze I could not avoid since she sat a couple of rows up on my immediate left, thus putting her at about eye level. She was a woman of rare beauty, but revealed nothing about her thoughts or feelings with her face or body language. Her dark eyes were piercing and I wondered if they were projecting friendliness or Iranian distrust of westerners. As a professor, you get accustomed to all kinds of gazes, body language, and mannerisms but making sense of them is an elusive and precarious enterprise at best.

Physically, I would describe her as a slimmer Iranian version of a young Sophia Loren. She was tastefully dressed, chic, tall and lean, and her Islamic attire was unsuccessful in hiding what had to be a very nice figure. She also was blessed with a perfect complexion, pitch black eyes, and even darker jet black hair that framed and highlighted a gorgeous face and some of the prettiest eyes and most perfect white teeth I have ever seen. All I could think of to describe her was "movie star" or "runway model."

After the talk, the mystery woman got in line with maybe a dozen other students, waiting her turn to visit. Upon reaching the front of the line, she told me in more than passable English she thought I was a great teacher and wanted to say so in person. As stated earlier, I had no idea what I expected, but was pleased with her kind words, of course. Unfortunately, in the crush of other students, I had no chance to get to know our Iranian runway model better.

Unbeknownst to me, while I was visiting with the long line of students, several others had cornered Mohammad on the other side of the room to express their concerns about my safety. It seems that an anti-American demonstration was scheduled for the next day at a location on or near the university. Mohammad assured his concerned students that I would be aboard a plane headed for Dubai at 0400, and safely in the airport there by 0700, long before the demonstrators got cranked up. It was nice to know the students were concerned about the welfare of someone who could easily be viewed as the oft-reviled, ugly American. Mohammad later told me the scheduled rally ended up being much more of an anti-government demonstration than an anti-US one.

As we prepared to leave inner city Tehran after the lecture, Gilda came up to say goodbye, and, wiping away tears, said something that was quite heartwarming: "I don't want you to go home. I like you so much, I want you to stay in Iran." The sentiment she expressed pretty much captures the essence of the really first class, sensitive, caring young woman that is Gilda Khalaj. I heard from her numerous times by email upon arriving back in the US, and she and her parents, both dentists by trade, were on campus in March of 2011 while Gilda looked into the possibility of gaining admission to the PhD program in Sport Management here. For a variety of reasons, mostly of a bureaucratic nature, she was not admitted to the PhD program. Instead, she recently finished her second master's degree at A&M in Sport Management. Not too long ago, I asked if she would re-apply to the PhD program in Sport Management at A&M, and she gave me a resounding "No!" She wanted to go to work in the sports industry, make some money, and stay away from academia for a while (or permanently). Where Gilda is today, I am not sure as we have lost contact with each other, but I think she is still in the US.

In Summation. By way of summarizing the experience in Iran, I can say without equivocation those four days were among the best in my life. I was treated like royalty, with total and absolute acceptance by every single person with whom I interacted. I have never met warmer and more gracious people than the Iranians at the conference. My feelings have been echoed by well-known author, chef, and erstwhile world traveler Anthony Bourdain who was taken aback at the Iran he encountered during a recent visit. He and his filming crew found the Iranians to be "…outgoing, friendly, welcoming to strangers to a degree we rarely experience very, very few places – and I'm talking Western Europe and allied nations." By way of summing up his visit, Bourdain said: "It was a very different Iran than I had been led to expect or could have imagined." Exactly my sentiments…

Governments are governments, and they are often at odds with each other, but people are pretty much people all over the world; most just want to get along. It is too bad that the Iranians, the US, and the world community cannot settle their differences and restore Iran and its human capital, historical riches, cultural diversity, and architectural wonders to its rightful place in a free world. I am fascinated by the potential of Iran and it is my fond hope there will come a day when the people are free to follow their dreams and be whatever they want to be. The Iranians have so much to offer and it is a shame to have it all hidden behind an oppressive wall of sanctions and secrecy. And it is mind-boggling to think that Mesopotamia, the cradle of civilization which flourished in the convergence of the Tigris and Euphrates and of which we heard so much about as school children, is off limits to much of the outside world.

Lagniappe

The remainder of this segment of the trip down memory lane will be devoted to what my Cajun friends might call *lagniappe*, a word with origins in the south and most closely associated with Louisiana and Mississippi. The website, answers.com, says the term is a mix of Spanish *la napa*, "the gift" and Louisiana Creole Quechua *pay*, "to give more." A similar term, *yapa*, is used in Andean markets to denote something added in freely to an existing purchase, so says Wikipedia. That same source indicates that the concept of lagniappe is practiced in parts of Southeast Asia where it is customary to throw in a few extra green chilies or a small bunch of cilantro with a food purchase. Those of a more Hispanic persuasion might label this largesse *olla podrida* (a Spanish stew). Essentially, then, lagniappe refers to something given gratuitously or thrown in for good measure.

The famous writer, Mark Twain (born Samuel Langhorne Clemens), writes of lagniappe in a chapter on New Orleans from his book, *Life on the Mississippi* (1883):

"We picked up an excellent word—a word worth traveling to New Orleans to get: a nice, limber, expressive, handy word—lagniappe." They pronounce it *lanny-yap*. It is Spanish—so they said. We discovered it at the head of a column of odds and ends in the *Picayune*, the first day; he heard twenty people use it the second; inquired what it meant on the third; adopted it and got facility in swinging it on the fourth. It has a restricted meaning, but I think all the people spread it out a little when they choose. It is the equivalent of the thirteenth roll in a "baker's dozen." It is something thrown in, *gratis*, for good measure. The custom originated in the Spanish quarter of the city. When a child or servant buys something in a shop—or even the mayor or the governor, for aught I know—he finishes the operation by saying—"Give me something for lagniappe." The shopman always responds; gives the child a bit of licorice-root, gives the servant a cheap cigar or a spool of thread, gives the governor—I don't know what he gives the governor; support likely. When you are invited to drink, this does occur now and then in New Orleans—and you say, "What again?—No I've had enough;" the other party says, "But just this one time more—this is for lagniappe." When the beau perceives that he is stacking his compliments a trifle too high, and sees by the young lady's countenance that the edifice would have better with the top compliments left off, he puts his "I beg pardon—no harm intended," into the briefer form of "Oh, that's for lagniappe."

I would like to devote the remainder of this humble document to the spirit of lagniappe as expressed so eloquently by the inimitable and infinitely wise Mr. Twain. Future prose will focus on my children, students, student evaluations of "teaching effectiveness", pleas for help from students in distress, the quirky nature of student letters of recommendation, former students, beer, barbecue, coffee, sports, athletes, celebrities, reflections on the quirks of daily life, and my take on the highly controversial topic of religion, just to name a few topics. The intent is to reveal to the reader some of the idiosyncratic thought processes that make me what I think I am. In addition to that modest goal, I hope what I have to say is informative. In the process, I hope to amuse.

I am an eternal optimist who relishes but does not dwell on the past, and I eagerly anticipate what the future holds in store. I have hopes of living another decade or two in good health and a positive frame of mind so that I may continue to validate my optimism. I would also like to stick around long enough to watch my kiddos and grandchildren develop into whatever it is they are destined to become. Alas, I am not sure there are enough years left to see what becomes of my great-grandchildren, Noah Cline, Anna Katherine Cline, and Henry Declan Powell, and others to follow. As well, I would like to enjoy the remaining years with my exciting, lovely wife, Judy Webb LeUnes. She has been my anchor, has kept me grounded in reality, and has seen to it that I avoid lapsing into bad habits. She is steadfast in her belief that the only reason civilization is able to endure is because of the socializing influence of females. She is convinced to the core of her existence that men would still be wandering around in outfits reminiscent of the once-popular comic strip caveman Alley Oop, dragging their knuckles on the ground and eating detritus from the floors of caves if it were not for the civilizing influence of women. I agree! I have friends without women in their lives, and their inattention to everyday social amenities is a constant source of wonderment. It is this spirit that I bring you my version of lagniappe, with topics covered in no particular order and with no binding theme, really.

Miss Hispanic Texas

The fall semester of 2003 was drawing to a close when a Hispanic coed, a Communications major named Vanessa, knocked on my office door to inquire about the possibility of making up some missed work in my Abnormal Psychology course. Here is my paraphrasing of what she related to me that day: "Dr. LeUnes I have missed quite a bit of school including the entire months of October and November and five of your six exams. I did take the first one on time, but I missed the last five. What I propose is to make them all up tomorrow starting at 0900, with each of the other four to be completed at hourly intervals. A few minutes rest in between should be plenty." I was, in a word, blown away by the disingenuousness of her proposal.

FOUR GENERATIONS OF WEBB/LEUNES FAMILIES-GRANDMOTHER JOYCE ELIZABETH WEBB, MOTHER JUDY KAY WEBB LEUNES, DAUGHTER KATIE ELIZABETH CRYER, GRANDAUGHTER ASHLYN GRACE CRYER

I asked Vanessa if she could provide extenuating circumstances that might justify allowing her to make up so much as one of the missed exams, let alone five. To this request, she said: "You are probably not aware of the reason I missed all your classes and exams during those two months but the answer is really quite simple. You see, I represent A&M as "Miss Hispanic Texas", and the duties associated with that title require that I travel a lot and make numerous personal appearances on behalf of the university. It is part of an attempt by A&M to reach out to the Mexican-American and larger Hispanic communities, and my obligations occasionally do interfere with my school work. However, it is an honor to be able to represent my school as "Miss Hispanic Texas" and I am sure you understand the significance of my mission."

I think I grasped the significance of her mission alright, but could not wrap my mind around the fact that the demands of that calling required that she miss two consecutive months of school. I thus denied her request out of hand but made what I thought was a most magnanimous counter-offer. To wit, I agreed to give her an incomplete in the course with certain stipulations. First of all, she had to completely repeat the course with my Honors section in the upcoming spring semester. Second, she had to take all exams, attend all field trips, make a forty-five minute power point presentation on a topic of her choice related to the course content, and attend each and every class with a zeal bordering on religious fanaticism. As Vanessa heard me out, I think she stopped breathing for a minute or two. Finally, and I am sure most reluctantly, she agreed that my proposal represented an acceptable compromise. In fact, it was the only option available and I think she understood that.

That following spring semester, Vanessa met all the coursework requirements I had set forth other than the attendance requirement which she more or less met. I am not sure it was in her DNA to attend any class with regularity unless forced to do so at gunpoint but I conceded her the relatively minor attendance shortcomings, and when all was said and done, she made a low C in the course. I never saw her again. I sometimes wonder if she is still out there somewhere among the huddled Mexican-American masses in Brownsville or Laredo or El Paso, title and tiara in hand, representing A&M across our great state as "Miss Hispanic Texas."

This anecdote reminds me of a story an old friend, Keith Rudasill, loved to tell about his days as a History instructor at Cisco Junior College, way out there in west Texas. With apologies to the locals, I once drove through Cisco and it is perhaps the ugliest city I have ever seen. Sorry, Cisco-ites! Anyway, back to the trials and tribulations of Professor Rudasill. It seems that a female student, batting her lovely blue eyes all the while, approached Keith with pretty much the same proposal as the one Vanessa had presented to me, though the source of the interference with academic performance differed. As she told Keith: "Professor Rudasill, I am sure you have wondered where I was for the last couple of months. It is unusual for me to miss class but I think you will agree that my reason in this instance is a good one. You see, I work for the GBI and my duties keep me away from campus a lot."

Keith, as might be expected, was not familiar with the GBI, so he asked for an explanation. His student continued: "Well, GBI stands for the Government Bureau of Investigation and I am with that super-secret agency, working as an undercover operative here in this part of Texas. The GBI is not the same as the FBI, but they share somewhat similar missions. My GBI duties have been intense and demanding this whole semester but there is a let-up in the action and I now have time to complete my courses. What do you think?"

Keith was not impressed and denied her request. She let him know she was unhappy with his decision and she could not vouch for how the leadership of the GBI might take the news. They could be quite upset, she said. Since I have not heard from Keith in nearly three decades, I have often wondered if he ended up a victim of a covert vendetta at the hands of her fellow GBI operatives there in Cisco. Certainly, the implied threat from our nefarious coed was thinly-veiled.

The Death of Willie Zapalac

A *Houston Chronicle* headline dated May 22, 2010 read: "Zapalac remembered fondly by Ags, Horns alike." The obituary goes on to indicate Willie Zapalac was a football legend at both The University of Texas and Texas A&M University, with numerous ties to both institutions as player and coach. Zapalac was just short of ninety years of age at the time of his death, and was survived by his wife of sixty-three years as well as two sons, Bill and Jeff. Both Zapalac boys played football on national championship teams with that scourge from Austin, the dreaded "teasips" (as the Longhorns are fondly known at A&M).

Willie Zapalac was a player of legendary proportions at Bellville (TX) High School which is located an hour south of College Station. Willie lettered twice at A&M before World War II and, upon returning from the war, captained the Aggie team in 1946. He subsequently coached at various Texas high schools and colleges including A&M and Texas, and spent a decade or so coaching in the NFL. His coaching stint at A&M was from 1953 to 1960, including four years with the legendary Paul "Bear" Bryant of A&M and Alabama fame. It was during his stay at A&M that Willie Zapalac and I crossed paths, however briefly.

Though some of the less significant details of my chance meeting with Coach Zapalac may be fuzzy because of the passage of almost six decades, the major facts of the case have been etched pretty firmly in my memory. It seems all undergraduate Physical Education majors at that time were required to take a course in the Coaching of Football, so I enrolled in it for the second semester of my sophomore year in 1957. The course met for the first few days in an auditorium on the second floor of the hallowed but now non-existent G. Rollie White, and we were sitting around in the classroom the first day waiting on the professor who we hoped in one short semester would miraculously transform us neophytes into full-fledged Knute Rockne's, Bud Wilkinson's, or "Bear" Bryant's. We had no idea who would be teaching the class, so there was an element of intrigue in the air. We were even naïve enough to believe that perhaps the "Bear" himself would be our professor, or at least make a grand appearance or two as guest guru.

Enter Willie Zapalac. Coach Zapalac was in his late thirties and still looked as if he could suit up and play. He was not a huge man, but had that unmistakable football coach look and demeanor...decent size, good muscularity for a man his age, pronounced jaw line, athletic swagger, an air of gruffness, and confidence out the wazoo.

COACH WILLIE ZAPALAC

To get our attention at the start of class that first day, Coach Zapalac tapped on the desk with a blackboard pointer, leading most everyone to quiet down as requested. However, a freshman running back, Eddie Van Dyke, if my memory serves me right, kept talking to the guy on his left. All of a sudden, Willie Zapalac sprang into action like a cat, grabbed the miscreant by the collar, lifted him out of his chair, and flung him to the front of the room where he landed in a heap against the blackboard. He then turned back toward the group and drawled, slowly but oh so resolutely: "Gentlemen, my name is Willie Zapalac. I am the Assistant Head Coach at A&M and I report to Coach "Bear" Bryant. From now on, when I walk into the room and tap on this desk, I want absolute silence. Do you read me loud and clear?" Needless to say, after that dramatic introduction, Willie had no trouble getting the group's attention on the few occasions we actually met for class after that.

I say "few occasions" for a reason. At our second meeting, Coach Zapalac announced that the football team would be using the coaching of football course to conduct three additional (he did not say illegal, though they were) hour-long workouts for the entire spring semester. His words went something like this: "The football team will practice each week during these three hours and attendance for all football players is mandatory. For those in the class who do not play football, you may come watch us work out if you like. If you are not interested in watching us practice, please bring me a twenty-page notebook on the coaching of football the first week of May, just before the semester final exams start."

I chose not to watch the team practice and never saw Willie Zapalac again. When the course grades were assigned, the football players all made A's and the rest of us made B's. I thought it was a good deal overall, getting a B for drinking coffee and bullshitting with my friends in the Memorial Student Center (MSC) snack bar. Interestingly, it was during this time period that the A&M football program was placed on probation by the NCAA, and one of the charges cited among many was using coaching of football classes to conduct illegal workouts.

Many people have fond memories of Willie Zapalac, and I have no doubts he was a good man. I do not know if my memories of him would be described as fond, but there is no doubt he left a lasting, indelible impression on me. Thus, it was with great interest that I read the various newspaper and electronic obituary accounts of his death. Willie, I hardly knew ye, but our one brief interaction has given me nearly sixty years of most interesting memories!

I am pleased to report the other major player in this drama, Eddie Van Dyke, survived his physical encounter with his displeased coach and has been a successful insurance agent in nearby Brenham for the intervening six decades. No harm, no foul, I guess!

The Untimely Passing of Coach Jim Culpepper

Speaking of Aggie athletics, in the early 1970's I developed a short-lived but cordial friendship with Jim Culpepper, the freshman basketball coach. Jim had been a highly successful high school coach in Dallas and subsequently had several outstanding teams at A&M in the days when universities fielded both varsity and freshman teams in a number of sports. For obvious reasons, mostly financial, that practice died a quick death around 1970.

Jim Culpepper and I, along with a friend and PhD student in Counseling Psychology named Don Williams, shared birthdays over a three-day period in mid-April. My birthday was on the sixteenth of April and Jim and Don, served as bookends for me, with birthdays on April fifteen and seventeen. The three of us celebrated what the Germans call "Alles gute zum Geburtstag" together for several years.

I happened to spot Jim eating breakfast one morning at a local restaurant and I joined him for some eggs, bacon, biscuits, and basketball banter. During the course of the meal, Jim told me he was hanging up his whistle and getting out of coaching. I was taken aback at the news and inquired about why he had decided to throw in the coaching towel. I was among the true believers who thought Jim had a bright future in basketball.

His response to my query was: "I am getting out because I can no longer look at myself in the mirror while shaving each morning. When I think about all the illegal, unethical and immoral things I have done to get basketball players into A&M and keep them eligible, I want to slit my throat right there on the spot. I just cannot do this any longer." My response was a terse and to-the-point query to the effect: "What keeps you from following through and cutting your throat, Jim?" His response was telling: "The only thing that keeps me from doing it is the realization that as dirty as we are in basketball, we are a hundred times cleaner than the football program." I suspect not much has changed in this regard since that chance meeting a half-century ago.

True to his word, Jim vacated his A&M coaching position shortly after our talk, left town, and, sadly, died a few years later after eating at a restaurant in the Rio Grande Valley. It seems that Jim rose from his chair and, according to newspaper reports, died on the spot of a massive heart attack. Jim was in his forties, tall, maybe 6'3" or 6'4", long and lean, and looked like anything but a candidate for a fatal heart attack. Jim Culpepper was a good guy who died far too early.

On a much happier note, early in Jim's coaching tenure, I approached him about the possibility of borrowing some old Aggie uniforms for a basketball team I was throwing together on a lark. It seems that while touring the Mexia State School, a residential treatment facility for intellectually disabled persons with one of my classes, we happened across some residents who were playing basketball in their gymnasium. A couple of my male students later proposed that we get a basketball team together to challenge the Mexia State School squad. This suggestion led me to approach Jim, and he gave us some faded old rags that more than adequately met our needs.

After a couple of practices, my guys and I motored the eighty-five miles to Mexia and when we took the floor for pre-game warm-ups that evening, their players thought they were competing against the real A&M team. Fortunately, for the Aggies, there was no resemblance between them and the ragtag, Bad News Bears collection of ballers I had thrown together for the occasion. As I recall, there were nine of us including me, and I was thirty-five or so and well past my basketball prime (if I ever had one). Several of my guys had played high school basketball and one, maybe two, had a bit of junior college experience, but overall I would characterize our team as mostly short, slow, and talent-challenged. We compensated for these shortcomings by being sadly out of shape. As a result, the young Mexia lads ran us ragged, but somehow we were able to eke out a 49-48 win. A month or so after we played them, the Mexia team won the state championship in a league made up of the other state schools of which there were a dozen or so. It took two overtimes for Mexia to defeat the Austin State School 69-68 in the title game.

We arranged to play the Mexia bunch again, but they were at a huge disadvantage the second time because their star player had been ruled ineligible for some kind of disciplinary violation. He had accounted for thirty-three of their forty-eight points the first time we played, and without him, the Mexia boys put up only token opposition and we won handily. My guys eventually graduated, and the TAMU-Mexia State School rivalry died in its infancy with Texas A&M holding a 2-0 advantage.

Student Cries for Help

I have visited with literally hundreds of students concerning a huge variety of topics and issues over the past what now seems like eons, and quite a few of those exchanges focused on personal problems. Though we have a full-blown and competently staffed student counseling center, some students feel more comfortable talking to a favorite professor or at least one they perceive to be an empathic or sympathetic listener. For example, the following email was sent to me ten years or so ago at 0653 hours (6:53am) by a student in my Abnormal Psychology class:

L****:
Dear Professor LeUnes:

> I cannot belive (sic) that I am writing you this email, it is so pathetic and belittling, but I have made a promise. As you may or may not know, I am a freshman. I took AP classes and 6 hours at a community college during my senior year- and tested high enough in them to allow me to come in with 27 hours. I graduated in the top 4.6% of my class of close to 600. I was such a wholesome, friendly, full of fire and ambitious young girl. I was the "social psychologist" for all my friends. I would listen to everyone's problems, and let them vent, would truly care and help them in any way. I was so happy to be away from my parents and on my own when college started. I didn't have any of my old friends come here, but I had gotten back with my old boyfriend J****. (We broke up last year when he came to A&M, and we had always planned to meet back up when I came here the next year.) Well college was going pretty good at first, I learned to really study, sleep less, and drink lots of coffee. But I wasn't happy with the situations I found myself in. All of my new "friends" were the girl friends of J****'s roommates, who would vent to me all (sic) their problems, and who I went out of live (sic) so many times to help (ex – taking one to get the morning-after pill

because her boyfriend didn't feel like it). The girls liked me superficially, the boys didn't. B/c whenever one of the roommates' girlfriends would leave – they would call 1 or 2 girls to come over for some fun. I hated all the lies, cheating, an (sic) complete ignorance that swarmed that apartment. When i would try to do the right thing- the girls didn't believe me or the guys would get really angry and tell me to leave their business along. I have not made 1 true friend up here. However, due to J****'s big mouth- he would get himself into parties by telling them at the door "My girlfriend is prescribed to." He personally never took them but he knew that Adderall to college students is like catnip to cats. But I never distributed it, even when people begged or offered money, never. I hated people who do that. It got so bad that I had to carry only my pill for that day in the bottle and leave the rest at home. And I am proud to say that none have gotten into improper hands, but my empty pill bottle has been taken numerous times. I was getting phone calls and people were nice to me soley (sic) on the hope that I would give them Adderol this time. It finally got to the point where I told people that i got caught by the cops and was no longer prescribed (sic), but still people ask. I was so likable and social before, and now if I wanted any friend, there was a price.

I will stop rambling and get to the point.

Over the past month, I have really been stressed, with school, my parents (they are divorced and fight via my brother and I), my lack of friends yet still going out of my way, and X-J****. He is a psyc major- you will get him eventually. He had evolved into a selfish, uncaring and unforgiving sociopath. And that is not my quote, it is his. He really thinks he is a sociopath. So over the past month and mainly last week, I have been in argument after argument, lie after lie, gossip, and depression. I finally broke up with J**** last week. I found myself in higher self-regard but very lonely. Despite the fact that I found out that J**** cheated on me- I still told him that I would forgive him and be his friend. We talk everyday- but about his life- he tells me rumors, his problems, his stressors (sic)- but at the slight chance that I began to talk about me- the conversation ends. I had so much hate and anger for him- but I pushed it aside- trying to be a good friend- his personal therapist- because I know he is severely disturbed mentally. Well I got on birth control this year and had to get an annual exam. I found out that I had an abnormal pap smear- which was caused by a STD that I got. I was lucky, and it can be cured with antiboitics (sic), but there is concern that there may be another problem so I am to be closely monitored for the next6 (sic) months. Upon hearing this, I tried to talk to j**** but he wouldn't answer- So I wrote him a letter with a copy of all the information to take to him. I found him with a girl that is well-known for sleeping around. It was 2 days after we had broken up. Thur- yesterday- I had to get his medical info. for an appt. thurs, but again no answer, and again I found a new girl. I never yelled- just aked (sic) the questions and quitely left. I got home. And then my mom called, she starting yelling about money and how I am drinking myself away, sleeping around, -all fanatical lies of a bipolar, bible-belt mother. It wasn't true- in fact I cant (sic) remeber (sic) the last time I even had 1 drink. The situation worsened when I tried to find someone to- talk with besides my family- who would freak out and utterly reject me. I found no one. No one who would even act like they cared. And I mean I tried everybody. Even people that I had known since grade school. I was so depressed, so alone. I had been trying so hard, have been doing the morally rigtht (sic) things, had helped others study when I should have- put every effort I had into it- and ended up alone, tainted, and disgusted by own self- how I had let myself become so shallow. So yesterday, I left school and prayed to god to let me be in a car accident. But- instead- I got a speeding ticket a quarter mile away from my house. I went inside and had so much emotion inside- that I did something very stupid, what i did when I was 13, I began cut my arm. I didn't want to kill myself- but just let the outside hurt as much as the inside- when I took a little Nyquil and cried myself to sleep. It is sad when your home was switched and changed so much that you dont even know where home is. And when you think of dying and it seems to benefit everybody, especially (sic) your parents- both for sympathy exploitation and life insurance money. That too can get a little discouraging. Of everybody I called, 2 people called back. My brother- who I love but he cannot handle the stress- it tears him up to see like this- like I was when I was 13. And my best friend D****, at UT- when he got off work. I told him everything- he came up immediately and got me. I have poured my heart and soul out and am doing much better. He made me promise to tell you, to let you know why I have been so out of it.

Please don't think less of me- I am not crazy, I am not suicidal, I am not desperate. I was just had to get it all out of all this semesters trials. I have not slept all night. I don't know why I reacted the way I did- but I just couldn't take it anymore. I have 4 classes tomorrow, 2 tests, assignments, and much to do. D**** has just now gone to sleep. I will be coming back tomorrow-but only for a little while- to get some things, and then I am staying here. D**** wants me to talk to some people tomorrow- I will. I have done it before. Therapy is not a stranger to my family. I am being more open with you than my other teachers. I need to ask how i go about doing this. D****'s roommate said that if I went up to each teacher and showed them the small cuts- that they would have to commit me. I don't need to be committed, I promise. But, I don't think that I can #1- have d**** get back to me in time and #2- attempt to explain to a teacher why I missed class.

It makes me seem stable and psychotic. My phone has died, and I can't charge it, but i will wait your email and seek your advice. When I do get back to college station- whatever time that is- I will try to visit you. If I miss my other classes, tests, quizzes (sic), etc- it doesn't matter to me. I will take a zero because I really need to get away. Had i stayed- things would have turned out far worse- not death- but further depression and grief that I am desperate to be rid of. I am so sorry for doing this to you, please don't judge me by what you have seen- I am actually a good person- just in a bad rut right now. Thank you so much, L****.

This email was one of a half dozen I received from this student, usually at odd hours and always about depression, desperation, and doom and gloom. L**** subsequently enrolled in my class in Sport Psychology, Q-dropped the course after about a month, and I have not seen or heard from her since.

Another strange email showed up on my computer in June of 2009 from a student who had also taken Abnormal Psychology with me. As well, we had several long conversations in my office, often focusing on the pathological parent-child interactional style of which she felt herself to be a victim. The email went as follows:

Hi Professor LeUnes:

How are you doing? I've been wanting to come by to say hi, but I'm usually working on Mondays during the day. So I'm hitting ya up on email! I'm guessing you might be in Germany with a summer school session.

And of course I do have a question for ya! What's the difference between recreational drug use and addiction. I take seroquel, buspar, and lexapro for my anxiety and unstable mood. It helps A LOT. I smoke dro every night for about 7 hours. I occasionally take like 30mg of adderall or I'll take a few vicodin or a klonopin or a xanax. Not usually all at once. Now, I'll do this for perhaps a week or two if I'm REALLY down. But normally I do it for a night and then lay off for a couple of days. Then I do it again. Then lay off a couple days. Sometimes I'll stay up for 2 days straight and sleep for 12 hours. Then lay off for a few days.

So, my caseworker at MHMR wants me to go to rehab for the pot. They don't know about the vicodin, klonopin, adderall, or xanax. Now, the people I buy from are hardcore into it. One of the guys takes vicodin all day long. He doesn't know how many he takes. He just takes them. He hides the pills in different spots throughout his house so that when he runs out goes searching for something to take, he finds one. He has 2 walmart size bags full of prescription bottles all for the same medication with his name on it. Thats just his personal stash. His dresser has about 10 pill bottles with different things in it that his boss fronts him so he can sell them. If he runs out of vicodin, he is sick. He sits around all day depressed and finds a way to get more. If I dont have vicodin, I take a tylenol and zantaq for the withdrawal and go to work and forget about it. Doesn't really matter to me. I'll be all right without it. Just nice to have it every once in a while to relax and distress. But I still go to my job. If I don't smoke at night, I'm real unstable the next day. If I smoke at night, the "pot hangover" makes me chill and unstable throughout the day so I don't get anxiety attacks.

So... what's the difference between addiction and recreational drug use? I stay away from blow and heroine (sic). I don't tweek. Hmm...it seems more like conservative opinion than actual concern and fact in my opinion. Wanted to know your thoughts on it...

K***:)

"And Ashley's doing real well! She graduated. Going into neuroscience."

Letters of Recommendation

A task that never seems to end if you have so much as one student-oriented bone in your body is the letter of recommendation for jobs, graduate school, medical school, physical therapy school, veterinary medicine programs, MBA programs, teaching positions, and on and on and on. Some border on onerous when you are not as familiar with the student as you would like. On the other hand, other letters are easy and flow right from the start, usually those concerning special students you have nurtured in the classroom, the laboratory, the office, on foreign soil, or elsewhere.

Most applications require that the potential candidate compose a statement of purpose or a biographical essay. In that regard, Professor Tim Cavell, late of A&M and currently a Professor at the University of Arkansas, placed the following essay to end all essays on my desk maybe twenty-five years ago. It is an actual letter and resulted in the applicant being successfully admitted to New York University. It reads as follows:

In order for the admission staff of our college to get to know you, the applicant, better, we ask that you answer the following question: Are there any significant experiences you have had, or accomplishments you have realized, that helped define you as a person?

I am a dynamic figure, often seen scaling walls and crushing ice. I have been known to remodel train stations on my lunch breaks, making them more efficient in the area of heat retention. I translate ethnic slurs for Cuban refugees, I write award-winning operas, I manage time efficiently. Occasionally, I tread water for three days in a row.

I woo women with my sensuous and godlike trombone playing, I can pilot bicycles up severe inclines with unflagging speed, and I cook Thirty Minute Brownies in twenty minutes. I am an expert in stucco, a veteran in love, and an outlaw in Peru.

Using only a hoe and a large glass of water, I once single-handedly defended a small village in the Amazon Basin from a horde of vicious army ants. I play bluegrass cello, I was scouted by the Mets, I am the subject of numerous documentaries. When I am bored, I build large suspension bridges in my yard. I enjoy urban hang gliding. On Wednesday's after school, I repair electrical appliances free of charge.

I am an abstract artist, a concrete analyst, and a ruthless bookie. Critics world-wide swoon over my original line of corduroy evening wear. I don't perspire. I am a private citizen, yet I receive fan mail. I have been caller number nine and have won the weekend passes. Last summer I toured New Jersey with a touring centrifugal-force demonstration. I bat .400.

My deft floral arrangements have earned me fame in international botany circles. Children trust me.

I can hurl tennis rackets at small moving objects with deadly accuracy. I once read *Paradise Lost, Moby Dick,* and *David Copperfield* in one day and still had time to refurbish an entire dining room that evening. I know the exact location of every food item in the supermarket. I have performed several covert operations with the CIA. I sleep once a week; when I do sleep, I sleep in a chair. While on vacation in Canada, I successfully negotiated with a group of terrorists who had seized a small bakery. The laws of physics do not apply to me.

I balance, I weave, I dodge, I frolic, and my bills are all paid. On weekends, to let off steam, I participate in full-contact origami. Years ago I discovered the meaning of life but forgot to write it down. I have made extraordinary four course meals using only a mouli and a toaster oven.

I breed prizewinning clams. I have won bullfights in San Juan, cliff-diving competitions in Sri Lanka, and spelling bees at the Kremlin. I have played Hamlet, I have performed open-heart surgery, and I have spoken with Elvis.

But I have not yet gone to college.

Butchered Words

There are a handful of words that get mispronounced more often than not. Perhaps a look at several of them would be a first step to remediating this problem.

Accreditation: This word invariably gets mispronounced as if the second t was a d, thus making it accredidation. It seems logical to me if you accredit something, such as a university, then it should follow that the process would be one of accreditation. Nevertheless, this one grates against the nerves when it is butchered, particularly by members of the local media who ought to know better.

Asterisk: Even the most educated among us refer to this one as an "asterick." As I tell my classes, the notation * is known among literate people as an asterisk. I accentuate the point by asking the students what they call an athlete who jumps out of an airplane or tries to climb Mount Everest. The usual response is "risk athlete." I then ask them how they would spell the work risk, and the answer is invariably r-i-s-k. I then query them as follows: "If r-i-s-k is risk in this context, how, how can it transmogrify into r-i-c-k in another?" I end the language lesson by telling them that if they say asterick, they risk being wrong. The word is asterisk, not asterick. I recently heard a sports color commentator, an ex-NFL jock, of all things, pronounce the word correctly. If an ex-NFL jock can get it right, surely my students and colleagues of above average intelligence can do so, too. Unfortunately, my efforts to clean up the language have proven to be largely futile. Most people who see this symbol * as an asterick before my phillipic still call them astericks after that. Bad verbal habits die hard.

Cavalry: When the horse soldiers come to rescue wagon train occupants, why are they referred to as the Calvary? Cavalry and Calvary are very different concepts. The local television sports anchor, Darryl Bruffet, took quite a beating recently from local viewers when he kept referring on air to the local semi-professional soccer team, the Brazos Valley Cavalry FC, as the Calvary. It still takes him a while to get the verbiage correct when reporting on the fortunes of the beloved Calvary. I assume Bruffet's Baptist upbringing and continuing church affiliation makes it difficult to handle this one adroitly.

Dour: This four letter word is always rhymed with sour but is correctly pronounced like your. But if you pronounce it correctly, you will almost always get a quizzical glance from your listener who is wondering why dour, pour, and sour can look so similar and be pronounced so differently. "Twould make one a bit dour, would it not?

Jaguar: This breed of cat closely resembles the leopard, is the third largest after the tiger and the lion, and is found in the Western Hemisphere. It is also the name of a high-dollar automobile which many people refer to as a "Jagwire" in lieu of the correct "Jagwahr" or the less preferred "Jag-you-ar."

Lackadaisical. This beauty is far too often pronounced as laxadaisical, due in great measure to the meaning of the word. But let's not get lax on this one.

Nauseated: This one is both misused and abused. Technically, if you are experiencing stress in the stomach, you are nauseated, but at least ninety percent of the people say they are nauseous. In the strictest sense of the word, when you say you are nauseous, it means you are making others sick. If you feel poorly (or perhaps dourly) you are, correctly speaking, nauseated. But I have given up on this one: Everyone chooses to use nauseous incorrectly, and I find the whole proposition to be positively nauseating!

Nuclear. A number of people, most particularly famous Texans like former President George W. Bush and presidential hopeful in both 2012 and 2016, Rick Perry, somehow have this in their vocabulary as "nucular." It really does not make them sound too smart, but neither has ever been thus accused.

Perusal: This puppy is not pronounced incorrectly very often but it may be one of the most abused entries in the dictionary. It is almost always invoked to denote a quick scan of a particular document or listing. Yet, according to *The American Heritage Dictionary*, to peruse is, "To read or examine with great care." Scan, yes. Peruse, no! They are not the same! It is my fond hope that the present readership is perusing this humble little document as opposed to scanning it. It is best perused!

Realtor: This nice little two syllable word almost universally ends up being pronounced as if it had three—"reel a ter" is the usual pronunciation, but it really ain't correct.

Wizened: Whiz, not wise, is the key wrinkle, if you will, necessary to get this one right. It is not a prominent offender only because so few people use the term.

A fast surface **perusal** of this folderol gives me a **laxadaisical** or sometimes **dour** perspective, makes me **nauseated**, and tempts me to go **nucular** on someone. All of this, in turn, gives me a **wizened** appearance. The whole thing makes me want to drive up in my **Jagwire** or call in the **Calvary** in hopes someone will put an **asterick** beside the word **reel a ter** while simultaneously retracting his or her **accredidation**. Yikes and God Save the Queen once again!

The Cell/Smart Phone: Can One Person's Drivel be Another Person's Spinach?

> Drivel (verb) 1. To slobber; drool. 2. To talk stupidly or childishly.
> Gibberish (noun) 1. Nonsensical, rapid talk.
> Palaver (noun) 1. Idle chatter.
> Prattle (verb) 1. To talk idly or meaninglessly; babble. 2. To utter in a childish way.

As I make my daily rounds about this colossus known as a university or the nearby provincial village, I sometimes feel I am drowning in a sea of people making cell/smart phone calls or sending/receiving text messages. And I often ask myself if there is any chance the vast preponderance of the verbiage dispensed in these exchanges is sheer gibberish? I think so, and the service providers count on it....the greater the volume of drivel, gibberish, palaver, and prattle, the greater the profit margins.

I am also convinced of a strong correlation between a rich mental life and the amount of time spent texting on a cell/smart phone, and the direction of that relationship does not speak well for the habitual user. A writer named Todd Holcomb has described cell/smart phones as the "world's longest umbilical cord." Someone else has called them the modern day "opiate of the masses."

In this connection, wise words from sages through the ages offer some interesting perspectives. The 19th Century Swiss philosopher and poet Henri Frederic Amiel once said, "The man who has no inner life is a slave to his surroundings." Another take on this line of thought is that of the Lebanese poet, Kahlil Gibran, mentioned elsewhere in this document: "You talk when you cease to be at peace with your thoughts; And when you can no longer dwell in the solitude of your heart, you live in your lips, and sound is a diversion and a pastime. And in much of your talking, thinking is half murdered. For thought is a bird in space that in a cage of words may indeed unfold its wings but cannot fly." Perhaps the Roman philosopher, statesman, and dramatist Seneca (4 BC-65 AD), who predated both Amiel and Gibran by almost two thousand years, captured the essence of my thoughts best: "Nothing, to my way of thinking, is a better proof of a well-ordered mind than a man's ability to stop just where he is and pass some time in his own company."

The three wise men of yore, Amiel, Gibran, and Seneca, were prescient in their musings and if around today would no doubt agree these cell/smart phone drones, these unwitting prisoners of techno-tyranny, are fearful of what they might find if they ever stowed the phone and delved into the barren landscape of their mental and emotional lives.

Our three philosophically-inclined sages would undoubtedly turn over in their graves if they had been privy to a cell/smart phone conversation I overheard recently. It seems that an A&M coed not of my acquaintance and yours truly were wending our way from the Academic Building to the Memorial Student Center, a leisurely five-minute stroll. At no point was my walking companion seemingly aware of my existence, chattering away to what I assume was a friend. Her entire conversational repertoire consisted of "No Way", "Get out of here", "Get out of town", and the exquisitely eloquent, "You don't mean it." There were times when six or eight consecutive "Get out of towns" were followed by a matched stream of "No way's." I finally concluded the poor woman had a dozen-word vocabulary and an incredibly stupid friend who is easily amused and possessed of an unlimited appreciation for drivel. Or is it palaver?

My recently deceased distinguished colleague and good friend, Jack Nation, always opined that these students walking around campus talking on cell/smart phones were actually social isolates or rejects, conversing with the phone company's time and temperature service to create the illusion they really did have friends. The ever-perspicacious Professor Nation may have been on to something.

Speaking of overhearing cell/smart phone conversations, I was working out at the now-defunct Aggieland Fitness Dome one afternoon a couple of years ago, abusing myself in the name of the holy grail of fitness by riding an instrument of torture known as an exercise bike. Once you get all geared up for a thirty-minute workout on one of those things, you do not want to have to get up in the middle and find a new one with which to flagellate yourself. Thus, I found myself stuck no more than five feet from a cell/smart phone addict on the adjacent stair-stepper machine who was regaling an obviously bullshit-tolerant friend with a half hour of pure, unadulterated, non-stop gibberish (folderol? palaver?). As I was finishing up the bike ride, my lovely wife, aka "she-who-must-be-obeyed", walked over and asked how it went. I said, "Fine, other than I had to listen to a fucking phone conversation the whole time." The coed with the cell/smart phone overheard my mildly muffled and consummately impolite response to Judy's query, and tears quickly formed in her eyes. She then offered an apology as follows: "You could have asked me not to talk so long. I did not know I was bothering you." To her *mea culpa*, I offered up a terse, to the point retort that went something along these lines: "Common courtesy and respect for others should have told you that no one wants to listen to someone else's cell/smart phone drivel (or is it prattle?) during a workout. You exercise to get away from those things. And I should not have to ask you to exercise good manners. That was the job of your parents."

Sometimes I despair for humanity when I see four university coeds eating at a restaurant and all are talking or texting to someone afar. The same is true when I see two of them walking across campus together, and both are talking or text messaging. Why not do something novel and give your friends and acquaintances a few minutes of undivided attention?

Can someone tell me why people talk so loud on their cell/smart phones, so much so that you can hear every word in the next county? Also, does it ever dawn on people who talk on cell/smart phones that the rest of us do not have the remotest interest in hearing their conversations? What is vitally intriguing to one individual is most likely another person's spinach!

Talking on the cell/smart phone has taken a serious back seat of late to something more insidious and odious, and it is called texting. Would someone please tell me why people text message while they are walking? And do these perps, almost always females, at least on our campus, know how utterly stupid they appear to others as they mindlessly text away? Is the message so important that it cannot wait until they sit down? And why can they not walk in a straight line while texting? I cannot tell you how many times I have had to alter my bicycle path to avoid being toppled by a mesmerized texter.

As an afterthought on this topic, several months ago, I followed a young coed across one of College Station's busiest streets, George Bush Drive, buried in a gaggle of other bicyclists making their way to campus for eight o'clock classes. When the street light gave us the "Go" sign, the coed whipped out her cell/not-so-smart-phone in this case from her back pocket, removed her hands from the handlebars, and texted away with both hands as she crossed George Bush in heavy 0800 traffic. Freud would have been pleased to know that Thanatos, Freud's death wish, was alive and well at Texas A&M that morning.

Speaking of text messaging, there is grave national concern about the problem of college graduates being underemployed or not able to find jobs at all. My solution is to send out a national, state, or local "Get Rid of Texters" task force, or maybe even a heavily armed SWAT team, to each college campus. Their mission would be to identify those students walking across campus texting and dispatch them (or at least dismiss them from the university on the spot). No, the more I think about it, dispatching them might not be a bad idea. These people are without a doubt the most dull and unimaginative subjects in the college student pool, and will end up unemployed or underemployed and living with their parents after graduation (assuming they do in fact graduate). At the very least, the dismissal of the texting riffraff could go a long way toward beautifying college campuses across America.

As a caveat to the present diatribe/rant and in an effort to be fair to cell phone drivelmeisters, I must acknowledge that a January 2006 segment from the all-news radio station WTOP in Washington, D. C., indicates that as dangerous as cell/smart phones are to driving safety, it may well be that farding while driving an automobile is a greater menace. For those of you not familiar with farding, the word comes to us from the French and refers to applying makeup. Thus, beautifying one's face while driving, or farding, constitutes a violation of the law in some places. However difficult it may be to process mentally and emotionally, farders may well be more dangerous than cell/smart phone users! I observed a serious lapse on the part of what I am sure is a serial farder just two days ago, and the woman had a small child unrestrained in the back seat. If farding in this case does not constitute reckless endangerment, I do not know what does!

Speaking of major, perhaps even unconscionable, violations of both the law and propriety, I was rummaging around some folders in my office recently when I came across an article that appeared in the crime section of the *Houston Chronicle* in April of 1991. It seems that Kyle Krebs, a first-year student at Baylor University in Waco, Texas, was ticketed by the campus police for the most heinous of criminal acts, breaking wind in violation of the university's ordinance prohibiting obnoxious odors. In defending himself against the charges, the villainous Krebs said he was not directing his sphincter emissions at the police. He added in his defense that he assumed the gendarmerie were far enough away they would neither hear nor smell his handiwork. Despite his protestations of innocence, the charge against Krebs was upheld by the presiding magistrate. I have often wondered if this transgression, this maiden run-in with the law, was the beginning of a life of crime for the obviously dangerous threat to society, Mr. Krebs who would now be in his mid- to late forties. And I have to ask: Would you want this man running loose on the streets of America, knowing he might serially offend? Given the recent reports of serial rape and utter disregard for such behavior under the "leadership" of Coach Art Briles at Baylor, it makes the offenses committed by Mr. Krebs look pretty tame.

Von Miller, a former football star at Texas A&M and presently an All-Pro linebacker for the NFL Seattle Seahawks, is trying to go one up on Krebs in the farting department. It seems that the multi-talented, multi-faceted, much-admired, filthy-rich Mr. Miller has been fined a number of times for on-the-field and off-the-field misbehaviors in the past several years, including a six-game suspension for violation of the league substance abuse policy, driving without a valid license, careless driving, no proof of insurance, failure to appear in court on the driving-related charges, speeding, and trying to buy a gun with an outstanding warrant for his arrest. His on-the-field problems, mainly penalties for late hits and unsportsmanlike conduct, by my humble estimate have probably cost him between $50,000 and $100,000 in past years.

His latest team-related violations were heralded all over the Internet on June 6, 2015, thus adding a new dimension to the misbehavior portfolio of our Aggie superstar. His off-the-field transgressions make the on-field acts look pretty tame. For example, recent media headlines read: "Von Miller reveals Broncos fine him for passing gas during meetings", "Broncos players have a fart tax and Miller is the fartiest...", "Von Miller says Broncos have a fart tax and he thinks he's been fined the most." And who says Texas A&M doesn't turn out leaders!

All of which brings us full circle to the interface of football and the cell/smart phone. One of my associates had a late adolescent daughter who regarded the passing of gas to be one of the most vile, objectionable, and unforgiveable of all human behaviors, a sentiment apparently shared by virtually no man and almost all women. To get inside his sister's head, the villainous, obviously unfeeling sibling would dial her up from time to time on his cell/smart phone and pass copious amounts of gas in the microphone as long and loudly as he could. My question: Does farting in a cell/smart phone also qualify as drivel?

Who Is It?

I do not know who to credit for this charming little ditty, but it is worth noting:

If you can start the day without caffeine,
If you can always be cheerful, ignoring aches and pains,
If you can resist complaining and telling people your troubles,

> If you can eat the same food every day and be grateful for it,
> If you can understand when your loved ones are too busy to give you any time,
> If you can take criticism and blame without resentment,
> If you can ignore a friend's limited education and never correct her or him,
> If you can resist treating a rich friend better than a poor friend,
> If you can conquer tension without medical help,
> If you can relax without liquor,
> If you can sleep without the aid of drugs,
> ….Then you are probably the family dog!!

There Oughta' be a Special Place

It dawned on me lately as I sat through a couple of funerals that the concepts of heaven and hell may not be as abstract as I once thought. I have not quite figured out what heaven is but I am now dead certain that hell is either (1) being forced to listen to rap music for the rest of eternity or (2) being forced to sit through an Episcopalian Church funeral service for perpetuity. I would not wish such fates on anyone, though exceptions should be made in cases of the person or persons who:

(1) First thought of bringing an air horn to athletic events or graduation ceremonies;
(2) Came up with the idea for television sitcom laugh tracks;
(3) Convinced women they look charming wearing cowboy boots with dresses or shorts;
(4) Created the labyrinthine phone systems that make it impossible to talk to a human being while making business calls;
(5) Decided that waving flags, towels, or streamers at athletic events was a good way to show team spirit. All those objects do is get in the way, plus I always have the sickening feeling I am getting ready to lose an eye to some out-of-control, beered-up sports fan caught up in the heat of the moment;
(6) Thought that brewing or mixing beer with lemonade, orange, or raspberry flavoring was a good idea;
(7) Decided that champagne was actually drinkable. I get no kick out of champagne… it is bilge water with a persuasive press agent;
(8) Came up the idea of half time interviewers at football and basketball games. These reporters, almost always women, ask stupid, predictable questions of players and coaches who respond with a litany of even more predictable clichés, and then only because it is required by their universities or conferences;
(9) Invented jet skis;
(10) Decided that killing animals should be promoted as a television sport. Listening to these breathless, sweaty, testosterone-driven, blood-thirsty types recall gory detail after gory detail of their kills makes me wretch. And to think that we have a television channel that devotes a lot of airspace to men (and some women) stalking and killing innocent animals. Hell might not be good enough for the creators of that television "entertainment". But,

then, it would not survive if there were not people to watch it. Steve Ruggeri, a former hunter turned animal activist, sums up my feelings nicely: "When we have exposed the specious reasoning of the hunters' apologists and stripped their sport of its counterfeit legitimacy, the naked brutality of hunting defines itself: Killing for the fun of it."

(11) Do not flush the urinals or toilets when they are finished with their chores. The same can be said for those who throw their gum, Kleenex, or paper towels in the men's urinals;

(12) Came up with the sentence-ending "blah, blah, blah…." or "yada, yada, yada" to summarize a series of things, events, or people;

(13) Invented the "puppy mill", those egregious, for-profit operations that in most cases torture dogs in the name of the almighty dollar. Most of the "puppy mills" are family-owned and are used to supplement family income from other sources, but that fact in no way excuses their presence. Estimates are that there are at least 4,000 of them and they produce half a million puppies per year, thus flooding the markets and forcing legitimate animal shelters to maintain unfortunately high euthanasia rates. Ditto someone who purchases a dog from a pet store. Almost without fail, those dogs are from "puppy mills" and the buyer often gets an unhealthy dog, and one that is not pure-bred as advertised. If someone is ignorant of the situation, that is one thing and a partial excuse can be made in those cases. On the other hand, if the buyer knows about "puppy mills" and still shops in puppy stores, maybe there should be an even harsher penalty. I would suggest being forced to watch episodes of *Cheaters* for two months;

(14) Came up with the hokey gimmick so popular with Madison Avenue advertising executives and the funniest home video crowd suggesting there is something hilarious or amusing about watching a male taking a shot to the testicles. That notion is abhorrent to me, and I hope those who think this is funny get locked up in a room and forced to listen to old Whitney Houston songs for eternity.

You Ain't Just A' Whistling Dixie

Have you ever heard someone whistle who was truly good at it? Whistling is one of the most fascinating of human endeavors because almost no one has any talent for it. Intelligence seems to be distributed fairly evenly along the spectrum, with some people very bright and some not so smart. Athletic ability appears to also lie along the normal curve, with some people gifted with speed and agility and others incapable of walking and chewing gum at the same time. But the ability to whistle defies the properties of the normal curve; virtually no one can do it.

Whistlers of all varieties and levels of talent seem to really believe the cacophonous noise emanating from their lips is in some way related to the symphonic sounds they are hearing in their heads. The harmonious internal dialogue and the cacophonous external representation thereof have almost nothing to do with each other. What may sound to you like a gaggle of honking geese seeking sanctuary from the Canadian cold is in the mind of a whistler a Mendelsohn concerto, or at the very minimum, *Annie's Song*, a la Placido Domingo.

One cannot help but be impressed with the enthusiasm of the typical whistler, though, just chirping away like a songbird in heat. Like Diogenes in search of the honest man, I am still seeking a whistler who can turn out something other than the run-of-the-mill, pedestrian, polyglot of loosely connected, cacophonous, largely unrelated notes.

If you think about it, women seldom whistle. I think they are blessed with an internal sensor that tells them whistling is a losing battle and not worth the effort. Once again we see evidence in support of my wife's assertion that women are more civilized than men.

Speaking of saving civilization, I think it is time we elected a woman to the Presidency of this great but struggling country. If you look at the mess George W. Bush and Donald J. Trump, both males, have made of national and world affairs, could a woman do any worse? And maybe a woman President would keep us out of stupid, wasteful, morally unjustifiable wars. Women often become mothers, and mothers sometimes ascend to positions of political power such as the presidency, and mothers do not like to see their male children killed. Thus, we need to put a woman in the Oval Office.

Academia at Its Boring Best

I once sat through a long thesis defense in 1981 for a graduate student whose study was entitled "The Effects of Item Difficulty on the Behavioral Assessment of Heterosocial Initiation Skill". During his nearly two-hour presentation, the student uncorked 434 incredibly distracting "Uh's". Those verbal gaffes were a source of some consternation but, upon sober reflection, they turned out to be the most interesting parts of the presentation!

Hot Item on My Personal Bucket List

Ever since the movie, "Bucket List" came out a few years ago, I have been compiling my own agenda for the future. In that connection, not too long ago I was watching a family of five dining at Mi Cocina, a Mexican restaurant, on Wellborn Road in College Station. All family members were seated save the mother, who came in maybe ten minutes later than the others. She was in her thirties, fit and athletic looking, wearing a baseball cap, short-sleeved shirt with a neckline that barely contained what I assumed were ample breasts, and sporting tight, black leotard-like pants suggestive of a toned figure. A workout addict maybe?

While one of her children, perhaps age five, no doubt a diagnosed ADHD kid, tried to destroy the menu by repeatedly stabbing it with his fork a la Jack the Ripper, another male child maybe age three, whined incessantly about anything and everything he could find worth pissing and moaning about. The mother proceeded to give her husband what appeared from a distance to be an animated, major league ass-chewing, all the while shooting him the evil eye and pointing a menacing finger in his face. She then snatched the fork from the hands of "El Destructo", grabbed the whiny little shit by the shoulder, and squeezed both of them with vise-grip force in hopes of quelling the noise and stopping the destruction. Then, in a moment of obvious weakness, she said something pleasant to her daughter who appeared to be seven or eight years of age.

All the tongue-lashing and child bashing was done while engaging in non-stop texting for at least the first fifteen minutes after she sat down at the table. I had a couple of thoughts about the situation. The first thing that came to mind was this woman may well be in that six percent of adults over age twenty-five in one survey who agreed it would be okay to give or receive text messages during sexual activity. My second thought, perhaps harsher in spirit, was, "Hey lady. Put the goddam cell phone away, be nice to your husband, and engage in some positive interactions with the boys, thus depriving them of their destructive or whiny tendencies." But the texting would then lose its pre-eminence in her life, and if one cannot text, what else is there? Palaver, maybe? Or could it be gibberish?

But let's get back to my bucket list item. Though most of my enmity was directed toward the mother, observations of the children reinforced my desire to place an item on my present bucket list, or at the very least, as a part of one in my next life. My bucket list or next-life goal is to own a restaurant in which everyone under the age of sixteen or perhaps even eighteen is expressly forbidden to enter. There will be a sign at the door that reads: "If you are under sixteen (eighteen?) and take one more step, you will be shot on sight and fed to the Dobermans out back who we have been poking with sticks and starving for a week."

My wish is borne of an overpowering obligation to humanity; I owe something back for all the good things that have happened in my life. Thus, I want to provide an opportunity for my clients to have sixty to ninety minutes of reprieve from children while dining at a fine restaurant. Children whine, mingle snot with their food, tear up the menus, run loose like little hellions once they are through with their chips or Big Reds, and if nothing else, ruin a potentially good meal by nothing more than their mere presence. Even if they are behaving reasonably well, just having to look at them is enough to ruin a meal. To make sure that everyone fully understands the zeitgeist of my futuristic restaurant, the marquis will feature larger than life neon letters that read: "Arnie's Sports Bar and Grill: Children Under the Age of 16 (18?) Never, Ever, Ever, Ever, Ever, Ever, Ever Allowed." Of late, I have gotten really grandiose in my ruminations and am thinking about building an entire mall where people can shop minus children under eighteen. And while I am at it, maybe I could start a movement to ban cell phones in the restaurants and bedrooms of America, too!

There would be another idiosyncrasy the patrons would have to indulge or they would be banned permanently from the premises, regardless of age. And you are asking yourself: What strange idiosyncrasy could he possibly be foisting on his clientele? It is this: All waitpersons would be free to reject tips they thought were an insult. I am not talking here of someone who might be chintzy enough to leave a dollar or two on a thirty dollar meal. In extreme cases where inconsiderate assholes leave only pocket change for a tip at a six-top (in waitperson lingo, a table for six), the servers would be instructed to throw the pennies, nickels, and dimes at their feet with exaggerated gusto as the "customer" vacates the premises, I am sure for the final time. There should be a witch doctor whose only duty in life is to put hoodoo's on bad tippers. Or maybe "haints' in their homes!

Favorite Sayings

"I try to never go outside when the temperature is below seventy."

R. C. Slocum, Texas A&M football coach

"Never kick a cow chip on a hot day."

Will Rogers, Satirist and Humorist

"Be master of your petty annoyances and conserve your energies for the big, worthwhile things. It isn't the mountain ahead that wears you out – it's the grain of sand in your shoe."

Robert Service, Writer

"The trouble with the world is that the stupid are cocksure and the intelligent are full of doubt."

Bertrand Russell, Writer and Philosopher

"The man who claims to be the boss in his own home will lie about other things as well."

Amish saying

"People demand freedom of speech as a compensation for the freedom of thought which they seldom use."

Soren Kierkegaard, Philosopher

"Familiarity is a magician that is cruel to beauty but kind to ugliness."

Ouida aka Marie Louse de la Ramee

"Always do right. This will gratify some people and astonish the rest."

Anonymous

"The man who is a pessimist before forty-eight knows too much; if he is an optimist after it, he knows too little."

Mark Twain, Humorist

"If you are going to have a sexual relationship with an animal, make it a horse. That way, if things don't work out, at least you'll have a ride home."

Singer Willie Nelson advising fellow singer, author, politician, and resident curmudgeon Kinky Friedman

"Tell me what company thou keepst, and I'll tell thee what thou art."

Miguel de Cervantes, Spanish novelist

"It has been my experience that folks who have no vices have very few virtues."

Abraham Lincoln, American President

"Football: A sport that bears the same relation to education that bullfighting does to agriculture."

Norman Chad, Sports Columnist and Humorist

"They came for the communists, and I did not speak up because I wasn't a communist;
They came for the socialists, and I did not speak up because I wasn't a socialist;
They came for the union leaders, and I did not speak up because I wasn't a union leader;
They came for the Jews, and I didn't speak up because I wasn't a Jew.
Then they came for me, and there was no one left to speak for me."

Martin Niemoller, Theologian and Philosopher

"A hand in the bush is worth any number of birds."

Unknown

"May the wind at your back be other than your own."

Unknown

"A hard man is good to find."

Graffiti, Duddley's Draw, College Station (TX)

"If it has tits or tires, it will eventually cause you trouble."

Resident Bathroom Philosopher, Dixie Chicken, College Station (TX)

"Sex: Something that begins at adolescence and ends as marriage."

Unknown

"Sex: The most fun you can have without smiling."

Unknown

Sentimental Journey Home I (1965-2018)

"I find each day too short for all the thoughts I want to think,
all the walks I want to take, all the books I want to read,
and all the friends I want to see."

John Burrough

"Some days you're the dog, some days you are the hydrant"

Anonymous

And finally, I would like to add my favorite quotes about or applicable to our forty-third President and, as noted repeatedly in these pages, my least favorite Texan, Mr. George W. Bush:
"A moment I've been dreading. George (Bush Sr.) brought his ne'er-do-well son around this morning and asked me to find the kid a job. Not the political one who lives in Florida. The one who hangs around here all the time looking shiftless. This so-called kid is already almost 40 and has never had a real job. Maybe I'll call Kinsley over at the *New Republic* and see if they'll hire him as a contributing editor or something. That looks like easy work."

President Ronald Reagan, 1986

This quote is among the more widely circulated of the various ones concerning George W. Bush. Alas, it turns out to be apocryphal. A perusal (as opposed to a scan) of President Reagan's autobiography reveals no such quote; it apparently never happened. The sad thing is that the quote captures the essence of "The Shrub" so aptly. One can only wish it were true!

"If ignorance ever gets to $40 a barrel, I want drilling rights on that man's head."

Texas political activist Jim Hightower

"How can 59,054,087 [American] people be so DUMB?"

***London Daily Mirror* front page headline the day after George W. Bush was re-elected President in 2004**

"I keep thinking we should include something in the Constitution in case
the people elect a fucking moron."

Anonymous cartoon published during The Shrub's reign depicting meeting of framers of the Constitution

"It seems like the less a statesman amounts to the more he adores the flag."

Kin Hubbard, Humorist

> "The whole aim of practical politics is to keep the populace alarmed (and hence clamorous to be led to safety) by menacing it with an endless series of hobgoblins, all of them imaginary."
>
> **H. L. Mencken, Satirist, Journalist, Essayist, "The Sage of Baltimore**

OK, OK, OK, Oooooooooooooooookay

For many years, A&M has sponsored brainwashing sessions for incoming freshmen euphemistically known as Fish Camps, and they are held at a retreat in Palestine, 120 miles northeast of College Station. As noted elsewhere, freshmen are called "Fish" at A&M, hence the term Fish Camp. These get-togethers are held annually in July and August to instill Aggie spirit and school pride among the new freshmen, or to put it more honestly, brainwash the next generation of Aggies. It is customary to name each camp after an A&M professor or staff member or former student who excels, at least in the eyes of students, in student relations and I was the namesake for the festivities in 1995 and 2005. As noted elsewhere, my wife, Judy, has received that honor for summer, 2018.

During one of the rah-rah sessions in Palestine, a fellow with some stature in the student leadership hierarchy was holding forth about what it takes to be a good Aggie. He was regaling a group of maybe a hundred new fish and a gaggle of more experienced camp counselors with tales of school spirit, and I noticed he ended many of his sentences with "Okay?" which I assumed was simply a nervous habit, and a really annoying one at that. Every time he said "Okay?", which was often, the older students in the group would follow up his "Okay" with a string of their own that went something like this: "Okay, Okay, Okay, Okay" in an ever-increasing crescendo, followed eventually by a long, drawn out "OOOOOOOOOOOOO-KAY" that seemed to last for at least fifteen seconds or more each time. The speaker remained unfazed, seemingly unaware his audience was making fun of him. Such, I guess, is life at Fish Camp.

"Daddy, Your Students Are Pigs"

When Lyndon, my twenty-nine-year old was six or seven, he would occasionally accompany me to my office while Judy took a well-earned break from the myriad manifestations of motherhood. He watched me pound away on my computer one morning and, after an hour of hit-or-miss observation, announced he did not want to be a college professor when he grew up since their work is so boring. He told me: "Daddy, all you do is stare at a computer screen all day." Out of the mouth of babes…

But an even more astute observation occurred in the midst of a trip to the restroom near my office. Lyndon sagely opined: "Daddy, your students are pigs." I asked, "Why do you say that, son?" His response was, "Because they never flush the toilets." Obviously, he had listened to his mother when she lectured him about proper toilet flushing behavior.

It is always a hoot to stop by the office over the weekend when Friday's left-over urine has had time to ferment. By Monday, the accumulated stagnation is enough to gag an anosmic maggot!

This pearl from Lyndon and subsequent observation on my own have led me to amend the Aggie honor code statement: "Aggies do not lie, cheat or steal, nor tolerate those who do." There is absolutely no question that Aggies do not commit the misdeeds mentioned in the honor statement, because the code says so, but the code needs amending since it stops short of being totally accurate; it should more accurately read, "Aggies do not lie, cheat, steal, or flush toilets, nor tolerate those who do." This is at least true for the males on campus and one can only hope that the females are more attuned to social niceties. It would be disconcerting to find out that we also have female pigs in the student body! Perhaps the university is where females start honing their civilizing influence over males, though they have had no impact on toilet-flushing behavior thus far.

Karen Pays the Price

Karen Price was a student in my Abnormal Psychology class in the fall semester of 1974, and her story is unusual, intriguing, and possibly inspiring to some. When I met Karen, she was nearer my age of thirty-six than she was to her undergraduate peers in the class. She was also one of the fairly numerous older locals coming back to school after a hiatus to work and raise a family, the norm for quite a few women in those days. Though I was unaware of it for quite some time, my course represented Karen's very first college experience, and she was able to eke out a solid B after a somewhat rocky start on exams one and two.

It turns out that Karen's enrollment in my course was the beginning of one of the most interesting approaches to getting a college degree I have witnessed in all my years of waxing pedantic from the podium. Karen worked full-time in the Office of the Registrar but arranged to take one course each semester for the next twenty years. She would take a fall course some years, a spring offering in others, and occasionally enroll in summer school. The net effect was that she got her degree at the rate of six hours per year for twenty-plus years, eventually accumulating the 128 hours required at that time (now 120) for a bachelor's degree in Psychology.

As a small token of my appreciation for her diligence, when she finally graduated in 1994, I xeroxed that portion of my grade book pertaining to her test scores and sent it along as a memento. Karen subsequently earned a master's degree in Educational Administration and continued working as Assistant Registrar in the Office of Admissions and Records until her recent retirement. Again, because of its uniqueness and inspirational qualities, recounting Karen Price's graduation story is one of my all-time favorites.

Descendants, Diogenes, and David's Ditzes

My sons, Chay (12/22/1966) and Lyndon (01/24/1989), were born twenty-three years apart, but share at least one common life experience. I overheard them talking years ago about their father's enjoyment of the now-deceased comedian Johnny Carson and the recently retired heir-apparent to the late night comedy throne, David Letterman. Chay told his younger brother that he often had trouble sleeping as a young boy because I would laugh so loud at Carson's zany antics, aided and abetted by his affable sidekick, Ed McMahon. Lyndon agreed that he had often had the same problem because of my enjoyment of the often outrageous David Letterman. Those two comedians have brought so much joy to my life, as have past Carson and Letterman guests Jonathan Winters and Robin Williams, among others. Now that Johnny is dead and David retired, the only other late night humorist who was even remotely funny was Jay Leno, the winner in the internecine NBC fiasco of 2010 involving the least funny comedian of them all, Conan O'Brien. Unfortunately, Leno is out again, replaced by the not even remotely amusing Jimmy Fallon. Perhaps Leno has nine lives and will use one of them to find a late night niche once again.

LEUNES BOYS, L TO R, LYNDON, ARNOLD, CHAY, 2011

I fear for late night humor, what with the likes of Craig Ferguson, Jimmy Kimmel, Jimmy Fallon, and Conan O'Brien, especially the latter. I have yet to muster up a smile or even a random chuckle at anything Conan O'Brien has said or done. I am reminded of that old iconic song, *Bye Bye, American Pie*, and the line about the day the laughter died. When Conan O'Brien hits the screen, laughter dies, and, oh, so painfully! No wonder the guy got canceled from *The Tonight Show* after only seven months. He cast the blame on Leno and NBC, but perhaps Conan ought to drum up something funny to say. Ditto Jimmy Fallon. Stephen Colbert took over the Late Show reins in

September of 2015 and it will be interesting to see if he can pump some life into late night television over the long haul. The early promos were silly and adolescent and afforded little hope that Colbert is the answer.

My wife put in her two cents worth on Chay's and Lyndon's discussion, writing down my top nine greatest flaws or worst habits, if you will. Included were the following: (1) Cussing barking dogs (I actually cuss all dogs, barking or not); (2) Terrorizing cats (I only did this once and almost lost an arm to four sets of claws); (3) Reading in the bathroom (a truly bad habit that I long ago kicked by getting in and getting out as recommended by my physician); (4) Washing clothes at all hours of the day and night (I only wash when she is out of the house now); (5) Bleached blondes (never could tell the difference between the real ones and the contrived variety); (6) Coaching our daughter (no more daughters to coach, praise Allah); (7) Clearing my throat (till my dying day bad habit #1); (8) Spitting on the pavement and stepping on it (my part in keeping the environment spic and span); and (9) Laughing loudly starting at 10:30 every night. For me, the laughter died when Letterman retired. I truly despair when I think of Conan O'Brien and assorted other pretenders as my late night laughter options.

As you have noted by now, I have a hard time omitting Diogenes from my dialogue. The poor bloke spent a lot of time looking for that eternally elusive honest man, and I am on a similar quest to find a female guest appearing on late night talk shows who is (1) interesting and/or (2) smart. Predictably, the female guests enter from off-stage dressed in the latest stylish short, tight skirt, and a blouse or sweater with a mandatory plunging neckline designed to show as much cleavage as propriety (or the censors) allows. Each ingénue sits down, crosses her often long and most of the time lovely legs, is told by the host how beautiful she is, handles (mishandles?) a few perfunctory questions about their young children, and then the ennui begins in earnest. If they are young, they have nothing of interest to talk about unless you think they themselves are interesting, which is damned rare. If they are a bit older, they can talk about their children, at which point I turn off my hearing aids (not really; just a figure of speech). There is a never-ending pool of these neuronally-challenged ingénues from which to draw but one wonders: Why? Why are they there? Who listens to them? Who gives a rat's ass what they think, if they think? And, to be honest, the male guests are really not much better. It sort of makes you wonder about the intelligence of thespians and musicians. But if one wants to really wonder about intelligence, listen to most young rock musicians talk about their craft. Mumbo-jumbo, fuzzy stuff, word salad, loose musings, rambling ruminations; literally palaver at its best!

A Coed Kicks the Book Habit

I accidentally fell in behind a young coed a few years ago, walking from the Academic Building to the far reaches of the parking lot near Kyle Field, an easy ten-minute trek. Semester final exams were coming to an end, and things apparently had not gone too well for our lovely protagonist. She was too preoccupied with abusing an increasingly battered textbook to notice me, deploying her right foot as a weapon of mass destruction. There was a rhythm and symmetry to it all, watching her kick the beaten and bedraggled book while mixing in a fusillade of vehement, heartfelt GD-bombs, F-bombs, MF-bombs, S-bombs, BS-bombs, and SOB-bombs aimed in its direction and, perhaps by proxy, at the professor who adopted it for the class. The barrage of kicks and utterance of expletives continued until we parted ways south of the football field. By then, the book had seen its better days. Since I had never seen the young lady before, I am assuming her rancor was not directed at my textbook or, by proxy, me. Thank the Lord for small favors!

One theory of aggression suggests that the venting of anger and aggression is cathartic, releasing and thus diminishing anger, aggression, and pent-up emotion, so I am guessing that this venting process eventually led to some state of cathartic release for her. Let's hope so, anyway. It is scary to think about what would happen if she were mad at a person instead of a poor, unsuspecting textbook that cannot defend itself!

Things I Forgot to Tell Rosario

In the mid-1990's, I was blessed by getting to know a young woman of South American heritage who hailed from the Rio Grande Valley in south Texas. Her name was Rosario Grajales, a classic Latina in looks and temperament....dark eyes, hair, and complexion, and uninhibited in a likeable, pleasant, extroverted way. She took my course in Abnormal Psychology and, later, an Independent Studies course in which she and I, along with my colleague, Tony Bourgeois, devised a study of college student perceptions of incarcerated juvenile delinquents.

Our methodology involved administering a pre-test attitude survey to students in my Abnormal Psychology class concerning three aspects of juvenile delinquency, juvenile delinquents themselves, juvenile delinquent residential treatment centers, and caretakers of juvenile delinquents. Later in the semester, four students from the nearby juvenile treatment facility in Giddings, Texas, came to class to talk about their backgrounds, lives of crime, the treatment they were receiving, their aspirations for the future, and anything else they wanted to throw out for later discussion. Shortly after their visit, I took the students on a tour and picnic of the Giddings facility. Once the students experienced the tour and the picnic, an attitude posttest measure was administered.

The preceding exposures essentially created four treatment conditions:

(1) Lecture on juvenile delinquency only;
(2) Lecture and classroom visit but no tour and picnic;
(3) Lecture and tour and picnic but no classroom visit;
(4) Lecture, classroom visit, tour and picnic.

Briefly summarizing our results, we found that students who experienced all four conditions had more favorable initial attitudes on all concepts. We also determined that the more conditions the students were exposed to, the more favorable were their attitudes about all three posttest concepts. The least favorable attitudes were held by those who attended only the class lecture on delinquency but did not take part in the other three exposures.

Because of our multiple associations, I got to know Rosario pretty well. She was a big help with the study and did her share to make it successful, and our results were eventually published in 1996 in the *Journal of Social Psychology*. Shortly after we finished the study, Rosario graduated, got married, and moved on to a job in Dallas. About eighteen months later, I received a phone call, and the conversation went something like this once we got past the usual pleasantries: "Arnold (with a lot of Latin tongue rolling emphasis on ar NOLD), you were my advisor and trusted mentor and friend throughout my undergraduate career. You were my professor. We talked a lot about school and life, love and marriage, childrearing, and careers. We worked on a research project together, you were truly my mentor. I trusted you in all things. You talked a lot about the real world I was getting ready to enter, and I believed all of the Pollyanna-ish predictions you made. You misled me over and over. Your truly lied to me." She then hesitated for ten or fifteen seconds to gain the desire effect before offering up the following: "You never told me that real world was shit!"

I had not heard from Rosario for nearly fifteen years until she sent me an email in late January, 2010. She was living in Chicago, had two boys in middle school, and was looking for something to occupy her time after years of being unemployed by choice. She had no earthly idea where this decision (indecision?) would lead, but I know it worked out for her. And it sure was great to hear from her. We laughed about the nearly two decades old "real world" conversation, and she admitted that her pessimistic utterances early on had softened over the years, and that life really was pretty doggone good. We also reminisced about the juvenile delinquency study, and generally had a nice time getting reacquainted. Having students such as Rosario get in touch after fifteen years is one of the perks associated with being a college professor. And as an added extra, when I returned to my office following the 2017 summer fiasco in Germany with pneumonia, I found two notes and a telephone number from none other than Rosario. I shall call soon and see what's going on with her.

Do Big-Time College Coaches Have Wives?

Do big-time sports coaches have wives? The reason I ask is, as stated several times elsewhere, my wife is certain that for the majority of men, the only reason they are remotely civilized is because they are married and thus acculturated on a daily basis by their wives. Over the years, I have seen some validity in her assumptions through single friends. The longer they have been single, the more idiosyncratic and socially unacceptable their behavior becomes.

Big time coaches manifest behaviors in public that suggest they have no wives to monitor their conduct. I am convinced beyond a shadow of a doubt that Bo Pelini, the football coach who was canned a few years ago at Nebraska cannot possibly have a wife. If he did, I know she would tell him to can the chewing gum. Pelini chewed gum at a Guinness Book of World Records pace unparalleled in my experience, and I found it most distracting. I know if Bo Pelini really had a wife, she would not allow him to chomp on gum on the sidelines. Pelini was also demonstrative in other ways, and his sideline antics got him in trouble during the 2012 season when he was captured on television engaged in a heated argument with one of his players. In response to this event, the apologetic Chancellor of the university offered up the following: "He [Pelini] has noticeably controlled his sideline behavior this year." One could easily ask, "What about the other years?" There must have been events that took place during earlier seasons that led the Chancellor to make his remarks. However, we all know in college and professional football, winning trumps character, and Pelini's Nebraska teams won quite a bit more than they lost early in his tenure in Lincoln. Pelini was eventually terminated when the losses started to approximate the number of wins. His sideline antics suddenly were no longer amusing and cute.

What about the case of Oklahoma's recently retired and highly successful football coach, Bob Stoops? Stoops was a great coach, one of the all-time best, but I am positive he would have behaved very differently during OU games if he had a wife. If there had been a Mrs. Stoops, the non-stop excoriation and expletive-filled lapidation of officials for four hours every Saturday during football season would have diminished or stopped altogether. Surely she could have put a stop to his chiding and cursing, ranting and raving, and bitching and berating of those poor officials. I know no self-respecting wife would let her husband behave in public like Stoops did. The cynical side of me says that almost any behavior is probably tolerated if one's husband makes five million bucks a year. One can learn to bite one's tongue and look the other way under those conditions.

I know what you are thinking about now. You're thinking to yourself…How about the legendary college basketball coach, Bobby Knight, that fiery, throat-grabbing, chair-throwing master of the sideline tantrum? Did he have a wife in his heyday? I can only answer this query by falling back on the wisdom of the Couch Slouch, Norman Chad, who always ends his syndicated, satiric, and almost always humorous sports column with the off-hand, "Pay the man, Shirley."

Beer, Beer for Old Dewey High

I absolutely adore the taste of beer, but have abandoned my mantra of past years which said the darker the better. I have to lighten up on the dark stuff, such as one-time favorite Guinness Stout, and I now only drink Shiner Bock, a beer brewed in the small town of Shiner, Texas, and an occasional 1554 from Fort Collins, Colorado when I can find it. For most of my life, I drank Budweiser Light which is pretty much the equivalent of drinking lightly tinted water with a trace of alcohol thrown in for good measure. This near-beer diet allowed me to consume six to twelve beers cans or bottles daily almost without exception commencing for the most part at age twenty-eight and continuing through the present, or fifty-two years. If you take the midpoint of the two daily consumption figures, that averages out to roughly nine beers per day, or just under 150,000 beers since my twenty-eighth year. Since there are twelve ounces in each beer and you multiply that by an average of nine per day, you come up with a total daily consumption figure of 108 ounces of essentially what amounts to water. Full calorie beers such as Shiner Bock and Guinness Stout are more difficult to consume in large amounts, and my consumption has dropped off quite a bit over the past five years or so. Also, my beer consumption while in Germany for the past sixteen summers has always gone down because those delightful beers, of which there are many, have little in common with their watery cousins in the US. Lest the reader think I am pickling my assorted internal organs and systems, I am pleased to report that my liver functioning at every checkup is superb, sugar readings normal, and other relevant signs reasonably positive.

Speaking of watery beer, a sport psychology colleague from Johann Wolfgang Goethe University in Frankfurt, after a nice professional lecture to my Study Abroad students a couple of summers ago, asked if any of them knew what Germans think of American beer. None of my minions were sure how to respond to his query, so he offered the following wisdom for their consumption: "Germans think American beer is like making love in a canoe." After a brief hesitation to let the thought sink in, he said: "You know, fucking close to water!" You could have heard a pin drop among the shocked students, but their easily-amused professor almost spit out his false teeth (Not really. The few I have are still mine) because he was laughing so hard.

One of the signs of alcohol abuse or out-and-out alcoholism is missing work and dysfunctional family relations. In that regard, I must confess to missing only one day of work in all my years in the Army or at A&M due to overconsumption of alcohol, and that was forty years ago. That absence in question was actually partial rather than total, and came following a night of softball and beer drinking at Duddley's Draw with Denny Seal, Vicki Vise, Sarah Murphy, Elda Perez, Wayne Nelius (I think), Tony Bourgeois, and a few other friends. When Duddley's closed, Denny suggested we continue the party at his house south of the university on Dexter Street in College Station. It turned out that Denny's landlord and next-door neighbor, Dr. David Woodcock, a Brit and Professor of Architecture, just happened to have an inviting swimming pool and conveniently was out of town on a family vacation. After briefly deliberating about the pros and cons of appropriating Dr. Woodcock's pool, we jumped over the fence and dove into the inviting water. We also brought along several bottles of wine and a cooler or two of beer and proceeded to party until the wee, wee, wee hours of the morning. The excessive alcohol intake and the keeping of late hours took its predictable toll, leaving me strung out, hung over, and manifestly miserable when I woke up the next morning. I struggled out of bed, cleaned up, got dressed, and made my way to school for my ten o'clock class. Ten minutes in, I knew it was not going to work! I let the class go and went home to hopefully recover. I can honestly say that was the only day I ever missed work due to abuse of alcohol. None is better than one, of course, but it could have been a lot worse, given my one-time fascination with both beer and late hours.

International Coffee Wars

Anna Kriebel, a native Costa Rican, was my Teaching Assistant in 1982 and we have kept up with each other fairly closely over the years. Anna completed her master's degree at A&M in the mid-1980's and shortly thereafter initiated a tradition of periodically replenishing my office coffee supply with some outstanding varieties from her home country. Over the past three decades she has sent coffee through an intermediary on several occasions, and in those rare instances in which she was in Texas or College Station, she would bring the gift in person. She often used her son, Andres, as the conduit for most of the coffee, though that stopped when he completed his degree in Chemical Engineering in 2010. Anna was in College Station earlier that same year, on March 2 to be exact, and came by my office for a brief visit where she presented me with a pound of Dota, a blend from the Tarrazu' region of Costa Rica famous for its coffee plantations.

It is an interesting aside to talk about how Andres found a job in the US after graduation. His initial job hunting produced nary an offer so he decided to go home for a while and contemplate his next move (or his navel). While awaiting his flight to Costa Rica from George Bush International in Houston, Andres struck up a casual conversation with a fellow traveler who just happened to be the owner of an engineering firm. It turns out that the soon-to-be-boss was in the market for a young, newly-minted chemical engineer and Andres got the offer on the spot! Talk about serendipity! Andres cancelled his flight, found a place to live in Houston, and began his new job the following Monday. It would be nice to say that the employer was an Aggie hiring an Aggie, thus substantiating the good old boy (girl?) network, but I honestly do not remember if the boss man was an A&M graduate or not.

But let us get back to the topic at hand, coffee. I once mentioned in one of my classes how much I have enjoyed my association with Anna and her generosity when it came to Costa Rican coffee. This comment got Jessica Frantzen, an undergraduate from Bolivia, to thinking. Jessica offered that Bolivian coffee was better than the various blends from Costa Rica, so she brought me a couple of pounds from her country. Later on, I mentioned this struggle between conflicting coffee ideologies to our departmental undergraduate advisor at the time, Zuleika Carrasco-Martinez, and she decided to weigh in to the competition by bringing me a pound of coffee from her native Puerto Rico. To top things off in the coffee wars, I had a young Ecuadoran in class in the fall of 2011 named Nicole Espinoza-Zerlanga who attended A&M for only that one semester, at which time she returned to Ecuador's capitol, Quito, to complete her degree in Clinical Psychology. We were visiting one day outside of class and with malice aforethought, I planted the idea in her head suggesting that maybe the Ecuadorans produce even better coffee than the Costa Ricans, Bolivians, and Puerto Ricans. Nicole promised that I would be receiving some Ecuadoran coffee when she returned home but, so far, nothing has been forthcoming. Nicole apparently has not taken the bait and my string of successes in the international coffee market appears to have been broken! Where is Anna Kriebel when I need her?

The long and short of all this warring is that I have been provided with a reasonably dependable supply of Caribbean, Central, and South American coffees for several years now. Which coffee is best depends on which of the beneficent young ladies I am talking to; being wishy-washy is imperative because I cannot afford to jeopardize my supply lines.

Playgirl, Inc.

I stopped by the departmental mailroom one morning when I was in my late thirties, and the following document was imbedded in the midst of the usual inter-campus mail envelopes, advertisements for textbooks, and memoranda from Deans and Provosts:

New York, New York

June 11, 1976

Dr. Arnold LeUnes
Dept. of Psychology
Academic Building
Texas A&M University
College Station, Texas 77843

RE: Centerfold

Dear Dr. LeUnes:

    We wish to thank you for the pictures you recently sent by your friends to our booth at the SWPA Convention in Houston. However, I regret to inform you that we will not be able to use them for our centerfold.
    On a scale of 9 to 10, your body was rated a -2 by our panel of women ages 65 to 75 years. We asked our panel of women in the 25-35 age bracket to evaluate you, but we could not get them to stop laughing long enough.
    Should the taste of the American Woman ever change so drastically that they would accept you as a centerfold, you will be notified by this office. In the meantime, don't call us———we'll call you.

Sympathetically,

Amanda Sue Smith, Editor
Playgirl Magazine
ASS/pdq

Things That Can Go Wrong With the Body

    It is interesting to note that the life expectancy in the US is well into the late seventies. It seems an oddity that this relative longevity is achieved despite the frailty of the human body and the seemingly endless number of things that can go wrong, some aggravating and others life-threatening. The genesis for this segment of the book arose from conversations over a period of thirty-five years with Jack Nation, my colleague, co-author, jogging partner, and deceased dear friend. When you jog at the pace we selected, say eight-minute miles, followed by a leisurely two-mile walk, give or take, there is plenty of time for idle chatter about life, liberty, and the pursuit of perpetuity through exercise. Jogging, working out, playing softball, working in the yard, having accidents, and suffering unexplainable illnesses, aches, and pains take their toll on the body and spirit. There seems to be no end to the subtle and sometimes negative nuances and manifestations of these myriad life events. Jack and I often talked about the wonder of it all, marveling at how many things can go wrong with the body and yet people somehow survive.

Since Jack's untimely and unfortunate death due to the effects of alcoholism on May 27, 2008, a sobering event to say the least, I have decided these afflictions he and I discussed can be dichotomized into illness and injuries that are aggravating and those that are life-threatening or fatal, though some overlap is probably inevitable. What is aggravating to one person may be life-threatening to another. With this caveat in mind, I have placed the following afflictions and events in the aggravating category, however arbitrary, I would include in alphabetical order:

Acne, acid reflux, air sickness, allergies, anemia, anorexia, athlete's foot, benign prostatic hyperplasia (VPH), bladder infections, boils, bronchitis, bruises, bulimia, bunions, burns, bursitis, carbuncles, carpal tunnel syndrome, cataracts, colds, conjunctivitis, constipation, corns, dandruff, diarrhea, diverticulitis, eczema, edema, erectile dysfunction, farding (How in the hell did this one get in here?), fever blisters, flatulence, food poisoning, frigidity, gastritis, gingivitis, glaucoma, halitosis, hangnails, hemorrhoids, hernias, hiccups, high blood pressure, hives, impetigo, influenza, ingrown toenails, insomnia, jaundice, keratosis, laryngitis, measles, mumps, necrosis, night sweats, osteomyelitis, osteoporosis, parasites, pimples, plantar fasciitis, pruritus ani, plantar warts, restless leg syndrome, rheumatic fever, ringworm, scoliosis, seborrhea, somnambulism, sprains, strains, stings, strep throat, styes, tremors, tumors, urethritis, vaginismus, vertigo, vitamin deficiency, warts, welts, yeast infections, yips (if you are an aging golfer), and zits (I know; it's a reach but it is the only affliction that starts with a z that anyone has ever heard about).

The preceding list of aggravations seems relatively benign compared to the more serious, disabling, life-threatening, or fatal afflictions we hear or read about each and every day. To wit:

Acquired Immunodeficiency Syndrome (AIDS), Alzheimer's, amyotrophic lateral sclerosis (ALS or Lou Gehrig's disease), aneurysm, angina pectoris, autism, bipolar illness, breast cancer, bubonic plague, cerebral palsy, chlamydia, cholera, colitis, cystic fibrosis, dementia, diabetes, Down Syndrome, Ebola, emphysema, epilepsy, fetal alcohol syndrome, flesh eating bacteria, genital herpes, glaucoma, gonorrhea, gout, hemophilia, hepatitis, Huntington's chorea, Kaposi's sarcoma, Korsakoff's syndrome, leukemia, lupus, macular degeneration, mad cow disease, mania, melanoma, meningitis, muscular dystrophy, nephritis, ovarian cancer, paranoia, Parkinson's disease, Peyronie's, pneumonia, polio, Q fever (what the hell is that?), respiratory failure, rheumatoid arthritis, rubella, schizophrenia, shingles, sickle cell anemia, spina bifida, Sudden Infant Death Syndrome (SIDS), syphilis, tetanus, tuberculosis, undulant fever, West Nile disease, whooping cough, x and y chromosomal anomalies, yaws, yellow fever, and zemmiphobia (I know; another reach but perhaps an abnormal fear of the great mole rat could be fatal).

The aggravations and afflictions cited here are admittedly arbitrarily placed and represent only the tip of the iceberg but, *in toto*, they raise an interesting question: How does the human race survive?!

In Search of the Ultimate Barbecue Experience

Friends Tony Bourgeois, Shane Hudson, and Paul Keiper are what I would call, for lack of a better term, "barbecue freaks." We are always on the lookout for the ultimate barbecue experience, and our search has led us to such establishments as Louie Mueller's in Taylor, Snow's in Lexington, Kreuz Market in the barbecue capital of Texas, Lockhart, City Market in Giddings, City Market in Luling, and perhaps the most famous venue of all, Franklin's in Austin. When you go to the area newspapers or *Texas Monthly* for a listing of the top barbecue restaurants in Texas, the preceding are always in the top ten. Of the top venues, the only one we have not graced with our presence is Cooper's in Llano. Llano is a bit out of the way for us but we have heard numerous rave notices about their barbecue. We have Cooper's targeted for the future. A couple of years ago, we tried their "satellite" in Fort Worth, and were generally disappointed, as has been the case with the Kreuz operation in Bryan.

Barbecue restaurants are cropping up like fire ants all over Texas, and Houston lays claim to quite a large number of the new attractions which I must confess we have not visited. Perhaps we will make some of those soon. As well, we need to make the long trek out to Llano and see if Cooper's is really as good as reports from many sources have it.

I think the four of us agree that the best of the ones we have visited is Franklin's in Austin. My only visit there thus far took place when Shane and I drove over one Saturday, arriving as they suggested in Austin about 0700 hours. We had a cooler of beer for the anticipated wait but ended up sharing mimosa's with a mid-thirties, female psychologist for the duration. Four hours later, at 1100 hours, Franklin's threw open the doors for business, and the line behind us was three- or four-hundred people deep. Shortly thereafter, Shane and I got to sink our teeth into absolutely the most fabulous brisket one could ever imagine. People often ask me if the four-hour wait was worth it, and my answer is a resounding "yes." Aaron Franklin, a Bryan native and A&M graduate, really knows what he is doing, and all those rankings that have him number one in the world are spot on as far as I am concerned.

All things considered, my own personal rankings have Franklins's at the top, followed by the City Market in Luling, and number three is the City Market in Giddings. Snow's in Lexington is right there in the mix, and Louie Mueller's comes in at number five. Because of the pork, Kreuz Market in Lockhart gets honorable mention. In addition to their overall good barbecue menu, Snow's does an outstanding job on pork. As for sausage, the two city markets in Luling and Giddings are, in our humble opinion, the best, and their ribs are also outstanding. My cohorts might quibble with me or each other over minor disagreements but they are in general agreement with the LeUnes ratings.

It is difficult these days to pick up a newspaper or magazine that does not have an article on barbecue and books on the topic abound in profusion. Attesting to this popularity, the Department of Meat Sciences at A&M hosts Camp Barbecue to anyone interested, and their allotment of 250 spots is filled every time in less than sixty seconds. Friends Jeff Savell and Ray Riley deserve a big pat on their backs for bringing barbecue aficionados together to help them prepare a better product. Go Jeff! Go Ray! Go barbecue!

The Gospel According to Arnold the Skeptic

"I like your Christ. I do not like your Christians. Your Christians are so unlike your Christ."
Mahatma Gandhi

"When the missionaries arrived, the Africans had the land and the missionaries had the Bible. The missionaries taught us to pray with our eyes closed.
When we opened them, the missionaries had the land and we had the Bible."
Jomo Kenyatta, Statesman, Author, and First President of Kenya

"Is man one of God's mistakes or is God one of man's?"
Friedrich Nietzsche, Philosopher (1844-1900)

"God is a comedian playing to an audience too afraid to laugh."
Voltaire, Philosopher (1694-1778)

"Forgive, O Lord, my little jokes on thee and I'll forgive the great big joke on me."
Robert Frost, Poet

"Faith is believing what you know ain't so."
Samuel Langhorne Clemens (aka Mark Twain) (1835-1910)

"In Heaven all the interesting people are missing."
Friedrich Nietzsche, Philosopher

"To profess to be doing God's will is a form of megalomania."
Joseph Prescott, Aphorist (1913-2001)

"Is God willing to prevent evil, but not able? Then he is not omnipotent. Is he able but not willing? Then he is malevolent. Is he both willing and able? Then whence cometh evil? Is he neither able or willing? Then why call him God?"
Epicurus, Philosopher (c. 341-270 BC)

Sentimental Journey Home I (1965-2018)

"And if there were a God, I think it is very unlikely that He would have such an uneasy vanity as to be offended by those who doubt his existence."

Bertrand Russell, Philosopher, Mathematician, Author (1872-1970)

"What can be asserted without proof can be dismissed without proof."

Christopher Hitchens, Author (1949-2011)

"A belief that leaves no place for doubt is not a belief: it is a superstition."

Jose Bergman, Author (1895-1983)

"If God exists, I hope he has a good excuse."

Woody Allen, Author, Actor, Film Maker (1935-)

"Man is certainly stark mad; he cannot make a flea, yet he makes gods by the dozens."

Michel E. de Montaigne, Renaissance Thinker (1533-1592)

"We establish no religion in this country. We command no worship. We mandate no belief, nor will we ever. Church and state are and must remain separate."

Ronald Reagan, Actor and 40th US President

"May all who love the Lord, love you and those who don't love you, may the Lord give them a limp so you can see them coming."

Irish Proverb

"Beer is living proof that God loves us and wants us to be happy."

Benjamin Franklin, Statesman (1706-1790)

"When I was a kid, I used to pray every night for a new bicycle. Then I realized that the Lord doesn't work that way so I stole one and asked Him to forgive me."

Emo Phillips

"da mihi castitatem et continetiam, sed noli modo"
"Grant me chastity and continence, but not yet."

Augustine of Hippo, Philosopher and Theologian (354-430)

"Homo sapiens is the species that invents symbols in which to invest passion and authority, then forgets that symbols are inventions."

Joyce Carol Oates (1938-) Writer and Professor of Humanities at Princeton University

"An atheist is a man who has no invisible means of support."

Bishop Fulton J. Sheen, Theologian

"I prayed for freedom for twenty years, but I received no answer until I prayed with my legs."

Frederick Douglass, Former slave, abolitionist, editor, and orator

"I've found that prayers work best when you have big players."

Knute Rockne, Legendary Notre Dame Football Coach

What Religious Outsiders and True Christians Think About Religion. In their 2007 book entitled *Unchristian: What a New Generation Thinks About Christianity...And Why it Matters*, David Kinnamon and Gabe Lyons state: "Christianity has an image problem." Using data from research conducted under the auspices of the Barna Group, an organization created to promote religious or spiritual transformation in people's lives, the authors spent years trying to understand what is taking place in America with regard to religion. Their survey involved analysis of questionnaire responses gathered from hundreds of what they call "Young Outsiders", or people ages sixteen to twenty-nine with little or no religious affiliation, and "Christian Churchgoers", believers who are regular in their observance of and attendance at religious services. Though it is unfair to try to summarize the totality of their work in a few words, some of the more salient findings are worth considering.

"Young Outsiders" believe that Christians have become famous more for what they oppose than what they are positive about. Also, there is a pronounced us-versus-them mentality that is divisive. Christians are seen as anti-homosexual (i.e., "God created Adam and Eve not Adam and Steve") by young people (ninety-one percent), judgmental (eighty-seven percent), and hypocritical (eighty-five percent). Other terms with which there is widespread agreement among "Young Outsiders" include old-fashioned, too involved in politics, out of touch with reality, insensitive to others, boring, not accepting of other faiths, and confusing. Interestingly, eighty percent of "Christian Churchgoers" believe that anti-homosexual accurately describes their views. As well, fifty-two percent find the term judgmental to be descriptive, half agree that there is too much involvement in politics, and nearly half are in agreement with the hypocritical label. The authors summarize their data by suggesting it is a wakeup call from an entire generation of young people who want reform and a return to a more Jesus-based, kinder religion. And not all of them are "Young Outsiders!" To quote the nineteenth century writer, Jules Renard (1864-1910), "I don't know if God exists, but it would be better for his reputation if he didn't."

Origins of Religion as Personal Mystery. Organized religion has always been a mystery to me, and I have never understood why I cannot wrap my mind around it when so many others seem to grasp its meaning. Organized religion just does not make any sense to me, what with its mysticism, inane rituals, demand for blind obedience to authority, obsession with negativity, and the striking lack of compassion and genuine love. Many of man's most inhumane moments throughout history have been carried out by religious zealots with a nefarious agenda. In the final analysis, better minds than mine have held forth on the various nuances of religious beliefs, so I can only enunciate here my own personal philosophy, as primitive as it might seem, while begging and borrowing here and there from others more insightful and more eloquent than me.

In tracing the family roots contributing to my manifest "ignorance" of matters religious, my mother, I think, was an atheist, though she seldom if ever mentioned religion. I do remember her speaking with considerable bitterness about sexual advances she alleges were made against her as a teenager by a man or men of the cloth from the Christian Church in my hometown of Dewey, Oklahoma. In all honesty, I do not know about the validity to her assertions, but I can say with certainty she believed them to be true and they greatly colored her views of religion.

As for my father, for a short time during my pre-adolescent years, he was a pillar in Texas City's First Presbyterian Church. As a result, we regularly attended church on Sundays for a few years, and from time to time had the minister and his wife over for Sunday dinner. That was until the leadership of the church decided to employ non-union labor to build the sanctuary, and my father and the Presbyterian Church went their separate ways over this issue. I was spared the gory details of the separation but I can only surmise that my father's commitment to the labor movement exceeded the valence he felt for matters of religion. It may well be that the labor union business in the 1940's and 1950's along the Gulf Coast of Texas was a religion of its own, at times exerting mystical powers over its adherents.

However, a most salient memory of my brief tenure as a Presbyterian was suffering unnecessarily at the hands of my Sunday School teacher, a Mrs. Jacobs, who specialized in humiliation tactics because I was not as familiar with the Bible as were some of my more informed (indoctrinated ? brainwashed?) peers. I learned nothing about religion from Mrs. Jacobs but she firmly entrenched a loathing for Sundays, Sunday School, organized religion, and most justifiable of all, Mrs. Jacobs herself. Even from the uninitiated perspective of the pre-teen, I saw what seemed to be a huge disconnect between the message of love and tolerance she spouted on Sundays and the behavior she manifested toward me and, to a lesser extent, some of the other kids in her Sunday School class. It struck me that using denigration tactics to humiliate eleven-year olds in Sunday School was not very Christian.

It was some consolation to me when I heard years later that the married daughter of Mrs. Jacobs had run off with the equally married youth minister of the church amid all kinds of juicy, scandalous rumors. Perhaps the birds really do come home to roost…

Dragging A "Slow One" Across Harlene as Religious Experience. As a teen, I do not think I went near a church except for a short time in junior high school. It turned out that if you attended the Methodist Youth Foundation (MYF) meetings on Sunday nights, you were invited to a dance afterwards, usually at the house of Janice Golden, a fellow MYF'er whose parents were most accommodating about such things. One of the big reasons guys attended these dances was because they offered multiple opportunities to dance with a classmate named Harlene who happened to have a wonderfully developed, sexy body. Some of the guys would brag about "dragging a slow one across her" while they danced. What they were referring to was the almost-certain twisted blue steel erection sometimes referred to as a "Woodie", as she rhythmically moved her sexy legs and flat, rock-hard abdomen against theirs during a slow song. There may have been other nymphets and nubiles at the MYF dances who provoked the same sort of response, but the talk among the guys centered on our supple, sexy, sixteen going on twenty-one classmate. Fortunately or unfortunately, and similar to almost everything else in life, the Sunday night dances had their fifteen minutes of fame, and much of our new-found, short-lived religious fervor waned with their demise. Opportunities to dance with Harlene also went by the wayside, much to the chagrin of more than one hormonal adolescent male in our cohort. One of those males was none other than Mike Rhea and I think he coined the phrase "dragging a slow one across Harlene."

Adult Experiences and Misgivings. As a young adult, I found the message at most religious services to be stifling and inconsistent with my generally optimistic view of the nature of man. There was far too much emphasis on the darkness lurking inside each of us for my taste. I also greatly disliked the "Look at me. Aren't I cute?" mentality of too many of the preachers. In this regard, I recently attended the funeral of one of my first college professors, Dr. Garland Bayliss, and got up in the middle of the proceedings and walked out of the church because I could no longer put up with the self-aggrandizing, grandstanding of the minister leading the service.

When I was in my mid-twenties, newly-married, and by a military man, my young bride Barbara was convinced I would love the minister at the Baptist church she attended in her hometown of Sherman, Texas. Against my better judgment but in the spirit of maintaining good marital relations (i.e., "Happy wife, Happy life") I gave in and attended church with her on a beautiful Easter morning in 1963. I came out of the sermon so incensed with the darkness and negativity of the message that I pretty much swore never to go back, and I have not been to church since except for occasional christenings, quite a number of weddings, and far too many funerals.

Jesus as a Charismatic Middle Eastern Peasant. I found a posting on the Internet in May of 2008 to be most thought-provoking. In Toronto, Canada, a minister named Gretta Vosper suggested the Virgin Birth, the Resurrection, and the many miracles alluded to in the Bible are convenient fictions with no basis in reality. She further asserted that Jesus was nothing more than a "Middle Eastern peasant with a few charismatic beliefs and a great posthumous marketing team." How wonderful! I could not have said it better if I tried! It is also interesting to compare Reverend Vosper's take on the Bible with that of Thomas Jefferson mentioned elsewhere in this document.

Religious Intolerance: A Redundancy? Another pearl of wisdom comes from a quote from the grade school dropout longshoreman, University of San Francisco professor and philosopher, Eric Hoffer, who said: "To know a person's religion we need not listen to his profession of faith but must find his brand of intolerance." So much is communicated here in so few words about hypocrisy, meanness, racism, and intolerance. In a similar vein, the recently deceased science fiction writer Arthur Clarke (1917-2008) said: "The greatest tragedy in mankind's entire history may be the hijacking of morality by religion."

The narrow-mindedness and intolerance alluded to in these quotes, and the misguided souls who believe such nonsense, allows nut cases like the Reverend John Hagee to actually attain some level of credibility. Hagee believes that the Jews are responsible for their own persecution and Adolf Hitler was an emissary of God put on earth to perpetrate the Holocaust and rid the planet of the Jewish scourge. At one time, Pastor Hagee was aligned very closely with the 2008 presidential campaign of John McCain. However, Hagee's extremism led the senator to dissociate himself from the man and his primitive, dangerous, and wrong-headed views.

The fifteenth century philosopher and mathematician, Blaise Pascal, said: "Men never do evil so completely and cheerfully was when they do it from religious conviction." In that vein, the words of the fifteenth century novelist, Daniel Defoe resonate, "Of all plagues with which mankind is cursed, ecclesiastic tyranny's the worst." Harking back to the time when witches were being burned at the stake, author and lecturer Gil Baillie (1944-) has said: "The people who burned witches at the stake never for one moment thought of their act as violence; rather they thought of it as an act of divinely mandated righteousness. The same can be said for most of the violence we humans have ever committed."

George W. Bush as Tartuffe. Almost 2,000 years ago, and proving that once again there is little new under the sun, the Greek philosopher Aristotle reminds us: "A tyrant must put on the appearance of uncommon devotion to religion. Subjects are less apprehensive of illegal treatment from a ruler whom they consider god-fearing and pious. On the other hand, they do less easily move against him, fearing that he has the gods on his side." Though not known as a philosopher and dispenser of sagacious words, the forty-third President, George W. Bush, appears to have understood Aristotle well for he practiced that variant of religious tyranny with uncanny skill. He was ably assisted by his evil-spirited henchpersons, Dick Cheney and Condoleezza Rice, both of whom greatly appreciated the potency of fear messages couched in religious terms and their powers to manipulate the human psyche and spirit. He also understood and practiced what the nineteenth century philosopher Ludwig Feuerbach called morality-based theology: "Whenever morality is based on theology, whenever right is made dependent on divine authority, the most immoral, unjust, infamous things can be justified and established." Perhaps George Bush, or "The Shrub", as he was dubbed by the late Texas social philosopher and profoundly wise humorist, Molly Ivins, was not as mentally challenged as he appeared on the surface. One thing is clear for sure; he understood the power of righteous propaganda.

When it comes to issues of religion and George W. Bush, I think the word "Tartuffe" is apropos. Tartuffe is defined as a hypocrite who feigns virtue, especially in religious matters. It is always difficult for me to give "The Shrub" credit for really believing in much of anything except his narrow and selfish interests and those of his wealthy, sycophantic cronies. However, I will give him full credit for being master propagandist, a skillful manipulator of public opinion who zealously used religion to further his ignoble agenda. Of course, there is always the specter of Dick Cheney lurking about when talking of George W. Bush, and he may well have orchestrated the propaganda and manipulation of thought.

It is fascinating that a man who gave so much credence to matters of religion in running his Presidency could be so uninformed and ineloquent in expressing his own personal and supposedly heart-felt views. "The Shrub" was interviewed about his religious beliefs in a 2008 *Nightline* episode and his message came across as shockingly primitive in both content and emotion. I was astounded at how little he had thought through the nuances of his own religious credo, and the iteration left me wondering if he had any beliefs that were heartfelt and devoid of political opportunism.

For eight years in the Oval Office, the man added a new dimension to the words vacuity and insincerity in both politics and religion. The astute New York Congressman, Charlie Rangel once said of the ex-President: "George Bush has once and for all put the myth of white superiority to rest." Wisely, Rangel also has said that the quickest way to end the needless wars Mr. Bush and his friends got us into in Iraq and Afghanistan would be to reinstate the draft. It is okay to field an army with lower-class kids from rural farms and the mean streets of Baltimore and Chicago but it would be an entirely different matter if the frat-rat sons and sorority sister daughters of businessmen and women, politicians, oil barons, and Silicon Valley computer geeks suddenly started getting draft notices, thus ticketing them for desert warfare.

"The Shrub" got this country involved in a most unpopular "war" with Iraq, ostensibly to eradicate the country of its weapons of mass destruction (which were never discovered), to depose its evil dictatorial leader (Why this evil dictator and not others?), and to cripple Al-Qaeda's stronghold in that country (which was never the case). War hawks, such as Mr. Bush are quick to send young men into harm's way, but they seem to give little thought to the consequences of war which, in the words of an old German proverb, "…leaves the country with three armies – an army of cripples, and army of mourners, and an army of thieves." These three armies have been visibly at work in Iraq where the war supposedly ended on December 15, 2011.

It is indeed ironic that "The Shrub" declared victory in Iraq with his monumentally misguided and moronic "Mission Accomplished" pronouncement aboard the USS Abraham Lincoln on May 1, 2003. Some 5,000 days (or fifteen years) after his premature pronouncement, the mission still has not been accomplished and American fighting men are still dying or getting mutilated in the indefensible middle-eastern wars.

Grim statistics tell us that 4,487 American soldiers died in Iraq (leaving behind an "army of mourners"), 32,226 GI's were wounded, many of them grievously, both physically and mentally (giving us our "army of cripples"), and an estimated 100,000 Iraqi's died (and they too were mourned), and over a trillion taxpayer dollars were spent to finance the fiasco. Many of those dollars were siphoned off by unscrupulous Iraqi government officials or went into the pockets of American profiteers (i.e., "the thieves"). Estimates are that the eventual long-term cost to the US taxpayer of the Bush debacle will ultimately be upwards of nearly two trillion dollars. Many of those dollars will be dedicated to our Veterans Administration hospitals and psychiatric facilities which will be populated by an "army of cripples" throughout the better part of the twenty-first century.

To add insult to injury, various authoritative reports indicated that twelve billion dollars was flown into Baghdad by 2004 and not one penny of that money was ever accounted for. One administration official called the affair, "…the largest theft of funds in national history." Seven years later, CBS News reported that six billion more taxpayer dollars simply disappeared upon arriving in Baghdad from aboard a US cargo plane. To be fair to Mr. Bush (who deserves damn little charity), this act of malfeasance took place under the watch of President Barack Obama.

On May 1, 2011, eight years to the day after "The Shrub" prematurely declared our "Mission Accomplished", Navy Seals raided a compound in Pakistan and killed Osama bin Laden, the terrorist blamed for many of the woes in the world at that time. It is both a sad and ironic commentary that Mr. Obama received a nice spike in his popularity polls for having orchestrated the much sought-after, visibly-popular, coldly-calculated murder of Osama bin Laden. It is also ironic that the Bush administration as well as that of Barack Obama focused so much time, energy, and money on tracking down Osama bin Laden and yet the 2012 Republican candidates used the killing of the Al-Qaeda leader against Mr. Obama as a waste of that same time, energy, and money. Politics at its worst.

I know it is not charitable in any Christian sense, but my fondest hopes are that George W. Bush, the warmonger and tartuffe *par excellence*, has trouble sleeping at night for what he has done to the citizens of America and Iraq. I find it hard to disagree with attorney and best-selling author Vince Bugliosi who advocated in his 2008 book, The Prosecution of George W. Bush for Murder" that "The Shrub" be brought to trial and prosecuted for 4,487 cases of first degree murder, one for each soldier killed in Iraq. It is Bugliosi's contention that bringing George W. Bush and Condoleezza Rice, the war criminals primarily responsible for the debacle in Iraq, to justice is a first step toward restoring the greatness of this country. I, for one, have a hard time disagreeing with Bugliosi.

Sigmund Freud on Religion. I suppose I would be remiss in my duties as a psychologist if I talked about religion without discussing the views of the patron saint of psychoanalysis, Sigmund Freud. In summarizing the life of the consummately brilliant Austrian physician and his psychoanalytic expostulations in their highly respected and legendary book on personality theory in psychology, Gardner Lindzey and Calvin S. Hall suggest that, "…[Freud] sees in the belief in God a fixation to the longing for an all-protecting father figure, an expression of a wish to be helped and saved, when in reality man can, if not save himself, at least help himself, only by waking up from childish illusions and by using his own strength, his reason, and skills." For these views and others of a similar nature, Freud has been labeled an atheist. Rather, I see him as a profound thinker and passionate philosopher of considerable clarity and perspicacity. Apparently so did Oliver Wendell Holmes who wrote: "Men are idolaters, and want something to look at and kiss and hug, or throw themselves down before; they always did and they always will; and if you don't make it of wood, you must make it of words." Another kindred spirit is Robert Green Ingersoll, a lawyer and orator of the late nineteenth century, who wrote: "It has always seemed absurd to suppose that a god would choose for his companions, during all eternity, the dear souls whose highest and only ambition is to obey." Albert Einstein (1879-1955), the physicist, put it this way: "Unthinking respect for authority is the greatest enemy of truth. According to the German philosopher and poet, Goethe (1749-1832), "There is nothing more frightful that ignorance in action."

U. S. Founding Fathers Views of Religion. Conservative politicians and a sizeable segment of the American population cling to the belief that this country was founded as a "Christian Nation." However, according to a piece posted on the Internet by www.examiner.com in 2014, some doubt is cast on this notion if one reads what some of the more prominent founders of this nation had to say about religion. For example:

"Christianity is the most perverted system that ever shone on man."
Thomas Jefferson

"It does me no injury for my neighbor to say there are twenty gods
or no god. It neither picks my pocket nor breaks my leg."
Thomas Jefferson

"This would be the best of all possible worlds if there were no religion in it."
Thomas Paine

"I do not believe in the creed professed by the Jewish Church, by the Roman Church,
by the Greek Church, by the Turkish Church, by the Protestant Church,
nor by any Church that I know of. My mind is my own Church. Each of those
churches accuse the other of unbelief; and for my own part,
I disbelieve them all."
Thomas Jefferson

"Lighthouses are more useful than churches."
Benjamin Franklin

"There is one redeeming feature in our superstition of Christianity. It has made
one half of the world fools, and the other half hypocrites."
Thomas Paine

"Religious bondage shackles and debilitates the mind and
unfits it for every noble enterprise."
James Madison

"All national institutions of churches, whether Jewish, Christian, or Turkish, appear to me no other than human inventions, set up to terrify and enslave mankind and monopolize power and profit."

Thomas Paine

"Religious controversies are always productive of acrimony and irreconcilable hatreds than those that spring from any other cause. Of all the animosities which have existed among mankind, those which are caused by the different sentiments in religion appear to be the most inveterate and distressing, and ought to be depreciated. I was in hopes that the enlightened and liberal policy, which has marked the present age, would at least have reconciled Christians of every denomination so far that we should never again see the religious disputes carried to such a pitch as to endanger peace of the society."

George Washington

"The Bible is not my book, nor Christianity my profession."

Abraham Lincoln

Arnold LeUnes

Dr. James Kaufman Takes on Dr. Laura Schlessinger

Dear Dr. Laura:

Thank you for doing so much to educate people about God's Law. I have learned a great deal from your show, and try to share that knowledge with as many people as I can. When someone tries to defend the homosexual lifestyle, for example, I simply remind them that Leviticus 18:22 clearly states that it is an abomination....End of debate. I do need some advice from you, however, regarding some other elements of God's Laws and how to follow them.

1. Leviticus 25:44 states that I may possess slaves, both male and female, provided they are purchased from neighboring nations. A friend of mind claims that only applies to Mexicans, but not Canadians. Can you clarify? Why can't I own Canadians?
2. I would like to sell my daughter into slavery, as sanctioned in Exodus 21:7. In this day and age, what do you think would be a fair price for her?
3. I know that I am allowed no contact with a woman while she is in her period of menstrual uncleanliness (Leviticus 1:19-24). The problem is how do I tell? I have tried asking but most women take offense.
4. When I burn a bull on the altar as a sacrifice, I know it creates a pleasing odor for the Lord (Leviticus 1:9). The problem is my neighbors. They claim the odor is not pleasing to them. Should I smite them?
5. I have a neighbor who insists on working on the Sabbath. Exodus 35:2 clearly states he should be put to death. Am I morally obligated to kill him myself, or should I ask the police to do it?
6. A friend of mine feels that even though eating shellfish is an abomination, (Leviticus 11:10) it is a lesser abomination than homosexuality. I don't agree. Can you settle this? Are there degrees of abomination?
7. Leviticus 21:20 state that I may not approach the altar of God if I have a defect in my sight. I have to admit that I wear reading glasses. Does my vision have to be 20/20, or is there some wiggle room here?
8. Most of my male friends get their hair trimmed, including the hair around their temples, even though it is expressly forbidden by Leviticus 19:27. How should they die?
9. I know from Leviticus 11:6-8 that touching the skin of a dead pig makes me unclean, but may I still play football if I wear gloves?
10. My uncle has a farm. He violates Leviticus 19:19 by planting two different crops in the same field, as does his wife by wearing garments made of two different kinds of thread. He also tends to curse and blaspheme a lot. Is it really necessary that we go to all the trouble of getting the whole town together to stone them (Leviticus 24:10-16)? Couldn't we just burn them to death at a private family affair, like we do with people who sleep with their in-laws (Leviticus 20:14)?"

I know you have studied these things extensively and thus enjoy considerable expertise in such matters, so I'm confident you can help.

Thank you again for reminding us that God's word is eternal and unchanging.

Your adoring fan.

James M. Kauffman
Ed.D. Professor Emeritus
Dept. of Curriculum, Instruction, and Special Education, University of Virginia.

P. S. (It would be a damn shame if we couldn't own a Canadian)

Power of Prayer. Other insights come from the musings of the brilliant if curmudgeonly Ambrose Bierce, who offered up a definition of the word, pray: "To ask the laws of the universe to be annulled on behalf of a single petitioner, confessedly unworthy." In this connection, the seventeenth century poet Samuel Butler says that "Prayers are to men as dolls are to children. They are not without use and comfort, but it is not easy to take them very seriously".

It has always been a source of amazement to me that when people's lives are spared, say in a horrific tornado, they often attribute their survival to God answering their prayers. As sure as my name is Arnold Dallas LeUnes, I can guarantee you their neighbors who died in the same tornado were praying their collective asses off, but to no avail. What happened to their plaintive pleas? Why were their prayers not answered? The self-centeredness of this invocation boggles my mind; do these people really believe they are so special as to be spared when other equally worthy people around them are dying right and left? The same thing is true for these egotistical athletes who point to the skies in supplication every time they hit a single in baseball or make a sack in football. Do they really believe God gives a big rat's ass about baseball or football? I would prefer He/She/It be out confronting the Four Horsemen of the Apocalypse, War, Famine, Pestilence, and Death,

Two thousand years ago, an ancient unnamed philosopher offered the following words of wisdom on the problematic nature of prayer: "If the gods listened to the prayers of men, all humankind would quickly perish since they constantly pray for so many evils to befall one another." Similarly, Herbert J. Muller (1905-1980), a historian, educator, and writer, said: "The doctrine of the material efficacy of prayer reduces the Creator to a cosmic bellhop of a not very bright or reliable kind." A former minister, Dan Barker, said: "Not thinking critically, I assumed that 'successful' prayers were proof that God answers prayer while the failures were proof that there was something wrong with me." Not to be outdone by philosophers and the clergy, actor, writer, and comedian Steve Allen (1921-2000) once said: "If you pray for rain long enough, it eventually does fall. If you pray for floodwaters to abate, they eventually do. The same happens in the absence of prayers." The famous scientist and science fiction writer, Isaac Asimov, chimes in his two cents worth: "If I were not an atheist, I would believe in a God who would choose to save people on the basis of the totality of their lives and not the pattern of their words. I think he would prefer an honest and righteous atheist to a TV preacher whose every word is God, God, God, and whose every deed is foul, foul, foul."

Speaking of televangelists and the power of prayer, the incredibly charismatic and unbelievably wealthy religious huckster, the Reverend Frederick J. "Reverend Ike" Eikerenkoetter II, was fond of saying, "…every time you get on your knees to pray, you leave yourself wide open to receive a kick in the butt."

Brann the Iconoclast. The writings of the brilliant if prickly nineteenth century Texas writer William Cowper Brann (1855-1898) lend yet another dimension to the present discussion and are thus instructive. Brann was widely known as a brilliant maverick who engaged in a life-long struggle to stamp out hypocrisy and religious bigotry. Much of what Brann had to say is found in B*rann, the Iconoclast*, writings collected and edited by J. D. Shaw in 1906. Brann alienated people right and left with his emotionally loaded and heretical thoughts, words, deeds, and expostulations, and this irreverence eventually led to his death. He met his maker, so to speak, while walking the streets of Waco, Texas, that Southern Baptist bastion of both reverence and hypocrisy, with a friend when an assassin shot him in the back. Brann turned and shot his perpetrator dead, but died as a result of his wounds a few hours later. Of Brann, Shaw says: "His religion was to do whatever he believed to be right, and to defy the wrong even though it should be found parading in the garb and livery of righteousness." Brann himself had the following to say about this issue: "Unquestionably there are many worthy church communicants in Texas, as elsewhere; but they appear to be in a hopeless minority—a few grains of sound corn in a pile of compost." He goes on to add: "There are broad-gauged men in the Protestant ministry here—men who serve the Lord in spirit and in truth, and in their kindly acts, progressive ideas, and noble tolerance dignify the cause; but they are the exception instead of the rule and are almost invariably unpopular with the great body of church communicants, whose ideal appears to be a preacher with just ability enough to deceive and just religion enough to persecute."

Today, if you were to drive by Brann's burial site in Waco, his headstone is reportedly pockmarked from bullets fired by disgruntled true believers, no doubt armed with righteousness in their cold, miserable, unforgiving hearts. Visiting this site is definitely on my bucket list. Speaking of goodness, Henry David Thoreau said: "There is no odour so bad as that which arises from goodness tainted. It is human, it is divine, carrion. If I knew for a certainty that a man was coming to my house with the conscious design of doing me good, I should run for my life as that dry and parching wind of the African deserts called the simoon, which fills the mouth and nose and ears and eyes with dust until you are suffocated, for fear I should get some of his good done to me, - some of its virus mingled with my blood."

Christians as Infidels. Returning to the heretical Ambrose Bierce for a moment, he took an interesting stance in defining the word infidel. Infidel: (n) "In New York, one who does not believe in Christian religion; in Constantinople, one who does." In this regard, my esteemed colleague, Dr. John McDermott, who teaches, among other things, a course in Philosophy of Religion, is fond of saying (and I am even fonder of quoting): "Ten percent of the people in the world are Christians and ninety percent of them hate each other." The numbers may be off a tad but the sentiment rings true! Jonathan Swift, the writer, weighs in on Professor McDermott's point as follows: "We have enough religion to hate each other, but not enough to love each other."

The eloquent essayist and prolific poet Ralph Waldo Emerson (1803-1882) aptly captured my feelings about the exceedingly erudite Professor McDermott well over one hundred years ago when he wrote the following: "A chief event of life is the day in which we have encountered a mind that startled us." Mc Dermott never ceases to startle me though I must confess to a certain dislike for the man because we view most things in life pretty much the same but he is able to frame his thoughts and utterances so much more eloquently.

In thinking about Professor McDermott's aforementioned pronouncement about Christians, I cannot help but recall an interesting takeoff on this theme arising from a casual conversation I had with one of my Asian students several years ago. He and I were visiting in my office, and he happened to mention his religion, Buddhism, while concurrently offering up the following observation about his Protestant peers: "I went to the Baptist Student Union for a meeting of the college student group last Wednesday evening and all they did was rag on the Mormons the whole time. I thought you Christians all loved each other." On a slightly different tack, a relatively obscure writer by the name of Anne Lamott stated that "You can safely assume that you've created God in your own image when it turns out that God hates all the same people you do."

Animal Rights and Religion. Speaking of nature, how can one talk out of one side of one's mouth about unending love and devotion for God and one's fellow man and, at the same time, talk in a bloodthirsty fashion about the killing of animals? As Anna Sewell (1820-1878) said: "There is no religion without love, and people may talk as much as they like about their religion, but if it does not teach them to be good and kind to other animals as well as humans, it is all a sham."

For several years, the area media glorified a former star quarterback at A&M who later played, sparingly and ineffectively at best, for the NFL franchises in Dallas and Houston for a short time. He was, and I would assume still is, a Bible-thumping, finger-waving, card-carrying poster child for Texans of an ultra-conservative, right wing, Christian persuasion. During his time at Texas A&M University, the adoring local media would fawn all over this guy, almost without fail making mention of his devotion to God and football coupled with references to his third passion in life, killing animals. The sad thing was that the unquestioning media treated this bloodlust as if it was a virtue, no doubt equating it with manliness and the killer instinct as a football player. I for one am not ready to accord iconic status to a high profile football player who amuses himself in his spare time by killing animals for entertainment and diversion, all the while spouting a good game of religion which in his case seemed devoid of compassion. I am always afraid deep down that this lack of compassion for animals also extends to one's fellow humans when push really comes to shove.

A Positive Perspective. Lest one think I am a curmudgeon cut from the same cloth as Ambrose Bierce and W. C. Brann, let me offer up for your consumption the following more positive views of the nature of religion. If religion were practiced as suggested by the following authorities, it is likely that the world would soon become a better place.

"This is my living faith, an active faith, a faith of verbs: to question, explore, experiment, experience, walk, run, dance, play, eat, love, learn, dare, taste, touch, smell, listen, argue, speak, write, read, draw, provoke, emote, scream, sin, repent, cry, kneel, pray, bow, rise, stand, look, laugh, cajole, create, confront, confound, walk back, walk forward, circle, hide, and seek. To seek: to embrace the questions, be wary of answers."

Terry Tempest Williams, naturalist and author (1955-):

"Let us face a pluralistic world in which there are not universal churches, no single remedy for all diseases, no one way to teach or write or sing, no magic diet, no world poets, and no chosen races, but only the wretched and wonderfully diversified human race."

Jacques Barzun, professor and writer (1907-2012):

"I see that sensible men and conscientious men all over the world were of one religion – the religion of well-doing and daring, men of sturdy truth, men of integrity and feeling for others."

Nineteenth century writer and philosopher Ralph Waldo Emerson

"When I do good, I feel good; when I do bad, I feel bad. That's my religion."

President Abraham Lincoln

"So many gods, so many creeds, So many paths that wind and wind, While just the art of being kind is all the sad world needs."

Ella Wheeler Wilcox, poet (1850-1919)

"God has no religion."

Mahatma Gandhi, (1869-1948)

"I believe in God, only I spell it Nature."

Frank Lloyd Wright, the famed architect (1867-1959)

For Aggies Only

"Sometimes you can't explain what you see in a person.
It's just the way they take you to a place where no one else can."
Curtis Mayne

"Rekindlers" and Others Who Made a Difference

This list of "rekindlers" who take you to places where no one else can is arranged in alphabetical order, with females first and males second, and covers the fifty-two years from 1966 through 2018. Everyone mentioned here can rest assured that, in some way or another, our association has exerted a significant influence on my life. One of the criteria for making this list is that I must be able to tell myself or others at least one anecdote about you that makes you memorable. If I look at the list and cannot remember something meaningful, then your name gets removed from the collection, and that has happened a few times over the years as this memoir has been crafted,

    I would also like to apologize for omissions of meaningful people; there have been far too many of you and it is unfortunately inevitable that a few treasured "rekindlers" got left out. Also, I have been stingy about including people from the past five years or so, for those associations have not stood the test of time. On the other hand, if you are a student from the 1960's and 1970's and have made this list, you can bet your sweet bippy you had a lasting impact. With these caveats in place, here we go.

A

K. C. Abrahamson, Jennifer Acklam, Kristi Albernaz, Holly Albert, Katie Alexander, Lisa Allee, Caroline Allen, Charlene Allen, Karen Allen, Christina Amo, Marnie McIntosh Anderson, Kathy Anding, Monica Andres, Alita Andrews, Michelle Arishita, Shirley Arizpe, Jeannie Arnold, Alia Atkinson, Carrie Austgen, Jasmine Autrey

Kyle Adams, Phil Adams, Dennis Allen, Grady Allen, Tom Allen, Mike Allender, Donnie Anz, Brian Apperson, Bob Arizpe, Ross Arth, Ian Arthur, Jason Atkinson, Reilly Avalos

B

Wanda Badgett, Katie Baird, Laura Ball, Bailey Barksdale, Haley Barnett, Kate Barnett, Victoria Barranco-Giovanetti, Tammie Barron, Teri Jo Bartlett, Claire Baudouin, Madison Bayliss, Bets Beck, Natasha Becka, Kristen Bell, Meredith Benkendorfer, Kim Berra, Tina Biffle, Barbara Bilski, Kimberly Black, Tamara Black, Morganne Blackstock, Bryn Blalack, Sarah Blalock, Betty Blevins, Brandi Bockhorn, Morgan Bolleter, Tonya Boozer, Amanda Borg, Sandy Bowen, Chandler Bowersox, Lisa Branch, Jamie Brantley, Ashley Breitigam, Annette Brooks, Anne Marie Brown, Beverly Brown, Kaitlyn Brown, Leslie Bruno, Emily Bryan, Damitria Buchanan, Katherine Buckley, Staci Burchett, Jolee Burger, Ashley Burgess, Beth Burkett, Shannon Burkett, Cindy Burkhalter, Alexandra Burks, Candy Butler, Tracy Butler

Brandon Baber, Thomas Ray Barnum, Duane Barone, Andy Barona, Scott Barto, Pete Bassett, Cedric Bates, Scott Bauer, Chris Baumbach, Bill Beach, James Beamer, Payton Beck, Glenn Beecher, Jonathan Berry, Taylor Bertolet, Bill Betts, Tom Bevans, Josh Bias, Clay Bibb, John Billig, Brian Bittiker, Matt Blume, Bobby Boenigk, Searcy Bond, Spencer Bond, Ken Bottom, Mike Bridges, Scott Brinker, Bill Broussard, Travis Broussard, Jace Brown, Jimmy Reagan Brown, Kevin Bryan, Tom Buchanan, Ozzie Burke, John Burkhalter, Sam Buser, Duke Butler, Ryan Byrne

C

Sandy Caballero, Herminia Callejas, Donyale Canada, Tamara Cannon, Samantha Caplan, Paige Castellino, Cari Cesaro, Samantha Chalupa, Brooke Chamblee, Shannon Champion, Donna Chaney, Julie Chapman, Leyla Choobineh, Nicole Chovan, Monique Cioffi, Raychel Clark, Charlene Cobb, Jana Cogswell, Terri Cole, Alana Collier, Barbara Collinsworth, Debbie Cook, Kate Cooper, Linda Cooper, Courtney Copeland, Patsy Copeland, Mary Corey, Nizie Cos, Christi Cossey, Frances Coulson, Carol Crain, Cristie Cramer, Amanda Craven, Edit Csuha

Joe Calao, Danny Callaway, Lou Camilli, Mark Caperton, Randall Caperton, Joel Castillo, Logan Chamberlain, Parker Chenevert, Steve Clodfelter, Alex Cohen, Shannon Cole, Douglas Coleman, Scott Coleman, Everton Cope, Tom Copeland, Jonathan Cornwell, Quentin Coryatt, Winston Crite, Bill Crockett, Skip Crow, Scott Cummings, George Cunningham

Sentimental Journey Home I (1965-2018)

D

Misty Dawn Dark, Sammye Darling, Deanna Davalos, Brittany Davis, Alyssa Day, Karol Decuir, Esther Dedrick, Jennifer Demarais, Abby Demiano, Donna DeOtte, Deneesa Diebel, Andrea DiGuardi, Jennifer Dobbertin, Carrie Dodd, Jennifer Dolim, Jennifer Douglass, Billie Douthitt, Kristin Drake, Tracy Driggars, Lydia Dubuisson, Cori Duke, Cristina Duke, Katie Dunn, Nicole Durossette, Hunter Dyer

Randy Dausin, Brandon Davidson, Don Delucia, Brian Demarais, Allen Denton, Gibbs Dibrell, Willie Dickup, John Diedenhofen, Nick Dobrovolsky, Wes Dorsett, Jay Downey, Ben Downs, Tim Drain, Ryan Dreyer, Leon Dreyfus, Mike Dromgoole, David Dubbelde, Richard Dubois, Vince Duchsmasclo, Ken Duesterhoft, Cliff Dugosh

E

Devanee Eberhard, Kristina Edfors, Jan Edwards, Alicia Egeberg, Lucretia Eiler, Brooke Emery, Kim English, Nicole Espinoza, Ryann Estakhri, Salina Eubanks, MK Evers, Brenda Ewald

Mark Eddy, Will Edmonds, Hamed El-Feky, Eric England, Efrain Escobedo, Moses Esquivel

F

Ginger Faught, Kathy Faulkner, Julie Fey, Marsha Fields, Crissa Fisher, Carlanne Flynt, Meagan Fondren, Evelyn Fontana, Lauren Forde, Cheryl Forehand, Kathy Foster, Sara Foster, Millie Foye, Bridget Frank, A'Quonesia Franklin, Jessica Frantzen, Jessica Frazier, Megan Freeman, Jacqui Freund

Scott Farrar, Stephen Farrar, Dru Fenimore, Tim Field, Matt Flippen, Clarke Flowers, Don Flynt, Glenn Fortner, Jeremy Frampton (victim of the bonfire collapse in 1999), George Franklin, Levi Franklin, Bill Franzen, Vic Frysinger

G

Amanda Gajdosik, Flor Galavis, Mary Cay Gallaway, Alex Gamez, Diane Ganzer, Ana Maria Garcia, Lauren Garza, Belinda Gardenhire, Katie Gardner, Morgan Gardner, Chelsea Garibay, Jessica Garner, Brea Garrett, Tracey Gehbauer, Rebekah Geistweidt, Kelly Gerrity, Lisa Gibbs, Karla Gilbert, Candy Gill, Shannon Gilley, Christa Glad, Carrie Glenn, Sondra Goad, Katrina Godbee, Perilou Goddard, Robin Goddard, Rebecca Grace, Rosario Grajales, Sherry Green, Sarah Gremmel, Barbara Grossman, Lisa Grubbs, Jennie Guinn, Valerie Grysinski, Rebecca Gunner, Jackie Gutierrez

Marcus Galle, Gerald Garcia, Roberto Garcia, Shane Garrett, Amos Gbunblee, Tommy Gergeni, Marshall Getz, James Giese, Jimmy Gilbert, Mike Gilhausen, David Gill, Matt Gindling, Brent

Glamann, Aaron Glenn, Mike Goldsby, Don Goldston, Clay Gould, Jeff Granger, Ken Gray, Charles Green, Richard Green, Sean Greenwald, Charlie Gremmel, D. D. Grubbs, Mike Grubbs, Robert Gruy, Dustin Guarnere, Al Guarnieri, Richard Gunn

H

Ja'net Hacker, Laura Haderxhanaj, Rhonda Halbert, Mel Hall, Megan Hammond, Karla Hancock, Carol Hansen, Peggy Harding, Cristina Harkrider, Dinah Harriger, McKenzie Harrison, Brooke Hathaway, Mary Havard, Patty Havelka, Dena Heffelfinger, Leslie Henderson, Catherine Hensley, Hazel Hernandez, Kalin Hill, Sabrina Hill, Carly Hilley, Rachel Holland, Fancy Adrian Hollis, Shelley Hollon, Morgan Hooker, Kerry Hope, Kriss Hope, Holly House, Paula House, Aimee Howarth, Heather Howbert, Danielle Howell, Amy Huebel, Meg Huebner, Nancy Huebner, Pat Huebner, Holly Hughes, Jamie Hullett, Karen Hungate, Kacie Hurta

Walter Haisler, James Haislet, Curley Hallman, Rex Hardaway, Mike Hare, James Harrington, Connor Harris, Billy Hart, Kenny Hassenteufel, Danny Hayes, Marcus Heard, George Heimann, John Henderson, Pat Henry, Richard Higgins, Billy Hobbs, Leroy Hodge, James Hodges, Ralph Hoegg, Samantha Hoenig, Jerry Honore, Jerry Honza, Alan Hopewell, Larry Horton, Tom Hosea, Ronny Hubby, Earl Humphreys, John Hurley, Jason Hutchins

I

Kris Ibrom, Arnette Ingram, Cheyenne Ivey

Warren Inman, Ahmed Issa, De' Lon Isom

J

Jenna Jacobson, Jennifer Jambor, Alyssa Johnson, Jenny Johnson, Donna Jones, Lauren Jordan, Nicole Judice

Kelly Jamail, Jim James, Lex James, Pat Jamison, Kamran Janjua, Jim Jeter, Adolph Johnson, Chad Johnson, Charles Jones, Robert Juda

K

Kim Kainer, Karen "KK" Kalhoefer, Jennifer Kalinec, Sarah Kannegieter, Jayanthi Kasiraj, Karyann Keaton, Cynde Keefe, Kathy Keng, Eleanor Key, Marli Kimball, Sarah Kirby, Sarah Kitchell, Jo Klatt, Kimberly Klein, Mary Knapp, Taylor Knox, Kirsten Knutson, Ula Kobeszcko, Virginia Koppa, Ali Kramer, Anna Kriebel, Chloe Krippner, Katherine Ksendzuk, Jean Kunkel, Lacy Kutcherousky

Sentimental Journey Home I (1965-2018)

Jason Kaspar, Bruce Katt, Jim Kazmierski, Mike Kazmierski, Robert Kehoe, Tim Kelly, Jamie Kern, Paul Keiper, Habib Kheribi, Tom King, Alexis Klegou, John Knauer, Danny Kniffin, Tom Knightstep, Jim Kotch, Austin Krajicek, Kyle Kutach

L

Laura Lampert, Laura Lancaster, Adrienne Langelier, Lisa Langston, Stacey Larkin, Lauren Laserna, Amanda Lawler, Kari Leavell, Cassidy Lebedzinski, Beverly Leonard, Lauren Lepori, Natalie LeUnes, Alice Liles, Shawn Lockie, Jordan Logue, Amy Loria, Karen Lovdahl, Laura Lowak, Barbara Loveless, Kelsey Luedtke, Sharon Lundgren

Robert Lagoudis, Sammy Lampo, Paul Laroche, Larry Lee, Logan Lee, Chay LeUnes, Darren Lewis, Darwin Link, James Link, Larry Linton, Mike Littell, Steve Lofton, Steve Logsdon, Bob Long, Randall Lopez, Dave Loving

M

Melissa Machac, Kalleen Madden, Martha Madison, Bahareh Mahdavi, Sandy Malatich, Anastasia Malavansos, Jo Manning, Holly Manos, Aimee Maple, Dana Marable, Anna Marshall, Jamie Martin, Kate Massey, Sarah Massey, Cathy McCandless, Debe McCandless, Jana McCleskey, Daffney McCool, Cathy McDonald, Julia McDonald, Chronika McDowell, Jennifer McFalls, Kay McGlashan, Anne McGowen, Tara McGowen, Megan McGrath, Linda McMillan, Ann McMurrey, Dorothy McMurrey, Nikki Mechem, Jessica Meers, Bobbie Melton, Farah Mensik, Raychelle Michalke, Angela Milburn, Stephanie Minnerly, Allyson Mohundro, Claudia Moise, Lisa Moore, Julie Molleston, Barbara Mora, Alyssa Morine, Ashley Morren, Eden Morris, Karmen Moss, Eunice Mudd, Christina Munoz, Evy Munro, Sara Murphey, Julie Musial, Sue Mutzel, Karissa Myers

Clint Machann, Fred Maddox, Paul Madison, Micah Mahaney, Rick Majewski, Jim Malatich, Keith Manning, Kevin Marks, Phil Massad, Don Mathews, Kevin Mathews, Tommy Maxwell, Keith McAfee, Matt McCall, Patrick McGinty, Danny McCray, Jordan McGowen, Mike McGown, Jeff McNutt, Tim Meekma, John Metoskie, Siegfried Meyer, Michael C. Meyers, Matt Milburn, Roger Moellenberndt, Brody Monceaux, Doug Montgomery, Jules Moor, Matt Moore, Todd Moore, Britt Mullins, Chace Murphy, Richard Murphy, William D. A. Musick, Ralph Mutschler

N

Lauren Negrete, Barbara Nemec, Gena Nivens, Maria Nietling, Jen Nixon, Amy Noack, Linda Nobles, Tiana Noffsker, Weatherly Nowak, Florida Nyanpinga

Mark Naftanel, John Nallon, Matthew Nancarrow, Derek Nation, Wayne Nelius, Max Nelson, Jason Nestor, Dat Nguyen, Alex Noriega, Jeff Noto

O

Patty Obenhaus, Cindy Oden, Tina Oggero, Collette Ohlendorf, Irene Olivares, Kathy Olson, Nancy Ondrovik, Diana Ortiz, Lainie Overton

Fernando Oberdieck, Sammy O'Brient, Donny Ohana, John Oliphant, Gary Oliver, Steve O'Neal, Dewey Overholser, Mike Owen

P

Patty Paisley, Simin Partovi, Kim Pate, Kim Pavlin, Macy Pawelek, Shelly Peacock, Peggy Pearson, Terry Peiskee, Victoria Pena, Sarah Peoples, Shelly Permenter, Lauren Perrin, Judy Plantowsky, Judy Pressley, Karen Price

Gary Pabst, Bill Page, Hank Paine, Ryan Palmer, Jeff Paradowski, Mance Park, Phillip Parkin, Brian Parsley, Danny Parsley, Corey Paulson, Greg Payne, Don Pegues, Tim Piekert, Michael Pierpoline, Jordan Peterson, Edgar Plemper, Ken Poenisch, Frank Pontelandolfo, Hayden Pottkotter, Ray Powell, Gene Power, Scotty Price

Q

Kristi Quammen

Cliff Quick

R

Kristen Raaum, Merrie Jo Raymond, Judy Reed, Jennifer Rhine, Kendall Richards, Marika Ripke, Natalie Ripper, Kellie Risk, Magaly Rivera, Emily Rhodes, Suzanne Rhodes, Cindy Riddle, Vickie Riddle, Hannah Riley, Sophie Roberts, Robbin Robertson, Amy Robinson, Dana Robinson, Lacey Robison, Tina Roel, Loren Rose, Pam Ross, Vickie Royall, Melba Royder, Sarah Rubenstein, Katie Rued, Carolyn Ruffino, Rose Ruffino, Dena Russo, Daryl Ryan

Tommy Ramirez, Vince Ramos, Russ Ramsey, Bashir Ramzy, John Raney, Alan Reuber, Gene Rhoton, Bob Rice, Bucky Richardson, Joe Richardson, Nick Robinson, Jimbo Robison, Jason Rockhold, Anthony Rodriguez, Reymundo Rodriquez, Steve Roop, Tom Royder, Jack Rubin, Brett Ruoff

S

Libby Sales, Vita Salvaggio, Suzanne Sartore, Marilda Scamardo, Matilda Scamardo, Lorie Schaeffer, Lois Schiavo, Shavonn Schneider, Stephanie Schulte, Amanda Schumann, Debbie Scott,

Kathy Seale, Judy Sears, Stacey Shaeffer, Maureen Shannon, Alexandra Sharp, Shae Shatto, Becky Sicilio, Mimi Sicilio, Diane Siebeneicher, Mary Catherine Siemsglusz, Sandra Siemsglusz, Carolina Silva, Patricia Simpson, Alison Skrehot, Daisy Mary Sloan, Kristie Smedsrud, D'Rinda Smith, Kim Smith, Maddie Smith, Michelle Smith, Kim Snedden, Suzanne Specht, Ashleigh Spencer, Katy Spencer, Martha Spencer, Kathy Sperry, Melesa Spreen, Lauren Stacell, Stacey Stewart, Cheryl Stiles, Essence Stowe, Cathy Straub (Copeland), Joyce Strawser, Patti Strawser, Madeline Street, Joanne Stringfellow, Rebecca Sturdy, Jan Sturm, Kaylani Sturrock, Melanie Styduhar, Tonya Sulak, Pat Sullivan, Wen Sun, Kristin Swan, Misty Dawn Swan, Angela Swanberg, Susie Swanson, Connie Sue Swartzwelder, Kailey Swick, Stacie Sykora

Mike Sagas, Arthur San Miguel, Mark Satterwhite, Joe Sauter, Francis "Doc" Savage, Charlie Saxon, Eric Schaefer, David Schares, Phillip Scherrer, Tim Schnettler, Mark Schoenemann, Brian Schrumpf, Denny Seal, Tom Semper, Mike Sharp, Bob Shaw, John Shellberg, Abeezar Shipchandler, Geoff Shute, Will Simmen, Randy Simmons, Wally Simpson, Wayne Smart, Doug Smith, Nathan Smith, Preston Smith, Loy Sneary, Sean Snedeker, Steve Snow, Steve Snowden, Jim Sparr, Jesse Spinner, Frank Stanford, Joe Staples, Joe Stark, Ric Steele, Noah Stein, Stewart Stephenson, Jimmy Sterling, Bob Steronko, Matt Steward, Larry Stout, Mickey Stratton, Jonathan Street, Mike Stulce, Scott Sturgeon, James Sulzer, Don Sweeney, Tommy Swygert

T

Caity Tarabocchia, Jeneba Tarmoh, Deidre Tarver, Tina Taylor, Yolanda Taylor, Jessica Tharp, Brenda Thomason, Heather Thompson, Val Thurman, Jeannie Thurmond, Angela Tombari, Shelley Toney, Diana Tovar, Tiffany Tracy, Billy Trail, Susan Trout, Julie Troy, Trudy Turla, Kelly Turk, Erinn Tuttle, Natalie Twyman

Michael Tamayo, Larry Taylor, Lance Teichelman, Jack Thomas, David Thompson, Eric Torres, Roger Torres, Philip Tremont, James Truemper, Paul Turner, John Turton

U

Ellen Umbach

Scott Ungaro

V

Debbie Valentine, Lydia Vandevoort, Kristin VanHooydonk, Allison Van Ness, Kelsey van Steenbergen, Kristen Vaughan, Dori Venhaus, Vivian Viera, Lisa Villa, Carrie Veltman, Vicki Vise

Ignacio Valdes, Luis Valdes, Jody Vanacek, Walter Varvel, Javier Vela, Art Vickland, Dick Vitek, Morris Vogel

W

Susan Wade, Julee Walker, Alison Wallace, Anne Wampler, Tiffany Ward, Toni Wayland, Tori Walters, Heather Watkins, Katherine Watson, Janie Weatherholt, Andrea Webb, Kathy White, Ramona White, Shanae Wilbert, Holly Wildrick, Barbara Williams, Faith Williams, Jean Williamson, Annie Willis, Natalie Wilson, Stephanie Wilson, Ellen Wimmer, Lindsey Witz, Kendall Wolkenstein, Kristi Wolkenstein, Audra Woods, Judy Wooten, Marla Wycoff

Percy Waddle, Carl Wagner, Keith Waguespack, David Walenta, Ernie Walkup, Lee Wallace, Andrew Walne, Steve Waples, Anthony Ware, Fred Warhol, Dennis Warrington, Mark Weaver, Ronny Werner, Dexter Wesley, Bob West, Tony Wheeler, Brian Wigley, Fred Wilganowski, Dennis Wilkerson, Jacob Wilson, Troyce Wilson, Don Williams, Andrew Wood, Bob Wooten

X

Y

Karen Edna Yost

Oura Yarbrough, Chris Yoder, Reverend Donald Young

Z

Caroline Zeid, Alicia Zemanek, Dorothy Zemanek, Ashley Zeppelin

Bruce Zaroskey, Rolando Zavala, Bill Zella, P. P. Zimmerhanzel, Matt Zisette, George Zukotynski

All Names Team

The following people have been chosen for inclusion because their names struck me an interesting or unusual along some ill-defined dimension. In each of these categories, there are some people for whom I have either no memory or just a vague recollection of who they are, but the names are interesting and worth mentioning. I have an All-Alliterative Team, a Four-Letter Word Surname Team, an All-First Names Team, All-Last Names Team, All-United Nations Team, All-European Names Team, and All-Time Ex-Students Football Team.

All-Alliteration Team

Brandi Bockhorn, Bobby Boenigk, Beverly Brown, Beth Burkett, Coni Claycamp, Don Delucia, Donna De Otte, Dempster Dobson, Deirdre Domes, David Dubbelde, Gerald Garcia, Heather Howbert, Jennifer Jambor, Janice Jeang, Jim Jeter, Kim Kainer, KaryAnn Keaton, Laura Lampert,

Larry Lee, Logan Lee, Lauren Lepori, Linda Lindamood, Laura Lowak, Micah Mahaney, Margaret Matocha, Peggy Pearson, Russell Ramsey, Robbin Robertson, Reymundo Rodriquez, Suzanne Sartore, Stacey Schaeffer, Shavonn Schneider, Cecily Silvernale, Sean Snedeker, Suzanne Specht, Stacey Stewart, Stuart Stewart, Stacey Sykora, Trudy Turla, Ptolemy Taylor, Tiffany Tuggle

All Four-Letter Word Surname Team

Bull (Kayla), Chew (Linda), Dark (Dusty Dawn), Dick (Sam), Dino (Dee), Eddy (Mark), Fish (Shay), Garb (Ronni), Ivey (Cheyenne), Link (Darwin), Neck (Erika), Path (Rocky), Risk (Kellie), Seal (Denny), Sorn (Sophy), Swan (Kristin), Swan (Misty Dawn), Wing (Evelyn), Work (Celia)

All First-Names Team

Abeezar (Shipchandler), Amethyst (Templer), Caughey (Richardson), Daffney (McCool), Dahr (Jamail), Daisy (Sloan), Dayspring (Brown), Dempster (Dobson), Dimple (Patel), Django (Hopps), Evangelin (Pangelian), Everdale (Gathcalian), Gulstan (Dart), Jenivie (Isgitt), Kaylani (Sturrock), Kiska (Howell), Kriggy (Beadling), Lanster (Martin), Lock (Tupper), Monalisa (Nguyen), Nature (Sargent), Nizie (Cos), Oura (Yarbrough), Soozy (Conrad), Summer (Flowers), Thelonius (Peugh), Thermelius (Glover), Weatherly (Nowak), Widdie (Kelly), Wispeny (Floyd), Zeinab (Scandarini)

All Last-Names Team

Bedgood (Cassie), Dickup (Willie), Fritter (Monica), Goodspeed (Amber), Harden (John Wesley), Hatmaker (Jodie), Hugebeck (DeeDee), Killen (Mada), Knightstep (Tom), Looker (Kathy), Meals (Rosemary), Miranda (Carmen), Organ (Allison), Peach (Amy), Pipes (Rikki), Po (Ben), Rambo (Philip), Ripper (Natalie), Sleeper (Trey), Valentine (Debbie), Wrinkle (Susan), Zeppelin (Ashley)

All United Nations Team

Ersen Arseven, Tunde Bolitiwa, Bandana Chadda, Mobeen Choudri, Hamed El-Feky, Efrain Escobedo, Stephanie Feiz-Mahdavi, Nanda Halaswamy, Hisham Hamed Hassen, Peimaneh Hedayati, Habib Kheribi, Anguizola Kieswetter, Cherrymayne Mandapat, Anu Mannathikuzhiyil, Giannini Mazzar, Kelechukwu Onwuchekwa, Fernando Oberdieck, Rachel Osaze-Ediae, Simin Partovi, Nirmala Sahadeo, Joseph Uomoleale, Pam Wanawichayen, Diya Wazirali

Arnold LeUnes

All European Names Team (Plus Canada)

Albania,
Laura Haderxhanaj

Canada,
Jean Sebastian Vocal

Croatia,
Poppy Cuculic

Czech Republic,
Amanda Gajdosik, Jennifer Kalinec, Andrea Kubala, Nancy Ondrovik,
Katerina Ruzickova, Richard Vitek

England,
Sherry Blatherwick

Finland,
Meredith Ylitalo

France,
Brianne Charbonneau, Richard Dubois, Collette Vache Ohlendorf,
Monique St. Laurent

Germany,
Ashley Breitigam, Devanee Eberhard, Kenny Hassenteufel, Melanie Holsaetter
Gretchen Holzapfel, Roger Moellenberndt, Dewey Overholser, H. E. Pflughaupt
Diane Siebeneicher, Mary Catherine Siemsglusz, Sandra Siemsglusz,
Kyska Srader, Dori Venhaus

Greece,
Nichole Loup, Anastasia Malavansos, Holly Manos, Anna Papaliodis

Hungary,
Edit Csuha

Sentimental Journey Home I (1965-2018)

Italy,
Cari Cesaro, Andrianne Giovanini, Al Guarnieri, Dustin Guanere, John Iacoponelli, Sammy Lampo, Tina Oggero, Michael Pierpoline, Frank Pontelandolfo, Carolyn Ruffino, Georgio Sant Ambrogio, Marilda Scamardo, Matilda Scamardo, Becky Sicilio, Mimi Sicilio, Reynaldo Spinelli

Netherlands,
Kristen van Hooydonk, Katie van Englehoven, Kelsey van Steenbergen

Poland,
Barbara Bilski, Ula Barbara Kubesczko, Agnieszka Mlodnicka, George Zukotynski

Spain,
Bartolemi Oropeza

All-Time Ex-Student A&M Football Team

In order to be on this team, the players must have taken at least one course with me. One, Javier Vela, took three! The following are my humble rankings by position:

Offense

TE, Tommy Buckman, Ross Brupbacher, Mark Weaver
T, Dexter Wesley, Matt McCall, Alan Reuber, Robert Cortez, Clarke Flowers
LG, Travis Koehn, Jim Kazmierski, Larry Taylor, Jason Rockhold
C, Kevin Matthews, Chris Yoder
WR, Bob Long, Chris Taylor, Ken (Dude) McLean, Leroy Hodge, Percy Waddle, Danny McCray, Gary Oliver, Larry Lee, Shane Garrett, Steve Lofton, Kary Vincent, Todd Moore, Phil Adams, Chris Caflisch
QB, Bucky Richardson, Brandon Stewart, Jeff Granger, Lex James
RB, Darren Lewis, Greg Hill, Keith McAfee, Jerry Honore', Randy Simmons, Ronnie Hubby, Tommy Gergeni
K, Tony Franklin, Keith Waguespack, Taylor Bertolet
P, Steve O'Neal

Defense

DL, Grady Allen, Sammy O' Brient, Marcus Heard, Pat Henry, Amos Gbunblee, Lance Teichelman, Mark Weaver, Kevin Bryan, Winston Beam, Gary Gruben, Kristofor Grimes, Isaac Flores
LB, Dat Nguyen, Billy Hobbs, William Thomas, Garth Ten Napel, Jason Atkinson, Kyle Mangan, Cedric Booker
CB, Aaron Glenn, Curley Hallman, Larry Horton, Javier Vela, Brandon Jennings, Leroy Hauerland
S, Kip Corrington, Tommy Maxwell, Dennis Allen, Jordan Peterson

12th Man

Ernie Walkup, Tom Bevans

Managers/Trainers

Danny Kniffin, Lydia Dubuisson, David Stenklyft, Sheila Spacek, Jim Kotch

CPSIA information can be obtained
at www.ICGtesting.com
Printed in the USA
FSHW01n2034160818
51311FS